THE HUMANITIES THROUGH THE ARTS

FIFTH EDITION

THE HUMANITIES THROUGH THE ARTS

F. DAVID MARTIN
Professor of Philosophy Emeritus
Bucknell University

LEE A. JACOBUS
Professor of English
University of Connecticut

THE McGRAW-HILL COMPANIES, INC.
New York St. Louis San Francisco Auckland Bogotá Caracas Lisbon
London Madrid Mexico City Milan Montreal New Delhi San Juan
Singapore Sydney Tokyo Toronto

McGraw-Hill

A Division of The ***McGraw-Hill*** *Companies*

THE HUMANITIES THROUGH THE ARTS

This book is printed on acid-free paper.

9 0 VNH VNH 0 0 9 8 7 6 5 4 3 2

ISBN 0-07-040820-3

This book was set in New Aster by York Graphic Services, Inc.
The editors were Cynthia Ward, Nancy Blaine, and Larry Goldberg;
the designer was Joan E. O'Connor;
the production supervisor was Richard A. Ausburn.
The photo editor was Kathy Bendo;
the photo researchers were Sax Freymann and Mia Galison.
Von Hoffmann Press, Inc. was printer and binder.

Cover photo credit: Jacques-Germain Sufflot, The Pantheon Interior, Paris (Lee A. Jacobus)

Library of Congress Cataloging-in-Publication Data

Martin, F. David, (date)
The humanities through the arts / F. David Martin, Lee A. Jacobus.–5th ed.
p. cm.
Includes bibliographical references and index.
ISBN 0-07-040820-3
1. Arts–Psychological aspects. 2. Art appreciation.
I. Jacobus, Lee A. II. Title.
NX165.M37 1997
700′. 1′ 04–dc20 96-20177

http:/www.mhcollege.com

ABOUT THE AUTHORS

F. DAVID MARTIN (Ph.D., the University of Chicago) taught at the University of Chicago and then at Bucknell University until his retirement in 1983. He was a Fulbright Research Scholar in both Florence and Rome from 1957 through 1959, and he has received seven other major research grants during his career as well as the Christian Lindback Award for Distinguished Teaching. Dr. Martin recently taught in the University of Pittsburgh's Semester at Sea, and is currently a consultant for Time-Warner for the development of CD-ROMs in the arts and the humanities. In addition to more than 100 articles in professional journals, Dr. Martin is the author of *Art and the Religious Experience* (Associated University Presses, 1972) and *Sculpture and the Enlivened Space* (The University Press of Kentucky, 1981). Although he has taught all fields of philosophy, Dr. Martin's main teaching interests have centered on the "why" questions of the arts and the humanities. Married with four children and twelve grandchildren, Dr. Martin lives on the Susquehanna River in Lewisburg, PA. His hobbies are nature, poetry, music, tennis, golf, and the world—especially Italy.

LEE A. JACOBUS (Ph.D., Claremont Graduate School) is Professor of English at the University of Connecticut. He graduated from Brown University and held a Danforth Teacher's Grant while earning his doctorate. His publications include *Shakespeare and the Dialectic of Certainty* (St. Martins, 1992); *Sudden Apprehension: Aspects of Knowledge in Paradise Lost* (Mouton, 1976); *John Cleveland: A Critical Study* (G. K. Hall, 1975); *Humanities: The Evolution of Values* (McGraw-Hill, 1985); *Writing as Thinking* (Macmillan, 1989); *Literature: An Introduction to Critical Reading* (Prentice-Hall, 1996); and several edited volumes: *A World of Ideas* (Bedford Books, 1993); *The Bedford Introduction to Drama* (Bedford Books, 1997); *The Longman Anthology of American Drama* (Longman, 1982); *Aesthetics and the Arts* (McGraw-Hill, 1968). Currently he is working on a book on James Joyce's *Ulysses.* Dr. Jacobus has held several research grants for his writing and for his photography. He has played jazz drums much of his life and now studies piano. He has published poetry, short fiction, and numerous scholarly articles, and has had two plays in showcase production in New York City. He is married with two children and lives near New Haven.

WE DEDICATE THIS STUDY
TO TEACHERS AND STUDENTS
OF THE HUMANITIES

CONTENTS

PREFACE

The Humanities Through the Arts, fifth edition, is an exploratory approach to the humanities that focuses on the special role of the arts. The relation of the humanities to values—objects and events important to people—is central to the book's purpose, while it makes a distinction between the role of artists and that of other humanists. Artists reveal values; other humanists examine or reflect upon values. This book provides a self-contained program for studying values as revealed in the arts, following the basic theory of revelatory aesthetics.

While most humanities texts study the arts chronologically within the frameworks of their social and stylistic environments, we have not organized our study historically, except incidentally. The book begins with a general introduction to the humanities, focusing on what they are and on the basic importance of the arts to the other humanities. The next two chapters, devoted to definitions of art and varieties of critical approaches to the arts, establish a foundation for critical response. Then individual chapters treat the various arts: painting, sculpture, architecture, literature, drama, music, dance, film, and photography. New to this edition is a chapter on the interrelationships of the arts.

The emphasis throughout the text is on participation and involvement with maximum understanding and thus maximum intensity of enjoyment—allowing each work of art to unfold its fullness. To help our readers sharpen their perceptive responses to a work of art, we have provided "perception keys," making this book unique among humanities texts. Concentrating on specific works of art, the perception keys include questions and suggestions designed to elicit more sensitive perception. Students can see immediately the extent or limit of their understanding of any given example. The perception keys also encourage both critical and creative activities by our readers. Through genuine participation, they are prevented from being passive receptors of absolute value statements about the arts. The perception keys invite students to question and test virtually all statements of interpretation and value—whether implicit or explicit—throughout the text as well as in the classroom and in their own general experience. Our analyses, which follow rather than precede the keys, are offered not as *the* way to perceive a given work of art, but rather as one possible way. We avoid dogmatic answers and explanations; our primary interest is in exciting our readers to perceive the splendid singularity of a work of art.

In the final chapter, the relationship of values in the arts to the other humanities—especially history, philosophy, and religion—is explored with the help of "conception keys." Similar in format to the perception keys, they involve the student in conceptual problems and explore the distinctions between perceiving and conceiving. Through its use of perception and conception keys, *The Humanities Through the Arts* comes as close to being self-instructional as a humanities book can be.

In the second edition we added a chapter on drama. The third edition added a chapter on photography. The third edition was also closely coordinated with the telecourse "Humanities Through the Arts," based on our book. Produced by KOCE-TV and Coast Community College District, consisting of thirty one-half-hour programs, and hosted by Maya Angelou, the telecourse is now widely distributed through Coast Telecourses. *A Study Guide for the Televised Course: The Humanities Through the Arts,* fourth edition (New York: The McGraw-Hill Companies, 1997), was written by Richard T. Searles and revised by Michele Dammon for the Coast Community College District. The study guide helps students master material in the text and videos, providing lesson overviews, learning objectives, assignments, additional readings, review quizzes, and suggestions for further study.

The fourth edition added a chapter on "almost art." Additionally, the fourth edition updated considerable material and refined many analyses. The theory of art as the revelation of values (along with the distinctions between subject matter, form, and content) was carried out more consistently throughout the whole text.

The fifth edition arrives with a brand new look. There are now color reproductions throughout the book, making it possible to make much subtler and much more interesting analyses of works of art. The addition of color also makes it possible to compare works more realistically with one another. Of course, even color reproductions are no substitutes for the originals, and we advise throughout this book to consult original works of art wherever possible. We have also added a chapter, long asked for, on the interrelationships among the arts. We have updated individual chapters on the arts with new examples and new analyses, while maintaining extended discussions that have pleased previous users of the book. In the music chapter, we have added timing for our analysis of Beethoven's *Eroica* symphony, keyed to George Szell's masterful interpretation now available on compact disk to users of this book. The music chapter has been streamlined and made more accessible to the general reader. The bibliographies for all chapters have been updated. New to this edition is a list of websites and gopher addresses to introduce computer users to the incredible resources of the World Wide Web in all areas of the arts.

The reception of this book, since its first edition, has been enormously warming. It has reassured us that the humanities thrive in the academy as well as in life. We wish to dedicate this book to the students and teachers who use it and to those who continue to examine values through a lifetime of contact with the arts.

ACKNOWLEDGMENTS

This book is indebted to more people than we can truly credit. Yet some names must be mentioned. The following reviewers read the manuscript at various stages, and for their help we are deeply grateful: Michael Berberich, Galveston College; Jim Doan, Nova University; Roberta Farrell, SUNY—Empire State; Michael Harsh, Hagerstown Junior College; Marsha Keller, Oklahoma City University; Paul Kessel, Mohave Community College; Henry Rinne, Westark Community College; Lorain Stowe, Highline Community College; and Robert Tynes, University of North Carolina at Asheville; Walter Doyle, Tidewater Community College; Edward Kies, College of Du Page; Susan Schmeling, Vincennes University; Bernard Selling, Los Angeles Community College. Harrison Davis, of Brigham Young University, had some important suggestions and valuable criticism which led to revisions that strengthened the book. The critical eye of such people as Selma Jeanne Cohen, editor of *Dance Perspectives,* led to changes and refinements. Conversations with numerous people involved in the humanities all led, in one way or another, to adjustments or insights that helped during the writing of this book—such people as Gerald Eager of the Department of Art and Harry Garvin of the Department of English of Bucknell University; Deborah Jowitt, dance critic of the *Village Voice;* the dance critic Marcia Segal; Martha Myers, former chair of the Department of Dance at Connecticut College; Joanna J. Jacobus, choreographer and dance teacher; Walter Wehner of the Music Faculty of the University of North Carolina at Greensboro; the late Marceau Myers, former Dean of the School of Music at North Texas State University; Bruce Bellingham of the Music Department at the University of Connecticut; William E. Parker, photographer in the Art Department at the University of Connecticut; our former editors, Alison Meersschaert, Cheryl Mehalik, Kaye Pace, and Peter Labella; and our present editors, Cynthia Ward and Nancy Blaine, who both read these pages with loving attention. We thank our students, who contributed to these pages in terms of their responses and insights. Katie Girard and Amy Page helped in manuscript preparation. Mrs. Nancy Johnson scrupulously cared for early versions of the manuscript. Finally, we thank Associated University Presses for permission to paraphrase and quote from *Art and the Religious Experience,* 1972, and the University Press of Kentucky for permission to paraphrase and quote from *Sculpture and Enlivened Space,* 1981, both by F. David Martin.

F. David Martin
Lee A. Jacobus

THE HUMANITIES THROUGH THE ARTS

CHAPTER 1

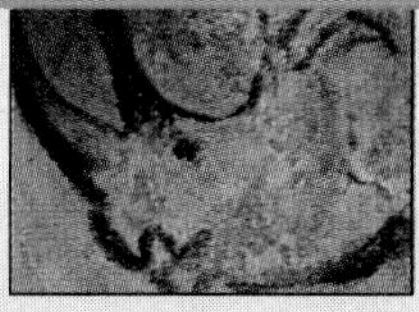

THE HUMANITIES: AN INTRODUCTION

THE HUMANITIES: A STUDY OF VALUES

In the medieval period the word "humanities" distinguished that which pertained to humans from that which pertained to God. Mathematics, the sciences, the arts, and philosophy were humanities: they had to do with humans. Theology and related studies were the subjects of divinity: they had to do with God. This distinction does not have the importance it once did. Today we think of the humanities as those broad areas of human creativity and study that are distinct from mathematics and the "hard" sciences, mainly because in the humanities strictly objective or scientific standards are not usually dominant.

The separation between the humanities and the sciences is illustrated by the way in which values work differently in the two areas. Consider, for example, the drinking of liquor: a positive value for some people, a negative value for others. The biologist describes the physiological effects. The psychologist describes the psychological effects. The sociologist takes a poll and tabulates value preferences concerning drinking. These scientists study values, but they are concerned with what "is" rather than what "ought to be." That is why they can apply strictly scientific standards to their investigations. If they make a value judgment, such as that liquor ought to be banned, they will tend—as scientists—to make it clear that their pronouncements are personal value judgments rather than scientific statements. With humanists, on the other hand, the sharp separation between the "is" and the "ought," between scientific statement and value judgment, is usually not so evident, primarily because the scientific method is not so basic to their work. Most scientists and humanists will agree that we must all make value judgments and that the sciences can often provide important information that helps us make sound decisions. For example, if biologists discovered that liquor significantly shortens the life span, this discovery would indeed be relevant to a value judgment about banning liquor. However, such consensus seems to be lacking with respect to the relevance of the humanities to value judgments. Scientists, more than humanists, probably would be dubious about an assertion that novels such as Dostoevski's *Brothers Karamazov* contribute important information for making sound value judgments about the banning of liquor.

The discoveries of scientists—for example, the bomb and the Pill—often have tremendous impact on the values of their society. Yet some scientists have declared that they merely make the discoveries and that others—presumably politicians—must decide how those discoveries are to be used. Perhaps it is this last statement that brings us closest to the importance of the humanities. If many scientists feel they cannot judge how their discoveries are to be used, then we must try to understand why they give that responsibility to others. This is not to say that scientists uniformly turn such decisions over to others, for many of them are humanists as well as scientists. But the fact remains that governments—from that of Hitler to that of Churchill and those of such nations as China, the Soviet Union, and the United States—have all made use of great scientific achievements without pausing to ask the "achievers" if they approved of the way their discoveries were being used. The questions are: Who decides how to use such discoveries? On what grounds should their judgments be based?

Studying the behavior of neutrinos or ion-exchange resins will not help us get closer to the answer. Such study is not related to the nature of humankind but to the nature of nature. What we need is a study that will get us closer to ourselves. It should be a study that explores the reaches of human feeling in relation to values—not only our own individual feelings and values, although that is first in importance, but also the feelings and values of others. We need a study that will increase our sensitivity to ourselves, others, and the values in our world. To be sensitive is to perceive with insight. To be sensitive is also to feel and believe that things make a difference. Furthermore, it involves an awareness of those aspects of values that cannot be measured by objective standards. To be sensitive is to respect the humanities because, among other reasons, they help develop our sensitivity to values, to what we as individuals place importance on.

There are numerous ways to approach the humanities. The way we have chosen here is the way of the arts. One of the contentions of this book is that values can be expressed in subtle and enduring ways in the arts. From what we can tell, human beings have had the impulse to express their values in arts since virtually the earliest times for which we have a record of human existence. Ancient tools have been recovered from the ice-age which have decorative features designed only to express an affection for beauty in addition to the tools' utility.

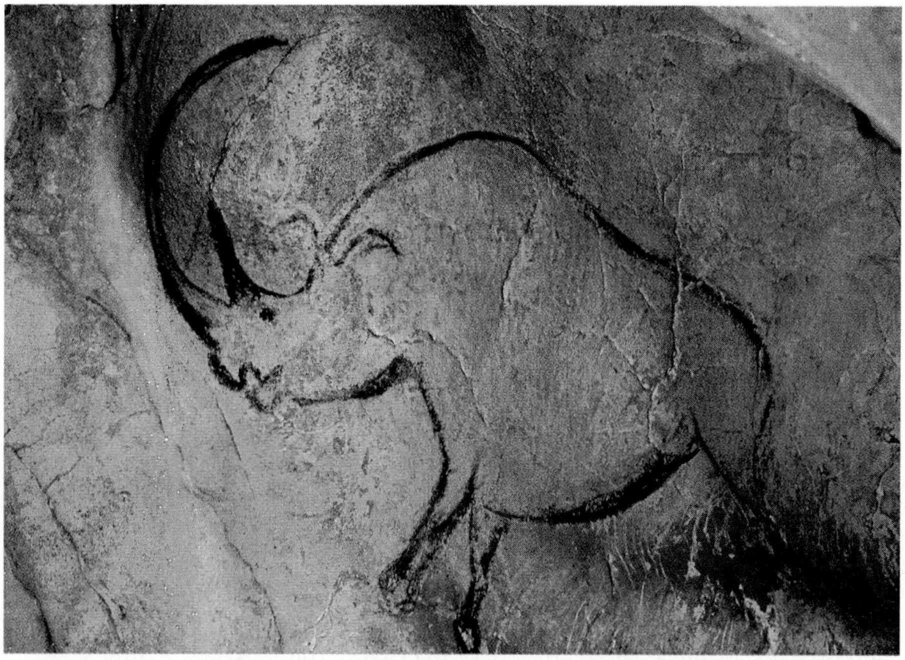

FIGURE 1-1
Photograph from Chauvet Caves. (LeSeuil/Sygma)

The consistency of the human experience in the arts is extraordinary. For example, the concept of progress in the arts is perpetually problematic. Who is to say whether the cave paintings of 30,000 years ago in present-day France are less excellent or advanced than the work of Picasso or Frida Kahlo? Until 1994 the oldest paintings discovered in the Lascaux caves dated to approximately 15,000 years ago. But in 1994 the Chauvet cave yielded a new trove of paintings that are yet another 15,000 years older (Figure 1-1). This discovery has upset theories about the development of styles in art and suggests that humans were highly advanced artists in the earliest years of the existence of our species. The discovery of these new paintings has left us with an interesting sense of reassurance about ourselves and the values of our forebears: their art rivals the best of contemporary efforts.

Among the numerous ways to approach the humanities we have chosen the way of the arts because, as we argue below, the arts clarify or reveal values. As we deepen our understanding of the arts, we necessarily deepen our understanding of values, for that is what the arts are about. We will study our experience with works of arts as well as the values others associate with them. And in the process of doing this we will also educate ourselves about the nature of our own values.

TASTE

Taste is an exercise in values. People who have already made up their minds about what art they like or do not like defend their choices as an expression of their taste. Some opera buffs think Italian opera is uniformly superior to opera in English, French, or German. Others feel that any opera Mozart wrote is wonderful, but all others are impossible. People have various kinds of limitations about the arts. Some cannot stand opera at all. Some cannot look at a painting or sculpture of a nude figure without smirking. Some think any painting is magnificent as long as it has a sunset in it, or a dramatic sea, or a battle, or as long as it is abstract and goes well with the couch. Some people will read any book that has horse racing as part of its subject matter, that has a scientific angle to it, or that is about their current hobby.

One thing we know is that the taste of the mass public shifts constantly. Movies, for example, survive or fail commercially on the basis of the number of people they can appeal to. In commercial art money is the factor that decides on values: a film is good if it makes plenty of money. Consequently, films make every effort to "cash in" on current popular tastes, usually by making sequels until the public's taste changes. Sometimes that happens quickly. For example, among the top fifty grossing films of all time, several have spawned sequels: *Star Wars* (1977), *The Empire Strikes Back* (1980), and *Return of the Jedi* (1983) are good examples, as are *Raiders of the Lost Ark* (1981), *Indiana Jones and the Temple of Doom* (1984), and *Indiana Jones and the Last Crusade* (1989); *Home Alone* I (1990) and II (1992); *Beverly Hills Cop* I (1984) and II (1987); and the ongoing *Batman* series (1989, 1992, 1995). However, sagging box office results for some sequels, such as the *Rocky* films, have doomed future versions. You can certainly add your own examples to this list.

One point our study of the humanities emphasizes is that commercial success is not the most important guide to values in the arts. The long-term success of works of art depends on their ability to interpret human experience at a level of complexity that warrants examination and reexamination over time. Most commercially successful arts give us what we think we want rather than what we really need with reference to insight and understanding. By satisfying us in an immediate and usually superficial way, commercial art can dull us to the possibilities of more complex and more deeply satisfying art.

Everyone has limitations as a perceiver of art. Sometimes we defend ourselves against stretching our limitations by assuming that we have developed our taste and that any effort to change it is bad form. An old saying—"Matters of taste are not disputable"—can be credited with making many of us feel very righteous about our own taste. What the saying means is that there is no accounting for what people like in the arts, for beauty is in the eye of the beholder. Thus, there is no use in trying to educate anyone about the arts. Obviously we disagree. We believe that all of us can and should be educated about the arts and should learn to respond to as wide a variety of the arts as possible: from rock, to jazz, to string quartets; from Charlie Chaplin to Ingmar Bergman; from Lewis Carroll to T. S. Eliot; from folk art to Picasso. Most of us defend our "taste" because anyone who challenges our taste challenges our deep feelings. Anyone who tries to change our responses to art is really trying to get inside our mind. If we fail to understand its purpose, this kind of education naturally arouses resistance in us.

Many facts are involved in the study of the arts. We can verify the dates of Beethoven's birth and death and the dates of his important compositions, as well as their key signatures and opus numbers. We can investigate the history of jazz and the claims of Jelly Roll Morton for having been its "inventor." We can decide who was or was not part of the Barbizon school of painting in nineteenth-century France, when Corot and Manet were painting. We can make lists of the Impressionist painters and those they influenced. Oceans of facts attach to every art form. But our interest is not in facts alone.

What we mean by a study of the arts penetrates beyond facts to the values that evoke our feelings—the way a succession of Eric Clapton's guitar chords when he plays the blues can be electrifying or the way song lyrics can give us a chill. In other words, we want to go beyond the facts *about* a work of art and get to the values implied in the work. How many times have we all found ourselves liking something that, months or years before, we could not stand? And how often do we find ourselves now disliking what we previously judged a masterpiece? Generally we can say the work of art remains the same. It is we who change. We learn to recognize the values expressed in such works as well as to understand the ways in which they are expressed. This is the meaning of "education" in the sense in which we have been using the term.

RESPONSES TO ART

Our responses to art usually involve processes so complex that they can never be fully tracked down or analyzed. At first, they can only be hinted at when we talk about them. However, further education in the arts permits us to observe more closely and thereby respond more intensely to the content of the work. Let us begin by looking at a painting by the Mexican painter David Alfaro Siquieros, *Echo of a Scream* (Figure 1-2, p. 6).

This is a highly emotional painting—in the sense that the work seems to demand a strong emotional response. What we see is the huge head of a baby crying, and then, as if issuing from its own mouth, the baby himself. What kinds of emotions do you find stirring in yourself as you look at this painting? What kinds of emotions do you feel are expressed in the painting? Your own emotional responses—such as shock, pity for the child, irritation at a destructive, mechanical society, or any other nameable emotion—do not sum up the painting. However, they are an important starting point, since Siquieros paints in such a way as to evoke emotion, and our understanding of the painting increases as we examine the means by which this evocation is achieved.

Consider another work, very close in temperament to Siquieros' painting: *Eternal City* by the American painter Peter Blume (Figure 1-3, p. 7).

After attending carefully to the kinds of responses awakened by *Eternal City,* take note of some background information about the painting that you may not have known. The date of this painting is the same as that of *Echo of a Scream:* 1937. *Eternal City* is a name reserved for only one city in the world: Rome. In 1937 the world was on the verge of world war: fascist Italy

FIGURE 1-2
David Alfaro Siqueiros, *Echo of a Scream*. 1937. Enamel on wood, 48 × 36 inches. The Museum of Modern Art, New York, Gift of Edward M. M. Warburg. (Photograph © 1997 The Museum of Modern Art, New York)

Perception Key
ECHO OF A SCREAM

1. Identify the mechanical objects in the painting.
2. What is the condition of these objects? What is their relationship to the baby?
3. What are those strange round forms in the upper right corner?
4. How might your response differ if the angular lines were smoothed out?
5. Why are the natural shapes in the painting, such as the forehead of the baby, distorted? Is awareness of such distortions crucial to a response to the painting?

and Germany against the democratic nations of Europe and the Americas. In the center of the painting is the Roman forum, close to where Julius Caesar, the alleged tyrant, was murdered by Brutus. But here we see fascist Black Shirts, the modern tyrants, beating people. At the left is a figure of Christ and beneath him is a beggar woman—a cripple. Near her are ruins of classic Roman statuary. The enlarged and distorted head, wriggling out like a jack-in-the-box, is that of Mussolini: the man who invented the Black Shirts and fascism. Study the painting closely again. Has your response to the painting changed?

Before going on to the next painting, which is quite different in character, we should pause to make some observations about what we have done. With added knowledge about its cultural and political implications—what we shall call the background of the painting—your responses to *Eternal City* may have changed significantly. Ideally they should have become more fo-

PERCEPTION KEY
ETERNAL CITY

1. What common ingredients do you find in the Blume and Siquieros paintings?
2. Is your reaction to this painting similar to or distinct from your reaction to the Siquieros?
3. Is the effect of the distortions similar or different?
4. How are colors used in each painting? Are the colors those of the natural world, or do they suggest an artificial environment? Are they distorted for effect?
5. In terms of the objects and events represented in each painting, do you think the paintings are comparable?

FIGURE 1-3
Peter Blume, *The Eternal City*. 1934–1937. Dated on painting 1937. Oil on composition board, 34 × 47⅞ inches. The Museum of Modern Art, New York. Mrs. Simon Guggenheim Fund. (Photograph © The Museum of Modern Art, New York; art © 1997 Estate of Peter Blume/Licensed by VAGA, New York)

cused, intense, and certain. Why? The painting is surely the same physical object you looked at originally. Nothing has changed in that object. Therefore, something has changed because something has been added to you: information that the general viewer of the painting in 1937 would have had and would have responded to much more emotionally than we do now. Consider how a fascist, on the one hand, or an Italian humanist and lover of Roman culture, on the other hand, would have reacted to this painting in 1937.

A full experience of this painting is not one thing or one system of things but an innumerable variety of things. Moreover, "knowledge about" a work of art can lead to you "knowledge of" the work of art, which implies a richer experience. This is important as a basic principle, since it means that we can be educated about what is in a work of art, such as its form, shapes, and objects, as well as what is external to a work, such as its political references. It means we can learn to respond more completely. It also means that artists such as Peter Blume sometimes produce works that demand background information if we are to appreciate them fully. This is particularly true of art that references historical circumstances and personages.

Perception Key
GUERNICA

1. Distortion is powerfully evident in this painting. How does its function differ from that of the distortion in Blume's or Siquieros' paintings?
2. Describe the objects in the painting. What is their relationship to one another?
3. Why the prominence of the light bulb?
4. What large geometrical shapes dominate the painting? How do they define the overall organization of the painting?
5. Because of reading habits in the West, we tend initially to focus on the left side of most paintings and then move to the right. Is this the case with your perception of *Guernica*? In the organization or form of *Guernica* is there a countermovement that, once our vision has reached the right side, pulls us back to the left? If so, what shapes in the painting cause this countermovement? How do these left–right and right–left movements affect the balance of the painting?
6. The bull seems to be totally indifferent to the carnage. Do you think the bull may be some kind of symbol? For example, could the bull represent the spirit of the Spanish people? Could the bull represent General Franco, the man who ordered the bombing? Or could the bull represent both? To answer these questions adequately do you need further background information, or can you defend your answers by referring to what is in the painting, or do you need to do both?
7. The bombing of Guernica occurred during the day. Why does Picasso portray it as happening at night?
8. Which is more visually dominant, human beings or animals? If you were not told, would you know that this painting was a representation of an air raid?
9. Is the subject matter—what the work is about—of this painting war? Death? Suffering?
10. What kinds of responses does the painting evoke in you?

FIGURE 1-4
Pablo Picasso, *Guernica*. 1937. Oil on canvas, 11 feet 6 inches × 25 feet 8 inches. (© 1997 Succession Picasso/Artist Rights Society (ARS), New York)

Therefore, we may find ourselves unable to respond to a work of art because we lack the background knowledge the artist presupposes.

Picasso's *Guernica* (Figure 1-4), one of the most famous paintings of the twentieth century, also dates from 1937. Its title comes from the name of an old Spanish town that was bombed during the Spanish Civil War—the first aerial bombing of noncombatant civilians in modern warfare. Examine this painting carefully.

The next painting (Figure 1-5) was completed in 1936 by Piet Mondrian, an influential Dutch painter. Mondrian, using the bold style of *Composition in White, Black and Red,* became a household name because his designs produced a sense of satisfaction in viewers around the world.

PERCEPTION KEY

COMPOSITION IN WHITE, BLACK AND RED

1. If you were to comment on "distortion" in this painting, what would that imply about what the painting represents? What is represented in the painting?
2. How would your responses differ if all the black areas were repainted orange? Would the balance of the painting be distorted?
3. Suppose the horizontal black line running across the width of the painting were raised nearer to the top. Would the balance of the painting be disturbed?
4. Suppose the little black rectangle at the upper left-hand corner were enlarged. Would the balance of the painting be disturbed? How important is visual balance in this work?
5. There is no frame around this painting. Do you think there should be?
6. Do you need any historical background to appreciate Mondrian's painting? Is what we have said about world conditions in 1937 irrelevant to this painting? Soon after that date, Mondrian's country, Holland, partially destroyed itself by

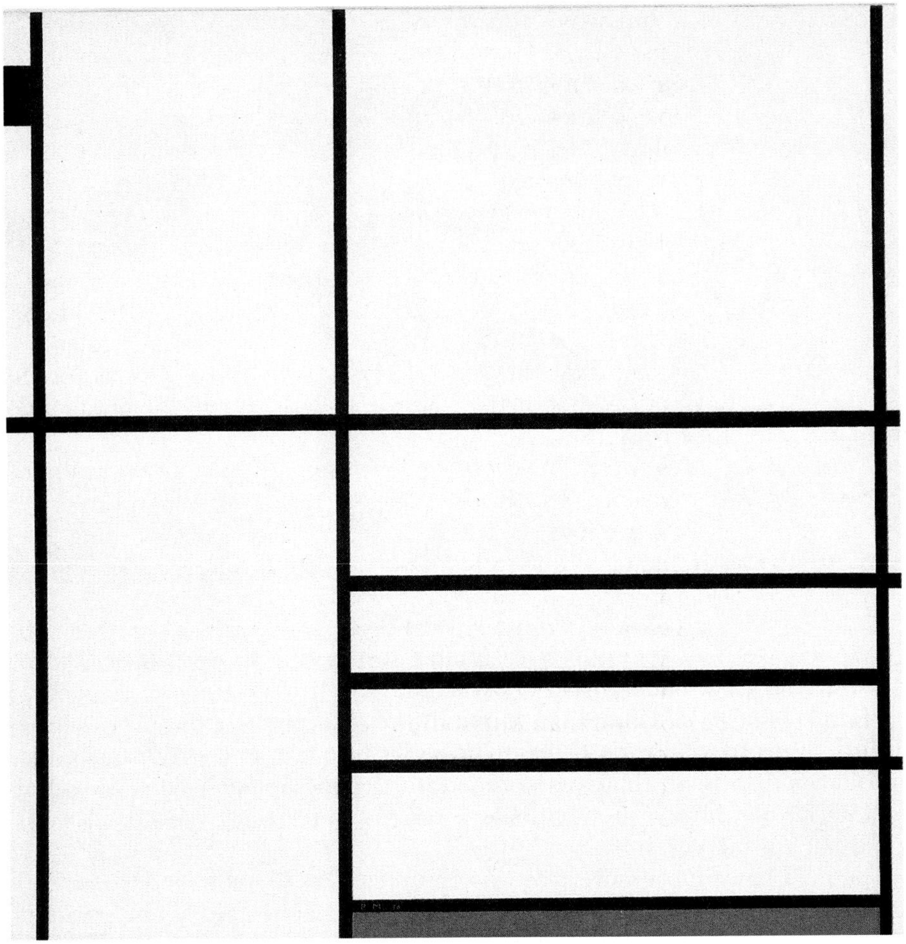

FIGURE 1-5
Piet Mondrian, *Composition in White, Black, and Red*. 1936. Oil on canvas, 40¼ × 41 inches. The Museum of Modern Art, New York. Gift of the Advisory Committee. (Photograph © 1997 The Museum of Modern Art, New York)

opening its dikes in an attempt to keep Hitler out. Does this fact influence the way you look at this painting?

7. Does the painting evoke strong responses in you? Do you have more difficulty articulating your responses to it than to the paintings by Siquieros, Blume, and Picasso? If so, how is this to be explained?
8. Suppose the Mondrian were hung with its vertical lines not parallel to the lines of the wall. Would you need to straighten it? If *Echo of a Scream* were crooked on a wall, would you feel as compelled to straighten it? Explain.
9. Is it true that the painting by Mondrian is more like music than the paintings by Siquieros, Blume, and Picasso?

ARTISTIC FORM

The Mondrian obviously is very different from the other paintings in subject matter. (In Chapter 4 we will consider the subject matter of Mondrian and abstract painting generally.) The responses you have when you look at it are probably quite different from those you had when you were viewing the other paintings, but why? You might reply that the Mondrian is pure form, an entirely sensuous surface. Unlike the other paintings, no objects or events are represented. And yet this painting can be very exciting. Form—the interrelationships of lines, colors, light, textures, and shapes—can be very moving. Most of us have the capacity to respond to pure form even in paintings whose subject distracts us from pure form. Thus, for us, responding to *Eternal City* involves responding not just to an interpretation of fascism taking hold in Italy but also to the painting's sensuous surface—its organization of shapes, colors, light, lines, and textures. This is certainly true of *Echo of a Scream;* if you look again at that painting, you will see that its sensuous surface, colors, forms, and shapes are not only interesting intrinsically but also that they deepen our response to what is represented. In the hands of a good artist, form is an instrument for producing in us subconscious responses.

Every painter uses form, but every painter does not necessarily call attention to it the way Mondrian does. And since we often respond to form without even being conscious that it is affecting us, it is of the first importance that a painter make sure form is successful. Study the composition of *Eternal City.* Figure 1-6 is a tracing of the basic form.

In the "center stage" of the composition is the scene of fascist Black Shirts brutalizing citizens: it is the government in its forum. To one side is Christ, not only removed but bricked off. Moreover, Christ is smaller and less important to the composition than Mussolini's head—the largest shape—close to the action and in control. The two shapes beneath Mussolini's head represent the smiling common people, the middle-class citizens who helped Mussolini gain power and who thought they would benefit from his government.

FIGURE 1-6
Line tracing of Blume's *Eternal City*.

The form of any painting can be analyzed because any painting has to be organized: parts have to be interrelated. Moreover, it is important to think carefully about the form of individual paintings. This is particularly true of paintings one does not respond to immediately—to "difficult" or apparently uninterestingly paintings. Often the analysis of form can help us gain access to such paintings so that they become genuinely exciting.

PERCEPTION

We cannot respond properly to a work of art that we do not perceive properly. What is less obvious is what we referred to previously—the fact that we can often give our attention to a work of art and still not really perceive very much. The reason for this should be clear from our previous discussion. Frequently, we need to know something about the background of a work of art that would aid our perception. Anyone who did not know who Christ was, or what fascism was, or what Mussolini meant to the world would have a difficult time making much sense of *Eternal City*. But it is also true that anyone who could not perceive the form of Blume's painting might have a completely superficial response to the painting. Such a person could indeed know all about the background and understand the more or less symbolic statements made by the painting, but that is only part of the painting. From seeing what Mondrian can do with line, shape, color, light, texture, and their relationships, you can understand that the formal qualities of a painting are neither accidental nor unimportant. In Blume's painting, the form acts in such a way as to focus attention and organize our perceptions by establishing the relationships between the parts of the composition.

Form is basic to all the arts and to everything that is organized. To perceive any work of art adequately, we must perceive the form. Examine the following poem—"l(a"—by e. e. cummings. It is unusual in its form and its effects.

l(a

le
af
fa

ll

s)
one
l

iness

This poem looks at first like a strange kind of code, like an Egyptian hieroglyph. But it is not a code—it is more like a Japanese haiku poem, a poem that sets a scene or paints a picture and then waits for us to get it. And to "get it" requires sensitive perception.

Perception Key
"L(A"

1. Study the poem carefully until you begin to make out the words. What are they?
2. One part of the poem is a general term; the other is the name of an event. What is the relationship between them?
3. Is the shape of the poem important to the meaning of the poem?
4. Why are the words of the poem difficult to perceive? Is that difficulty important to the poem?
5. Does the poem evoke an image or images?
6. Once you have perceived the words and imagery of the poem, does your response change? Compare your analysis of the poem with ours, which follows.

In this poem a word is interrupted by parenthesis: "l one l iness"—"loneliness"—a feeling we have all experienced. Because of its isolating, biting power, we ordinarily do not like this feeling. Then, inside the parentheses, there is a phrase, "a leaf falls," the description of an event. In poetry such a description is usually called an image. In this poem the image illustrates the idea, or theme, of loneliness, melding the specific with the abstract. But how is this melding accomplished? First of all, notice the devices that symbolize or represent oneness, an emblem of loneliness. The poem begins with the letter "l," which in the typeface used in the original poem looks like the number "one." Even the parenthesis separating the "a" from the "l" helps accent the isolation of the "l." Then there is the "le," which is the singular article in French. The idea of one is doubled by repetition in the "ll" figure. Then cummings brazenly writes "one" and follows it by "l" and then the ultimate "iness." Furthermore, in the original edition the poem is number one of the collection. Secondly, notice how these representations of oneness are wedded to the image: "a leaf falls."

As you look at the poem, your eye follows a downward path that swirls in a pattern similar to the diagram in Figure 1-7. This is merely following the parentheses and consonants. As you follow the vowels as well, you see curves that become spirals, and the image is indeed much like that of a leaf actually falling. This accounts for the long, thin look of the poem. Now, go back to the poem and reread it. Has your response changed? How?

Of course, most poems do not work in quite this way. Most poems do not rely on the way they look on the page, although this is one of the most important strategies of cummings. But what most poets are concerned with is the way the images or verbal pictures fit into the totality of the poem, how they make us experience the whole poem more intensely. In cummings' poem the single, falling, dying leaf—one out of so many—is virtually perfect for helping us understand loneliness from a dying person's point of view. People are like leaves in that they are countless when they are alive and together. But like leaves, they die singly. And when one person separates himself or herself from the community of friends, that person is as alone as the separate leaf.

FIGURE 1-7
Diagram of e. e. cummings' "l(a."

ABSTRACT IDEAS AND CONCRETE IMAGES

Cummings' poem presents an abstract idea fused with a concrete image or word picture. It is concrete because what is described is a physical event: a falling leaf. Loneliness, on the other hand, is abstract. Take an abstract idea: love, hate, indecision, arrogance, jealousy, ambition, justice, civil rights, prejudice, revenge, revolution, coyness, insanity, or any other. Then link it with some physical object or event that you think expresses the abstract idea. "Expresses" means simply to make us see the object as portraying the abstract idea, the way a leaf expresses loneliness. Of course, you need not follow cummings' style of splitting words and using parentheses. You may use any way of lining up the letters and words that you think is interesting.

In *Paradise Lost* John Milton describes hell as a place with "Rocks, Caves, Lakes, Fens, Bogs, Dens, and shades of death." Now, neither you nor the poet has ever seen "shades of death," although the idea is in Psalm 23, "the valley of the shadow of death." Milton gets away with it because he has linked the abstract idea of shades of death to so many concrete images in this single line. He is giving us images that suggest the mood of hell just as much as they describe the landscape, and we realize that he gives us so many topographic details in order to get us ready for the last detail—the abstract idea of shades of death—which in many ways is the most important.

There is much more to be said about poetry, of course, but on a preliminary level poetry worked in much the same way in seventeenth-century England as it does in twentieth-century America. The same principles are at work: described objects or events are used as a means of bringing abstract ideas to life. The descriptions take on a wider and deeper significance—wider in the sense that the descriptions are connected with the larger scope of abstract ideas, deeper in the sense that because of these descriptions the abstract ideas become vividly focused and more meaningful. Thus cummings' poem gives us insight—a penetrating understanding—into what we all must face: the isolating loneliness of death.

The following poem is particularly telling for us because its theme is highly complex: the memory of an older culture (simplicity in this poem) and the consideration of a newer culture (complexity). It is an African poem by the Nigerian poet Gabriel Okara; and knowing that it is African, we can

PERCEPTION KEY
"PIANO AND DRUMS"

1. What are the most important physical objects in the poem? What cultural significance do they have?
2. Why do you think Okara chose the drum and the piano to help reveal the clash between the two cultures? Where are his allegiances?

begin to appreciate the extreme complexity of Okara's feelings about the clash of the old and new cultures. He symbolizes the clash in terms of music, and he opposes two musical instruments: the drum and the piano. They stand for the African and the European cultures. But even beyond the musical images that abound in this poem, look closely at the images of nature, the pictures of the panther and leopard, and see how Okara imagines them.

PIANO AND DRUMS

When at break of day at a riverside
I hear jungle drums telegraphing
the mystic rhythm, urgent, raw
like bleeding flesh, speaking of
primal youth and the beginning,
I see the panther ready to pounce,
the leopard snarling about to leap
and the hunters crouch with spears poised;
And my blood ripples, turns torrent,
topples the years and at once I'm
in my mother's lap a suckling;
at once I'm walking simple
paths with no innovations,
rugged, fashioned with the naked
warmth of hurrying feet and groping hearts
in green leaves and wild flowers pulsing.
Then I hear a wailing piano
solo speaking of complex ways
in tear-furrowed concerto;
of far-away lands
and new horizons with
coaxing diminuendo, counterpoint,
crescendo. But lost in the labyrinth
of its complexities, it ends in the middle
of a phrase at a daggerpoint.
And I lost in the morning mist
of an age at a riverside keep
wandering in the mystic rhythm
of jungle drums and the concerto.

Such a poem speaks directly to legions of the current generation of Africans. But consider some points in light of what we have said earlier. In order to perceive the kind of emotional struggle that Okara talks about—the subject matter of the poem—we need to know something about Africa and the struggle African nations have in modernizing themselves along the lines of more technologically advanced nations. We also need to know something of the history of Africa and the fact that European nations, such as Britain in the case of Nigeria, once controlled much of Africa. Knowing these things, we know then that there is no thought of the "I" of the poem accepting the "complex ways" of the new culture without qualification. The "I" does not think of the culture of the piano as manifestly superior to the culture of the drum. That is why the labyrinth of complexities ends at a "daggerpoint." The new culture is a mixed blessing.

We have argued that the perception of a work of art is aided by background information and that sensitive perception must be aware of form, at least implicitly. But we believe there is much more to sensitive perception. Somehow the form of a work of art clarifies or reveals values, and our response is intensified by our awareness of those revealed values. But how does the form do this? And how does this awareness come to us? In the next chapter we shall consider these questions, and in doing so we will also raise that most important question: what is a work of art? Once we have examined each of the arts, it will be clear, we hope, that the principles developed in these opening chapters are equally applicable to all the arts.

SUMMARY

Unlike scientists, humanists generally do not use strictly objective standards. The arts reveal values; other humanities study values. Judging from the most ancient of artistic efforts, we can assert that the arts represent one of the most basic of human activities. They satisfy a need to explore and express the values that link us all together. By observing our responses to a work of art and examining the means by which the artist evokes those responses, we can deepen our understanding of art. Our approach to the humanities is through the arts and our taste in art connects with our deep feelings. Yet our taste is continually improved by education. Usually, background information about a work of art and increased sensitivity to its form intensify our responses.

CHAPTER 1 BIBLIOGRAPHY

Barthes, Roland. *Image, Music, Text.* New York: Hill and Wang, 1977.

Beardsley, Monroe C. *Aesthetics: Problems in the Philosophy of Criticism.* New York: Harcourt Brace, 1961.

Blocker, H. Gene. *Philosophy of Art.* New York: Scribners, 1979.

Chadwick, Whitney. *Women, Art, and Society.* London: Thames and Hudson, 1990.

Dewey, John. *Art as Experience.* New York: Capricorn Books, 1934.

Gombrich, E. H. *The Story of Art,* 16th ed., expanded and redesigned. London: Phaidon, 1995.

Jacobus, Lee A. (ed.). *Aesthetics and the Arts.* New York: McGraw-Hill, 1968.

Jarrett, James L. *The Humanities and Humanistic Education.* Reading, Mass.: Addison-Wesley, 1973.

Langer, Susanne K. (ed.). *Problems of Art.* Kyoto: Appollon-sha, 1981.

———. *Reflections on Art.* New York: Arno, 1979.

Lipman, Matthew. *What Happens in Art?* New York: Appleton-Century-Crofts, 1967.

Maslow, Abraham. *New Knowledge in Human Values.* Chicago: Henry Regnery, Gateway, 1971.

Neill, Alex, and Aaron Ridley. *Arguing About Art.* New York: McGraw-Hill, 1995.

———. *The Philosophy of Art: Readings Ancient and Modern.* New York: McGraw-Hill, 1995.

Pearce, Lynne. *Woman, Image, Text.* Toronto: University of Toronto Press, 1991.

Rader, Melvin, and Bertram Jessup. *Art and Human Values.* Englewood Cliffs, N.J.: Prentice-Hall, 1976.

Read, Herbert. *Art and Alienation*. New York: Viking, 1969.
———. *Education Through Art*, new rev. ed. New York: Pantheon, 1963.
Santayana, George. *The Sense of Beauty*, critical ed. Cambridge, Mass.: MIT Press, 1988.
Whitehead, Alfred North. *Adventures of Ideas*. New York: Free Press, 1967.

CHAPTER 1 WEBSITES

To make use of these sources you will need a computer and a connection to the Internet and thus the World Wide Web. Your library will help you gain access to these sites if you do not have your own computer. Many of these sources will link you with other sites that have special interest for you. Most of them are updated regularly so that you will have access to recently added sites. A useful book to help acquaint you with the Internet is Alfred Glossbrenner's *Internet 101: A College Student's Guide* (McGraw-Hill, 1995).

Art Museums and Exhibits

World Wide Web: **http://www.yahoo.com/Art/Museums**

Art on the Internet

World Wide Web: **http://www.art.net/**

Art Sites

World Wide Web: **http://bastille.gatech.edu/adam/art.html**

ArtSource

World Wide Web: **http://www.uky.edu/Artsource**

ArtWorld

World Wide Web: **http://www.anima.wis.net/ARTWORLDhome.html**

Digital Picture Archive

Gopher: **olt.et.tudelft.n1 1251**

Fine Art Forum Home Page

World Wide Web: **http://www.msstate.edu/Fineart_Online/home.html**

The FineArt Forum World Wide Web Resource List

World Wide Web: **http://www.msstate.edu/Fineart_Online/art-resources.html**

French Cave Paintings

World Wide Web: **http://www.culture.fr/culture/gvpda-en.html**

Index World Arts Resources

World Wide Web: **http://www.cgrg.ohio-state.edu/Newark/artres.html**

New York Art Line Collection of Art and Art Resources

Gopher: **panix.com**

CHAPTER 2

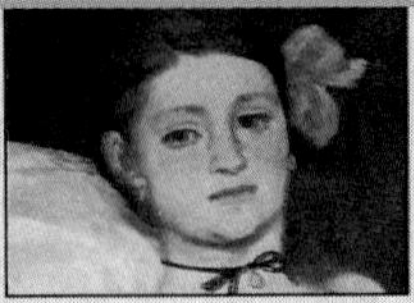

WHAT IS A WORK OF ART?

No definition for a work of art seems completely adequate, and none is universally accepted. Thus we shall not propose a definition here, but rather attempt to clarify some criteria or distinctions that can help us identify works of art. Since the term "work of art" implies the concept of making in two of its words—"work" and "art" (short for "artifice")—a work of art is often said to be something made by a person. Hence sunsets, beautiful trees, "found" natural objects such as grained driftwood, "paintings" by insects or birds, and a host of other natural phenomena are not considered works of art, despite their beauty. You may not wish to accept the proposal that a work of art must be of human origin, but if you do accept it, consider the construction shown in Figure 2-1, Jim Dine's *Shovel.*

Shovel is part of a valuable collection of art and was first shown at an art gallery in New York City. Furthermore, Dine is considered an important American artist. He did not make the shovel himself, however. Like most shovels, the one in his construction, although designed by a person, was mass-produced. Dine mounted the shovel in front of a beautifully painted panel and presented this construction for serious consideration. The construction is described as "mixed media," meaning it consists of several materials, paint, a panel, the box beneath the shovel, wood, a cord, and the metal of the shovel. Given these credentials, is it then a work of art?

We can hardly discredit the construction as a work of art simply because Dine did not make the shovel; after all, we often accept objects manufactured to specification by factories as genuine works of sculpture (see the Calder construction, Figure 5-16). Collages by Picasso and Braque, which include objects such as paper and nails mounted on a panel, are generally accepted as works of art, as is Kurt Schwitters' *Merz Konstruktion* (Figure

5-26). Museums have even accepted such objects as a signed urinal by Marcel Duchamp, one of the Dadaist artists of the early twentieth century, who in many ways anticipated the works of Dine, Warhol, Oldenburg, and others in the Pop Art movement of the 1950s and 1960s.

IDENTIFYING ART CONCEPTUALLY

Three of the most widely accepted criteria for determining whether or not something is a work of art are (1) that the object or event is made by an artist, (2) that the object or event is intended to be a work of art by its maker, and (3) that important or recognized experts agree that it is a work of art. Unfortunately, one cannot always determine these criteria only by perceiving the work. In many cases, for instance, we may confront an object like *Shovel* and not know whether Dine constructed the shovel very carefully in imitation of the mass-produced object, thus satisfying the first criterion that the object be made by an artist; or whether Dine intended it to be a work of art; or whether experts agree that it is a work of art. In fact, Dine did not make this particular shovel; but since this fact cannot be established by perception, one has to be told.

FIGURE 2-1
Jim Dine's *Shovel*. 1962. Mixed media. (Sonnabend Gallery, photograph by Eric Pollitzer)

PERCEPTION KEY
IDENTIFYING A WORK OF ART

1. If Dine actually made the shovel, would *Shovel* then unquestionably be a work of art? If he constructed the panel and box and placed the shovel where it is, would that satisfy the criterion that the "object or event" be made by an artist?
2. Suppose Dine made the shovel himself, and it was absolutely perfect in the sense that it could not be readily distinguished from a mass-produced shovel. Would that kind of perfection make the piece more a work of art or less a work of art?
3. Find people who hold opposing views about the question of whether or not *Shovel* is a work of art. Ask them to argue the point in detail, being particularly careful not to argue simply from personal opinion. Ask them to point out what it is about the object itself that qualifies it for or disqualifies it from being identified as a work of art.

IDENTIFYING ART PERCEPTUALLY

Perception, what we can observe, and conception, what we know or think we know, are closely related. We are often led to see what we expect or want to see; we recognize an object because it conforms to our conception of it. For example, in architecture we recognize churches and office buildings as distinct because of our conception of churches and office buildings. The ways of identifying a work of art mentioned above depend on the conceptions of the artist and experts on art and perhaps not enough on our perceptions of the work itself. Objects and events have qualities that can be perceived without the help of artists or experts, although these specialists are often helpful. If we wish to consider the artistic qualities of objects or events, we can easily do so. Yet to do so implies an attitude or an approach.

We are going to suggest an approach here that is simple and flexible and that depends largely on perception, although not so exclusively as to rule out important conceptual aspects. The distinctions of this approach will not lead us necessarily to a definition of art, but they will offer us a way to examine objects and events with reference to whether they possess artistically perceivable qualities. And in some cases at least, it should bring us to reasonable grounds for distinguishing certain objects or events as art. We will consider three terms related primarily to the perceptual nature of the work of art.

1. Artistic form
2. Content
3. Subject matter

A fourth term relates primarily to what our perception of the work of art does to us:

4. Participation

ARTISTIC FORM

All objects and events have form. They are bounded by limits of time and space, and they have parts with distinguishable relationships to one another. Form is the interrelationships of part to part and part to whole. To say that some object or event has form means it has some degree of perceptible unity. Thus a single isolated tone played on a piano has form, but only in relation to the silences that precede and succeed it. To say that something has artistic form, however, usually implies that there is a strong degree of perceptible unity. Artistic form distinguishes art from objects or events that are not works of art.

"Artistic form" implies that the parts or elements we perceive—line, color, and shape in a painting—have been organized for the most profound effect possible. Not all works of art have organic form (in which all elements relate functionally to one another)—for instance, Mondrian's *Composition in White, Black and Red* (Figure 1-5) does not need it. Our daily experiences are characterized more by disunity than by unity. Consider, for instance, the order of your experiences during a typical day or even a segment of that day. Compare that order with the order most novelists give to the experiences of their characters. One impulse for reading novels is to experience the tight unity that artistic form usually imposes, a unity almost none of us comes close to achieving in our daily lives. Much the same is true of music. Noises and random tones in everyday experience lack the order that most composers impose. Indeed, even nature's models of unity are usually far less strongly perceptible than the unity of most works of art.

Consider, for example, birdsongs, which are clearly precursors of music.

Even the song of the meadowlark, which is longer than most birdsongs, is fragmentary and incomplete. It is like a theme that is simply a statement and repetition, lacking development or contrast. Thus the composer, finding the meadowlark's short melody monotonous when repeated again and again, enriches it by such devices as adding notes to those already sounded, by varying the melody through alternation of rhythm, or by changing the pitch of some of the notes to higher or lower positions on the musical scale, or by adding a completely different melody to set up a sense of contrast and tension with the initial melody.

Since strong, perceptible unity appears so infrequently in nature, we tend to value the perceptible unity of artistic form. Works of art differ in the power of their unity. If that power is weak, then the question arises: Is this a work of art? Consider the Mondrian with reference to its artistic form. If its elements and parts were not carefully proportioned to the overall structure of the painting, the tight balance that produces a strong unity of structure would be lost. Mondrian was so concerned with this problem that he worked out the areas of lines and rectangles to be sure they had a clear, almost mathematical relationship to the totality. Of course, disunity or playing against expectations of unity can also be artistically useful at times. Some artists realize how strong the impulse toward unity is in those of us who have perceived many works of art. For some people, the contemporary attitude toward the loose organization of formal elements is something of a norm, and the highly unified work of art is thought of as old-fashioned. However, it seems that the effects achieved by a lesser degree of unity succeed only because we recognize them as departures from our variations upon well-known, highly organized forms.

Artistic form as distinct from nonartistic form, we have suggested, involves a high degree of perceptible unity. But how do we determine what is a high degree? And if we cannot be clear about this, how can this distinction be of much help in distinguishing works of art from things that are not works of art? Consider, for example, the following news photograph—taken on one of the main streets of Saigon in February 1968 by Eddie Adams, an Associated Press photographer—showing Brig. Gen. Nguyen Ngoc Loan, then South Vietnam's national police chief, killing a Vietcong captive (Figure 2-2).

Adams stated that his picture was an accident, that his hand moved the camera reflexively as he saw the general raise the revolver. The lens of the camera was set in such a way that the background was thrown out of focus. The blurring of the background helped bring out the drama of the foreground scene. Does this photograph have a high degree of perceptible unity? Is it a work of art? Certainly the skill and care of the photographer are evident. Not many amateur photographers would have had enough skill to catch such a fleeting event with such stark clarity. Even if an amateur had accomplished this, we would be inclined to believe that it was more luck than skill. Adams' care for the photograph is even more evident. He risked his life to get it. If this photograph had not been widely publicized and admired, we can imagine the dismay he would have felt. But do we admire this work the way we admire Siquieros' *Echo of a Scream* (Figure 1-2)? Do we experience these two works in the same basic way?

FIGURE 2-2
Eddie Adams, *Execution in Saigon*. 1968. Silver halide. (AP/Wide World Photos)

Compare a painting of a somewhat similar subject—Goya's *May 3, 1808* (Figure 2-3).

Goya chose the most terrible moment, that split second before the crash of the guns. There is no doubt that the executions will go on. The desolate mountain pushing down from the left blocks escape, while from the right the firing squad relentlessly hunches forward. The soldiers' thick legs—planted wide apart and parallel—support like sturdy pillars the blind, pressing wall formed by their backs. These are men of a military machine. Their rifles, flashing in the bleak light of the ghastly lantern, thrust out as if they belonged to their bodies. It is unimaginable that any of these men would defy the command of their superiors. In the dead of night, the doomed are packed up against the mountain like animals being slaughtered. One man alone flings up his arms in a gesture of utter despair—or is it defiance? The uncertainty increases the intensity of our attention. Most of the rest of the men bury their faces, while a few, with eyes staring out of their sockets, glance out at what they cannot help seeing—the sprawling dead smeared in blood.

With the photograph of the execution in Vietnam, despite its immediate and powerful attraction, it takes only a glance or two to grasp what is presented. Undivided attention, perhaps, is necessary to become aware of the significance of the event, but not sustained attention. In fact, to take careful notice of all the details—such as the patterns on the prisoner's shirt—

Perception Key

GOYA'S *MAY 3, 1808*, AND ADAMS' *EXECUTION IN SAIGON*

1. Is the painting different from Adams' photograph in the way the details work together? Be specific.
2. Could any detail in the painting be changed or removed without weakening the unity of the total design? What about the photograph?
3. Does the photograph or the painting more powerfully reveal human barbarity?
4. Are there details in the photograph that distract your attention?
5. Do buildings in the background of the photograph add to or subtract from the power of what is being represented here? Compare the looming architecture in the painting.
6. Do the shadows on the street add anything to the significance of the photograph? Compare the shadows on the ground in the painting.
7. Does it make any significant difference that the Vietcong prisoner's shirt is checkered? Compare the white shirt on the gesturing man in the painting.
8. Is the expression on the soldier's face, along the left side of the photograph, appropriate to the situation? Compare the facial expressions in the painting.
9. Can these works be fairly compared when one is in black and white and the other is in full color?
10. What are basic differences between seeing a photograph of a real man being killed and a painting of that event?

FIGURE 2-3
Francisco Goya, *May 3, 1808*. 1814–1815. Oil on canvas, 8 feet 9 inches × 13 feet 4 inches. The Prado, Madrid. (Scala/Art Resource, NY)

does not add to our awareness of the significance of the photograph. If anything, our awareness will be sharper and more productive if we avoid such detailed examination. Is such the case with the Goya? We believe not. Indeed, without sustained attention to the details of this work, most of what is revealed would be missed. For example, block out everything but the dark shadow at the bottom right. Note how differently that shadow appears when it is isolated. We must see the details individually and collectively, as they work together. Unless we are aware of their collaboration, we are not going to grasp fully the total design.

Close examination of the Adams photograph reveals several artistic efforts to increase the unity and power of the print. For example, the flak jacket of General Loan has been blocked out so as to remove distracting details. The high contrast of the soldier on the left intensifies his grimace at the terrifying moment of the gun's explosion. The buildings in the background have been "dodged out" (held back in printing so that they are not fully visible) so that they are mere suggestions of habitation and form. The shadows of trees on the road have been softened so as to lead the eye inexorably with the hand that holds the gun toward the body of the victim. The victim's face has been dodged slightly to make it more recognizably human, and the space around the head of the victim is completely dodged out so that it appears virtually as if there is a halo around the head. All this is done artistically in the act of printing.

We are suggesting that the Goya has a much higher degree of perceptible unity than Adams' photograph, that perhaps only the Goya has artistic form. We base these conclusions on what is given for us to perceive: the fact that the part-to-part and the part-to-whole relationships are much stronger in the Goya. Now, of course, you may disagree. No judgment about such matters is indisputable. Indeed, that is part of the fun of talking about whether something is or is not a work of art—we can learn how to perceive from each other.

PARTICIPATION

Both the photograph and the Goya tend to grasp our attention. Initially for most of us, probably, the photograph has much more pulling power than the painting. But the term "participate" is much more accurately descriptive of what we are likely to be doing in our experience of the painting. With the painting, we must not only give but also sustain our undivided attention. If that happens, we lose our self-consciousness, our sense of being separate, of standing apart from the painting. We participate. And only by means of participation can we come close to a full awareness of what the painting is all about.

Works of art are created, exhibited, and preserved for us to perceive with not only undivided but also sustained attention. Artists, critics, and philosophers of art or aestheticians generally are in agreement about this. Thus if, in order to understand and appreciate it fully, a work requires our participation, we have an indication that the work is art. Therefore—unless our analyses have been incorrect, and you should satisfy yourself about this—the Goya would seem to be a work of art. Conversely, the photograph is not as obviously a work of art as the painting, and this is the case despite the fascinating impact of the photograph. Yet these are highly tentative judgments. We are far from being clear about why the Goya requires our participation and the photograph apparently does not. Until we are clear about these "whys," the grounds for these judgments remain shaky.

Goya's painting tends to draw us on until, ideally, we become aware of all the details and their interrelationships. For example, the long dark shadow at the bottom right underlines the line of the firing squad, and the line of the firing squad helps bring out the shadow. Moreover, this shadow is the darkest and most opaque part of the painting. It has a forbidding, blind, fateful quality that, in turn, reinforces the ominous appearance of the firing squad. On the other hand, the dark shadow on the street just below the forearm of General Loan seems less powerful. The photograph has fewer meaningful details. Thus our attempts to keep our attention on the photograph tend to be forced—which is to say that they will fail. Sustained attention or participation cannot be achieved by acts of will. The splendid singularity of what we are attending to must fascinate and control us to the point where we no longer need to will our attention. We can make up our minds to give our undivided attention to something. But if that something lacks the pulling power that holds our attention, we cannot participate with it.

The ultimate test for recognizing a work of art, then, is how it works in us, what it does to us. Participative experiences of works of art are communions—experiences so full and final that they enrich our entire lives. Such experiences are life-enhancing not just because of the great satisfaction they may give us at the moment but also because they make more or less permanent contributions to our future life. Does Mondrian's *Composition in White, Black and Red* (Figure 1-5) heighten your perception of the relationships between sharply edged vertical and horizontal lines, the neatness and "spatial comfortableness" of these kinds of rectangles, and the rich qualities of white, black, and red? Does cummings' "l(a" heighten your perception of falling leaves and deepen your understanding of loneliness and death? Do you see shovels differently, perhaps, after experiencing *Shovel* (Figure 2-1) by Dine? If not, presumably they are not works of art. But this assumes that we have really participated with these works, that we have allowed them to work properly in our experience, so that if content were present it had a chance to come forth into our awareness. Of the four basic distinctions—participation, artistic form, content, and subject matter—the most fundamental is participation. We must not only understand what it means to participate but also be able to participate. Otherwise, the other basic distinctions, even if they make good theoretical sense, will not be of much practical help in making art more important in our lives. The central importance of participation requires further elaboration.

Participation involves undivided and sustained attention. However, spectator attention dominates most of our experiences. Spectator attention is more commonsensical, and it works much more efficiently than participative attention in most situations. We would not get very far changing a tire if we only participated with the tire as art. We would not be able to use the scientific method if we failed to distinguish between ourselves and our data. Practical success on every level requires problem solving. This requires distinguishing the means from the end, and then we must manipulate the means to achieve the end. In so doing, we are aware of ourselves as subjects distinct from the objects involved in our situation. In turn, the habit of spectator attention gets deeply ingrained in all of us because of the demands of survival. That is why, especially after we have left the innocence of childhood, participative attention is so rarely achieved. A child who has not yet had to solve problems, on the other hand, is dominated by participative attention. In this sense, to learn how to experience works of art properly requires a return to the open, receptive attitudes of childhood, for in childhood we were more likely to think from things than at things. As children, we did not always try to dominate things but, rather, let them reveal themselves to us. Watch young children at play. Sometimes they will just push things around, but often they will let things dominate them. Then, if they are looking at flowers, for example, they will begin to follow the curves and textures with their hands, be entranced with their smell, perhaps even the taste—so absorbed that they seem to listen, as if the flowers could speak.

As participators we do not think of the work of art with reference to categories applicable to objects—such as what kind of thing it is. We grasp the work of art directly. When, for example, we participate with Cézanne's *Mont Sainte Victoire* (Figure 2-5), we are not making geographical or geological observations. We are not thinking of the mountain as an object. For

FIGURE 2-4
Mont Sainte Victoire. (Courtesy John Rewald)

FIGURE 2-5
Paul Cézanne, *Mont Sainte Victoire*. 1886–1887. Oil on canvas, 23½ × 28½ inches. The Phillips Collection, Washington, D.C.

if we did, Mont Sainte Victoire would pale into a mere instance of the appropriate scientific categories. We might judge that the mountain is a certain type. But in that process the vivid impact of Cézanne's mountain would dim down as the focus of our attention shifted beyond in the direction of generality. This is the natural thing to do with mountains if you are a geologist. It is also the natural thing to do with this particular photograph of the mountain (Figure 2-4). The photograph lends itself to the direction of generality because its form fails to hold us to the photograph in all its specificity. But, on the other hand, to be only a spectator of the Cézanne is unnatural in the sense that we block off much of the satisfaction we might have.

When we participate, we *think from.* The artistic form initiates and controls every thought and feeling. When we are spectators, we *think at.* We set the object into our framework. We see the Cézanne—name it, identify its maker, classify its style, recall its background information—but this approach will never get us into the Cézanne as a work of art. Of course, such knowledge can be very helpful. But that knowledge is most helpful when it is under the control of the work of art working in our experience. This happens when the artistic form not only suggests that knowledge but also keeps it within the boundaries of the painting. Otherwise the painting will fade away. Its splendid specificity will be sacrificed for some generality. Its content will be missed.

Participators are thrust out of their ordinary, everyday, business-as-usual attitude. They are thrust out of themselves. The content of the work of art makes contact. And then the "concrete suchness" of the work of art penetrates and permeates their consciousness. Even if they forget such experiences, which is unlikely, a significant change has taken place in their perceptive organs. New sets of lenses, so to speak, have been more or less permanently built into their vision. After participating with Cézanne's *Mont Sainte Victoire,* participators will automatically see mountains differently.

These are strong claims, and they may not be convincing. In any case, before concluding our search for what a work of art is, let us seek further clarification of our other basic distinctions—artistic form, content, and subject matter. This is worth our trouble. Even if we disagree with the conclusions, clarification helps understanding. And understanding helps appreciation.

PARTICIPATION AND ARTISTIC FORM

The participative experience—the undivided and sustained attention to an object or event that makes us lose our sense of separation from the object or event—is induced by strong or artistic form. Participation is not likely to develop with weak form because weak form tends to allow our attention to wander. Therefore, one of the indications of a strong form is the fact that participation occurs. Another indication of artistic form is the way it clearly identifies a whole or totality. In the case of the visual arts, a whole is a visual field or design limited by boundaries that separate that field from its surroundings. Both Adams' photograph and Goya's painting have visual designs, for both have forms that produce boundaries.

No matter what wall these two pictures are placed on, the Goya probably stands out more distinctly and sharply from its background. Part of this is because the Goya is in color and on a gigantic scale: eight feet nine inches by thirteen feet four inches, whereas the Adams photograph is normally exhibited as an eight by ten inch print. However carefully such a photograph is printed, it will include some random details. No detail in the Goya fails to play a part in the total design. To take one further instance, notice how the lines of the soldiers' sabers and their straps reinforce the ruthless forward push of the firing squad. The photograph, on the other hand, has a weak form because a large number of details fail to cooperate with other details. For example, running down the right side of General Loan's body is a very erratic line. This line fails to tie in with anything else in the photograph. If this line were smoother, it would connect more closely with the lines formed by the Vietcong prisoner's body. The connection between killer and killed would be more vividly established. But as it is, and after several viewings, our eye tends to wander off the photograph. The unity of its form is so slack that the edges of the photograph seem to blur off into their surroundings. That is another way of saying that the form of the photograph fails to establish a clear-cut whole or identity.

Artistic form normally is a prerequisite if our attention is to be grasped and held. Artistic form makes our participation possible. Some philosophers of art, such as Clive Bell and Roger Fry, even go so far as to claim that the presence of artistic form—what they usually call "significant form"

—is all that is necessary to identify a work of art. And by "significant form," in the case of painting, they mean the interrelationships of elements: line to line, line to color, color to color, color to shape, shape to shape, etc. The elements make up the artistic medium, the silver halides, the paint, the substances the form organizes. According to Bell and Fry, any reference of these elements and their interrelationships to actual objects or events should be basically irrelevant in our awareness.

According to the proponents of significant form, if we take notice of the executions as an important part of Goya's painting, then we are not perceiving properly. We are experiencing the painting not as a work of art but rather as an illustration telling a story, thus reducing a painting that is a work of art to the level of communications. When the lines, colors, etc., pull together tightly, independently of any objects or events they may represent, there is a significant form. That is what we should perceive when we are perceiving a work of art, not some portrayal of some object or event. Anything that has significant form is a work of art. If you ignore the objects and events represented in the Goya, significant form is evident. All the details depend on each other and jell together, creating a strong structure. Therefore, the Goya is a work of art. If you ignore the objects and events represented in the Adams photograph, significant form is not evident. The organization of the parts is too loose, creating a weak structure. Therefore, the photograph, according to Bell and Fry, is not a work of art. "To appreciate a work of art," according to Clive Bell, "we need bring with us nothing from life, no knowledge of its ideas and affairs, no familiarity with its emotions."

Does this theory of how to identify a work of art satisfy you? Do you find that in ignoring the representation of objects and events in the Goya much of what is important in that painting is left out? For example, does the line of the firing squad carry a forbidding quality partly because you recognize that this is a line of men in the process of killing other men? In turn, does the close relationship of that line with the line of the long shadow at the bottom right depend to some degree upon that forbidding quality? If you think so, then it follows that the artistic form of this work legitimately and relevantly refers to objects and events. Somehow artistic form, at least in some cases, has a significance that goes beyond just the design formed by elements such as lines and colors. Artistic form somehow goes beyond itself, somehow refers to objects and events from the world beyond the design. Artistic form informs us about things outside itself. These things—as revealed by the artistic form—we shall call the content of a work of art. But how does the artistic form do this?

CONTENT

Let us begin to try to answer this question by examining more closely the meanings of the Adams photograph and the Goya painting. Both basically, although oversimply, are about the same abstract idea—human barbarity. In the case of the photograph, we have an example, an instance of this barbarity. Since it is very close to any knowledgeable American's interests, this instance is likely to set off a lengthy chain of thoughts and feelings. These thoughts and feelings, furthermore, seem to lie "beyond" the photograph. Suppose a debate developed over the meaning of this photograph. The photograph itself would play an important role primarily as a starting point. From there on the photograph would probably be ignored except for dramatizing points. For example, one person might argue, "Remember that this occurred during the Tet offensive and innocent civilians were being killed by the Vietcong. Look again at the street and think of the consequences if the terrorists had not been eliminated." Another person might argue, "General Loan was one of the highest officials in South Vietnam's government, and he was taking the law into his own hands like a Nazi." What would be very strange in such a debate would be a discussion of every detail or even many of the details in the photograph.

In a debate about the meaning of the Goya, on the other hand, every detail and its interrelationships with other details become relevant. The meaning of the painting seems to "lie within" the painting. And yet, paradoxically, this meaning, as in the case of the Adams photograph, involves ideas and feelings that "lie beyond" the painting. How can this be? Let us first consider some background information. On May 2, 1808, guerrilla warfare had flared up all over Spain against the occupying forces of the French. By the following day, Napoleon's men were completely back in control in Madrid and the surrounding area. Many of the guerrillas were executed. And, according to tradition, Goya represented the execution of forty-three of these guerrillas on May 3 near the hill of Principe Pio just outside Madrid. This background information is important if we are to understand and appreciate the painting fully. Yet notice how differently this information works in our experience of the painting compared with the way background information works in our experience of the Adams photograph.

The execution in Eddie Adams' photograph was of a man who had just murdered one of General Loan's best friends and had then knifed to death the rest of his family. The general was part of the Vietnamese army fighting with the assistance of the United States and this photograph was widely disseminated with a caption describing the victim as a suspected terrorist. What shocked Americans who saw the photograph was the summary justice that Loan meted out. It was not until much later that the details of the victim's crimes were revealed. A century from now, the photograph may be largely ignored except by historians of the Vietnam war. If you are dubious about this, consider how quickly most of us pass over photographs of similar scenes from World War I and even World War II. The value of Adams' photograph seems to be closely tied to its historical moment.

With the Goya, the background information, although very helpful, is not as essential. Test this for yourself. Would your interest in Adams' photograph last very long if you completely lacked background information? In the case of the Goya, the background information helps us understand the where, when, and why of the scene. But even without this information, the painting probably would still grasp and hold the attention of most of us because it would still have significant meaning. We would still have a powerful image of barbarity, and the artistic form would hold us on that image. In the Prado Museum in Madrid, Goya's painting continually draws and holds the attention of innumerable viewers, many of whom know little or nothing about the rebellion of 1808. Adams' photograph is also a powerful image, of course—initially far more powerful probably than the Goya—but the form of the photograph is not strong enough to hold most of us on that image for very long.

With the Goya, the abstract idea (human barbarity) and the concrete image (the firing squad in the process of killing) are tied tightly together because the form of the painting is tight, i.e., artistic. We see the barbarity in the lines, colors, masses, shapes, groupings, and lights and shadows of the painting itself. The details of the painting keep referring to other details and to the totality. They keep holding our attention. Thus the ideas and feelings that the details and their organization awaken keep merging with the form. We are prevented from separating the meaning or content of the painting from its form because the form is so fascinating. The form constantly intrudes, however unobtrusively. It will not let us ignore it. We see the firing squad killing, and this evokes the idea of barbarity and the feeling of horror. But the lines, colors, mass, shapes, and shadowings of that firing squad form a pattern that keeps exciting and guiding our eyes. And then the pattern leads us to the pattern formed by the victims. Ideas of fatefulness and feelings of pathos are evoked, but they, too, are fused with the form. The form of the Goya is like a powerful magnet that allows nothing within its range to escape its pull. Strong or artistic form fuses or embodies its meaning with itself.

In addition to participation and artistic form, then, we have come upon another basic distinction—content. Unless a work has content—meaning fused or embodied with its form—we shall say that the work is not art. Content is the meaning of artistic form. If we are correct (for our view is by no means universally accepted), artistic form always informs, that is, has meaning or content. And that content, as we experience it when we participate, is always ingrained in the artistic form. We do not perceive an artistic form and then a content. We perceive them as inseparable. Of course, we can separate them analytically. But that is also to say that we are not having a participative experience. Moreover, when the form is weak—that is, less than artistic—we experience the form and its meaning separately. We see the form of Adams' photograph, and it evokes thoughts and feelings, indeed, a very powerful meaning. But the form is not strong enough to keep its meaning fused with itself. The photograph lacks content, not because it lacks meaning but because the meaning is not merged with a form. Idea and image break apart.

Perception Key

GOYA'S *MAY 3, 1808*, AND ADAMS' *EXECUTION IN SAIGON*

We have argued that the painting by Goya is a work of art and the photograph by Adams is not. Even if the three basic distinctions we have made so far—artistic form, participation, and content—are useful, we may have misapplied them. Bring out every possible argument against the view that the painting is a work of art and the photograph is not a work of art.

SUBJECT MATTER

The content is the meaning of a work of art. The content is embedded in the artistic form. But what does the content interpret? We shall call it "subject matter." Content is the interpretation—by means of an artistic form—of subject matter. Thus, subject matter is the fourth basic distinction that helps identify a work of art. Since every work of art must have a content, every work of art must have a subject matter, and this may be any aspect of experience that is an object of some vital human interest. Anything related to a human interest is a value. Some values are positive, such as pleasure and health. Other values are negative, such as human barbarity and executions. But they are values because they are related to human interests. Negative values are the subject matter of both Adams' photograph and Goya's painting. But the photograph, unlike the painting, one of us argues, has no content. The less than artistic form of the photograph simply presents its subject matter. The form does not transform the subject matter, does not enrich the meaning of the subject matter. On the other hand, the artistic form of the painting enriches or interprets its subject matter, says something significant about it. In the photograph the subject matter is directly given. But the subject matter of the painting is not just there in the painting. It has been transformed by the form. What is directly given in the painting is the content.

The meaning or content of a work of art is what is revealed about a subject matter. But in that revelation you must imagine the subject matter. If someone had taken a news photograph of the May third executions, that would be a record of Goya's subject matter. The content of the Goya is its interpretation of human barbarity in those executions. Adams' photograph lacks content because it merely shows us an example of this barbarity. That is not to disparage the photograph, for its purpose was news, not art. A similar kind of photograph—that is, one lacking artistic form—of the May third executions would also lack content. Now, of course, you may disagree with these conclusions for very good reasons. You may find more transformation of the subject matter in Adams' photograph that in Goya's painting. For example, you may believe that transforming the visual experience in black and white distances it from reality and intensifies content. In any case, such disagreement can help the perception of both parties, provided the debate itself is focused. It is hoped that the basic distinctions we are making—subject matter, artistic form, content, and participation—will aid that focusing.

SUBJECT MATTER AND ARTISTIC FORM

Whereas a subject matter is a value that we may perceive before any artistic interpretation, the content is the significantly interpreted subject matter as revealed by the artistic form. Thus, the subject matter is never directly presented in a work of art, for the subject matter has been transformed by the form. Artistic form transforms and, in turn, informs about life. The conscious intentions of the artist may include magical, religious, political, economic, and other purposes; the conscious intentions may not include the purpose of clarifying values. Yet underlying the artist's activity is always the creation of a form that illuminates something from life, some subject matter. Content is the subject matter detached by means of the form from its accidental or insignificant aspects. Artistic form makes the significance of a subject matter more manifest. Artistic form is the means whereby values are threshed from the husks of irrelevancies. A form that only entertains or distracts or shocks is less than artistic. Whereas nonartistic form merely presents a subject matter, artistic form makes that subject matter more vivid and clearer.

On the other hand, artistic form draws from the chaotic state of life—which, as Van Gogh describes it, is like "a sketch that didn't come off"—a distillation. In our interpretation, Adams' photograph is like "a sketch that didn't come off," because it has numerous meaningless details. Goya's form eliminates meaningless detail. The work of art creates an illusion that illuminates reality. Thus, such paradoxical declarations as Delacroix's are explained: "Those things which are most real are the illusions I create in my paintings." Or Edward Weston's: "The photographer who is an artist reveals the essence of what lies before the lens with such clear insight that the beholder may find the recreated image more real and comprehensible than the actual object." Aristotle asserts: "Art completes what nature cannot bring to a finish. The artist gives us knowledge of nature's unrealized ends." Hegel: "Art is in truth the primary instructress of peoples." Camus: "If the world were clear, art would not exist." Artistic form is an economy that produces a lucidity that enables us better to understand and, in turn, manage our lives. Hence the informing of a work of art reveals a subject matter with value dimensions that go beyond the artist's idiosyncrasies and perversities. Whether or not Goya had idiosyncrasies and perversities, he did justice to his subject matter: he revealed it. The art of a period is the revelation of the collective soul of its time.

Values in everyday situations are confused and obscured. In art values are clarified in artistic form. Art helps us to perceive what we have missed. Anyone who has participated with cummings' "l(a" will see autumn leaves with heightened sensitivity, and will understand the isolation of loneliness and death a little more poignantly. In clarifying values, art gives us an understanding that supplements the truths of science. Dostoevski teaches us as much about ourselves as Freud. All of us require something that fascinates us for a time, something out of the routine of the practical and the theoretical. But such nonroutine experiences influence our routine experiences, making them more meaningful. Accordingly, if a work of art "works" successfully in us, it is more than a momentary delight, for it deepens our understanding of what matters most. Art adds to the permanent richness of our soul's self-attainment. Art helps us arrange our environment for authentic values. Art makes possible civilization.

PARTICIPATION, ARTISTIC FORM, AND CONTENT

Participation is the necessary condition that makes possible our insightful perception of form and content. Unless we participate with the Goya, we will fail to see the power of its artistic form. We will fail to see how the details work together to form a totality. We also will fail to grasp the content fully, for artistic form and content are inseparable. Thus we will have failed to gain insight into the subject matter. We will have collected just one more instance of human barbarity. The Goya will have basically the same effect upon us as Adams' photograph except that it will be less important to us because it happened long ago. But if, on the contrary, we have participated with the Goya, we probably will never see such things as executions in quite the same way again. The insight that we have gained will tend to refocus our vision so that we will see similar subject matters with a heightened awareness.

Look, for example, at the photograph by Kevin Carter (Figure 2-6), which was published in the *New York Times* March 26, 1993, and which won the Pulitzer Prize for photography in 1994. In terms of form, it isolates two dramatic figures. The closest is a starving Sudanese child making her way to a feeding center. The other figure is a plump vulture waiting for the child to die. This photograph raised a hue and cry, and the *New York Times* published a commentary explaining that the child recovered and made her way to the center. Carter meanwhile chased away the vulture. Unfortunately, Carter, who had seen more than his share of such horrors in his native Africa (see Figure 12-11), committed suicide in July 1994.

FIGURE 2-6
Kevin Carter, *Vulture and Child in Sudan*. Silver halide. (Kevin Carter/Sygma)

PERCEPTION KEY

ADAMS' *EXECUTION IN SAIGON*, CARTER'S *VULTURE AND CHILD IN SUDAN*, AND GOYA'S *MAY 3, 1808*

1. Does our discussion of Adams' photograph refocus your vision in any important way upon Carter's photograph?
2. Does our discussion of Goya's painting refocus your vision in any important way upon Carter's photograph?
3. Why are your answers to these questions fundamentally important in determining whether Adams' photograph or Goya's painting or both are works of art?
4. What is your experience regarding your participation with either photograph or Goya's painting? Can you measure the intensity of your participation with each of them? Which work do you reflect upon most when you relax and are not thinking directly on the subject of art?

PARTICIPATION AND THE WORK OF ART

ARTISTIC FORM: EXAMPLES

Let us examine artistic form in a series of examples taken from the work of Roy Lichtenstein, a contemporary American painter, in which the subject matter, compared with *May 3, 1808,* is not so obviously important. With such examples, a purely formal analysis should seem less artificial. In the late 1950s and early 1960s, Lichtenstein became interested in comic strips as subject matter. The story goes that his two young boys asked him to paint a Donald Duck "straight," without the encumbrances of art. But much more was involved. Born in 1923, Lichtenstein grew up before television. By the 1930s, the comic strip had become one of the most important of the mass media. Sex, sentimentality, sadism, terror, adventure, and romance found expression in the stories of Tarzan, Flash Gordon, Superman, Steve Roper, Mickey Mouse, Donald Duck, Batman and Robin, etc.

Because of the very large market for the comic strip, a premium has always been put on making the processes of production as inexpensive as possible. And so generations of mostly unknown commercial artists, going well back into the nineteenth century, developed ways of cheap, quick color printing. They had to develop a technique that could turn out their cartoons like the products of an assembly line. Moreover, because their market included a large number of children, they developed ways of producing images that were immediately understandable and of striking impact. They evolved a tradition that became a common vocabulary. Both the technique and its product became increasingly standardized. The printed images became increasingly impersonal. Donald Duck, Bugs Bunny, and Batman all seem to come from the same hand.

FIGURE 2-7 (left)
Pair 1a.

FIGURE 2-8 (right)
Pair 1b.

Lichtenstein reports that he was attracted to the comic strip by its stark simplicity—the blatant primary colors, the ungainly black lines that encircle the shapes, the "balloons" that isolate the spoken words or the thoughts of the characters. He was struck by the apparent inconsistency between the strong emotions of the stories and the highly impersonal, mechanical style in which they were expressed. Despite the crudity of the comic strip, Lichtenstein saw power in the strong directness of the medium. Somehow something very much about ourselves was mirrored in those cartoons. Lichtenstein set out to clarify what that "something" was. At first people laughed, as was to be expected. He was called "the worst artist in America." Today he is considered one of our best.

The accompanying examples (Figures 2-7 through 2-12) pair the original cartoon with Lichtenstein's transformation.[1] Both the comic strips and the transformations originally were in color, and Lichtenstein's paintings are very much larger than the comic strip. For the purposes of analysis, however, our reproductions are presented in black and white, and the sizes more or less equalized. The absence of color and the reduction of size all but destroy the power of Lichtenstein's work, but these changes will help us compare the structures. They will also help us to concentrate upon what is usually the most obvious element of two-dimensional visual structure—line.

Compare your analyses with ours. We think it is only in b that the shape of the lettering plays an important part in the formal organization. Conversely, the shape of the lettering is distracting in a. In b the bulky balloons are eliminated and only two words are kept—"torpedo . . . LOS!" The three alphabetic characters of which "LOS" is composed stand out very vividly. The balloon's simple shape helps, a regular shape among so many irregular shapes. Also, "LOS" is larger, darker, and more centrally located than "torpedo." Notice, on the other hand, how no word or lettering stands out

[1]These examples were suggested to us by an article on Lichtenstein's balloons by Albert Boime, "Roy Lichtenstein and the Comic Strip," *Art Journal*, vol. 28, no. 2, pp. 155–159, Winter 1968–1969.

FIGURE 2-9
Pair 2a.

FIGURE 2-10
Pair 2b.

Perception Key
COMIC STRIPS AND LICHTENSTEIN'S TRANSFORMATIONS

Decide which are the comic strips and which are Lichtenstein's transformations. Defend your decisions with reference to the strength of organization. Presumably Lichtenstein's works will possess much stronger structures than those of the commercial artists. Be as specific and detailed as possible. For example, compare the lines and shapes as they work together in each example. Consider the strength and certainty of the line, the interrelationship of shapes in the composition, the use of centrality or asymmetry in the composition, and the impact of the overall design. Take plenty of time, for the perception of artistic form is something that must "work" in you. Such perception never comes instantaneously. Compare your judgments with others.

Perception Key
COMIC STRIPS AND LICHTENSTEIN'S TRANSFORMATIONS, PAIR 1

Limit your analysis to the design functioning of the lettering in the balloons.

1. Does the shape of the lettering in a play an important part in the formal organization? Explain your reasons.
2. Does the shape of the lettering in b play an important part in the formal organization? Explain your reasons.

FIGURE 2-11
Pair 3a.

FIGURE 2-12
Pair 3b.

very vividly in a. Moreover, as Boime points out, the shapes of "LOS" are clues to the structure of the panel:

The "L" is mirrored in the angle formed by the captain's hand and the vertical contour of his head and in that of the periscope. The "O" is repeated in the tubing of the periscope handle and in smaller details throughout the work. The oblique "S" recurs in the highlight of the captain's hat just left of the balloon, in the contours of the hat itself, in the shadow that falls along the left side of the captain's face, in the lines around his nose, and in the curvilinear tubing of the periscope. Thus the dialogue enclosed within the balloon is visually exploited in the interests of compositional structure. Now analyze Pair 2 (Figures 2-9 and 2-10), and Pair 3 (Figures 2-11 and 2-12).

Perception Key

COMIC STRIPS AND LICHTENSTEIN'S TRANSFORMATIONS, PAIRS 2 AND 3

1. Decide once again which are the comic strips and which the transformations.
2. If you have changed any of your decisions or your reasons, how do you account for these changes?

It should not be surprising to you if you have changed some of your decisions, and it may be that your reasoning has been expanded. Other people's analyses, even when you disagree with them, will usually suggest new ways of perceiving things. In the case of good criticism, this is almost always the case. The correct identifications follow, and they should help you test your perceptive abilities.

Pair 1a Anonymous comic book panel.
Pair 1b Lichtenstein, *Torpedo . . . LOS!* 1963. Magna on canvas. (Courtesy Leo Castelli Gallery, New York)
Pair 2a Anonymous comic book panel.
Pair 2b Lichtenstein, *Image Duplicator.* 1963. Magna on canvas. (Courtesy Leo Castelli Gallery, New York)
Pair 3a Anonymous comic book panel.
Pair 3b Lichtenstein, *Hopeless.* 1963. Magna on canvas. (Courtesy Leo Castelli Gallery, New York)

If you have been mistaken, do not be discouraged. Learning how to perceive sensitively takes time. Furthermore, it is not possible to decide beyond all doubt, as with the proof that two plus two equals four, whether Lichtenstein is a creator of artistic form and comic-strip makers are not. We think it is highly probable that this is the case, but absolute certainty here is not possible. And it should be noted that the comic-strip makers generally look upon Lichtenstein's work as "strongly 'decorative' and backward looking."

Lichtenstein is a master at composing forms. But are these paintings works of art? Do these forms inform? Do they have a content? If so, what are their subject matters? What is the subject matter of "Torpedo . . . LOS!"? The aggressiveness of submarine commanders? Or, rather, the energy, passion, directness, and mechanicality of comic strips? Or could the subject matter be made up of both these things? Perhaps there is no interpreted subject matter—perhaps the event in the submarine is just an excuse for composing a form. Perhaps this form is best understood and appreciated not as informing but, rather, as simply attractive and pleasing. This kind of form we shall call "decorative form."

SUBJECT MATTER AND CONTENT

The female nude constitutes a subject matter fundamental to Western art. It has figured in sculpture, architectural decoration, and painting from its beginnings. The variety of treatment of the nude is almost bewildering, ranging from the *Playboy* centerfold cliché to the radical reordering of Picasso's *Nude Under a Pine Tree.* A number of well-known female nude studies follow (Figures 2-13 through 2-20). Consider, as you look at them, how the form of the painting interprets the female body. Does it reveal it in such a way that you have an increased understanding and sensitivity to the female body? In other words, does it have content? Also ask yourself whether the content is different in a painting by a woman from that by a man.

Most of these paintings are very highly valued—some as masterpieces. Why? These paintings are highly valued as works of art because they are powerful interpretations of their subject matter, not just renderings of the

FIGURE 2-13
Giorgione, *Sleeping Venus*. 1508–1510. Oil on canvas, 43 × 69 inches. Gemaldegalerie, Dresden. (Super Stock)

FIGURE 2-14
Pierre Auguste Renoir, *Bather Arranging Her Hair*. 1893. Oil on canvas, 36⅜ × 29⅛ inches. National Gallery of Art, Washington, D.C., Chester Dale Collection.

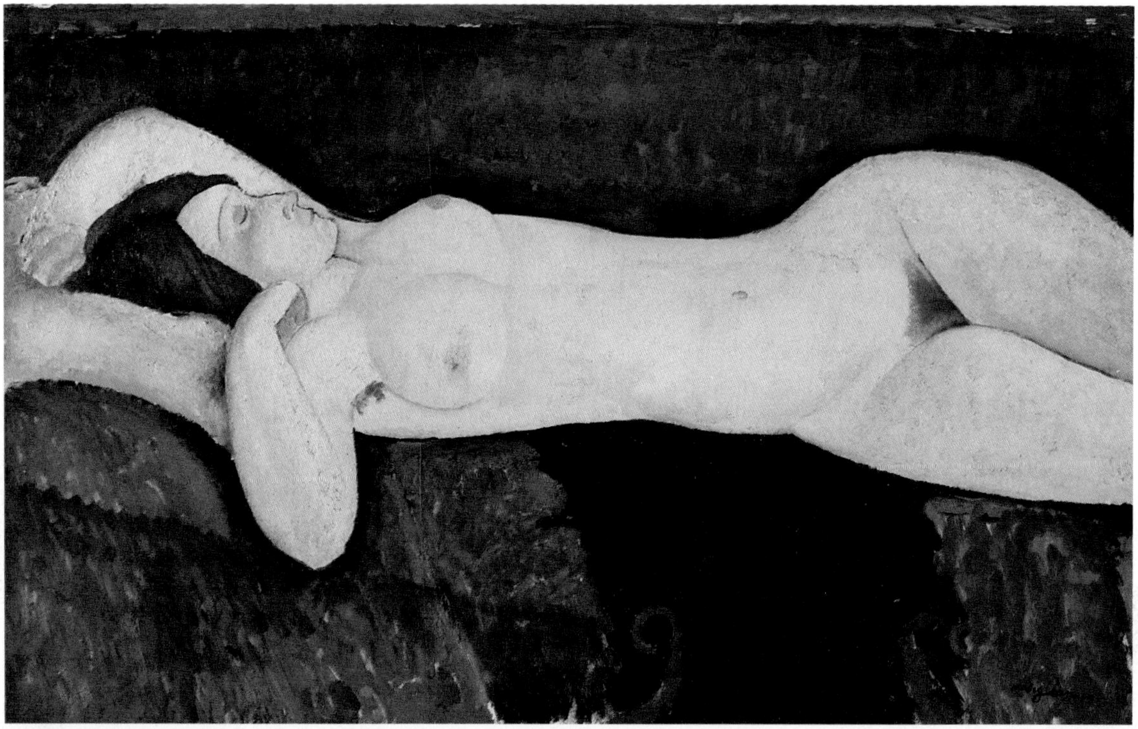

FIGURE 2-15
Amedeo Modigliani, *Reclining Nude*. Circa 1919. Oil on canvas, 28½ × 45⅞ inches. The Museum of Modern Art, New York. Mrs. Simon Guggenheim Fund. (Photograph © 1997 The Museum of Modern Art, New York)

FIGURE 2-16
Pablo Picasso, *Nude under a Pine Tree*. 1959. Oil on canvas, 72 × 96 inches. The Art Institute, Chicago. Bequest of Grant J. Pick. (1965.687). (© 1997 Succession Picasso/Artist Rights Society [ARS], New York)

FIGURE 2-17
Tom Wesselmann, *Great American Nude*. 1977. Oil on canvas, 54½ × 19 inches. Sidney Janis Gallery, New York. (© 1997 Tom Wesselmann/ Licensed by VAGA, New York)

FIGURE 2-18
Edouard Manet, *Olympia*. 1863. Oil on canvas, 51¼ × 74¾ inches. (Scala/Art Resource, NY)

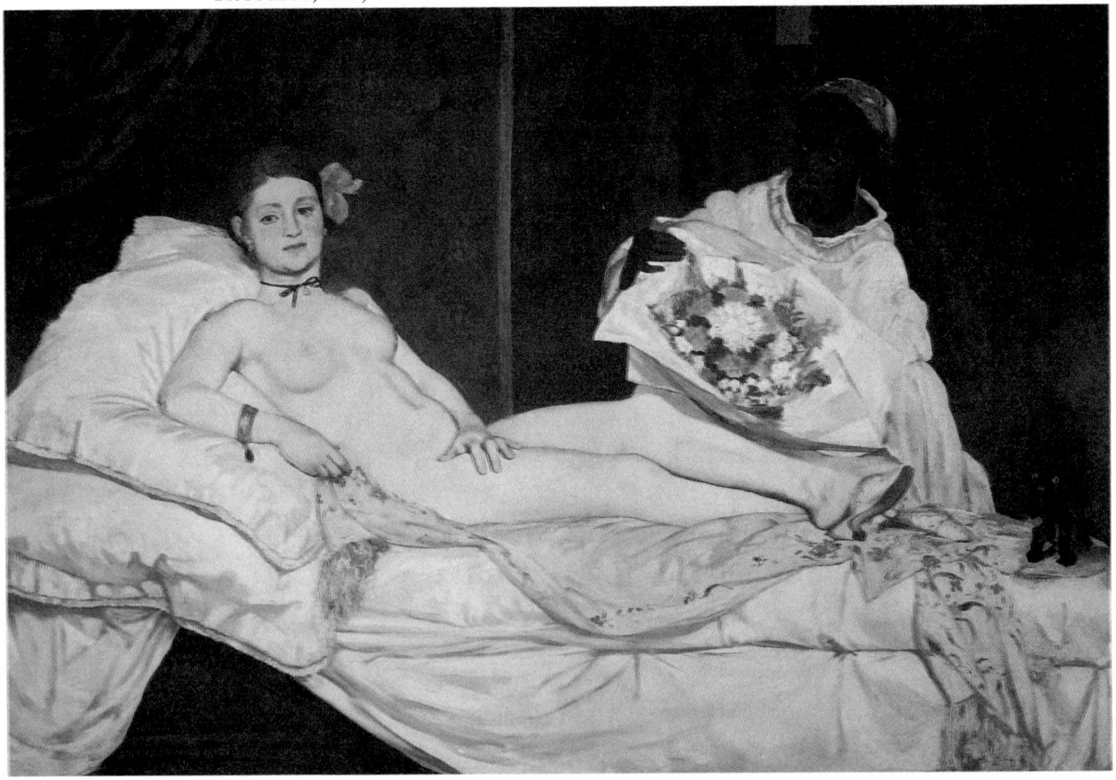

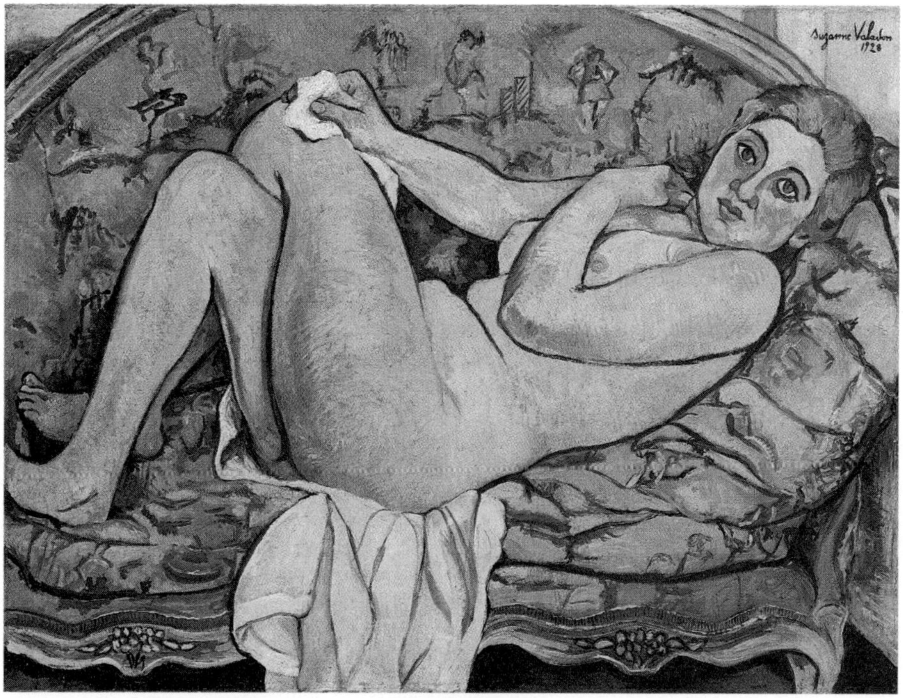

FIGURE 2-19
Suzanne Valadon, *Reclining Nude*. 1928. Oil on canvas, $23\frac{5}{8} \times 30\frac{11}{16}$ inches. The Metropolitan Museum of Art, New York. Robert Lehman Collection, 1975.

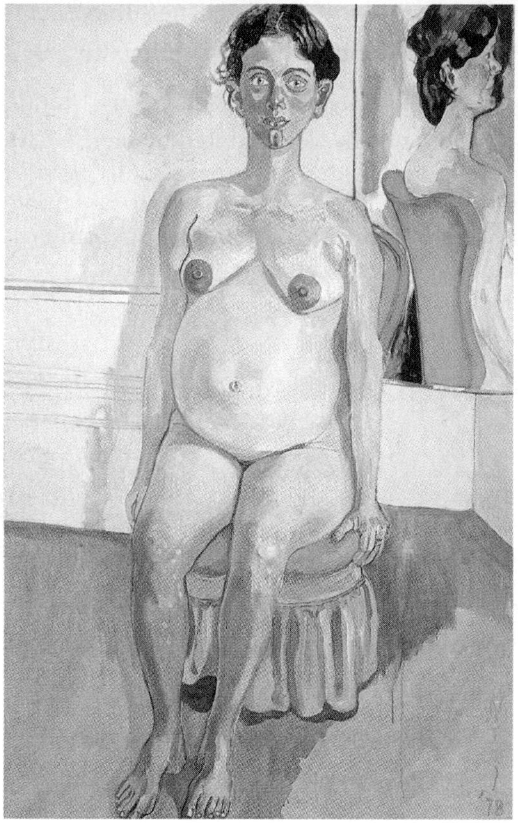

FIGURE 2-20
Alice Neel, *Margaret Evans Pregnant*. 1978. Oil on canvas, $57\frac{3}{4} \times 38$ inches. Collection, The John McEnroe Gallery. (By permission of the estate of Alice Neel, courtesy of Robert Miller Gallery, New York)

human body. Think from rather than at these paintings. Then notice how different the interpretations are. Any important subject matter has many different facets. That is why shovels and soup cans have limited utility as subject matters. They have very few facets to offer for interpretation. The female nude, on the other hand, is almost limitless. The next artist interprets something about the female nude that had never been interpreted before, because the female nude seems to be inexhaustible as a subject matter.

More precisely, these paintings all have somewhat different subject matters. All are about the nude. But the painting by Giorgione is about the nude as idealized, as a goddess, as Venus. Now there is a great deal that all of us could say in trying to describe Giorgione's interpretation. We see not just a nude, but an idealization that presents the nude as Venus, the goddess whom the Romans felt best expressed the ideal of woman. She represents a form of perfection which humans can only strive toward, but never achieve. A description of the subject matter can help us perceive the content if we have missed it. In understanding what the form worked on—that is, the subject matter—our perceptive apparatus is better prepared to perceive the "form-content."

The subject matter of Renoir's painting is the nude more as an earth mother. In the Modigliani, the subject matter is the sensual nude. In the Picasso, it is the nude enfleshed in her sex. In the Wesselmann, it is the nude as exploited. In the Manet, it is the nude as prostitute. In all six paintings the subject matter is the female nude—but qualified. The subject matter is qualified in relation to what the artistic form focuses upon and makes lucid.

The last two paintings, by Suzanne Valadon and Alice Neel, treat the female nude differently from all the others, which were painted by men. Neel's painting emphasizes an aspect of femaleness that the men usually ignore, pregnancy. Her painting does not show the alluring female, but the female who is beyond allure. Valadon's nude is more traditional, but a comparison with Renoir and Giorgione should demonstrate that she is far from the ideal as those painters imagine her.

Perception Key
THE FEMALE NUDE

1. Is it clear to you that Suzanne Valadon and Alice Neel have treated the female nude very differently from the way the male painters did? What are the differences? Do the women painters treat the nude more subjectively?
2. If you feel there is a difference between the way the men and women painted the female nude, do you feel the difference is perceptible in the paintings' form-content? Would you have known without being told that Valadon's and Neel's paintings were created by women?

SUMMARY

A work of art is a form-content. An artistic form is a form-content. An artistic form is more than just an organization of the elements of an artistic medium, such as the lines and colors of painting. The artistic form interprets or clarifies some subject matter. The subject matter, strictly speaking, is not in a work of art. Thus the subject matter is only imaginable, not perceptible. It is only suggested by the work of art. The interpretation of the subject matter is the content or meaning of the work of art. Content is embodied in the form. The content, unlike the subject matter, is in the work of art, fused with the form. We can separate content from form only by analysis. The ultimate justification of any analysis is whether it enriches our participation with that work, whether it helps that work "work" in us. Good analysis or criticism does just that. But, conversely, any analysis not based on participation is unlikely to be very helpful. Participation is the way—the only way—of getting into direct contact with the form-content. And so any analysis that is not based upon a participative experience inevitably misses the work of art. Participation and good analysis, although necessarily occurring at different times, always end up hand in hand.

In this chapter, we have elaborated one set of guidelines. Of course, other sets are possible. We have discussed one other set very briefly: that a work of art is significant form. If you can conceive of other sets of guidelines, make them explicit and try them out. The ultimate test is clear: which set helps you most in appreciating works of art? We think the set we have proposed meets that test better than other proposals. But this is a very large question indeed, and your decision should be delayed. In any event, we will now investigate the principles of criticism. These principles should help show us how to apply our set of guidelines to specific examples. Then we will be properly prepared to examine the uniqueness of the various arts.

CHAPTER 2 BIBLIOGRAPHY

Aldrich, Virgil C. *The Philosophy of Art.* Englewood Cliffs, N.J.: Prentice-Hall, 1963.

Bell, Clive. *Art.* New York: Putnam, 1981.

Collingwood, R. G. *The Principles of Art.* Oxford: Clarendon Press, 1971.

Dewey, John. *Art as Experience.* New York: Perigree Books, 1980.

Ducasse, Curt J. *The Philosophy of Art.* New York: Dover, 1963.

Langer, Susanne K. *Feeling and Form.* New York: Scribner's, 1953.

Maritain, Jacques. *Creative Intuition in Art and Poetry.* Princeton, N.J.: Princeton University Press, 1978.

Merleau-Ponty, Maurice. *The Primacy of Perception.* James M. Edie (ed.). Evanston, Ill.: Northwestern University Press, 1964.

Pepper, Stephen C. *The Work of Art.* Bloomington: Indiana University Press, 1955.

Rader, Melvin. *A Modern Book of Aesthetics,* 5th ed. New York: Holt, Rinehart & Winston, 1979.

Read, Herbert. *The Meaning of Art.* London: Faber and Faber, 1972.
Reid, Louis Arnaud. *Meaning in the Arts.* London: Allen & Unwin, 1969.
Tolstoy, Leo. *What Is Art? and Essays on Art.* Aylmer Maude (trans.). London: Bristol Classical Press, 1994.
Weiss, Paul. *Nine Basic Arts.* Carbondale: Southern Illinois University Press, 1966.
Weitz, Morris. *Philosophy of the Arts.* New York: Russell & Russell, 1964.

CHAPTER 2 WEBSITES

Art Exploration
World Wide Web: **http://solar.rtd.utk.edu/friends/art/art.html**

Art History Server
World Wide Web: **http://rubens.anu.edu.au/**

Art on the Net
World Wide Web: **http://www.art.net**

Art Projects on the Internet
World Wide Web: **http://ziris.syr.edu/**

Arts Archive
World Wide Web: **http://pmwww.cs.vu.nl/archive/images/arts/**

Worldwide Art Resources
World Wide Web: **http://www.concourse.com/wwar/default.html**

Yale University
World Wide Web: **http://www.library.yale.edu/Internet/arthistory.html**

CHAPTER 3

BEING A CRITIC OF THE ARTS

In this chapter, we are concerned with establishing the methods and means of becoming a good critic and understanding the goals of responsible criticism. Our purpose is to intensify our experiences in the arts to the fullest. The act of responsible criticism aims for the fullest understanding and the fullest participation possible. Being a responsible critic is being at the height of awareness, examining a work of art in detail, establishing its context, and clarifying its achievement. It is not to be confused with popular journalism, which more often sidetracks the critic into being flashy, negative, and cute.

YOU ARE ALREADY AN ART CRITIC

Almost everyone operates as an art critic much of the time. Choosing a film or changing the television channel to look for something better implies a critical act. When turning a radio dial looking for good music, we become critics of music. The same is true when we stop to admire a building or a painting. What qualifies us to make such critical judgments? What training underlies our constant criticism of such arts as film, music, and architecture? Experience is one factor. We probably have listened to music on the radio, gone to the movies, and watched television since before we can remember. We can count on a lifetime of seeing architecture, of responding to the industrial design of automobiles and furniture, of seeing public sculpture. This is no inconsiderable background, and it helps us make critical judgments without hesitation.

But even though all this is true, we realize something further. Everyone has limitations as a critic. When left to our own devices we grow up with little specific critical training, even in a society rich in art, and find ourselves capable of going only so far. If we do nothing to increase our critical skills, they may not grow. By learning some essentials about criticism and how to put them to work, we develop our capacities as critics.

PARTICIPATION AND THE CRITIC

One of the reasons many of us resist our roles as critics is that we value very highly the participative experience we get from the works of art. Criticism interferes with that participative delight. For example, most of us lose ourselves in a good film and never think about the film in an objective way. It "ruins" the experience to stop and be critical, because the act of criticism is quite different from the act of participative enjoyment. And if we were to choose which act is the most important, then, of course, we would have to stand firm behind enjoyment. Art is, above all, enjoyable. Yet the kinds of enjoyment it affords are sometimes complex and subtle. Good critics make the complexities and subtleties more available both to themselves and to others. In other words, reflecting upon the participative experience we have had may help deepen our next participation. Thus the critical act is—at its very best—an act that is very much related to the act of participatory enjoyment. The reason is simple: a fine critical sense helps us develop the perceptions essential to understanding what's "going on" in a work of art.

Seeing a film twice, for instance, is often interesting. At first our personalities may melt away, and we become involved and "lost" in the experience. Competent and clever filmmakers can cause us to do this quickly and efficiently—the first time. But if the filmmaker is only competent and clever, as opposed to being creative, then the second time we see the film its flaws are likely to be obvious and we are likely to have a less complete participatory experience. However, when we see a really great film, then the second experience is likely to be more exciting than the first. If we have become good critics and if we have reflected wisely on our first experience, we will find that the second experience of any great work of art is likely to be more intense and our participation deeper. For one thing, our understanding of the artistic form and content is likely to be considerably more refined in our second experience and in all subsequent experiences.

It is obvious that only those works of art that are successful on most or all levels can possibly be as interesting the second time we experience them as they were the first. This presumes, however, a reliable perception of the work. For example, the first experience of most works of art will not be very satisfying—perhaps it will not produce the participative experience at all—if we fail to perceive the form-content to some significant extent. Consequently, it is possible that the first experience of a difficult poem, for instance, will be less than enjoyable. If, however, we have gained helpful information from the first experience and thus have made ourselves more capable of perceiving the poem, the second experience will be more satisfying.

One of the first critical questions we should ask concerns whether or not we actually have had a participative experience. Has the work of art taken us out of ourselves? If it is a good work of art, we should find ourselves "lost" in the delight of experiencing it. However, as we have been suggesting all along, if we are not so carried away by a given work, the reason may not be because it is not successful. It may be because we do not perceive all there is to perceive. We may not "get it" well enough for it to transport us into participation. Consequently, we have to be critical of ourselves some of the time in order to be sure we have laid the basic groundwork essential to participation. When we are sure that we have done as much as we can to prepare ourselves, then we are in a better position to decide whether the deficiency is in the work or in us. In the final analysis, the participative experience can be said to be something that we not only can but must have if we are to fully comprehend a work of art.

KINDS OF CRITICISM

With our basic critical purpose clearly in mind—that is, to learn, by reflecting on works of art, how to participate with these works more intensely and enjoyably—let us now analyze the practice of criticism more closely. If, as we have argued in Chapter 2, a work of art is essentially a form-content, then good criticism will sharpen our perception of the form of a work of art and increase our understanding of its content.

PERCEPTION KEY
KINDS OF CRITICISM

Seek out at least two examples of criticism from any available place, including, if you like, Chapters 1 and 2 of this book. Film or book reviews in newspapers or magazines or discussions of art in books may be used. Analyze these examples with reference to the following questions:

1. Does the criticism focus mainly on the form or the content?
2. Can you find any examples in which the criticism is entirely about the form?
3. Can you find any examples in which the criticism is entirely about the content?
4. Can you find any examples in which the focus is on neither the form nor the content but on evaluating the work as good or bad or better or worse than some other work?
5. Can you find any examples in which there is no evaluation?
6. Which kinds of criticism do you find most helpful—those bearing on form, content, or evaluation? Why?
7. Do you find any examples in which it is not clear whether the emphasis is on form, content, or evaluation?

This Perception Key points to three basic kinds of criticism: (1) descriptive—focusing on form, (2) interpretive—focusing on content, and (3) evaluative—focusing on the relative merits of a work. In later chapters on painting and photography we will also present examples of criticism that are historically oriented. However, all schools of criticism—formalist, historicist, feminist, response theory, and poststructuralist—employ all three basic kinds of criticism.

DESCRIPTIVE CRITICISM

Descriptive criticism concentrates on the form of a work of art, describing, sometimes exhaustively, the important characteristics of that form in order to improve our understanding of the part-to-part and part-to-whole interrelationships. At first glance this kind of criticism may seem unnecessary. After all, the form is all there, completely given—all we have to do is observe. But most of us know all too well that we can spend time attending to a work we are very much interested in and yet not perceive all there is to perceive. We miss things, and oftentimes we miss things that are right there for us to observe. For example, were you immediately aware of the visual form of e. e. cummings' "l(a"—the spiraling downward curve (Figure 1-7)? Or in Goya's *May 3, 1808* (Figure 2-3) were you aware of the way the line of the long dark shadow at the bottom right underlines the line of the firing squad?

Good descriptive critics call our attention to what we otherwise might miss in an artistic form. And even more important, they help us learn how to do their work when they are not around. We can, if we carefully attend to descriptive criticism, develop and enhance our own powers of observation. That is worth thinking about. None of us can afford to have a professional critic with us at all times in order to help us see the art around us more fully. No other learning is as likely to improve our participation with a work of art, for such criticism turns us directly to the work itself.

PERCEPTION KEY
DESCRIPTIVE CRITICISM AND *THE LIBERATION OF AUNT JEMIMA*

1. Relying on our discussions of Blume's *Eternal City* in Chapter 1 and Goya's *May 3, 1808,* in Chapter 2, descriptively criticize Betye Saar, *The Liberation of Aunt Jemima* (Figure 3-1). Point out every facet of the form that seems important. Look for shapes that relate to each other, examine color relationships; examine the figure of Aunt Jemima in relation to figures and images surrounding her. Discuss your criticism with others if possible.
2. Examine in particular the images that are used repetitively in the work. Are any of the images in conflict with each other?
3. After this criticism, return to the work and consider what the descriptive details you have uncovered imply for a political interpretation of the imagery.

DETAIL AND STRUCTURAL RELATIONSHIPS

As you worked through question 1 of this Perception Key, you may have found it difficult to organize your descriptions. After all, we have defined form as the interrelationships of part to part and part to whole in a work

FIGURE 3-1
Betye Saar, *The Liberation of Aunt Jemima*. 1972. Mixed media, assemblage box, 11¾ × 8 × 2½ inches. (Courtesy of the artist)

of art, and connections like this may seem endless. Betye Saar, an African-American artist, plays with imagery of the African-American domestic that has been visible in American commercial advertising since the early part of this century. Her use of repetition emulates advertising's repetition of Aunt Jemima as a brand name. In a sense, this work of art is critical of a cultural icon, but in a very complex fashion.

A connection of one part or region of form to another part or region we shall call a "detail relationship." For example, the relationship among the three primary images of Aunt Jemima—the image holding the white child, the larger image with the broom, and the image on the back wall—derived from advertising interact in complex ways. Observing these three images carefully leads us to question the title of the work and ask what kind of liberation is implied. What we see, if it is liberation, is ultimately ironic.

Details in poetry involve the relation of one word to another, one phrase to another, one image to another, or any of these to any other. In the dance, details involve the connections of a dancer's movement at one moment to a subsequent movement. In music details involve tones or phrases sounded at the same time or sounded one after another, as well as details of rhythm, harmony, or melody. Even if you do not read music, you can see that there is a considerable difference in the examples of music shown in Figures 3-2 and 3-3.

FIGURE 3-2
Two bars from Mendelssohn's Violin Concerto.

FIGURE 3-3
Three bars from Chopin's Prelude in C major.

Perception Key
MUSIC AND DETAIL RELATIONSHIPS

1. Which example has the fewer detail relationships?
2. Chopin's Prelude is marked *agitato,* suggesting that the passage should be played to exemplify a state of emotional agitation. Is it possible that emotional agitation is somehow related to the way tempo affects detail relationships?

In contrast to "detail relationships," "structural relationships" involve connecting one part or region of a work of art to the entirety of the work. Structure concerns itself with the totality of the work of art and the relationship of any details or parts to that totality. In most works of art the structure is not immediately perceptible. For example, in forms that take time to unfold because what is perceptible comes to us successively, such as literature, music, dance, and film, we are not aware of the totality of the structure until the unfolding is over or nearly over. Only then can we begin to grasp the complete structure. Plot—the sequence of actions or events—is usually the key to the structure of a literary or dramatic narrative or a film. The statement, development, and repetition of themes are usually key to the structure of a symphony or a popular song. In addition, symphonic structure consists of several movements whose relationships may be marked in terms of tempo: fast, slow, moderate, fast. Plays have plot with carefully marked pacing implied in their one- to five-act structure. Moreover, even when, as in most paintings, the structure is "all-present," we may need considerable time to perceive the organizational relationships. The structure of Picasso's *Guernica* (Figure 1-4) needs considerable time to work out because so much seems to be going on simultaneously in terms of detail.

FIGURE 3-4
Jackson Pollack, *Autumn Rhythm*. 1950. Oil on canvas, 105 × 207 inches. The Metropolitan Museum of Art. George A. Hearn Fund, 1957. (57.92). (© 1997 The Pollack-Krasner Foundation/Artist Rights Society [ARS], New York)

PERCEPTION KEY
DETAIL OR STRUCTURAL DOMINANCE

The dominance of either detail or structural relationships or their equality, more or less, often varies widely from work to work. Compare Mondrian's *Composition in White, Black and Red* (Figure 1-5), Picasso's *Guernica* (Figure 1-4), and Jackson Pollock's *Autumn Rhythm* (Figure 3-4). In which painting or paintings, if any, do detail relationships dominate? In which do structural relationships dominate?

Detail relationships dominate *Autumn Rhythm*, so much so that at first sight, perhaps, no structure is apparent. The loops, splashes, skeins, and blots of color were dripped or thrown on the canvas, which was laid out flat on the floor during execution. Yet there is not as much chaotic chance as one might suppose. Most of Pollock's "actions" were controlled accidents, the result of his awareness, developed through long trial-and-error experience, of how the motion of his hand and body along with the weight and fluidity of the paint would determine the shape of the drips and splashes as he moved around the borders of the canvas. Somehow the endless details finally add up to a self-contained totality holding the rhythms of autumn. Yet, unlike Mondrian's painting, there are no distinct parts or regions. In the Mondrian one can easily identify, for example, the region of the red rectangle as clearly distinct from the region of the black rectangle. Moreover, the structure is so evident and so overpowering that every detail and region is inevitably referred to the totality. Picasso's *Guernica*, on the other hand, is more or less balanced with respect to detail, region, and structure. The detail relationships are organized into three major regions: the great triangle—with the apex at the candle and two sides sloping down to the lower corners—and the two large rectangles, vertically oriented, running down along the left and right borders. Moreover, these regions—unlike the regions of Mondrian's painting—are hierarchically ordered because the triangular region takes precedence in both size and interest, while the left rectangle, mainly because of the fascination of the impassive bull, dominates the right rectangle, even though both are about the same size. Despite the complexity of the detail relationship in *Guernica*, we gradually perceive the power of a very strong, clear structure.

The relationship of Pollock's *Autumn Rhythm* to music is implied in its title, but even without the title it is evident in the fact that the painting is nonobjective—it does not represent or interpret objects from life. Its form is color, line, and space and its subject matter, as in the case of music, is at least in part the emotions it evokes in its viewer. The form-content is the interpretation of those emotions along with the events of autumn. Pollock usually painted with jazz playing loudly in his studio, using the rhythms of the music to guide his hand and brush. Both the Pollock and the Picasso are immense paintings that demand total attention when you stand before them. Their power is astonishingly diminished in the reproductions in a book. Part of the job of the descriptive critic is to account for the experience of looking at the genuine work, and not relying on reproductions. However, since most of us cannot go to Madrid or New York, we must make what observations we can using reduced-size photographs of the originals. The observations we make prepare us for looking at the real thing.

INTERPRETIVE CRITICISM

Interpretive criticism explicates the content of a work of art. It helps us understand how form transforms subject matter into content: what has been revealed about some subject matter and how that has been accomplished. The content of any work of art will become clearer when the structure is perceived in relationship to the details and regions. The following examples (Figures 3-5 and 3-6) demonstrate that the same principle holds for architecture as holds for painting. The subject matter of a building—or at

PERCEPTION KEY
SULLIVAN'S BANK AND LE CORBUSIER'S CHURCH

1. Which of these structures suggests solidity? Which suggests flight and motion? What have these things got to do with the function of each building?
2. Which of these buildings places more emphasis on visual details?
3. How do the details of each building relate to its overall structure? Are details in either work irrelevant (or superfluous) to the structure?
4. Explain the content of each building.

FIGURE 3-5
Le Corbusier, Notre Dame-du-Haut, Ronchamps, France, 1950–1955. (Photograph Ezra Stoller © ESTO; art © 1997 Artists Rights Society [ARS], New York/SPADEM, Paris)

least an important component of it—is usually the practical function the building serves. We have no difficulty telling which of these buildings was meant to serve as a bank and which was meant to serve as a church. In the Perception Key on page 54, consider why it is so easy to identify these buildings, even though neither is typical of its kind of architecture.

FIGURE 3-6
Louis Henry Sullivan, Guaranty (Prudential) Building, Buffalo, New York. 1894. (Buffalo and Erie County Historical Society)

Form-Content The interpretive critic's job is to find out as much about an artistic form as possible in order to explain its meaning. This is a particularly useful task for the critic—which is to say, for us in particular—since the forms of numerous works of art seem important but are not immediately understandable. When we look at the examples of the bank and the church, we ought to realize that the significance of these buildings is expressed by means of the form-content. It is true that without knowing the functions of these buildings we could appreciate them as abstract structures, but knowing about their functions deepens our appreciation. Thus the lofty arc of Le Corbusier's roof soars heavenward more mightily when we recognize the building as a church. The form takes us up toward heaven, at least in the sense that it moves our eyes upward. For a Christian church such a reference is perfect. The bank, on the other hand, looks like a pile of square coins or banknotes. Certainly the form "amasses" something, an appropriate suggestion for a bank. We will not belabor these examples, since it should be fun for you to do this kind of critical job yourself. Observe how much more you get out of these examples of architecture when you consider each form in relation to its meaning—that is, the form as form-content. Furthermore, such analyses should convince you that interpretive criticism operates in a vacuum unless it is based on descriptive criticism. Unless we perceive the form with sensitivity—and this means that we have the basis for good descriptive criticism—we simply cannot understand the content. In turn, any interpretive criticism will be useless.

Consider now Donald Justice's love poem and give some thought to the job an interpretive critic might have in explaining the poem to someone who does not understand or like it. What are the kinds of questions critics might ask about the work as a poem?

A MAP OF LOVE

Your face more than others' faces
Maps the half-remembered places
I have come to while I slept—
Continents a dream had kept
Secret from all waking folk
Till to your face I awoke,
And remembered then the shore,
And the dark interior.

This is the kind of poem that one needs to think about for quite a while, for its content is not obvious. And while thinking about it, one could be asking some questions that might help the poem to come into sharper focus.

PERCEPTION KEY
"A MAP OF LOVE"

1. Why is a map a useful metaphor for someone's face?
2. What does "dark interior" usually mean when we connect the term with a map?
3. Why would the narrator ("I") think in terms of a map?
4. What is the relationship between sleeping and waking in this poem?

In a way, everyone's questions about this poem are relevant, no matter how strange they may seem at first. This is particularly true if we have the opportunity to talk about our questions with others. Listening to the questions of others should give us some useful ideas about the ways in which works of art are understood by other people, providing us also with ideas about new ways in which we can understand works of art for ourselves. When you see it from this point of view, you realize that an open discussion, far from being vague and irrelevant to the sharpening of our understanding, ought to be one of the most valuable kinds of instruction we can get about the arts.

The relativity of explanations about the content of works of art is important for us to grasp. Even descriptive critics, who try to tell us about what is really there, will perceive things in a way that is relative to their own perspective. In Cervantes' *Don Quixote* there is an amusing story that illustrates the point. Sancho Panza had two cousins who were expert wine tasters. However, on tasting a wine, they disagreed. One found the wine excellent except for an iron taste; the other found the wine excellent except for a leathern taste. When the barrel of wine was emptied, an iron key with a leather thong was found. As N. J. Berrill points out in *Man's Emerging Mind:*

> The statement you often hear that seeing is believing is one of the most misleading ones a man has ever made, for you are more likely to see what you believe than believe what you see. To see anything as it really exists is about as hard an exercise of mind and eyes as it is possible to perform. . . .[1]

Two descriptive critics can often "see" quite different things in an artistic form. This is not only to be expected but is also desirable; it is one of the reasons great works of art keep us intrigued for centuries. But even though they may see quite different aspects when they look independently at a work of art, when they get together and talk it over, they will usually come to some kind of agreement about the aspects each of them sees. The work being described, after all, has verifiable, objective qualities each of us can perceive and talk about. But it has subjective qualities as well, in the sense that the qualities are observed only by "subjects."

In the case of interpretive criticism, the subjectivity and, in turn, the relativity of explanations are more obvious than in the case of descriptive criticism. The content is "there" in the form, and yet, unlike the form, it is not there in such a directly perceivable way. It must be interpreted. Thus, if someone were to read "A Map of Love" and think that the only "map" in the poem was the face of the beloved, that person might well be surprised to learn that there are other references to maps and to kinds of geography—the "interior" usually refers to the unmapped and "dark" places beyond the coasts of continents as yet not totally explored. Then, even if the reader did sense that maps were being used in a very large sense, he or she might not be fully aware that the beloved in the poem was being loved the way explorers love the country they explore, with all the surprises, terror, uncertainty, and excitement of discovery that famous explorers have written about. The reader might not be fully aware that the act of love can be a way of getting new knowledge, of being in an unfamiliar relationship with someone, and of being in an unfamiliar relationship with oneself. Few people will deny that the concept of the map is present in the poem, but many may disagree that it implies the other ideas we have suggested. For you it may imply something else. But before we can begin to decide what is implied by the poem, we must know what is there that we can agree upon as equally perceivable and conceivable. This is descriptive criticism, preliminary to interpretive criticism—to the coming to terms with the content of the poem.

Interpretive critics, more than descriptive critics, must be familiar with the subject matter. Interpretive critics often make the subject matter more explicit for us, at the first stage of their criticism. In doing so, they bring

[1]N. J. Berrill, *Man's Emerging Mind,* Dodd, Mead, New York, 1955, p. 147.

us closer to the work. Perhaps the best way initially to "get at" Picasso's *Guernica* (Figure 1-4) is to discover its subject matter. Is it about a fire in a barn or something else? If we are not clear about this, perception of the painting is obscured. But after the subject matter has been elucidated, good interpretive critics go much further: exploring and discovering meanings about the subject matter as revealed by the form. Now they are concerned with helping us grasp the content directly, in all of its complexities and subtleties. This final stage of interpretive criticism is, undoubtedly, the most demanding of all criticism.

EVALUATIVE CRITICISM

To evaluate a work of art is to judge its merits. At first glance, this seems to suggest that evaluative criticism is prescriptive criticism, which prescribes what is good as if it were a medicine and tells us that this work is superior to that work.

PERCEPTION KEY
EVALUATIVE CRITICISM

1. Suppose you are a judge of an exhibition of painting and the paintings discussed in Chapter 2 have been placed into competition. You are to award first, second, and third prizes. What would your decisions be? Why?
2. Suppose, further, that you are asked to judge which is the best work of art from the following selection: cummings' "l(a," Cézanne's *Mont Sainte Victoire* (Figure 2-5), Betye Saar's *The Liberation of Aunt Jemima* (Figure 3-1), and Le Corbusier's church (Figure 3-5). What would your decision be? Why?

It may be that this kind of evaluative criticism makes you uncomfortable. If so, we think your reaction is based on good instincts. In the first place, each work of art is such an individual thing that a relative merit ranking of several of them seems arbitrary. This is especially the case when the works are in different media and have different subject matter, as in the second question of the Perception Key. In the second place, it is not very clear how such judging helps us in our basic critical purpose—to learn from our reflections about works of art how to participate with these works more intensely and enjoyably.

Generally, evaluative criticism of some kind is necessary. We have been making such judgments continually in this book—in the selections for illustrations, for example. You make such judgments when, as you enter a museum of art, you decide to spend your time with this painting rather than that. Obviously, directors of museums must also make evaluative criticisms, because they cannot display every work they own. If a Van Gogh is on sale—and one of his paintings was bought for $82.5 million—someone has to decide its relative worth in a museum's collection. Evaluative criticism, then, is always functioning, at least implicitly. Even when we are participating with a work, we are implicitly evaluating its worth. Our participation implies its worth. If it were worthless to us, we would not even attempt participation.

The problem, then, is how to use evaluative criticism as constructively as possible. How can we use such criticism to help our participation with works of art? Whether Giorgione's painting (Figure 2-13) deserves first prize over Modigliani's (Figure 2-15) seems trivial. But if almost all critics agree that Shakespeare's poetry is far superior to Edward Guest's and if we have been thinking Guest's poetry is better, we would probably be wise to do some reevaluating. Or if we hear a music critic we respect state that Charles Ives' music is worth listening to—and up to this time we have dismissed it—then we should indeed make an effort to listen. Perhaps the basic importance of evaluative criticism lies in its commendation of works that we might otherwise dismiss. This may lead us to delightful experiences. Such criticism may also make us more skeptical about our own judgments. If we think that the poetry of Edward Guest and the paintings of Norman Rockwell are among the very best, it may be very helpful for us to know that other informed people think otherwise.

Evaluative criticism presupposes three fundamental standards—perfection, insight, and inexhaustability. When the evaluation centers on the form, it usually values a form highly only if the detail relationships are tightly organized. If detail fails to cohere with structure, the result is distracting and thus inhibits participation. An artistic form in which everything works together may be called perfect. A work may have perfect organization, however, and still be evaluated as poor unless it satisfies the standard of insight. If the form fails to inform us about some subject matter—if it just pleases us but doesn't make some significant difference in our lives—then that form may be called decorative rather than artistic. And decorative form may be valued below artistic form because the participation it evokes, if it evokes any at all, is not as intense, delightful, or lastingly significant. Finally, works of art may differ greatly in the depth of their content. The subject matter of Mondrian's *Composition in White, Black and Red* (Figure 1-5)—colors, lines, and space—is not as broad as Cézanne's *Mont Sainte Victoire* (Figure 2-5). And the depth of penetration into the subject matter is far deeper in the Cézanne, we believe, than in the photograph of the mountain (Figure 2-4). The stronger the content—that is, the richer the interpretation of the subject matter—the more intense our participation, because we have more to keep us involved in the work. Such works resist monotony, no matter how often we return to them. Such works apparently are inexhaustible, and evaluative critics usually will rate only those kinds of works as masterpieces.

Perception Key
EVALUATIVE CRITICISM

1. Evaluate the nudes (Figures 2-13 through 2-20) with reference to the perfection of their artistic forms, the tightness of the interrelationship of details to each other, and details to structure.
2. Evaluate these works with reference to their insight. How intensely does the form inform?
3. Evaluate these works with reference to their inexhaustibility.

Notice how unimportant it is how you ultimately rank these works. But notice, also, how these questions provide precise contexts for your attention.

SOME EXAMPLES FOR CRITICISM

The following are some examples to approach as a critic. You can decide whether or not you have any sense of participation with the works here—but remember that a photograph of a sculpture is not a sculpture, any more than a photograph of a building is a building. No one can hope to have a very intense participative experience except in the presence of the genuine work of art itself if for no other reason than that the scale of a work of art is usually impossible to realize in a reproduction. Still, with a little imagination we can sometimes get something of a participative experience even from a photograph.

The following figures are set up in pairs because useful criticisms are more likely to occur when we criticize works of the same artistic medium and at least roughly the same subject matter. Most criticisms are at least implicitly comparative, even when they seem entirely noncomparative. As we begin to develop our critical sense, comparative judgments are usually easier and more valuable than judgments about individual works in isolation. They also offer us more to discuss and, when we can share our interpretations with others, they can offer us alternative points of view.

Consider the following Perception Keys as mere starting points for your criticisms. Go as far beyond them as is useful.

PERCEPTION KEY

INTERIORS OF ST. PAUL'S CATHEDRAL, LONDON (FIGURE 3-7), AND ST. ZACCARIAH, VENICE (FIGURE 3-8)

1. Consider the differences between these two church interiors in terms of the attention paid to detail. Which is more intricately detailed? In which is the detail more tightly organized? Consider the power of repetition, such as vertical and curved lines. Evaluate the effect of the emphasis or the lack of emphasis on detail in relation to the function of each space in which spiritual matters are dominant.
2. What are the main regions observable in each interior? What is their effect on the space enclosed by these structures? Which space seems larger? Which seems more intimate? Which space is more dramatic? Which space is more peaceful?
3. Is it possible to evaluate responsibly the effect of the space in these churches without taking into account their function as churches? Which shape is more suited for public ceremony? Which is more suited for private prayer? How can you tell?

FIGURE 3-7
Choir of St. Paul's Cathedral, London. (Lee A. Jacobus)

FIGURE 3-8
Interior, Chapel, St. Zaccariah, Venice. (Lee A. Jacobus)

PERCEPTION KEY

THREE PORTRAIT BUSTS: EGYPTIAN MUMMY MASK (FIGURE 3-9); GREEK BUST OF ASKLEPIOS (FIGURE 3-10); AFRICAN MASK (FIGURE 3-11)

1. All three of these busts portray the human face. Describe each carefully in terms of its detail. Which is most dominated by detail? Which by structure?
2. Which of these portraits is most lifelike? Does the least realistic portrait have a strong sense of design? Examine that mask for its apparent content.
3. Which of these portraits seems to express the strongest sense of personality? Why? How is that personality interpreted?
4. Which of these portraits expresses power most intensely? What kind of power?
5. Which kind of criticism—descriptive, interpretive, or evaluative—do these portraits seem most to demand?

FIGURE 3-9
Egyptian mummy mask. Plaster. British Museum. (Lee A. Jacobus)

FIGURE 3-10
Greek portrait of Asklepios (the physician). Marble. British Museum. (Lee A. Jacobus)

FIGURE 3-11
African ritual mask. Wood. Museum of Ethnography, London. (Lee A. Jacobus)

FIGURE 3-12
Arch of Constantine. Rome. (Lee A. Jacobus)

Perception Key

ARCH OF CONSTANTINE (FIGURE 3-12)
AND POST AND LINTEL: STONEHENGE (FIGURE 3-13)

1. Both of these stone pieces were very carefully erected and dressed (finished and smoothed). Which is more emphatically structural in appearance? Which emphasizes detail?
2. What is the basic structure of the more detailed of these two pieces? Is it difficult to perceive?
3. Enumerate some of the important details of the Arch of Constantine. What does the presence of fluted columns, circular relief sculpture on the arch, and freestanding sculpture suggest about the richness of Roman society? What does the starkness of the Stonehenge post and lintel structure (two upright columns with a stone across their tops) suggest about the little known society that erected it?
4. Which of these pieces reveals more about the basic elemental force of nature? Which reveals more about the history of a civilization? Which of these structures is more timeless?
5. Compare these works for their relative emphasis on detail and structure.

FIGURE 3-13
Stonehenge, post and lintel. Salisbury, England. (Lee A. Jacobus)

Perception Key

THE HÔTEL DES INVALIDES (FIGURE 3-14)
AND THE GEORGES POMPIDOU CENTER FOR THE ARTS
(FIGURE 3-15)

1. The Hôtel des Invalides was built as a hospital and residence for wounded soldiers during the period of Louis XIV (1638–1715). Louis supervised a large number of huge architectural achievements during his lifetime. His ambition was great, and his ideals are reflected in buildings such as this wing of the Hôtel des Invalides. Does the form of the hospital give expression to ambition or grandeur? Does the form give expression to values you associate with hospitals? Does the form give expression to the values of a museum? This section is called Musée de L'Armée and is no longer used as a residence or hospital.
2. Does the Georges Pompidou Center for the Arts look like a museum? If not, is that bad?
3. Does the Pompidou Center emphasize structure or detail? Compare it in this respect with the Hôtel des Invalides. How well do the details of each building interrelate with its structure?

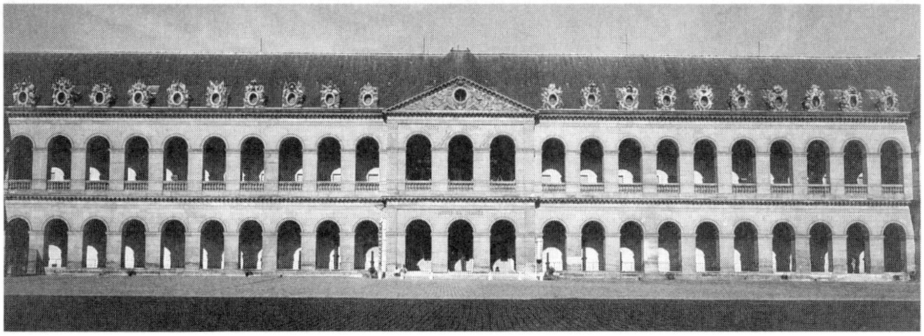

FIGURE 3-14
Liberal Bruant, Hôtel des Invalides. Paris, 1670–1677. (Lee A. Jacobus)

FIGURE 3-15
Richard Rogers and Enzo Piano, The Georges Pompidou Center for the Arts. Paris, 1976. (Lee A. Jacobus)

4. The Pompidou Center was built in 1976 and is currently one of the most popular buildings in Paris. It is often called the inside-out building, an example of a modern "high-tech" style. Make an evaluative comparison between the success of this contemporary style and the traditional style of the Hôtel des Invalides, which depends on the Roman arch and repeated patterning of structure.

PERCEPTION KEY

EAKINS' *PORTRAIT OF THOMAS EAKINS* (FIGURE 3-16) AND MÜNTER'S *BOATING* (FIGURE 3-17)

1. In which of these paintings is the structure simpler and more dominant?
2. How does the use of color aid the tightness of structure in each painting? Which colors are dominant in each painting? How do the colors contribute to the mood of each painting?
3. How has Münter used line and shape to help integrate the details in her painting so that it has a coherent structure? Do you feel it has a coherent structure?
4. Which of these paintings would you prefer to have in your own room to look at for, say, a year or two? Which seems more inexhaustible to you?
5. Discuss the content of each painting.

FIGURE 3-16
Susan MacDowell Eakins, *Portrait of Thomas Eakins*. 1889. Oil on canvas, 50 × 40 inches. Philadelphia Museum of Art. Given by Charles Bregler.

FIGURE 3-17
Gabriele Münter, *Boating*. 1910. Oil on canvas, 49¼ × 28⅞ inches. Milwaukee Art Museum collection. (© Artists Rights Society [ARS], New York/VG Bild-Kunst, Bonn, Germany)

PERCEPTION KEY

MASK (FIGURE 3-18) AND NAIL FIGURE (FIGURE 3-19)

1. How are the major details of the mask organized? Is the mask a recognizable mask? What emotions might be evoked by seeing this mask?
2. Comment on the organizing effect of the use of color and pigment in this mask.
3. Does the nail figure organize more or fewer details than the mask? How does the coloration contribute to or distract from its overall structural unity?
4. Which of these figures seems to have more unity? Why?
5. Which of these figures uses symmetry (repetition of shapes, balance of the right and left side or of the top and bottom, etc.) more effectively?
6. Can you imagine functions for these figures?

FIGURE 3-18
Mask. Wee peoples, Liberia and Ivory Coast, twentieth century. Wood, raffia, cloth, teeth, horn, feathers, hair, fiber, cord, cowrie shells, mud, pigment; height 32 inches. Seattle Art Museum. Gift of Katherine White and the Boeing Company. (81.17.193)

These African figures are carefully constructed for specific purposes. The mask is designed to be used in a dance in firelight to frighten away spirits that might cause dissension or sickness in the village. Villagers believe spirits abound and that they can be made visible in ritual ceremonies through the use of masks. The standing nail figure was designed to be used in healing ceremonies and was a container for powerful magic. The nails in this figure were pounded in as it was used. It is called *nkisi nkondi* and was also valuable in peace ceremonies or even in legal dealings. Sometimes blades were driven into the figure to initiate its powers.

FIGURE 3-19
Nail figure. Yombe group, Kongo peoples, Shilango River area, Zaire, nineteenth century. Wood, metal, raffia, cloth, pigment, clay, resin, cowrie shell; height 44½ inches. The Field Museum, #A109327c, Chicago.

SUMMARY

Good critics can help us understand works of art while also giving us the means or techniques which will help us become good critics ourselves. Principally, we can learn a good deal about what kinds of questions to ask about given works of art. Each of the following chapters on the individual arts is designed to do just that—to give some help about what kinds of questions a serious viewer should ask in order to come to a clearer perception and deeper understanding of any specific work. With the arts, unlike many other areas of human concern, the questions are often more important than the answers. The real lover of the arts will often not be the person with all the answers but rather the one who has the best questions. And the reason for this is not that the answers are worthless but that the questions, when properly applied, lead us to a new awareness, a more exalted consciousness of what works of art have to offer. Then, when we get to the last chapter, we will be better prepared to understand something of how the arts are related to other branches of the humanities.

CHAPTER 3 BIBLIOGRAPHY

Adams, Hazard (ed.). *Critical Theory Since Plato*, rev. ed. Fort Worth: Harcourt Brace Jovanovich, 1992.

Aschenbrenner, Karl. *The Concepts of Criticism*. Dordrecht, The Netherlands: Reidell, 1975.

Boas, George. *Wingless Pegasus*. Baltimore: The Johns Hopkins University Press, 1967.

Frye, Northrop. *Anatomy of Criticism*. Princeton, N.J.: Princeton University Press, 1990.

Greene, Theodore M. *The Arts and the Art of Criticism*. Princeton, N.J.: Princeton University Press, 1940.

Hirsch, E. D. *The Aims of Interpretation*. Chicago: University of Chicago Press, 1976.

Jacobus, Lee A., and Regina Barreca (eds.). *Lit: Literature Interpretation Theory*. 1989– .

Krieger, Murray. *Theory of Criticism*. Baltimore: The Johns Hopkins University Press, 1981.

Margolis, Joseph. *The Language of Art and Art Criticism: Analytic Questions in Aesthetics*. Detroit: Wayne State University Press, 1965.

Olson, Elder. *On Value Judgments in the Arts and Other Essays*. Chicago: University of Chicago Press, 1976.

Osborne, Harold. *Aesthetics and Criticism*. London: Routledge, 1955.

Sontag, Susan. *Against Interpretation and Other Essays.* New York: Farrar, Straus, and Giroux, 1964.

Wellek, René. *Concepts of Criticism.* New Haven: Yale University Press, 1973.

CHAPTER 3 WEBSITES

Art Criticism Forum (mailing list)

Name: **artcrit.** Address: **Listserve@vm1.yorku.ca**

Art Education Materials

World Wide Web: **http://www.ncsa.uiuc.edu./SDG/Experimental/anu-art-history/home.html**

Art History Information

World Wide Web: **http://www.ahip.getty.edu/ahip/home.html**

Fine Art Forum's Web Page (online fine arts journal)

World Wide Web: **http://www.msstate.edu/Fineart_Online/home.html**

Museums on the Web

World Wide Web: **http://www.comlab.ox.ac.uk/archive/other/museums.html**

Online Museums

World Wide Web: **http://gate.okc.com/morr/**

Web Museum: The Louvre

World Wide Web: **http://www.emf.net/wm/**

Women Artists

World Wide Web: **http://www.sonoma.edu/library/waa/**

CHAPTER 4

PAINTING

Painting is the art that has most to do with revealing the visual appearance of objects and events. The eye is the chief sense organ involved in our participation with painting, and one of the chief sense organs involved in our dealings with our everyday world. But our ordinary vision of our everyday world is usually very fragmentary. We usually see scenes with their objects and events only to the degree necessary for our practical purposes. Even in such a simple act as walking on a sidewalk, we tend to ignore the qualities of colors, lines, etc. Otherwise we would be late for our appointment or get run down by a car. We hurry on. When we are behind the wheel of a car, our lives depend on our judgment of how far away and how fast-moving that oncoming car really is. We just do not have time to enjoy its splendor of speeding color. Of course, someone else may be driving, and then the qualities of the visually perceptible may be enjoyed for their own sake. Or we may be walking leisurely in the mountains on a safe path, and then the fullness of the scene has a chance to unfold.

Our lives are dominated by practical concerns to the extent that we sometimes do not perceive the world about us with sensitivity. Test your visual powers for yourself (see Perception Key).

If you have found yourself tending to answer the questions of this Perception Key negatively or if you see the assignments about the green and the rock as being difficult and perhaps pointless, you should not be surprised or discouraged. Like the great majority of us, you probably have been educated away from sensitivity to the qualities of things and things as things. We have been taught how to manage and control things by thinking at them, as in the scientific method. This does not mean that such ed-

Perception Key
YOUR VISUAL POWERS

1. What are the eye colors of members of your family and those of your best friends?
2. Have you ever followed closely the swirl of a falling leaf?
3. Are you aware of the spatial locations of the buildings on the main street of your home town? Are they pleasing or distressing?
4. Are you aware very often of the detailed qualities of things—such as the fluidity of water, the roughness of rocks, or the greenness of grass?
5. Take some green paint and some red paint, a brush, and paper. Or, if these are not readily available, take any materials at hand, such as marbles and chips that are green and red. Now place the green and red side by side in such a way that, as far as possible, you make the greenness of the green shine forth. Maybe this will require a different tone of green or red or a different placement. Or maybe you have to remove the red altoghter and substitute another color. Notice how, as you go about this, you must really see the green. You must let the green dominate and control your seeing.
6. Are you aware very often of things as things, their "thingness"—such as the mountainness of mountains, the marbleness of marble, the glassiness of glass? Do you care about things in this sense?
7. Go into the fields if this is possible and seek a rock that will enhance the appearance of an area of the yard or building or room where you live. Select both the rock and the area so that the physical qualities of the rock—its hardness, roughness or smoothness, shape, and especially its solidity—will be perceivable.
8. John Ruskin, the great nineteenth-century critic, noted in his *Modern Painters*

   that there is hardly a roadside pond or pool which has not as much landscape in it as above it. It is not the brown, muddy, dull thing we suppose it to be; it has a heart like ourselves, and in the bottom of that there are the boughs of the tall trees and the blades of the shaking grass, and all manner of hues, of variable pleasant light out of the sky; nay the ugly gutter that stagnates over the drain bars in the heart of the foul city is not altogether base; down in that, if you will look deep enough, you may see the dark, serious blue of the far-off sky, and the passing of pure clouds. It is at your own will that you see in that despised stream either the refuse of the street or the image of the sky—so it is with almost all other things that we kindly despise.

   Do you agree with Ruskin? If not, why not?

ucation is bad. Without this education the business of the world would come to a halt. But if not supplemented, this training may blind us like some terrible disease of the eye. For help we must go to the artists, especially the painter—those who are most sensitive to the visual appearances of things. With their aid, our vision can be made whole again, as when we were children. Their paintings accomplish this, in the first place, by making things and their qualities much clearer than they are in nature. The artist purges from our sight the films of familiarity. Second, painting, with its "all-at-onceness," more than any other art, gives us the time to allow our vision to focus and participate.

ELEMENTS OF PAINTING

The most basic elements of painting are line, shape, light, texture, and color. The basic elements of composition are centrality, symmetry, asymmetry, and balance. These terms are important to developing a vocabulary to describe visual artifacts of many kinds, but they are especially valuable for discussing painting. Rather than speak of these elements in the abstract, let us begin with an examination of Cézanne's *Mont Sainte Victoire* (Figure 2-5). The line is sometimes indistinct in this painting in part because Cézanne inherited the Impressionist's technique of implying line so as to concentrate on color. Critics have observed that for Cézanne, "form and color were indissoluble." "When color is at its richest," Cézanne said, "form is at its fullest." The most distinct lines in this painting result from the definition of colors, such as the green fields and the lighter road moving from lower right diagonally to middle left, drawing the eye toward a structure. The same may be said of the colors of the viaduct moving horizontally just above the mid-line of the painting. The line of the mountain against the sky is not sharp, but sketchy and suggestive, as if it were at moments merging with the sky. The sinuous horizontal lines of the tree branches moving from the right side of the canvas to the left are also careful to avoid being so distinct as to be artificial. They suggest movement, as if the breeze were disturbing them. The shapes we see are mostly those of the fields, the close trees and bushes, the buildings, and then the massive mountain itself. They are essentially variations on parallelograms and triangles—man-made buildings and fields. Some of the buildings are defined by black lines, but most are defined by contrasting color, earth tones in contrast with the green fields and the purplish-hazy mountain.

The composition is carefully asymmetrical. The peak of the mountain is off-center to the left. In order to balance the painting visually, Cézanne places a mass of green on the right at the bottom. Following a line to the left from that mass of trees, using the line of the road as a guide, your eye moves to the building, but also to a mass of green limbs from the tree on the left. The bottom half of the painting is dominated by the diagonal lines of the road and the green fields. The top half of the painting is dominated by the mass and bulk of the mountain and the lines of the branches above it, all rhythmically balanced against one another.

This kind of visual analysis is useful for descriptive criticism, since it helps establish exactly what we see in the painting. It also gives us a guide to changes in style and changes in emphasis. For example, you may profitably compare the Cézanne with any of the comic strip panels in Chapter 2, where you will see that line is strong and defined, shapes are usually balanced and symmetrical, and centrality is important.

THE CLARITY OF PAINTING

Now examine again the photograph of Mont Sainte Victoire (Figure 2-4). The photograph was taken many years after Cézanne was there, but, aside from a few more buildings and older trees, the scene of the photograph shows essentially what Cézanne saw. Compare the photograph of the mountain with the painting. At first glance, you might conclude that the photograph is clearer than the painting, for there is a kind of blurry effect about the painting. But look again. See what the painting reveals that the photograph does not.

Perception Key
MONT SAINTE VICTOIRE

1. Why did Cézanne put the two trees in the foreground at the left and right edges? Why are they cut off by the frame? Why are the trees trembling?
2. In the photograph, there is an abrupt gap between the foreground and the middle distance. In the painting, this gap is filled in. Why?
3. In the painting the viaduct has been moved over to the left. Why?
4. In the painting the lines of the viaduct appear to move toward the left. Why?
5. Furthermore, the lines of the viaduct lead to a meeting point with the long road that runs toward the left side of the mountain. The fields and buildings within that triangle all seem drawn toward that apex. Why did Cézanne organize this middle ground more geometrically than the foreground or the mountain? And why is the apex of the triangle the unifying area for that region?
6. Why is the peak of the mountain in the painting given a slightly concave shape?
7. In the painting, the ridge of the mountian above the viaduct is brought into much closer proximity to the peak of the mountain. Why?
8. In the painting, the lines, ridges, and shapes of the mountain are much more tightly organized than in the photograph. How is this accomplished?

The subject matter of Cézanne's painting is surely the mountain. Suppose the title of the painting were *Trees*. This would strike us as strange because when we read a title we usually expect it to tell us what the painting is about—that is, its subject matter. And although the trees in Cézanne's painting are important, they obviously are not as important as the mountain. A title such as *Viaduct* would also be misleading.

The form reveals the mountainness of the mountain in so many ways that a complete description is very difficult. Some of the ways have already been suggested by the questions of the accompanying Perception Key. Every way helps bring forth the energy of Mont Sainte Victoire, which seems to roll down through the valley and even up into the foreground trees. Everything is dominated and unified around the mountain. The roll of its ridges is like waves of the sea—but far more durable, as we sense the impenetrable solidity of the masses underneath.

You will notice that the brushstrokes are usually perceptible, angular, and organized in units that function something like pieces in a mosaic. These units move toward each other in receding space, and yet their intersections are rigid, as if their impact froze their movement. Almost all the colors reflect light, like the facets of a crystal, so that a solid color or one-piece effect rarely appears. Generally, you will find within each unit a series of color tones of the same basic tint. The colors, moreover, are laid on in small overlapping patches, often crossed with dark and delicate parallel lines to give shading. These hatchings also model the depth dimension of objects, so we perceive the solidity of their volumes more directly, strangely enough, than we perceive them in nature. Compare again the photograph of Mont Sainte Victoire with the painting. The lines of the painting are not drawn around objects like outlines; rather, the lines emerge from the convergence of color, light, shadow, and volume much as—although this also may seem strange—lines emerge from the objects of nature. And the color tones of the painting, variously modulated, are repeated endlessly throughout the planes of space. For example, the color tones of the mountain are repeated in the viaduct and the fields and buildings of the middle ground and the trees of the foreground. Cézanne's color animates everything, mainly because the color seems to be always moving out of the depth of everything rather than being laid on flat like house paint. The vibrating colors, in turn, rhythmically charge into one another and then settle down, reaching an equilibrium in which everything except the limbs of the foreground trees seems to come to rest.

Cézanne's form distorts reality in order to reveal reality. He makes Mont Sainte Victoire far clearer in his painting than you will ever see it in nature or even in the best of photographs. Once you have participated with this and similar paintings, you will find that you will begin to see mountains like Mont Sainte Victoire with something like Cézanne's vision.

THE "ALL-AT-ONCENESS" OF PAINTING

In addition to revealing the visually perceptible more clearly, paintings give us time for our vision to focus, hold, and participate. Of course, there are times when we can hold on a scene in nature. We are resting with no pressing worries and with time on our hands, and the sunset is so striking that our attention fixes on its redness. But then darkness descends and the mosquitoes begin to bite. In front of a painting, however, we find that things "stand still," like the red in Mondrian's *Composition in White, Black and Red* (Figure 1-5). Here the red is peculiarly impervious and reliable, infallibly fixed and settled in its place. It can be surveyed and brought out again and again; it can be visualized with closed eyes and checked with open eyes. There is no hurry, for all of the painting is present and, under normal conditions, it is going to stay present; it is not changing in any significant perceptual sense.

Moreover, we can "hold on" any detail or region or the totality as long as we like and follow any order of details or regions at our own pace. No region of a painting strictly presupposes another region temporally. The sequence is subject to no absolute constraint. Whereas there is only one route in listening to music, for example, there is a freedom of routes in seeing paintings. With *Mont Sainte Victoire,* for example, we may focus on the foreground trees, then on the middle ground, and finally on the mountain. The next time around we may reverse the order. "Paths are made," as the painter Paul Klee observed, "for the eye of the beholder which moves along from patch to patch like an animal grazing." There is a "rapt resting" on any part, an unhurried series of one-after-the-other of "nows," each of which has its own temporal spread.

Paintings make it possible for us to stop in the present and enjoy at our leisure the sensations provided by the show of the visible. That is the second reason paintings can help make our vision whole. They not only clarify our world but also free us from worrying about the future and the past, because paintings are a framed context in which everything stands still. There is the "here-now" and nothing but the "here-now." Our vision, for once, has time to let the qualities of things and the things themselves unfold.

ABSTRACT PAINTING

The artistic medium of painting is made up of qualities such as colors, textures, lines, shapes, and light, the elements or aspects of the visible which lend themselves to being organized. They are the qualities of the work that stimulate our visual organ—the eye—qualities which we shall call "sensa." They are the "stuff" that the painter forms in order to reveal some subject matter—that is, to transform that subject matter into a content. By eliminating reference to everything but colors, lines, shapes, and light from their work, abstract painters liberate us from the habits of always referring these elements to specific objects and events. They make it easy for us to focus on the sensa themselves even though we are not artists. Then the radiant and vivid values of the sensuous are enjoyed for their own sake, satisfying a fundamental need. Abstractions can help fulfill this need to behold and treasure the images of the sensuous. Instead of our controlling the sensa, transforming them into data or signs that represent objects or events, the sensa control us, transforming us into participators.

Moreover, because references to specific objects and events are eliminated, there is a peculiar abstraction from the future and the past. Abstract painting, more than any other art, gives us an intensified sense of "here-now" or presentational immediacy. When we perceive representational paintings such as *Mont Sainte Victoire,* we may think about our chances of getting to southern France some time in the future. Or when we perceive *May 3, 1808,* we may think about similar executions. These suggestions bring the future and past into our participation, causing the "here-now" to be somewhat compromised. But with abstract painting—because there is no portrayal of specific objects or events that suggest the past or the future—the sense of presentational immediacy is more intense.

Although sensa appear everywhere, in paintings sensa shine forth. This is especially true with abstract paintings, because there is nothing to attend to but sensa. In nature the light usually appears as external to the colors and surface of sensa. The light plays on the colors and surface. In paintings the light usually appears immanent in the colors and surface, seems to come—in part at least—through them, even in the flat polished colors of a Mondrian. When a light source is represented—the sunlight coming through windows in the paintings of Rembrandt or Vermeer—the light often seems to be absorbed into the colors and surfaces. There is a depth of luminosity about the sensa of paintings that rivals nature. Generally the colors of nature are more brilliant than the colors of painting; but usually in nature sensa are either so glittering that our squints miss their inner luminosity or the sensa are so changing that we lack the time to participate and penetrate. To ignore the allure of the sensa in a painting, and, in turn, in nature, is to miss one of the chief glories life provides. It is especially the abstract painter—the shepherd of sensa—who is most likely to call us back to our senses.

Study the Mondrian (Figure 1-5) or the Rothko (Figure 4-1). Then reflect on how you experienced a series of durations—"spots of time"—that are ordered by the relationships between the regions of sensa. Compare your experience with listening to music.

Perception Key
ROTHKO AND MUSIC

1. Can the color tones of Rothko be compared with tones of music? What qualities of the colors suggest musical tonalities? If you have access to a musical instrument, play the tones that you find suggested in the painting.
2. The sensa or tones of music come to us successively, and they usually interpenetrate. For example, as we hear the tone C, we also hear the preceding G, and we anticipate the coming E. Do the tones of the music usually interpenetrate more than the sensa of the Rothko? Do you see a succession of colors when you look at the Rothko, or do you see an "all-at-onceness"?
3. Is the process of listening to musical tones different from the process of seeing abstract paintings? In what way?

The sensa of abstract paintings (and the same is largely true of representational paintings) are divided from one another, we think, in a different way from the more fluid progressions of music. Whereas when we listen to music the sensa interpenetrate, when we see an abstract painting the sensa are more juxtaposed. Whereas the process of perceiving music is continuous, the process of perceiving abstract painting is discontinuous. Whereas music is perceived as motion, abstract painting is perceived as motionless. We are fascinated by the vibrant novelty and the primeval power of the red of an abstract painting for its own sake, cut off from explicit consciousness of past and future. But then, sooner or later, we notice the connection of the red to the blue, and then we are fascinated by the blue. Or then, sooner or later, we are fascinated by the interaction or contrast between the red and blue. Our eye travels over the canvas step by step, free to pause at any step as long as it desires. With music this pausing is impossible. If we "hold on" a tone or passage, the oncoming tones sweep by us and are lost. Music is always in part elsewhere—gone or coming—and we are swept up in the flow of process. The processes of hearing music and seeing abstract paintings are at opposite poles.

INTENSITY AND RESTFULNESS

Abstract painting reveals sensa in their primitive but powerful state of innocence. In turn, this intensity of vision renews the spontaneity of our perception and enhances the tone of our physical existence. We clothe our vi-

FIGURE 4-1
Mark Rothko, *Earth Greens*. 1955. Oil on canvas, 90¼ × 73½ inches. Museum Ludwig, Koln. (Photograph Rheinisches Bildarchiv, Koln, Germany; art © 1997 Kate Rothko-Prizel & Christopher Rothko/Artists Rights Society [ARS], New York)

sual sensations in positive feelings, living in these sensations instead of using them as means to ends. And such sensuous activity—sight, for once, minus anxiety and eyestrain—is sheer delight. Abstract painting offers us a complete rest from practical concerns. Abstract painting is, as Matisse in 1908 was beginning to see,

> an art of balance, of purity and serenity devoid of troubling or depressing subject matter, an art which might be for every mental worker, be he businessman or writer, like an appeasing influence, like a mental soother, something like a good armchair in which to rest from physical fatigue.[1]

[1]*La grande revue*, Dec. 25, 1908.

Or, as Hilla Rebay remarks:

> The contemplation of a Non-objective picture offers a complete rest to the mind. It is particularly beneficial to business men, as it carries them away from the tiresome rush of earth, and strengthens their nerves, once they are familiar with this real art. If they lift their eyes to these pictures in a tired moment, their attention will be absorbed in a joyful way, thus resting their minds from earthly troubles and thoughts.[2]

PERCEPTION KEY
ROTHKO'S *EARTH GREENS* AND MATISSE'S *PINEAPPLE AND ANEMONES*

1. Rothko's *Earth Greens* (Figure 4-1) is, we think, an exceptional example of timelessness. Matisse's *Pineapple and Anemones* (Figure 4-2) also emphasizes sensa, especially the rich palette of red, oranges, and greens. How can we compare the timelessness of these paintings? What qualities make either more timeless?
2. Examine the sensa in Matisse's painting. Does the fact that the painting is a still life representing real things distract you from observing the sensa? How crucial are the sensa to your full appreciation of the painting?
3. What differences do you perceive in Rothko's and Matisse's approach to sensa?

The underlying blue rectangle of *Earth Greens* is cool and recessive with a pronounced vertical emphasis (91 inches by 74 inches), accented by the way the bands of blue gradually expand upward. However, the green and rusty-red rectangles, smaller but much more prominent because they "stretch over" most of the blue, have a horizontal "lying down" emphasis that quiets the upward thrust. The vertical and the horizontal—the simplest, most universal, and potentially the most tightly "relatable" of all axes, but which in everyday experience usually are cut by diagonals and oblique curves or are strewn about chaotically—are brought together in perfect peace. This fulfilling harmony is enhanced by the way the lines, with one exception, of all these rectangles are soft and slightly irregular, avoiding the stiffness of straight lines that isolate. Only the outside boundary line of the blue rectangle is strictly straight, and this serves to separate the three rectangles from the outside world.

Within the firm frontal symmetry of the world of this painting, the green rectangle is the most secure and weighty. It comes the closest to the stability of a square; the upper part occupies the actual center of the picture, which, along with the lower blue border, provides an anchorage; and the location of the rectangle in the lower section of the painting suggests weight because in our world heavy objects seek and possess low places. But even

[2]Hilla Rebay, "Value of Non-Objectivity," *Third Enlarged Catalogue of the Solomon R. Guggenheim Collection of Non-Objective Paintings*, Solomon R. Guggenheim Collection, New York, 1938, p. 7.

FIGURE 4-2
Henri Matisse, *Pineapple and Anemones*. 1940. Oil on canvas, 29 × 36 inches. Private collection. (© 1997 Succession H. Matisse/Artists Rights Society [ARS], New York)

more importantly, this green, like so many earth colors, is a peculiarly quiet and immobile color. Wassily Kandinsky, one of the earliest abstract painters, finds green generally an "earthly, self-satisfied repose." It is "the most restful color in existence, moves in no direction, has no corresponding appeal, such as joy, sorrow, or passion, demands nothing" Rothko's green, furthermore, has the texture of earth thickening its appearance. Although there are slight variations in hue, brightness, and saturation in the green, their movement is congealed in a stable pattern. The green rectangle does not look as though it wanted to move to a more suitable place.

The rusty-red rectangle, on the other hand, is much less secure and weighty. Whereas the blue rectangle recedes and the green rectangle stays put, the rusty-red rectangle moves toward us, locking the green in depth between itself and the blue. Similarly, whereas the blue is cold and the rusty-red warm, the "temperature" of the green mediates between them. Unlike the blue and green rectangles, the rusty-red seems light and floating, radiating vital energy. Not only is the rusty-red rectangle the smallest but also its winding, swelling shadows and the dynamism of its blurred, obliquely oriented brushstrokes produce an impression of self-contained movement that sustains this lovely shape like a cloud above the green below. This effect is enhanced by the blue, which serves as a kind of firmament for this sensuous world, for blue is the closest to darkness, and this blue, especially the middle band, seems lit up as if by starlight. Yet despite its amorphous inner activity, the rusty-red rectangle keeps its place, also serenely harmonizing with its neighbors. Delicately, a pervasive violet tinge touches everything. And everything seems locked together forever, an image of eternity.

REPRESENTATIONAL PAINTING

Matisse has also emphasized sensa in his painting, representing the pineapple and the anemones—as well as the table and leaves in brilliant, intense colors that are carefully harmonized. The red-colored background provides a basis from which to observe the fruit and the flowers. The power of Matisse's red is similar to the power of Rothko's red. However, as Rothko has placed the green rectangle beneath the red, he has made it an important dominant force. Matisse's greens are less dominant, yet they attach the visual experience of the painting to nature. Rather, the reds and yellows provide the exuberant power in the painting, almost rising from the canvas. If a sense of timelessness attaches to Rothko's painting more intensely than to Matisse's, it may be partly because the temporality of the fruit and the flowers is so apparent in *Pineapple and Anemones* (Figure 4-2).

In the participative experience with representational paintings, the sense of "here-now," so overwhelming in the participative experience with abstractions, is somewhat weakened. Representational paintings situate the sensuous in specific objects and events. A representational painting, just like an abstraction, is "all there" and "holds still." But past and future are more relevant than in our experience of abstract paintings because we are seeing representations of definite objects and events. Inevitably we are aware of place and date, and, in turn, a sense of past and future is a part of that awareness. Our experience is a little more ordinary than it is when we feel the extraordinary isolation from specific objects and events that occurs in the perception of abstract paintings. Representational paintings always bring in some suggestion of "once upon a time." Moreover, we are kept a little closer to the experience of everyday, because images that refer to specific objects and events usually lack something of the strangeness of images that refer only to sensa.

Representational painting furnishes the world of abstractions with definite objects and events. The horizon is sketched out more closely and clearly, and the spaces of the sensuous are filled, more or less, with things. But even when these furnishings (subject matter) are the same, the interpretation (content) of every painting is always different. This point is clarified any time paintings of basically the same subject matter are compared, as, for example, the Madonna holding her Child, a subject matter that fascinated Florentine painters from the twelfth through the sixteenth centuries.

INTERPRETATION OF THE MADONNA AND CHILD

Compare two great Florentine works that helped lead the way into the Italian Renaissance: a *Madonna and Child* (Figure 4-3) by Cimabue, completed around 1290, and a *Madonna Enthroned* (Figure 4-4) by Giotto, completed around 1310.

PERCEPTION KEY

MADONNA AND CHILD ENTHRONED WITH ANGELS AND *MADONNA ENTHRONED*

These paintings have basically the same subject matter, as their titles indicate. Yet their forms inform about their subject matter very differently. Describe the differences between the forms of these two pictures. Be as specific and detailed as possible. Then elaborate your understanding of the differences between the contents—the meanings—of these two works. Then compare our attempt at the same analysis. Do not, of course, take our analysis as definitive. There simply is no such thing as a criticism that cannot be improved.

The figures in Cimabue's panel at first sight seem utterly lacking in human liveliness. The fine hands of the Madonna, for example, are extremely stylized. Moreover, the geometricized facial features of the Madonna, very similar to those of the angels, and the stiff, unnaturally regular features of the Child seem almost as unnatural as masks. But Cimabue's *Madonna and Child* begins to grow and glow in liveliness when Cimabue's panel is juxtaposed with contemporary paintings, such as Coppo di Marcovaldo's *Madonna and Child* (Figure 4-5), circa 1275, and only in the context of its tradition can a work of art be fully understood and in turn fully appreciated. Thus historical criticism—which attempts to illuminate the tradition of works of art—provides the often indispensable background information for descriptive, interpretive, and evaluative criticism.

Coppo di Marcovaldo Everything in this slightly earlier work by Coppo is subordinated to the portrayal of theoretical, practical, and sociological expressions of the medieval Catholic conception of the sacred. For example, the Child is portrayed as divine, as the mediator between us and God, and as a king or prince. Conventional Christian symbols, such as halos, crowns, and the blessing gesture of the Child, dominate everything. Moreover, the sacred comes very close to being represented as totally separate from the secular, for the Madonna and Child are barely incarnated in this world. Coppo's panel is typical of the way the artists of the thirteenth and the immediately preceding centuries came as close as possible to representing the sacred absolutely. The Madonna and Child, compactly and symmetrically enclosed by the angels, are interpreted more as emblems than as living em-

FIGURE 4-3
Cimabue, *Madonna and Child Enthroned with Angels*. Circa 1285–1290. Panel painting, 151¾ × 78⅞ inches. Uffizi, Florence. (Scala/Art Resource, NY)

FIGURE 4-4
Giotto, *Madonna Enthroned.* Circa 1310. Panel painting, 128 3/16 × 80 3/8 inches. Uffizi, Florence. (Alinari/Art Resource, NY)

FIGURE 4-5
Coppo di Marcovaldo, *Madonna and Child.* Circa 1275. 93 3/4 × 53 1/8 inches. Church of San Martino ai Servi, Orvieto. (Scala/Art Resource, NY)

bodiments of the divine. "Love not the world, neither the things that are in the world. . . . For all that is in the world . . . passeth away"(John 2:15–17). And so the human qualities of the Madonna and Child are barely recognizable. Note, for example, how the fish-shaped, longtailed eyes of the Madonna cannot blink, and how the popping pupils stare out in a Sphinx-like glance that seems fixed forever. Her features are written large and seem added to rather than molded with the head. Only in the tender way she holds the Child is there any hint of human affection. The spirits of this Madonna and Child belong to a supernatural world; and their bodies are hardly bodies at all but, in the words of St. Thomas Aquinas, "corporeal metaphors of spiritual things." The secular is mainly appearance, a secondary reality. The sacred is the primary reality.

Nevertheless, the secular, even if it is interpreted as appearance, appears very powerfully indeed, for this panel is a very fine work of art. The sensa shine forth, especially in the glimmering gold and the rhythmic, sharply edged lines. We are lured by the sensa and their designs beyond mere illustrations of doctrine by images. We are caught in durations of the "here-now." But, unlike our experience of abstractions, these durations include, because of the conventional symbols, doctrinal interpretations of the sacred. And if we participate, we "understand"—even if we disagree—rather than having mere "knowledge of" these doctrines. The expressions of ultimate concern, reverence, and peace in Madonna, Child, and angels provide a context in which the intent of the Christian conventional symbols is unlikely to be mistaken by sensitive participators, even if they do not know the conventions of the symbols.

Cimabue When we compare Cimabue's panel with Coppo's, we can readily see that something of the rigid separation between the sacred and the secular has been relaxed. Cimabue was one of the first to portray, however haltingly, the change in Florentine society toward a more secular orientation. In the twelfth and thirteenth centuries Florence was making great strides in bending nature to human needs for the first time since the Roman Empire. A resurgence in confidence in human powers began to clash with the medieval view that people were nothing without God, that nature was valuable only as a stepping-stone to heaven, that—as St. Peter Damiani in the first half of the eleventh century asserted—"the world is so filthy with vices that any holy mind is befouled by even thinking of it." The emerging view was not yet "man is the measure of all things," but the honor of being human began to be taken seriously, an idea that "was to traverse all later Italian art like the muffled, persistent sound of a subterranean river" (Malraux).

Cimabue had assimilated from the Byzantine tradition its conventions, hierography, technical perfection, and richness of detail. He enriched that inheritance, and in turn helped break ground for the Renaissance, by endowing the old style with more liveliness and mixing the divine into the human, as in this panel, which reveals human emotions in the Madonna. The inert passivity of the Byzantine and the hard dogmatic grimness of the Tuscan style, both so evident in Coppo's work, are revitalized with a spiritual subtlety and psychic awareness, a warmth and tenderness, that make unforgettable the Madonna's benevolently inclined face, to which one returns with unwearying delight. With this face begins the scaling down of the divine into this world. The anthropocentric view—human beings at the center of things—is beginning to focus. A human face has awakened! And it leans forward to come more closely into spiritual contact with us. Its liveliness fell like a refreshing shower on a parched and long-neglected soil, and from that soil a new world began to rise.

Brown-gold tones play softly across the Madonna's features, merging them organically despite the incisive lines, setting the background for the sweeping eyebrows and large, deep eye sockets that form a stage on which the pathetic eyes play their drama of tragic foreknowledge. These eyes seem to pulsate with the beat of the soul because they are more flexible than the eyes in contemporary paintings—the irises rest comfortably and dreamily within their whites; the delicately curved lids, now shortened, detach themselves gracefully to meet neatly at the inner pockets; and the doubling line of the lower lid is replaced by fragile shadows that flow into the cheeks and nose. Furthermore, although the Greek, or bridgeless, nose is still high and marked by a conspicuous triangle, the sensitive modeling of the nose, its dainty shape, and the tucking in of the pinched tip help blend it into the general perspective of the face. Light shadows fall under the shapely chin to the slender neck and around the cheeks to merge indistinctly with the surrounding veil, whose heavy shadows add to the contemplative atmosphere. But the full lips, depressed at the corners and tightly drawn to the left, add a contrasting touch of intensity, even grimness, to what otherwise would be pure poignancy.

The immense, exquisitely decorated throne, with the bristling and curiously vehement prophets below, enhances by its contrasting monumentality the feminine gentleness of the Madonna. Her large size relative to the angels and prophets is minimized by her robe, which, with its close-meshed lines of gold feathering over the cascading folds, is one of the loveliest in Western art. In a skillfully worked counterpoint, the angel heads and the rainbow-colored wings form and angular rhythm that tenses toward and then quietly pauses at the Madonna's face. This pause is sustained by the simple dotted edge of the centered halo and by the shape of the pedimental top of the rectangular frame. The facial features of the angels resemble the Madonna's, especially the almond-shaped eyes, separated by the stencillike triangles, and the heavy mouths squared at the corners. Nevertheless, they lack the refined qualities and liveliness that betray so feelingly the soulful sadness of the Madonna. Now in the city of Florence

. . . Mercy has a human heart,
Pity a human face,
And Love, the human form divine,
And Peace, the human dress.

William Blake

But into this peaceful hush that spreads around her sound with anguished apprehension the tragic tones of the Pietà, like the melody of a requiem continued by our imaginations into the pregnant pause.

In Cimabue's panel, unlike Coppo's, there is no longer the sure suggestion of the sacred as almost completely separate from the secular. The sacred and the secular are only narrowly joined, but the juncture seems much more secure. The sacred is portrayed as clearly immanent in at least some things of our world—the Madonna, Child, and saints having some earthly aspects—but the emphasis, of course, is upon the transcendency of the sacred. There is not the slightest hint of the secular taking precedence over the sacred.

Giotto According to the legend reported by Ghiberti and embellished by Vasari, Cimabue

> going one day on some business of his own from Florence to Vespignano, found Giotto, while his sheep were browsing, portraying a sheep from nature on a flat and polished slab, with a stone slightly pointed, without having learnt any method of doing this from others, but only from nature; whence Cimabue, standing fast all in a marvel, asked him if he wished to go live with him. The child answered that, his father consenting, he would go willingly. Cimabue then asking this from Bondone, the latter lovingly granted it to him, and was content that he should take the boy with him to Florence; whither having come, in a short time, assisted by nature and taught by Cimabue, the child not only equalled the manner of his master, but became so good an imitator of nature that he banished completely that rude Greek manner and revived the modern and good art of painting, introducing the portraying well from nature of living people.[3]

Giotto's *Madonna Enthroned* and Cimabue's *Madonna and Child,* both originally placed in churches, now hang side by side in the first room of the Uffizi Gallery in Florence. The contrast between the panels is striking. Cimabue's Madonna, who seems to float into our world, is abruptly brought to earth by Giotto; or, as Ruskin puts it, now we have Mama. She sits solidly, bell-shaped, without evasion, in three-dimensional space subject to gravitational forces, her frank, focused gaze alerted to her surroundings, whereas Cimabue's Madonna is steeped in moodiness. The forms of Giotto's Madonna seem to have been abstracted, however radically, from nature, whereas Cimabue seems to have started from Byzantine forms. In subject matter Giotto seems to have begun more from "here," whereas Cimabue seems to have begun more from "hereafter."

The eyes of Giotto's Madonna, surrounded by her high forehead and the immense cheeks, have a fascinating asymmetry that gives her face a mark of idiosyncrasy and adds to its liveliness. The fish-shaped left eye with its half-covered pupil twists to the left, so that it appears to be looking in a different direction than the more realistic right eye. The resulting tension fixes our attention and heightens our feelings of being caught in her level gaze, which gains further intensity by being the focus of the gazes of the saints and angels. Since the open space below the Madonna provides us with a figurative path of access, we are directly engaged with her in a way

[3]Giorgio Vasari, *Lives of the Most Eminent Painters,* Gaston Duc Devere (trans.), Macmillan, London, 1912, vol.1, p. 72.

that Cimabue carefully avoids by, among other devices, putting the throne of his Madonna on a high-arched platform and then placing the little prophets within the arches.

The smallness of the sensual mouth of Giotto's Madonna, barely wider than the breadth of her long and snouty nose, accentuates its expressiveness. Also, for the first time, the lips of a Madonna open—however slightly, shyly revealing two teeth—as if she were about to gasp or speak. It does not matter, for the mobility of inner responsiveness is conveyed. Everything else expresses her stoicism, a rocklike kind of endurance—the untooled, centered halo, the steady gaze, the calm, impersonal expression, the cool and silvery skin color with green underpainting that suggests bone structures beneath, the heavy jaw and towerlike neck, the long unbroken verticals and broad sweeping curves of the simply colored robe and tunic, the firm hand that no longer points but holds, and above all her upright monumental massiveness, as solid as if hewn in granite. The saints and angels, compactly arranged in depth, stand on the same ground as the earthly throne. Although the saints express peace and the angels awe, they are natural beings, not imaginary supporters of a heavenly throne as in Cimabue's picture.

The Child shares with his mother the monumentality of Giotto's style—the square, forthright head, the powerful body, the physical density and solidity that make Giotto's figures so statuesque. Giotto's Child, compared with Cimabue's, seems almost coarse, especially in the shaping of the hands and feet, and the somewhat insecure placement of his body from a naturalistic standpoint is physically much more uncomfortable, primarily because such a standpoint is almost irrelevant in Cimabue's picture. The hair and ears are not so stylized as in Cimabue's Child, light and shadow sink more organically into the flesh, the eyes and nose are given the most realistic rendition since Roman times, and the expression is dynamically alert. Yet the lack of irregularity and flexibility in these less conventional features, combined with the effect of maturity in miniature, keep the Child from being a Baby. The content of Giotto's painting is clearly Christian, but not quite so obviously as in the paintings of Coppo and Cimabue. The portrayal of religious feeling is not quite so strong, and for the first time in Florence there is the suggestion, however muted, of the secular challenging the sacred. If Mama gets much more earthly and independent, the sacred no longer will be so obviously in control.

Parmigianino Compare now Giotto's painting with *The Madonna with the Long Neck* (Figure 4-6), painted by Francesco Parmigianino in the waning years of the Italian Renaissance, circa 1535 (see Perception Key, p. 86).

Although natural structures in Parmigianino's painting are suggested, they are not interpreted as natural. The light is neither quite indoors nor outdoors, the perspectives are odd, gravity is defied, the bodies are artificially proportioned and drained of mass and physical power, the protagonists are psychologically detached from one another, and above all the porcelain facial features allow no hint of liveliness. The head of the Madonna is shaped like a well-wrought urn, while the ears, set out abnormally in order to emphasize their serpentine calligraphy, look like its han-

Perception Key

GIOTTO'S *MADONNA ENTHRONED* AND PARMIGIANINO'S *THE MADONNA WITH THE LONG NECK*

1. *The Madonna with the Long Neck* was never quite finished, and so far as we know, Parmigianino did not provide a title. Later in the sixteenth century, Vasari baptized it *The Virgin and Sleeping Child.* Do you believe Parmigianino would have accepted this naming as appropriate? What about the appropriateness of its present title—*The Madonna with the Long Neck*?
2. How does the content of this picture differ from Giotto's?
3. How does Parmigianino's form accomplish a different interpretation of what apparently is the same subject matter?
4. Jacob Burckhardt, a knowledgeable nineteenth-century critic and historian, complained of Parmigianino's work's "unsupportable affectation," and, somewhat more tolerantly, of "the bringing of the manners of the great world divertingly into the holy scenes." Generally, until recent times, this work has been an object of derision. Judging from the Cimabue, Giotto, and Coppo di Marcovaldo, why would this be so?

dles. The nerveless skin is unnaturally cold and pale, glazed like ceramic, and beneath that polished surface the urn seems hollow. Hence the pure geometrical design of the fastidious lines of the eyebrows, eyes, nose, and mouth is assembled on a surface without organic foundation—no pulsating blood coursing through arteries and veins integrates these features, and no muscular structure can move them. And so the gaze down upon the Child—the most lifeless Child of the Renaissance—is too stylized and superficial to be expressive of any psychic, let alone sacramental, meaning. Like an Attic amphora, the head of the Madonna rises from its swanlike neck, while the hair decorates the lid with the preciosity of fine goldwork.

If the subject matter of *The Madonna with the Long Neck* is a sacred scene, Burckhardt's denunciation of "unsupportable affectation" is certainly justified. If, however, the Christian symbols are no more than a support or an excuse for an interpretation of line, color, texture, shape, and volume, Burckhardt's denunciation is irrelevant. To meet this painting halfway—and surely this is the responsibility of every serious perceiver—the religious symbols can be dismissed, and then the subject matter can be experienced as secular. The design of this delicate work, this splendor of form shining on the proportionate parts of matter, ought to bring one to a better understanding and appreciation of the rhythmic qualities of line; the cooling, calming powers of smooth surfaces and colors; the sinuous sensuousness of spiraling shapes; and the fluidity of bulkless volumes. But this heretical design, despite its lifting flow, will never waft you to a Christian heaven on the wings of faith.

The Madonna with the Long Neck is such a magnificently secular work of art that the excommunication of the Christian symbols is rather easily accomplished, at least in our day. That is why the present title probably seems more appropriate to most of us than Vasari's title. Abstract painting has opened our eyes to the intrinsic values of sensa, and a strong case can

FIGURE 4-6
Parmigianino, *The Madonna with the Long Neck*. Circa 1535. Panel painting, 36⅜ × 53¾ inches. Uffizi, Florence. (Erich Lessing/Art Resource, NY)

be made that *The Madonna with the Long Neck* is a kind of abstract painting. An appropriate title today might be *Sinuous Spiraling Shapes.*

DETERMINING THE SUBJECT MATTER OF A PAINTING

Consider a contemporary example by Helen Frankenthaler (Figure 4-7).

The third question of the Perception Key is tricky. We suggest the fol-

PERCEPTION KEY
FRANKENTHALER'S *FLOOD*

1. Is this painting abstract or representational? Take plenty of time before you decide, but disregard the title.
2. The title is *Flood.* Do you see a flood when you ignore the title? Do you see a flood when you take the title into consideration?
3. If you do, in fact, see a flood when taking notice of the title, does this make the painting representational? Consider the colors of the painting. How do they complement each other?
4. If you do not see a flood, what do you see?

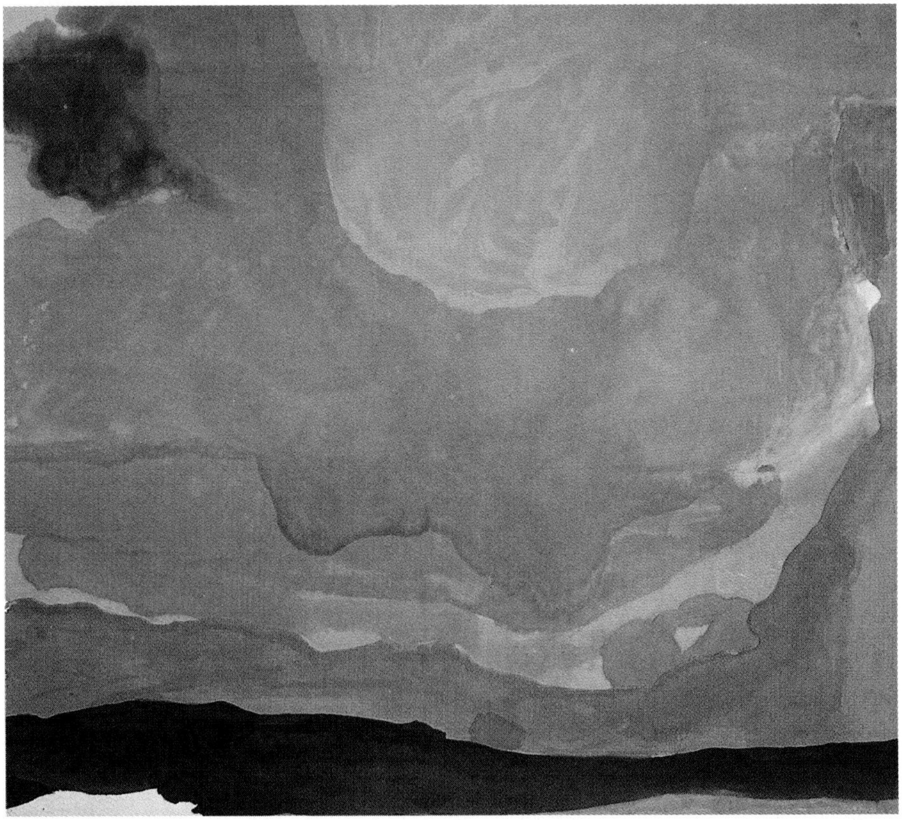

FIGURE 4-7
Helen Frankenthaler, *Flood*. 1967. Synthetic polymer on canvas, 124 × 140 inches. Collection of Whitney Museum of American Art. Purchase, with funds from the friends of Whitney Museum of American Art. (Photograph © 1997 Whitney Museum of American Art)

lowing principle as a basis for answering such questions. If a work "only shows" (presents) but does not interpret (reveal) the objects and events that the title indicates, this is not enough to make it representational. These objects and events must be interpreted if the work is to be usefully classified as representational. Our view is that a flood in Frankenthaler's painting is interpreted, that our perception of the spreading, merging earthy stains, soft as water, intensifies our awareness of flooding, especially the rhythms of backwater eddies. If this judgment is correct, the work is representational. On the other hand, your view may be that recognition of flooding in the painting only helps intensify your perception of sensa—the swirling rhythm of colors. If this judgment is correct, the work is abstract. Study Jean Arp's *Mountain, Table, Anchors, Navel* (Figure 4-8).

PERCEPTION KEY

ARP'S *MOUNTAIN, TABLE, ANCHORS, NAVEL*

1. What is the subject matter of this work?
2. What effect does the title have on what you "see" in the painting?
3. Does Arp succeed in revealing a mountain, a table, anchors, and a navel so that you have a heightened awareness of similar objects?

If your answer to question 2 in the Perception Key is "none," you should deny that the objects listed in the title are the subject matter of this paint-

FIGURE 4-8
Jean Arp, *Mountain, Table, Anchors, Navel*. 1925. Oil on cardboard with cutouts, 29⅝ × 23½ inches. The Museum of Modern Art, New York. Purchase. (Photograph © 1997 The Museum of Modern Art, New York; art © 1997 Artists Rights Society [ARS], NY/VG Bild-Kunst, Bonn)

ing. It is true, of course, that the references of the title are supported by the painting, for we can see a mountain, etc., in the painting once we have noted the title. But these references are misleading, if taken as anything more than identification tags, because the recognition of the objects designated is of little importance in our perception. *Colors and Shapes*—for they seem to us to be the subject matter of Arp's painting—would perhaps be a more appropriate title.

Sometimes, as we have seen with Frankenthaler's *Flood,* it is extremely difficult to distinguish between abstract and representational painting. Whether the recognition of definite objects and events in a painting intensifies perception may differ with the differences in temperament and background of the recipients. Nevertheless, the distinction between abstract and representational painting is very useful because it points up this important fact: whereas in abstract painting definite objects and events are not a part of the content, in representational paintings they are. Even when the distinction is difficult to make, as with *Flood,* focusing on the issue of abstraction and representation can help us clarify what is most important in any particular painting.

INTERPRETATION OF THE SELF: FRIDA KAHLO, ROMAINE BROOKS, AND REMBRANDT VAN RIJN

The self-portrait is a specialized subgenre of painting, but it is one which often fascinates great painters. Rembrandt, for example, painted himself again and again throughout his life, leaving us a record of changing fortunes, changing personality, and changing appearances. The modern Mexican artist Frida Kahlo did much the same, giving us numerous images of herself in often enigmatic poses and enigmatic states of mind. Romaine Brooks, on the other hand, did relatively few self-portraits, but the one reproduced here has a strength and straightforwardness that is especially captivating.

PERCEPTION KEY
THREE SELF-PORTRAITS

1. Which of these paintings is more dominated by detail? How does color contribute to that domination?
2. If the subject matter of each painting is similar, in what lies the difference?
3. What is revealed by each of these paintings?
4. In which of these paintings does light work most mysteriously?
5. Are all of these paintings equally representational?

The self-portrait, by its nature, usually benefits from some background information. For example, Frida Kahlo was a painter and the wife of one of Mexico's most famous muralists, Diego Rivera, who was twenty years her senior. She had suffered polio as a child and as a teenager was in a ter-

FIGURE 4-9
Frida Kahlo, *Self-Portrait with Thorn Necklace and Hummingbird*. 1940. Oil on masonite, 24½ × 18¾ inches. Harry Ransom Humanities Research Art Collection, The University of Texas at Austin. (By permission of Instituto Nacional de Bellas Artes, Mexico)

rible bus and streetcar crash that left her with three fractured vertebrae, a crushed pelvis, and broken ribs. She was actually impaled through the pelvis by a rail from the streetcar. The result was a life filled with pain. She had to wear orthopedic shoes and a restraining corset that gave her almost no relief throughout her life. Moreover, her marriage to Diego Rivera involved innumerable infidelities and many stormy scenes. Yet it remained in place throughout her life. She was involved with the Communist party in Mexico in the 1940s and spent much of her time in protest against exploitation and war. Her *Self-Portrait with Thorn Necklace and Hummingbird* (Figure 4-9) naturally connects her to the suffering of Christ, symbolized by the hummingbird. The monkey and cat were family pets and the leaves behind her are derived from Mexican folk art. Her gaze is not direct to the viewer; instead, it is distracted—possibly by psychic pain or remembrance—as if to reveal her vulnerability. The straight-on face, hair worn aloft, as she usually wore it, is unrelenting, unembarrassed, unyielding. Her eyebrows, growing together as they do, and her slight moustache were signature details in almost all her portraits—marks of natural strength.

The poet Clayton Eshleman reflected on Frida Kahlo and contemplates her as a Tehuana, a woman of Tehuanapec, a region whose costume she often wore, sometimes describing herself as a Tehuana:

TEHUANA FRIDA BY VICTORIAN HORRAH

Two bodies linked veinriverwise to the desire to be double
enough to live—and Frida does truly live, with her insect smile
and her locked woolyworm eyebrows.
Her greeting card balloons would spiral off happy birthdays
but stayed on to float folksong melodies over Frida and Diego
in the rimless forever of a fixated bird skull I see held by Frida's
fragile pelvis which needed to be cupped! yes, as Christ cupped
the Grail and drank from it, all of his head except his lips
covered by eyes.
Frail, frail Frida, borne in like scarlet bougainvillea strewn
across a casket.
The darts in your spine reangled the cantina word-drapery.
Your insolent courage forced Surrealism to frame your
honest face.

Romaine Brooks had a very difficult life as well. She had wealthy parents, but they essentially abandoned her at age six, when she was sent off to school. She was American, born in Rome, with an older, paranoid and dangerous brother. She was taken in by her grandfather. Her mother and brother died when she was twenty-eight, leaving her independently wealthy. She married apparently for society's sake, but lived openly as a lesbian in London and Paris. She specialized in portraits, usually of friends. She seems to have willfully restricted her range of colors, which emphasize gray and black, and often luminescent whites, because she was influenced by the American painter James McNeill Whistler, whose compositions were often titled *Arrangement in Gray and Black*. Her self-portrait emphasizes uprightness, aloneness, and, in the essentially masculine dress, independence (Figure 4-10). The architectural details in the background imply an urban lifestyle, while the direct, unashamed look encompasses the viewer in a frank, perhaps challenging fashion.

Rembrandt's self-portrait was painted when he was fifty-three. He had just ten more years to live. He made approximately 100 self-portraits

FIGURE 4-10
Romaine Brooks, *Self Portrait*. 1923. Oil on canvas, 46¼ × 26⅞ inches. National Museum of American Art, Smithsonian Institution, Washington, D.C. Gift of the artist. (Art Resource, NY)

FIGURE 4-11
Rembrandt van Rijn, *Self Portrait*. 1659. Oil on canvas, 33¼ × 26 inches. Andrew W. Mellon Collection. National Gallery of Art, Washington, D.C.

throughout his life, and this one is among the most poignant (Figure 4-11). Rembrandt had been extraordinarily successful as a painter. His impressive commissions made him a wealthy man, but a number of years before this portrait, Rembrandt was financially ruined and had to work all the harder just to survive. The range of color in this painting is limited to earth tones, subdued, controlled, limited. His gaze is steady, but not directly at the viewer—he paints himself as if he were staring into a mirror. His expression is not especially secure, not especially definite. You may decide for yourself what his expression implies, but one can see how different it is from the expressions on the faces of Frida Kahlo and Romaine Brooks. Rembrandt is inward looking, reflective, in deep meditation. The organization of the painting differs from Kahlo and Brooks in that it is dark and mysterious and in some ways deeply religious.

RECENT PAINTING

Painting, whether abstract or representational, sets forth the visually perceptible in such a way that it works in our experience with heightened intensity. Every style of painting finds facets of the visually perceptible that had previously been missed. For example, the painting of the last hundred years has given us, among many other styles, Impressionism, a style that reveals the play of sunlight on color, as in the work of Renoir (Figure 2-14); Post-Impressionism, using the surface techniques of Impressionism but drawing out the solidity of things, as in Cézanne (Figure 2-5); Expressionism, scenes portraying strong emotion, as in Blume (Figure 1-3); Cubism, showing the three-dimensional qualities of things as splayed out in a tightly closed two-dimensional space—without significant perspective or cast shadow—through geometrical crystallization, a technique partially exhibited in Picasso's *Guernica* (Figure 1-4); Dada, poking fun at the absurdity of everything including sculpture, as in Duchamp's *Bottle Rack* (Figure 5-27); Surrealism, the expression of the subconscious, as perhaps in Siquieros' *Echo of a Scream* (Figure 1-2); Suprematism or Constructivism, the portrayal of sensa in sharp geometrical patterns, as in Mondrian (Figure 1-5); Abstract Expressionism, the portrayal of sensa in movement with—as in Expressionism—the expression of powerful emotion or energy, as in Pollock (Figure 3-4); Pop Art, the revelation of mass-produced products, as in Dine and Lichtenstein (Figures 2-1 and 2-8); etc. And today and tomorrow new dimensions are and will be portrayed. Never in the history of painting has there been such rapid change and vitality. Never in history has there been so much help available for those of us who, in varying degrees, are blind to the fullness of the visually perceptible. If we take advantage of this help, the rewards are priceless.

SUMMARY

Painting is the art that has most to do with revealing the visual sensa and the visual appearance of objects and events. Painting shows the visually perceptible more clearly. Because a painting is usually presented to us as an entirety, with an all-at-onceness, it gives us time for our vision to focus, hold, and participate. This makes possible a vision that is both extraordinarily intense and restful. Sensa are the qualities of objects or events that stimulate our sense organs. Sensa can be disassociated or abstracted from the specific objects or events in which they are usually joined. Sensa are the primary subject matter of abstract painting. Specific objects and events are the primary subject matter of representational painting.

CHAPTER 4 BIBLIOGRAPHY

Alpers, Svetlana. *The Art of Describing.* Chicago: The University of Chicago Press, 1983.

Armstrong, Richard. *Mind Over Matter: Concept and Object.* New York: Whitney Museum of Art, 1990.

Arnheim, Rudolf. *Art and Visual Perception,* new rev. ed. Berkeley: University of California Press, 1974.

Bell, Clive. *Art.* New York: Putnam, 1981.

Canaday, John. *Keys to Art.* New York: Tudor, 1964.

———. *Mainstreams of Modern Art.* New York: Holt, Rinehart and Winston, 1959.

Elsen, Albert E. *Purposes of Art,* 4th ed. New York: Holt, Rinehart and Winston, 1981.

Fine, Elsa Honig. *Women and Art.* Montclair, N.J.: Allanheld & Schram/Prior, 1978.

Fry, Roger. *Vision and Design.* New York: New American Library, 1974.

———. *Transformations.* London: Chatto and Windus, 1970.

Gardner, Helen, et al. *Art Through the Ages,* 10th ed. New York: Harcourt Brace, 1995.

Gombrich, E. H. *The Story of Art,* 16th ed. London: Phaidon, 1995.

———. *Art and Illusion,* 5th ed. London: Phaidon, 1977.

Hauser, Arnold. *The Social History of Art.* 4 vols. New York: Vintage Books, 1964.

Hughes, Robert. *The Shock of the New.* London: BBC Books, 1991.

Janson, H. W. *History of Art,* 5th ed., revised and expanded by Anthony F. Janson. London: Thames & Hudson, 1995.

Panofsky, Erwin. *Meaning in the Visual Arts.* Princeton: Princeton University Press, 1995.

Rosenberg, Harold. *The Anxious Object.* Chicago: University of Chicago Press, Phoenix, 1982.

Steinberg, Leo. *Other Criteria: Confrontations with Twentieth-Century Art.* New York: Oxford University Press, 1972.

Wölfflin, Heinrich. *Principles of Art History.* W. D. Hottinger (trans.). New York: Dover, 1979.

CHAPTER 4 WEBSITES

Andy Warhol Museum (museum tours and event schedules)

World Wide Web: **http://www.usaor.net/warhol/** or **http://www.warhol.org/warhol/tour/tour.html**

Art Noveau (movement overview; individual artists, including Antonio Gaudí)

World Wide Web: **http://www.enst.fr/~derville/AN/AN.html**

Asian Art Gallery (exhibits and information on the Far East)

World Wide Web: **http://www.webart.com/asian art/index.html**

New York Artline

Gopher: Name: **Panix.** Address: **Gopher.panix.com** Select: **New York Art Line**

Sistine Chapel (artwork and historical information)

World Wide Web: **http://www.christusrex.org/www1/sistine/O-Tour.html**

Vermeer Paintings (art samples and biography)

World Wide Web: **http://www.ccsf.caltech.edu/~roy/vermeer/**

Web Museum for the Louvre

World Wide Web: **http://mistral.enst.fr/~pioch/louvre/louvre.html**

Women Artists Archive

Anonymous FTP: Address: **ftp.cascade.net** Path: **/pub/Womens_Studies/Art**

CHAPTER 5

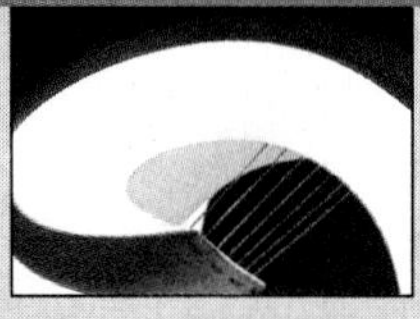

SCULPTURE

SCULPTURE AND TOUCH

Sculpture, along with painting and architecture, is usually, but not very usefully, classified as one of the visual arts. Such classification suggests that the eye is the chief sense organ involved in our participation with sculpture. Yet observe participants at an exhibition of both paintings and sculptures. Usually at least a few will touch some of the sculptures despite the "do not touch" signs. Some kinds of sculpture invite us to explore and caress them with our hands, and even, if they are not too large or heavy, to pick them up. Marcel Duchamp noticed this and experimented with a kind of sculpture not to be seen but only to be touched. Within a box with an opening at the top large enough to allow passage of the hand, he placed

PERCEPTION KEY
EXPERIMENT WITH TOUCH

Using scissors or some similar tool, cut out four approximately six-inch cardboard squares. Shape them with curves or angles into abstract patterns (structures that do not represent definite objects), and put one into a bag. Ask a friend to feel that sample in the bag without looking at the sample. Then ask your friend to (1) draw with pencil on paper the pattern felt, and then to (2) model the pattern in putty. Continue the same procedure with the other three samples. Have your friend make four samples for you, and follow the same procedures yourself. Analyze both your results. Were the drawings or the modelings more closely imitative of the samples?

forms with varying shapes and textures. Several well-known sculptors have created works for blind patrons.

SCULPTURE AND DENSITY

Sculpture engages our senses differently than painting does. This is because sculpture occupies space as a three-dimensional mass, whereas painting is essentially a two-dimensional surface that can only represent ("re-present") three-dimensionality. Of course, painting can suggest density—for example, *Mont Sainte Victoire* (see Figure 2-5)—but sculpture *is* dense. Henry Moore, one of the most influential modern sculptors, states that the sculptor "gets the solid shape, as it were, inside his head—he thinks of it, whatever its size, as if he were holding it completely enclosed in the hollow of his hand. He mentally visualizes a complex form *from all round itself;* he knows while he looks at one side what the other side is like; he identifies himself with its center of gravity, its mass, its weight; he realizes its volume, as the space that the shape displaces in the air."[1] Apparently we can only fully apprehend sculpture by senses that are alive not only to visual and tactile (touchable) surfaces but also to the weight and volume lying behind those surfaces.

SENSORY INTERCONNECTIONS

It is surely an oversimplification to distinguish the various arts on the basis of any one sensation or the sense organ; for example, to claim that painting is experienced solely by sight and sculpture solely by touch. Our nervous systems are far more complicated than that. Generally no clear separation is made in experience between the faculties of sight and touch. The sensa of touch, for instance, are normally joined with other sensa—visual, aural, oral, and olfactory. Even if only one kind of sensum initiates a perception, a chain reaction triggers off other sensations, either by sensory motor connections or by memory associations. We are constantly grasping and handling things as well as seeing, hearing, tasting, and smelling them. And so when we see a thing, we have a pretty good idea of what its surface would feel like, how it would sound if struck, how it would taste, and how it would smell if we approach. And if we grasp or handle a thing in the dark, we have some idea of what its shape looks like.

As we approach a stone wall, we see various shapes. And these shapes recall certain information. We know something about how well the surface of these stones would feel and that it would hurt if we walked into them. We do not know about the surface, volume, and mass of those stones by sight alone but by sight associated with manual experience. Both painting and sculpture involve especially sight and touch. But touch is much more involved in our participation with sculpture. If we can clarify such differ-

[1]Henry Moore, "Notes on Sculpture," in David Sylvester (ed.), *Sculpture and Drawings* 1921–1948, 4th rev. ed., George Wittenborn, Inc., New York, 1957, pp. xxxiii ff.

ences as these, our understanding of sculpture will be deeper and, in turn, our participation more rewarding.

SCULPTURE AND PAINTING COMPARED

Compare Rothko's *Earth Greens* (Figure 4-1) with Arp's *Growth* (Figure 5-1).

Both works are abstract, we suggest, for neither has as its primary subject matter specific objects or events (see Chapter 4). Arp's sculpture has something to do with growth, of course, as confirmed by the title. But is it human, animal, or vegetable growth? Male or female? Clear-cut answers do not seem possible. Specificity of reference, just as in the Rothko, is missing. And yet, if you agree that the subject matter of the Rothko is the sensuous, would you say the same for the Arp? To affirm this may bother you, for Arp's marble is dense material. This substantiality of the marble is very much a part of its appearing as sculpture. Conversely, *Earth Greens* as a painting—that is, as a work of art rather than as a physical canvas of such and such a weight—does not appear as a material thing. The weight of the canvas is irrelevant to our participation with *Earth Greens* as a work of art. Indeed, if that weight becomes relevant, we are no longer participating with the painting. That weight becomes relevant if we are hanging *Earth Greens* on a wall, of course, but that is a procedure antecedent to our participation with it as a painting.

Rothko has abstracted sensa, especially colors, from objects or things, whereas Arp has brought out the substantiality of a thing—the marbleness of the marble. Earth and grass and sky are not "in" Rothko's painting. Conversely, Arp has made the marble relevant to his sculpture. This kind of difference, incidentally, is perhaps the underlying reason the term "abstract painting" is used more frequently than the term "abstract sculpture." There is an awkwardness about describing something as material as most sculpture as abstract. Picasso once remarked: "There is no abstract art. You must always start with something. There is no danger then anyway because the idea of the object will have left an indelible mark." This may be an over-

PERCEPTION KEY
EARTH GREENS AND *GROWTH*

1. Would you like to touch either of these works?
2. Would you expect either the Rothko or the Arp to feel hot or cold to your touch?
3. Which work seems to require the more careful placement of lighting? Why?
4. Is space perceived differently in and around these two works? How?
5. Which of the two works appears to be the more unchangeable in your perception?
6. Which of the two works is more abstract?

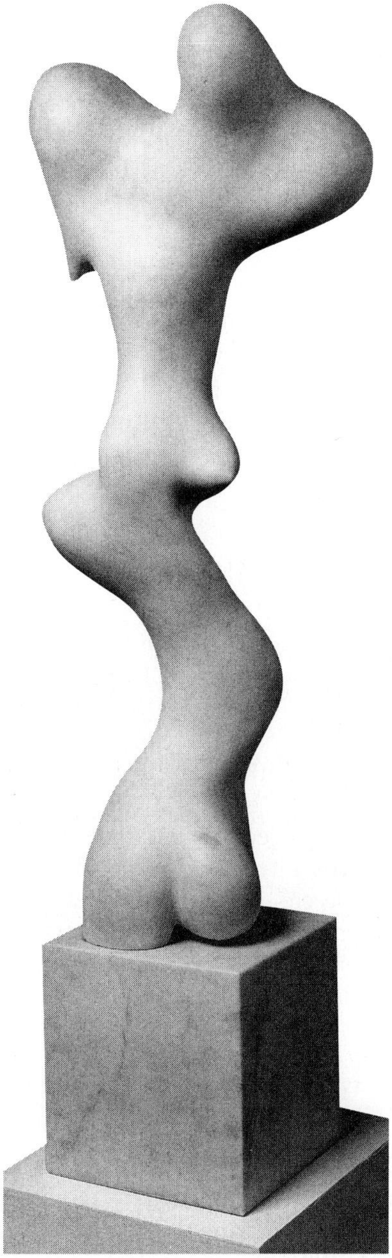

FIGURE 5-1
Jean Arp, *Growth*. 1938. Marble, 39½ inches high. (Art © 1997 Artists Rights Society [ARS], NY/VG Bild-Kunst, Bonn)

statement with respect to painting, but this point rings true with sculpture. Still, the distinction between abstract and representational sculpture is worth making, just as with painting, for being clear about the subject matter of a work of art is essential to all sensitive participation. It is the key to understanding the content, for the content is the subject matter interpreted by means of the form.

Most sculpture, whether abstract or representational, returns us to the voluminosity (bulk), density (mass), and tactile quality of things. Thus sculpture has touch or tactile appeal. Even if we do not actually "handle" a work of sculpture, we can imagine how it would feel with reference to its surface, volume, and weight. Sculpture brings us back into touch with things by allowing the thickness of things to permeate its surface. Most sculptures make us feel them as resistant, as substantial. Hence the primary subject matter of most abstract sculpture is the density of sensa. Sculpture is more than skin deep. Abstract painting can only represent density, whereas sculpture, whether abstract or representational, presents that density. Abstract painters generally emphasize the surfaces of sensa, as in *Earth Greens*. Their interest is in the vast ranges of color qualities and the play of light to bring out the textural nuances. Abstract sculptors, on the other hand, generally restrict themselves to a minimal range of color and textural qualities and emphasize light not only to play on these qualities but also to bring out the inherence of these qualities in things. Whereas abstract painters are shepherds of surface sensa, abstract sculptors are shepherds of depth sensa.

SUNKEN-RELIEF SCULPTURE

Compare, for example, Figure 5-2, a detail of an Egyptian work in limestone from about 2100 B.C., with Pollock's *Autumn Rhythm* (Figure 3-4). We usually think of sculpture, with its emphasis on density, as projecting out into space. Yet sometimes some of the lines and patches of paint in Pollock's paintings are laid on so thickly that they stand out as much as a half inch or so from the flat surface of the canvas. In the Egyptian work there is no projection whatsoever. Rather, the carving cuts grooves of various depths into the surface plane of the stone to outline each object, a technique called "sunken relief." The firmness, clarity, and brilliance of these linear grooves in the Egyptian work is brought out by the way their sharp outside edges catch the light. Did this technique in this instance produce sculpture rather than painting? Only if it brings out in some significant sense the voluminosity or density or surface feel of its materials: only then will the tactile as well as the visual appeal be significant.

This work, when you stand before it much more than when you see it in a photograph, has significant tactile appeal. The density of the limestone is especially evident. In other words, we are suggesting that this work is more than a linear drawing. Pollock's work, on the other hand, lacks significant tactile appeal despite the projection of its heavy thick oils. It is conceivable that this work could have been made in some other medium—aluminum paint or paint with more white lead, for example—and still be essentially the same work. It is inconceivable that the Egyptian relief could have been carved out of different material and still be essentially the same work. The surface as seen is what counts in Pollock's painting—the materials that make that surface possible are basically irrelevant in perceiving the work as painting (although for a restorer of the painting, the materials would be very relevant indeed). In the Egyptian relief, the surface is perceived more tactually than the surface of the Pollock. And yet, the differences between Pollock's painting and this Egyptian work are hardly clear-cut. You may disagree with good reasons.

FIGURE 5-2
King Akhenaten and Queen Nefertiti. Egyptian sunken relief from El-Amarna. XVIII dynasty. (The Metropolitan Museum of Art)

SURFACE-RELIEF SCULPTURE

Study Ghiberti's bronze doors of the Baptistry of Florence (Figure 5-3), completed in 1452, and called by Michelangelo "The Gates of Paradise." How different are the panels of these doors from representational paintings? There are some clearly noticeable projections out into space, but almost every device available to the Florentine painter of the fifteenth century for creating the illusion rather than the actuality of spatial depth—foreshortening, landscape vistas, perspective effects, etc.—is used. When used with sculptural materials, these pictorial methods produce what is called "surface relief." The surface planes of Ghiberti's panels are part of the composition, and there is no clear perceptual distinction between the relief that comes out into space and the surface planes. Behind the surface planes the backgrounds are nonplanar; thus, no limits to the backgrounds are perceptible, suggesting an infinity of space. The perspective of such things as the lines of trees, the retreating undulations of the ground, the receding arches, the overlapping and diminishing sizes of people, the increase in delicacy of modeling as the size of objects decreases, and even a progression from clear to hazy atmosphere all suggest an unlimited background space in which the various biblical actions take place. In other words, there are no background starting points that function as the bases for the planar organizations. Rather, the surface planes of the panels function as the basic organizing planes: hence the expression "surface relief." Does Ghiberti's "surface relief" produce sculpture? We think so (although some critics think otherwise), because the tactile qualities of the bronze significantly stimulate our tactile senses.

LOW-RELIEF SCULPTURE

Relief sculpture projects from a background plane such as a wall or column. Low-relief sculpture projects relatively slightly from its background plane, and so its depth dimension is very limited. Medium- and high-relief sculpture project further from their backgrounds, and so their depth dimensions are expanded. Sculpture in the round is freed from any background plane, and so its depth dimension is unrestricted. *Times Square Sky* (Figure 5-4) is, we think, most usefully classified as sculpture of the low-relief species. The materiality of the steel, the neon tubing, and especially the aluminum is brought out very powerfully by their juxtaposition. Unfortunately, this is difficult to perceive from a photograph. Because of its three-dimensionality, sculpture generally suffers even more than painting from being seen only in a photograph. Chryssa Vardea was born in Greece and when she came to America she was fascinated by the garishness of Times Square. She worked extensively with neon lighting. In *Times Square Sky* Chryssa is especially sensitive to aluminum, the neon light helping to bring out the special sheen of that metal, which flashes forth in smooth and rough textures through subtle shadows.

Yet *Times Square Sky,* as the title suggests, is representational. The subject matter is about a quite specific place, and the content of *Times Square*

FIGURE 5-3
Lorenzo Ghiberti, Doors of the Baptistry of Florence. 1425–1452. (Scala/Art Resource, New York)

Sky—by means of its form—is an interpretation of that specific subject matter. Times Square is closed in almost entirely by manufactured products, such as aluminum and steel, animated especially at night by a chaos of flashing neon signs. Letters and words—often as free of syntax as in the sculpture—clutter that noisy space with an overwhelming senselessness. The feel of that fascinating square is Chryssa's subject matter, just as it is in Mondrian's *Broadway Boogie Woogie* (Figure 5-5). Both works reveal something of the rhythm, bounce, color, and chaos of Time Square, but *Times Square Sky* interprets more of its physical character. Whereas Mondrian abstracts from the physicality of Broadway, Chryssa gives us a heightened sense of the way Broadway feels as our bodies are bombarded by the

FIGURE 5-4
Chryssa, *Times Square Sky*. 1962. Neon, aluminum, steel, 60 × 60 × 9½ inches. Collection, Walker Art Center, Minneapolis. Gift of the T. B. Walker Foundation, 1964.

street and its crowds. Those attacks—tactile, visual, aural, and olfactory—can have a metallic, mechanical, impersonal, and threatening character, and something of those menacing qualities is revealed in *Times Square Sky*. The physicality of that effect is, we suggest, what distinguishes this work as sculpture rather than painting. And yet the line here cannot be too sharply drawn. For if the neon tubing and aluminum were flattened down on the steel somewhat, or if Pollock had laid on his paints an inch or so thicker, would these works then be sculpture or painting?

PERCEPTION KEY

TIMES SQUARE SKY AND *BROADWAY BOOGIE WOOGIE*

1. Note the dates of each work. What does Mondrian's painting reveal about urban life in his time? Does it seem static and regular, or does it seem dynamic and energetic?
2. In what sense is Chryssa's sculpture revelatory of the confusion of life in a large urban environment?
3. Which of these works seems more representative, in that it "re-presents" aspects of an urban landscape? How does that affect its revelatory value?

Relief sculpture—with a few exceptions such as those previously discussed—allows its materials to stand out from a background plane, as in *Times Square Sky.* Thus relief sculpture in at least one way reveals its materials simply by showing us—directly—their surface and something of their depth. By moving to a side of *Times Square Sky,* we can see that the steel, neon tubing, and aluminum are of such and such thickness. However, this three-dimensionality in relief sculpture, this movement out into space, is not allowed to lose its ties to its background plane. Hence relief sculpture, like painting, is usually best viewed from a basically frontal position. You cannot walk around a relief sculpture and see its back side as sculpture any more than you can walk around a painting and see its back side as painting. That is why both relief sculptures and paintings are usually best placed on walls or in niches.

Charles Biederman's *Structurist Relief, Red Wing #6* (Figure 5-6), like *Times Square Sky,* is in high relief.

Structurist Relief, Red Wing #6 differs from most sculpture in several respects. In the first place, Biederman—unlike Chryssa, for example—covers up his material, the aluminum. Second, he uses a wider color range than most sculptors and even painters such as Mondrian. Yet we think *Struc-*

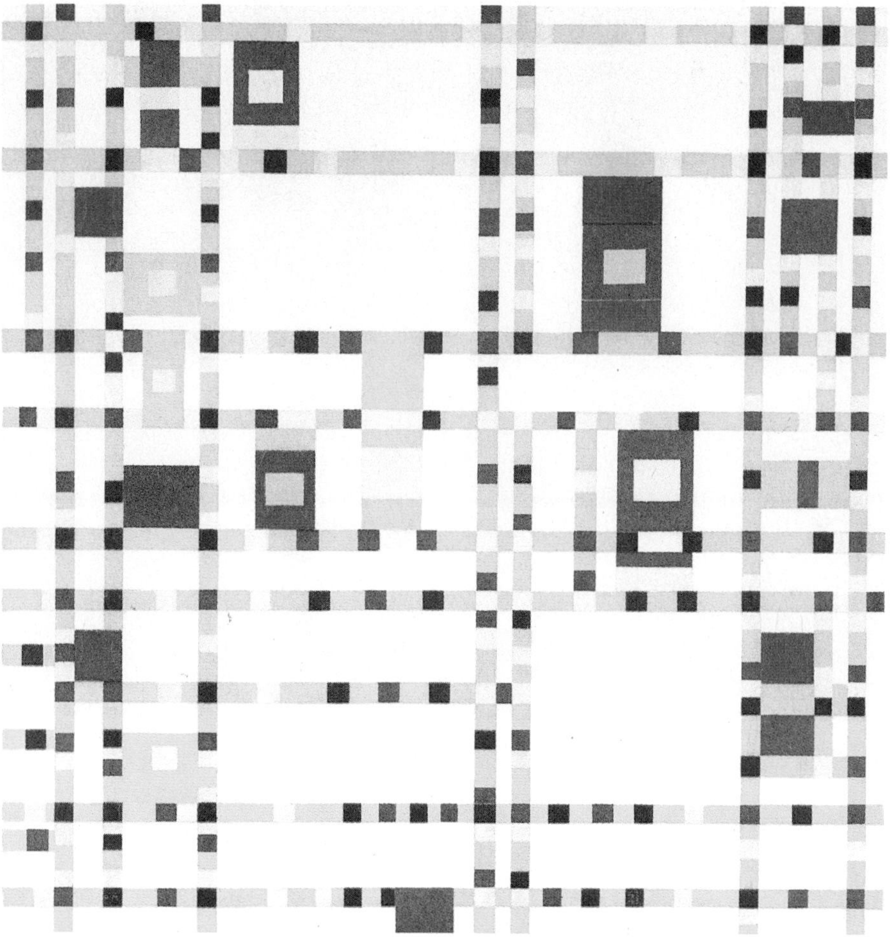

FIGURE 5-5
Piet Mondrian, *Broadway Boogie Woogie*. 1942–1943. Oil on canvas, 50 × 50 inches. The Museum of Modern Art, New York. Given anonymously. (Photograph © 1997 The Museum of Modern Art, New York)

FIGURE 5-6
Charles Biederman, *Red Wing #6*. 1957–1963. Painted aluminum, 38$\frac{7}{16}$ × 26¼ × 8⅝ inches. Collection, Walker Art Center, Minneapolis. Gift of the artist through the Ford Foundation Purchase Program, 1964.

Perception Key
STRUCTURIST RELIEF, RED WING #6

Biederman's sculpture is made of sheet aluminum, machine-tooled and sprayed with several coats of paint in order to build up bright, lustrous surfaces. The placement of the squares and rectangles with their right-angled lines is reminiscent of Mondrian's style (Figures 1-5 and 5-5). And, in fact, Biederman was strongly influenced by Mondrian. Unlike *Times Square Sky,* the metallic character of the aluminum of *Structurist Relief, Red Wing #6* is painted over rather than brought out. Despite the close relationship in style to Mondrian's paintings, would you be satisfied describing Biederman's work as a painting? Explain.

FIGURE 5-7
Dancing Asparas. XII to XIII century. Rajasthan, India. Relief, sandstone, 28 inches high. The Metropolitan Museum of Art. Gift of Mrs. John D. Rockefeller, Jr., 1942.

turist Relief, Red Wing #6 is an example of sculpture. The squares and rectangles, unlike Mondrian's, possess some significant three-dimensionality. Moreover, they move strongly with clean simplicity out into space, and their smooth surfaces lure our hands. In contrast to our participation with *Broadway Boogie Woogie* (see Figure 5-5), our tactile sense is strongly aroused. If we were blindfolded and felt this work, we would be able to make some sense of it. Furthermore, these sharply edged planes with their high-luster skins reflect the play of light out into and through space in a way that suggests the luminosity of crystals. And perhaps this is the key to the content of this sculpture—the interpretation of the molecular and crystal structures of nature. And perhaps, also, there is the suggestion of how the kinetics of modern technology are derivative from these natural structures, for in the absolute precision of this work there is something very machinelike. Biederman covers his aluminum, but in such a way that he uncovers something of the matter of nature and its relationship to the machine. This is a highly debatable interpretation, of course.

HIGH-RELIEF SCULPTURE

The Hindu deity, *Dancing Asparas* (Figure 5-7), from a temple of the thirteenth century A.D. at Rajasthan in India, is an example of high-relief sculpture. Bursting with energy, the deity stands out from the wall and almost escapes from her pillar. On the other hand, the small admiring handmaiden is in relatively low relief, closely integrated with the pillar. Partly because the deity is almost completely in the round, we sense her bulk and mass with exceptional force.

SCULPTURE IN THE ROUND

Michelangelo's *Pietà* (Figure 5-8), one of his last sculptures, circa 1550–1555, was unfinished. According to Vasari and Condivi, Michelangelo originally

FIGURE 5-8
Michelangelo Buonarroti, *Pietà*. Circa 1550–1555. Marble, 7 feet 8 inches high; in Florence Cathedral. (Alinari/Art Resource, New York)

wanted to be buried at the foot of this sculpture, which was to be placed in Santa Maria Maggiore in Rome. Hence he portrayed his own features in the head of Joseph of Arimathea, the figure hovering above, and apparently was making good progress. But then a series of accidents occurred, some involuntary and some probably voluntary. In carving the left leg of Christ, a vein in the marble broke, and the leg was completely destroyed. There are also breaks above the left elbow of Christ, in his chest on the left, and on the fingers of the hand of the Virgin. The story goes that, in despair, Michelangelo did some of this damage himself. In any case, he gave it up as a monument for his tomb and sold it in 1561, deciding that he preferred burial in Florence.

Perception Key
PIETÀ

1. Of the four figures in this statue—Joseph, Christ, the Virgin to the right, and Mary Magdalene to the left—one seems to be not only somewhat stylistically out of harmony with the other three but of lesser artistic quality. Historians and critics generally agree that this figure was not done or at least not completed by Michelangelo but rather by a second-rate sculptor, presumably Tiberio Calcagni. Which figure is this? What are your reasons for choosing it?
2. Michelangelo, perhaps more than any other sculptor, was obsessed with marble. He spent months at a time searching the hills of Carrara near Pisa for those marble blocks from which he could help sculptural shapes emerge. Something of his love for marble, perhaps, is revealed in this *Pietà*. Do you perceive this?
3. Is this sculpture in the round? The figures are freed from a base as background, and one can walk around the work. But is this *Pietà* in the round in the same way as Arp's *Growth* (Figure 5-1)?

The answer to the first question is the Magdalene. Her figure and pose, relative to the others, are artificial and stiff. Her robe—compare it with the Virgin's—fails to integrate with the body beneath. For no accountable reason she is both very aloof and much smaller, and the rhythms of her figure fail to harmonize with the others. Finally, the marbleness of the marble fails to come out with the Magdalene.

In the other figures—and this is the key to the second question—Michelangelo barely allows his shapes, except for the polished surfaces of the body of Christ, to emerge from the marble block. The features of the Virgin's face, for example, are very roughly sketched. It is as if she were still partially a prisoner in her stone. The Virgin is a marble Virgin; the Magdalene is a Magdalene and marble. Or, to put it another way, Michelangelo saw the Virgin in the marble and helped her image out without allowing it to betray its origin. Calcagni, or whoever did the Magdalene, saw the image of Magdalene and then fitted the marble to the image. Thus the claim that the face of the Virgin was unfinished is mistaken. It is hard to conceive, for us at least, how more chiseling or any polishing could have avoided weakening the expression of tender sorrow. The face of the Magdalene is more finished in a realistic sense, of course, but the forms of art reveal rather than reproduce reality. In the case of the body of Christ—compared with the rest of the statue except the Magdalene—the much more "finished" chiseling and the high polish were appropriate because they helped reveal the bodily suffering.

Since there is no background plane from which the figures emerge, the *Pietà* is usually described as sculpture in the round. Yet when compared with Arp's *Growth*, it is obvious that the *Pietà* is not so clearly in the round. There is no "pull" around to the rough-hewn back side, except our need to escape from the intensity of the awesome pity. And when we do walk behind the *Pietà*, we find the back side unintegrated with the sides and front and of little interest. Michelangelo intended this essentially three-sided pyramid, as with practically all of his sculptures, to be placed in a niche so that it could be seen principally from the front. In this sense, the *Pietà* is a transition piece between high-relief sculpture, such as the *Dancing Asparas* (Figure 5-7), and unqualified sculpture in the round, such as *Growth*.

SCULPTURE AND ARCHITECTURE COMPARED

Architecture is the art of separating inner from outer space in such a way that the inner space can be used for practical purposes. There is much more to architecture than that, of course, as we shall discuss in the next chapter. But how can sculpture be distinguished from architecture? Despite the architectural monumentality of Goeritz's *Five Towers of the Satellite City* (Figure 5-9), this is clearly sculpture because there is no inner space. But what about the Sphinx and the Pyramid at Memphis (Figure 5-10)? Like *The Five Towers of the Satellite City,* both the Sphinx and the Pyramid are among the densest and most substantial of all works. They attract us visually and tactilely. Since there is no space within the Sphinx, it is sculpture. But within the Pyramid, space was provided for the burial of the dead. There is a separation of inner from outer space for the functional use of the inner space. Yet the use of this inner space is so limited that the living often have a very difficult time finding it. The inner space is functional only in a very restricted sense—for the dead only. Is then this Pyramid sculpture or architecture? We shall delay our answer until the next chapter. The difficulty of the question, however, points up an important factor that we should keep in mind. The distinctions between the arts that we have and will be making are helpful in order to talk about them intelligibly, but the arts resist neat pigeonholing and any attempt at that would be futile.

SENSORY SPACE

The space around a sculpture is sensory rather than empty. Despite its invisibility, sensory space—like the wind—is felt. Sculptures such as *Growth* are like magnets from which radiating vectors flow. As we focus on such sculptures, we find ourselves being drawn in and around by these invisible but perceptible radiating forces. With relief sculptures, except for very high relief such as *Dancing Asparas* (Figure 5-7), our bodies tend to get stabilized in one favored position. The framework of front and sides meeting at sharp angles, as in *Times Square Sky* (Figure 5-4), limits our movements to 180 degrees at most. Although we are likely to move around within this limited range for a while, our movements gradually slow down, like finally getting settled in a comfortable chair. We are not Cyclops with just one eye, and so we see something of the three-dimensionality of things even when restricted to one position. But even low-relief sculpture encourages some movement of the body, because we sense that a different perspective, however slight, may bring out something we have not directly perceived, especially something more of the three-dimensionality of the materials.

FIGURE 5-9
Mathias Goeritz, *The Five Towers of the Satellite City.* 1957. Painted concrete pylons, 121 to 187 feet high, near Mexico City. (Photograph from *Matrix of Man*, 1968, by Sibyl Moholy-Nagy, Praeger Publishers. Courtesy Hattula Moholy-Nagy Hug)

When I visit Jean Arp's *Growth,* I find a warm and friendly presence. I find myself reaching toward the statue rather than keeping my distance. (If a chair were available I would not use it.) Whereas my perceptual relationship to a painting requires my getting to and settling in the privileged

FIGURE 5-10
Great Sphinx and Pyramid at Memphis, Egypt. IV dynasty, circa 2850 B.C. Rock-cut limestone and masonry; base of Pyramid, about 13 acres; Sphinx, 66 feet high, 172 feet wide. (Egyptian State Tourist Administration)

position, similar to finding the best seat in the theater, my perceptual relationship to the Arp is much more mobile and flexible. The smooth rounded shapes with their swelling volumes move gently out into space, turn my body around the figure, and control the rhythm of my walking. My perception of the Arp seems to take much more time than my perception of a painting, but in fact that is not so.

The Arp seems not only three-dimensional but four-dimensional, because it brings in the element of time so discernibly—a cumulative drama. Not only does each aspect make equal demands upon my contemplation, but, at the same time, each aspect is incomplete, enticing me on to the next for fulfillment. As I move, volumes and masses change, and on their surfaces points become lines, lines become curves, and curves become shapes. As each new aspect unrolls, there is a shearing of textures, especially at the lateral borders. The marble flows. The leading border uncovers a new aspect and the textures of the old aspect change. The light flames. The trailing border wipes out the old aspect. The curving surface continuously reveals the emergence of volumes and masses in front, behind, and in depth. What is hidden behind the surfaces is still perceived, for the textures indicate a mass behind them. As I move, what I have perceived and what I will perceive stand in defined positions with what I am presently perceiving. My moving body links the aspects. A continuous metamorphosis evolves, as I remember the aspects that were and anticipate the aspects to come, the leaping and plunging lights glancing off the surface helping to blend the changing volumes, shapes, and masses. The remembered and anticipatory images resonate in the present perception. My perception of the Arp is alive with motion. The sounds in the museum room are caught, more or less, in the rhythm of that motion. As I return to my starting point, I find it richer, as home seems after a journey.

SCULPTURE AND THE HUMAN BODY

Sculptures generally are more or less a center—the place of most importance which organizes the places around it—of actual three-dimensional space: "more" in the case of sculpture in the round, "less" in the case of low relief. That is why sculpture in the round is more typically sculpture than the other species. Other things being equal, sculpture in the round, because of its three-dimensional centeredness, brings out the voluminosity and density of things more certainly than any other kind of sculpture. First of all, we can see and touch all sides. But more importantly our sense of density has something to do with our awareness of our bodies as three-dimensional centers thrusting out into our surrounding environment. Philosopher-critic Gaston Bachelard remarks that

> immensity is within ourselves. It is attached to a sort of expansion of being which life curbs and caution arrests, but which starts again when we are alone. As soon as we become motionless, we are elsewhere; we are dreaming in a world that is immense. Indeed, immensity is the movement of a motionless man.[2]

Lachaise's *Floating Figure* (Figure 5-11), with its ballooning buoyancy emerging with lonely but powerful internal animation from a graceful ellipse, expresses not only this feeling but also something of the instinctual longing we have to become one with the world about us. Sculpture in the round, even when it does not portray the human body, often gives us something of an objective image of our internal bodily awareness as related to

[2]From *The Poetics of Space* by Gaston Bachelard. Translation ©1964 by the Orion Press, Inc. Reprinted by permission of Grossman Publishers.

FIGURE 5-11
Gaston Lachaise, *Floating Figure*. 1927. Bronze (cast in 1935), 51¾ × 96 × 22 inches. The Museum of Modern Art, New York. Given anonymously in memory of the artist. (Photograph © 1997 The Museum of Modern Art, New York)

Perception Key
EXERCISE IN DRAWING AND MODELING

1. Take a pencil and paper. Close your eyes. Now draw the shape of a human being but leave off the arms.
2. Take some clay or putty elastic enough to mold easily. Close your eyes. Now model your material into the shape of a human being, again leaving off the arms.
3. Analyze your two efforts. Which was easier to do? Which produced the better result? What do you mean by "better"? Was your drawing process guided by any other factor than your memory images of the human body? What about your modeling process? Did any significant factors other than your memory images come into play? Was the feel of the clay or putty important in your shaping? Did the awareness of your internal bodily sensations contribute to the shaping? Did you exaggerate any of the functional parts of the body where movement originates, such as the neck muscles, shoulder bones, knees, or ankles? Could these exaggerations, if they occurred, have been a consequence of your inner bodily sensations?

its surrounding space. Furthermore, when the human body is portrayed in the round, we may have the most vivid material counterpoint of our internal feelings and mental images of our bodily existence.

FIGURE 5-12
Aphrodite (Venus Anadyomene). Circa first century B.C. Marble, slightly under life size. Found at Cyrene. Museo Nazionale delle Terme, Rome. (Alinari/Art Resource, New York)

SCULPTURE IN THE ROUND AND THE HUMAN BODY

No object is more important to us than our body, and it is always "with" us. Yet when something is continually present to us, we find great difficulty in focusing our attention upon it. Thus we usually are only vaguely aware of air except when it is deficient in some way. Similarly, we usually are only vaguely aware of our bodies except when we are in pain. Nevertheless, our bodies are part of our most intimate selves—we are our bodies—and, since most of us are narcissists to some degree, most of us have a deep-down driving need to find a satisfactory material counterpoint for the mental images of our bodies. If that is the case, we are lovers of sculpture in the round. All sculpture always evokes our outward sensations and sometimes our inward sensations. Sculpture in the round often evokes our inward sensations, for such sculpture often is anthropomorphic in some respect. And sculpture in the round that has as its subject matter the human body—as in the *Aphrodite* (Figure 5-12), Michelangelo's *David* (Figure 5-13), or Rodin's *Danaïde* (Figure 5-14)—not only often evokes our inward sensations but also interprets them.

Rodin, one of the greatest sculptors of the human body, wrote that

> instead of imagining the different parts of the body as surfaces more or less flat, I represented them as projections of interior volumes. I forced myself to express in each swelling of the torso or of the limbs the efflorescence of a muscle or a

Perception Key
APHRODITE

The marble *Aphrodite* (Figure 5-12), slightly under life size, found at Cyrene, is a Roman copy of a Greek original of the first century B.C. It is extraordinary both for the delicacy of its carving—for most Roman copies of Greek works crudely deaden their liveliness—and the translucency of its marble, which seems to reflect light from below its surface. Compare this work with Giorgione's *Venus* (see Figure 2-13).

1. In both these works, graceful lassitude and sexuality have something to do with their subject matter. Yet they are interpreted, we think, quite differently. What do you think?
2. If the head and arms of the *Venus* were represented as broken off, would this injure the work as much as the *Aphrodite*? Some critics claim that the Aphrodite is not very seriously injured as an artistic object by the destruction of her head and arms. Yet how can this be? Suppose the *Aphrodite* were to come off her pedestal and walk. Would you not find this monstrous? Yet many people treasure her as one of the most beautiful of all female sculptures. How is this to be explained?

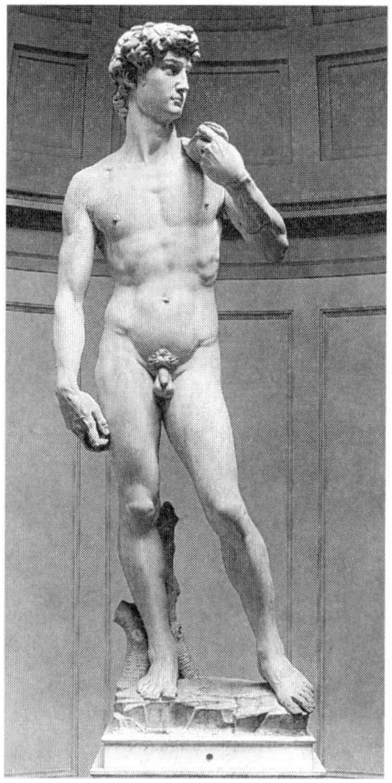

FIGURE 5-13
Michelangelo Buonarroti, *David*. 1501–1504. Marble, 13 feet high. Accademia, Florence. (Alinari/Art Resource, New York)

> bone which lay beneath the skin. And so the truth of my figures, instead of being merely superficial, seems to blossom from within to the outside, like life itself.[3]

Such sculpture presents an objective correlative—an image that is objective in the sense that it is "out there" and yet correlates or is similar to a

[3]Auguste Rodin, *Art*, Romilly Fedden (trans.), Small, Boston, 1912, p. 65.

FIGURE 5-14
Auguste Rodin, *Danaïde*. 1885. Marble, 35 × 73 × 57 centimeters. Musée Rodin, Paris. (Giraudon/Art Resource, New York)

subjective awareness—that clarifies our internal bodily sensations as well as our outward appearance.

These are large claims and highly speculative. You may disagree, of course, but we hope they will stimulate your thinking.

When we participate with sculpture such as the *Aphrodite,* we find something of our bodily selves confronting us. If we demanded all of our bodily selves, we would be both disappointed and stupid. Art is always a transformation of reality, never a duplication. Thus the absence of head and arms in the *Aphrodite* does not shock us as it would if we were confronting a real woman. Nor does their absence ruin our perception of the beauty of this statue. Even before the damage, the work was only a partial image of a female. Now the *Aphrodite* is even more partial. But even so, she is in that partiality exceptionally substantial. The *Aphrodite* is substantial because the female shape, texture, grace, sensuality, sexuality, and beauty are interpreted by a form and thus clarified.

The human body is supremely beautiful. To begin with, there is its sensuous charm. There may be other things in the world as sensuously attractive—for example, the full glory of autumnal leaves—but the human body also possesses a sexuality that greatly enhances its sensuousness. Moreover, in the human body, mind is incarnate. Feeling, thought, purposefulness—"spirit"—have taken shape. Thus, the absent head of the *Aphrodite* (Figure 5-12) is not really so absent after all. There is a dignity of spirit that permeates her body. It is the manifestation of Aphrodite's composed spirit in the shaping of her body that, in the final analysis, explains why we are not repulsed by the sight of the absent head and arms.

Compare Michelangelo's *David* (Figure 5-13) and *Pietà* (Figure 5-8) with the *Aphrodite*.

Perception Key
DAVID, APHRODITE, AND THE *PIETÀ*

1. Suppose the head of the *David* were broken off and, like the head of *Aphrodite,* you had never seen it. It is conceivable that a head something like that of the Christ of the *Pietà* could be satisfactorily substituted?
2. The *Pietà*, the *Aphrodite,* and the *David* are in marble, although of very different kinds. Which statue is more evocative of your outward sensations? Your inward sensations? Henry Moore claims that "sculpture is more affected by actual size considerations than painting. A painting is isolated by a frame from its surroundings (unless it serves just a decorative purpose) and so retains more easily its own imaginary scale." He makes the further claim that the actual physical size of sculpture has an emotional meaning. "We relate everything to our own size, and our emotional response to size is controlled by the fact that men on the average are between five and six feet high."[4] Does the fact that the *David* is much larger in size than the *Aphrodite* make any significant difference with respect to your tactile sensations?

[4]Moore, "Notes on Sculpture," p. xxxiv.

TECHNIQUES OF SCULPTURE

Sculpture in relief and in the round generally is made either by modeling or carving. Space sculpture, such as Calder's *Gates of Spoleto* (Figure 5-16), generally is made by assembling preformed pieces of material.

The modeler starts with some plastic or malleable material such as clay, wax, or plaster and "builds" the sculpture. If the design is complex or involves long or thin extensions, the modeler probably will have to use an internal wooden or metal support (armature) that functions something like a skeleton. Whereas *Floating Figure* (Figure 5-11) required armatures, much smaller modeled sculptures do not. In either case, the modeler builds from the inside outward to the surface finish, which then may be scratched, polished, painted, etc. But when nonplastic materials such as bronze are used, the technical procedures are much more complicated. Bronze cannot be built up like clay. Nor can bronze be carved like stone, although it can be lined, scratched, etc. And so the sculptor in bronze or any material that is cast must use further processes. We can present here only a grossly oversimplified account. For those who want to pursue the techniques of sculpture further—and this can be very helpful in sharpening our perceptual faculties—a large number of excellent technical handbooks are available.[5]

The sculptor in bronze begins with clay or some similar material and builds up a model to a more or less high degree of finish. This is a solid or positive shape. Then the sculptor usually makes a plaster mold—a hollow or negative shape—from the solid model. This negative shape is usually divisible into sections, so that the inside can easily be worked on to make changes or remove any defects that may have developed. Then, because plaster or a similar material is much better than clay for the casting process, the sculptor makes a positive or solid plaster cast from his negative plaster mold and perfects its surface. This plaster cast is then given to a specialized foundry, unless the sculptor does this work for himself or herself, and a negative mold is again made of such materials as plaster, rubber, or gelatin. Inside this mold—again usually divisible into sections to allow for work in the interior—a coating of liquid wax is brushed on, normally at least one-eighth inch in thickness but varying with the size of the sculpture. After the wax dries, a mixture of materials, such as sand and plaster, is poured into the hollow space within the mold. Thus the wax is completely surrounded.

Intense heat is now applied, causing the wax to melt out through channels drilled through the outside mold, and the molds on both sides of the wax are baked hard. Then the bronze is poured into the space the wax has vacated. After the bronze hardens, the surrounding molds are removed. Finally, the sculptor may file, chase, polish, or add patinas (by means of chemicals) to the surface. One of the most interesting and dramatic descriptions

[5]For example, William Zorach, *Zorach Explains Sculpture,* American Artists Group, New York, 1947. (Learning the techniques of handling various artistic media is one of the best ways of improving our perception and understanding of the arts. We do not have the space to go into these techniques, but good technical handbooks in all the arts abound.)

of casting, incidentally, can be found in the *Autobiography of Benvenuto Cellini,* the swashbuckling Renaissance sculptor whose *Perseus* was almost lost in the casting process.

The carver uses nonmalleable material, such as marble, that cannot be built up, and so the carver must start with a lump of material and work inward from the outside by removing surplus material until arriving at the surface finish. Thus for his *David* (Figure 5-13), Michelangelo was given a huge marble block that Agostino di Duccio had failed to finally shape into either a David or, more likely, a prophet for one of the buttresses of the Cathedral of Florence. Agostino's carving had reduced the original block considerably, putting severe restrictions upon what Michelangelo could do. This kind of restriction is foreign to the modeler, for there is no frame such as the limits of a marble block to prevent the expansion of the sculpture into space. And when a model is cast in materials of great tensile strength, such as bronze, this spatial freedom becomes relatively unlimited.

It should be noted that many carvers, including Michelangelo, sometimes modeled before they carved. A sketch model often can help carvers find their way around in such materials as marble. It is not easy to visualize before the fact the whereabouts of complicated shapes in large blocks of material. And once a mistake is made in nonplastic materials, it is not so easily remedied as with plastic materials. The shapes of the *David* had to be ordered from the outside inward, the smaller shapes being contained within the larger shapes. Whereas the modeler works up the most simplified and primary shapes that underlie all the secondary shapes and details, the carver roughs out the simplified and primary shapes within which all the secondary shapes and details are contained. For example, Michelangelo roughed out the head of the *David* as a solid sphere, working down in the front from the outermost planes of the forehead and nose to the outline of the eyes and then to the details of the eyes, etc. Hence the primary shape of the head, the solid sphere, is not only preserved to some extent but also points to its original containment within the largest containing shape, the block itself. Consequently, we can sense in the *David* something of the block from which Michelangelo started. This original shape is suggested by the limits of the projecting parts and the high points of the surfaces. We are aware of the thinness of the *David* as a consequence of the block Michelangelo inherited. There remains the huge imprint of that vertical block that had been sliced into. This accounts in part for the feeling we may have with some carved works of their being contained within a private space, introverted and to some extent separate. Modeled sculpture generally is more extroverted.

Alexander Calder's *Antennae with Red and Blue Dots* (Figure 5-15) and *The Gates of Spoleto* (Figure 5-16) obviously were neither modeled nor carved. Their wires and sheets of metal have little mass to be shaped and no interior to be structured. Although the materials of these works exist in three-dimensional space, as does everything else in this world, they are not themselves significantly three-dimensional. Calder preformed these pieces and then assembled them, attached, furthermore, at clearly discernible joints and intersections. These pieces relate across and frame space; in the case of *Antennae with Red and Blue Dots,* there is even movement through

FIGURE 5-15
Alexander Calder, *Antennae with Red and Blue Dots*. 1960. Kinetic metal sculpture (mobile), 43¾ × 50½ × 50½ inches (range). (Photograph The Tate Gallery, London/Art Resource, New York; Art © 1997 Artists Rights Society [ARS], NY/ADAGP, Paris)

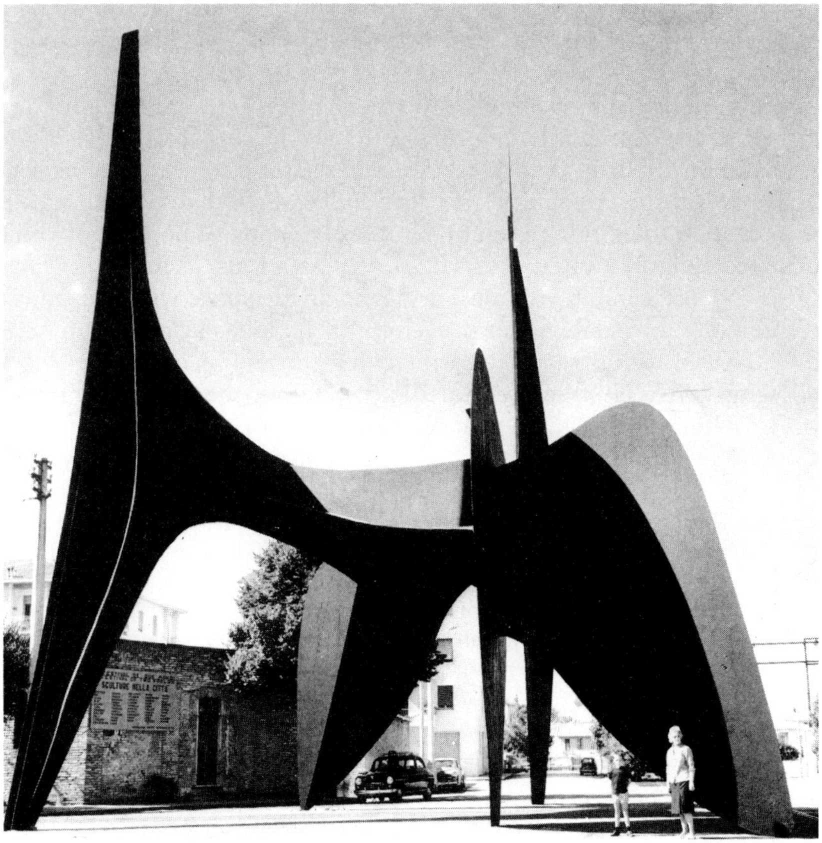

FIGURE 5-16
Alexander Calder, *The Gates of Spoleto*. 1962. Steel. (Photograph Edvard Trier; Art © 1997 Artists Rights Society [ARS], NY/ADAGP, Paris)

space. The appeal of these works, therefore, is more visual than that of earlier sculpture. Calder's materials fill space only slightly, and so their tactile appeal, while still present, is considerably reduced.

Calder's *Antennae with Red and Blue Dots* (Figure 5-15), made of wire and sheet metal, is an especially lovely example of spatial relationships. It is as if we were standing under a large insect, as the title suggests. The sinuous wires expand in all directions, and the graceful disks, like wings, ride the breezes. Here our visual perception of spatial relationships is clearly more important than the tactile qualities of wire and metal. We have little desire to touch these pieces. Yet in their flowing movement to and from each other, they help bring out the tactile qualities of the open air. Calder's mobiles, kinetic sculpture whose movement depends on balance and the motion of the air, can be described as "space drawings." Their primarily visual appeal, like very low-relief sculpture, has close affinities to painting. On the other hand Calder's *Gates of Spoleto* (Figure 5-16) has close affinities to architecture. As with many of the materials of architecture, Calder's materials sometimes are not only preformed and assembled but also massive. This makes it easily possible for inner space to be separated from outer space for practical purposes. If, for example, Calder had extended the upper steel sheets of *The Gates of Spoleto* horizontally, this work could serve as a functional shelter.

TACTILITY, MASS, AND SPACE

Space sculpture never completely loses its ties to the materiality of its materials. Otherwise tactile qualities would be largely missing also, and then it would be doubtful if such work could usefully be classified as sculpture. The materials of *Antennae with Red and Blue Dots* and *The Gates of Spoleto*, despite their thinness, appear heavy. Naum Gabo, one of the fathers of space sculpture, often uses translucent materials, as in *Spiral Theme* (Figure 5-17). Although the planes of plastic divide space with multidirectional movement, no visual barriers develop. Each plane varies in translucency as our angle of vision varies, and in seeing through each, we see them all—allowing for freely flowing transitions between the space without and the space within. In turn, the tactile attraction of the plastic, especially its smooth surface and rapid fluidity, is enhanced. As Gabo has written:

> Volume still remains one of the fundamental attributes of sculpture, and we still use it in our sculptures. . . . We are not at all intending to dematerialize a sculptural work. . . . On the contrary, adding Space perception to the perception of Masses, emphasizing it and forming it, we enrich the expression of Mass, making it more essential through the contact between them whereby Mass retains its solidity and Space its extension.[6]

[6]Quoted by Herbert Read and Leslie Martin in *Gabo: Constructions, Sculpture, Drawings, Engravings,* Harvard University Press, Cambridge, Mass., 1957, p. 168.

FIGURE 5-17
Naum Gabo, *Spiral Theme*. 1941. Construction in plastic, 5½ × 13¼ × 9⅜ inches, on base 24 inches square. The Museum of Modern Art, New York. Advisory Committee Fund. (Photograph © 1997 The Museum of Modern Art, New York)

Perception Key
RECLINING FIGURE, PELAGOS, AND *BRUSSELS CONSTRUCTION*

1. Compare Hepworth's *Pelagos* (Figure 5-18), Rivera's *Brussels Construction* (Figure 5-19), and Moore's *Reclining Figure* (Figure 5-20). Is there in these works, as Gabo claims for his, an equal emphasis on mass and space? If not, in which one does mass dominate space? Vice versa?
2. Moore has written that "The first hole made through a piece of stone [or most three-dimensional materials] is a revelation. The hole connects one side to the other, making it immediately more three-dimensional. A hole can itself have as much shape-meaning as a solid mass."[7] Is Moore's claim equally applicable to all of these works?
3. How many holes are there in *Pelagos?* What is the function of the strings? Why did Hepworth color the inside white? Hepworth said, "The colour in the concavities plunged me into the depth of water, caves or shadows . . . the strings were the tension I felt between myself and the sea, the wind, and the hills." Are her comments helpful in responding to the work?
4. *Brussels Construction* is mounted on a flat disk turned by a low-revolution motor. Is it useful to refer to holes in this sculpture? The three-dimensional curve of *Brussels Construction* proceeds in a long, smooth, continuous flow. Does this have anything to do with the changing diameter of the chromium-plated

[7]"Notes on Sculpture," op. cit., p. xxxiv.

stainless steel? Suppose the material absorbed rather than reflected light. Would this change the structure significantly? Do you think this sculpture should be displayed under diffused light, or in dim illumination with one or more spotlights? Is there any reference to human life in the simplicity and elegant vitality of this work? Or is the subject matter just about stainless steel and space? Or is the subject matter about something else? Do you agree that this work is an example of space sculpture? And what about *Pelagos?* Note that there is no assemblage of pieces in the case of *Brussels Construction,* whereas, because of the addition of strings, there is some assemblage in *Pelagos.* Would you classify these works in Figures 5-17 to 5-20 as space sculptures?

It seems to us that *Pelagos* and *Reclining Figure* are not space sculptures because, although they open up space within, the density of their materials dominates space. *Brussels Construction,* on the other hand, is space sculpture because the spatial relationships are at least as interesting as the stainless steel. The fact that *Pelagos* was assembled in part and *Brussels Construction* was not is not conclusive. Assemblage is the technique generally used in space sculpture, but what we are perceiving and should be judging is the product, not the producing process. Of course, the producing process affects what is produced, and that is why it can be helpful to know about the producing process. That is why we went into some detail about the differences between modeling, carving, and assemblage. But the basis of a sound judgment about a work of art is that work as it is given to us in perception. Any kind of background information is relevant provided it aids that perception. But if we permit the producing process rather than the work of art itself to be the basis of our judgment we are led away from, rather than into, the work. This destroys the usefulness of criticism.

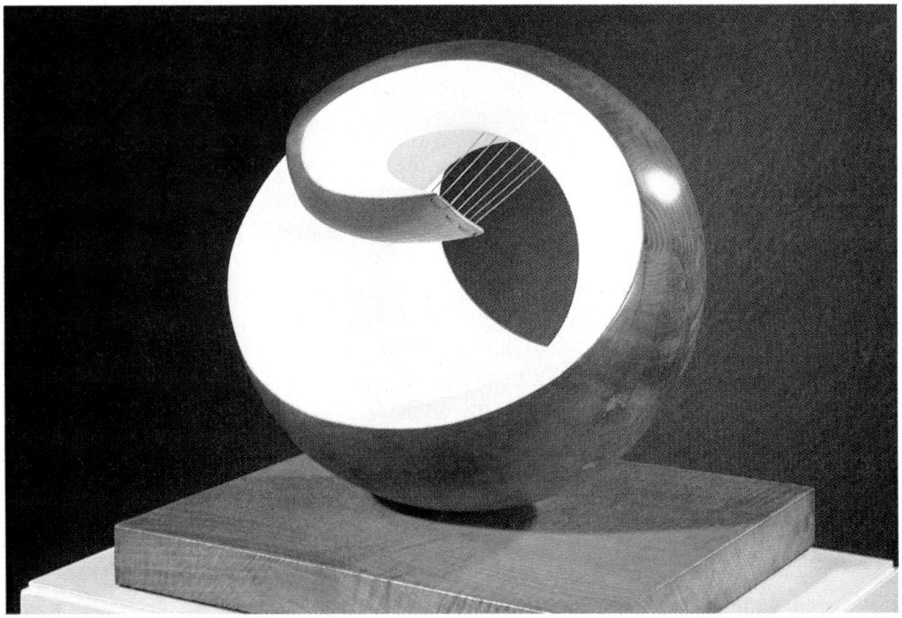

FIGURE 5-18
Barbara Hepworth, *Pelagos*. 1946. Wood with color and strings, 16 inches in diameter. (The Tate Gallery, London/Art Resource, New York)

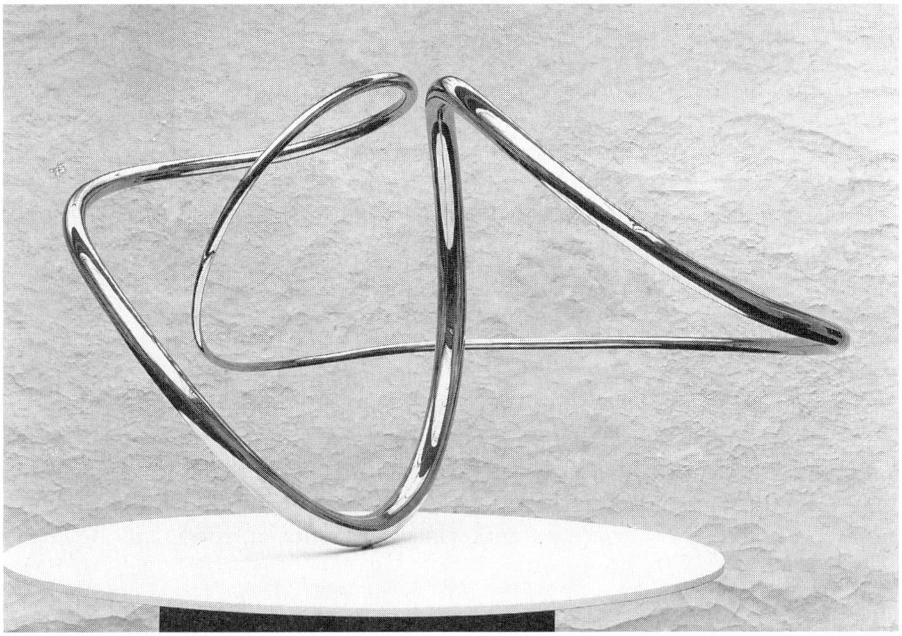

FIGURE 5-19
Jose de Rivera, *Brussels Construction*. 1958. Stainless steel. The Art Institute of Chicago. Gift of Mr. and Mrs. R. Howard Goldsmith. (Photograph © 1997 The Art Institute of Chicago)

FIGURE 5-20
Henry Moore, *Reclining Figure*. 1938. Green Hornton stone, 54 inches long. (The Tate Gallery, London/Art Resource, New York)

CONTEMPORARY SCULPTURE

Developments in sculpture are emerging and changing so quickly that no attempt can be made here even to begin to classify them. These developments fall into the species of low, medium, and high relief, sculpture in the round, space sculpture, earth sculpture, and some hybrids of these. But beyond that not-very-helpful generalization, the innovations of contemporary sculptors escape pigeonholing.

TRUTH TO MATERIALS

There is, however, at least one tendency, more of a reaffirmation than an innovation, that is fairly pervasive—respect for the materials used in the sculpture. In the flamboyant eighteenth-century Baroque, in the early-nineteenth-century Neoclassicism, and in some of the Romanticism of the later nineteenth century, respect for materials was ignored. Karl Knappe refers to

> the crisis through which art [sculpture] is passing [is] one that concerns . . . the artistic media. An image cannot be created without regard for the laws of nature, and each kind of material has natural laws of its own. Every block of stone, every piece of wood is subject to its own rules. Every medium has, so to speak, its own tempo; the tempo of a pencil or a piece of charcoal is quite different from the tempo of a woodcut. The habit of mind which creates, for instance, a pen drawing cannot simply be applied mechanically to the making of a woodcut; to do this would be to deny the validity of the spiritual as well as the technical tempo.[8]

In contemporary sculpture, perhaps in part as a reaction, respect for materials has come back with a vengeance. It has even been given a name—"truth to materials."

PERCEPTION KEY
TRUTH TO MATERIALS

1. Review the examples of twentieth-century sculpture we have discussed. Assuming that these examples are fairly representative, do you find a pervasive tendency to truth to materials? Do you find exceptions, and, if so, how might these be explained?
2. Henry Moore has stated that "Every material has its own individual qualities. It is only when the sculptor works direct, when there is an active relationship with his material, that the material can take its part in the shaping of an idea. Stone, for example, is hard and concentrated and should not be falsified to look like soft flesh—it should not be forced beyond its constructive build to a point of weakness. It should keep its hard tense stoniness."[9] Figures 5-14 and 5-20 are both in stone. Do they illustrate Moore's point? If so, point out as specifically as possible how this is done.

[8]Karl Knappe, quoted in Kurt Herberts, *The Complete Book of Artists' Techniques,* Thames and Hudson, London, 1958, p. 16. Published in the United States by Frederick A. Praeger.
[9]Quoted by Herbert Read, *Henry Moore, Sculptor,* A. Zwemmer, London, 1934, p. 29.

3. Can you imagine how human figures could be made in wax, and yet truth to wax as a material be maintained? If you think wax is a weak or even impossible material for the sculpture of human figures, try to see a wax work by Medardo Rosso (1858–1928). Some of his wax sculptures are in the Hirshhorn Museum in Washington, D.C. Kiki Smith, a contemporary sculptor, also produced a powerful group of sculptures portraying battered women, using wax as her medium.

The *Maternity Group Figure* (Figure 5-21), from Nigeria, is especially notable in its respect for materials. The wood is grooved, ridged, and carved in ways that make its "woodness" all the more apparent. Societies in which technology has not been dominant sometimes live closer to nature than we do, and so their feeling for natural things, such as stone and wood, feathers and bone, usually is reverent. Examine, for instance, Figures 3-18 and 3-19, the mask and the nail figure.

As technology has gained more and more ascendancy, reverence toward natural things has receded. In highly industrialized societies, people tend to revere artificial things, and the pollution of our environment is one result. Another result is the flooding of the commercial market with imitations of primitive sculpture, which are easily identified because of the lack of truth to the materials (test this for yourself). Even the contemporary sculptors have lost some of their innocence toward things simply because they live in a technological age. Many sculptors still possess something of the natural way of feeling things, and so they find in primitive sculpture inspiration, even if to reach it requires repentance. Despite its abstract subject matter, Barbara Hepworth's *Pelagos,* with its reverence to wood, has a close spiritual affinity to the *Maternity Group Figure* (Figure 5-21). Truth to materials sculpture is an implicit protest against technological ascendancy.

FIGURE 5-21
Maternity Group Figure. Afo peoples, Nigeria, nineteenth century wood. 27¾ inches high. The Horniman Museum & Gardens, London. (31.42)

PROTEST AGAINST TECHNOLOGY

Explicit social protest is part of the subject matter of all these works by Trova, Segal, and Giacometti, although perhaps only in *Wheel Man* (Figure 5-22) is that protest unequivocally directed at technology. Flaccid, faceless, and sexless, this anonymous robot has "grown" spoked wheels instead of arms. Attached below the hips these mechanisms produce a sense of eerie instability, a feeling that this antiseptically cleansed automaton with the slack, protruding abdomen may tip over from the slightest push. In this inhuman mechanical purity, no free will is left to resist. Human value, as articulated in Aldous Huxley's *Brave New World,* has been reduced to humanpower, functions performed in the world of goods and services. Since another individual can also perform these functions, the given person has no special worth. His or her value is a unit that can easily be replaced by another.

The Bus Driver (Figure 5-23) is an example of "environmental sculpture." Grimly set behind a wheel and coin box taken from an old bus, the driver is a plaster cast made in sections over a living well-greased model. Despite the "real" environment and model, the stark white figure with its rough and generalized features is both real and strangely unreal. In the air around

FIGURE 5-22
Ernest Trova, *Study: Falling Man (Wheel Man)*. 1965. Silicon bronze, 60 × 48 × 20 13/16 inches. Collection, Walker Art Center, Minneapolis. Gift of the T. B. Walker Foundation, 1965.

him, we sense the hubbub of the streets, the smell of fumes, the ceaseless comings and goings of unknown customers. Yet despite all these suggestions of a crowded, nervous atmosphere, there is a heartrending loneliness about this driver. Worn down day after day by the same grind, Segal's man, like Trova's, has been flattened into an x—a quantity.

In Giacometti's emaciated figures, the huge, solidly implanted feet suggest nostalgia for the earth; the soaring upward of the elongated bodies suggests aspiration for the heavens. The surrounding environment has eaten away at the flesh, leaving lumpy, irregular surfaces with dark hollows that bore into the bone. Each figure is without contact with anyone, as despairingly isolated as *The Bus Driver.* They stand in or walk through an utterly alienated space, but, unlike *Wheel Man,* they seem to know it. And whereas the habitat of *Wheel Man* is the clean, air-conditioned factory or office of *Brave New World,* Giacometti's people, even when in neat galleries, always seem to be in the grubby streets of our decaying cities. The cancer of the city has left only the armatures of bodies stained with pollution and scarred with sickness. There is no center in this city square (Figure 5-24) or any exit, nor can we imagine any communication among these citizens. Their very grouping in the square gives them, paradoxically, an even greater feeling of isolation. Each Giacometti figure separates a spot of space from the common place. The disease and utter distress of these vulnerable creatures demands our respectful distance, as if they were lepers to whom help must come, if at all, from some public agency. To blame technology entirely for the dehumanization of society interpreted in these sculptures is a gross oversimplification, of course. But this kind of work does bring out something of the horror of technology when it is misused.

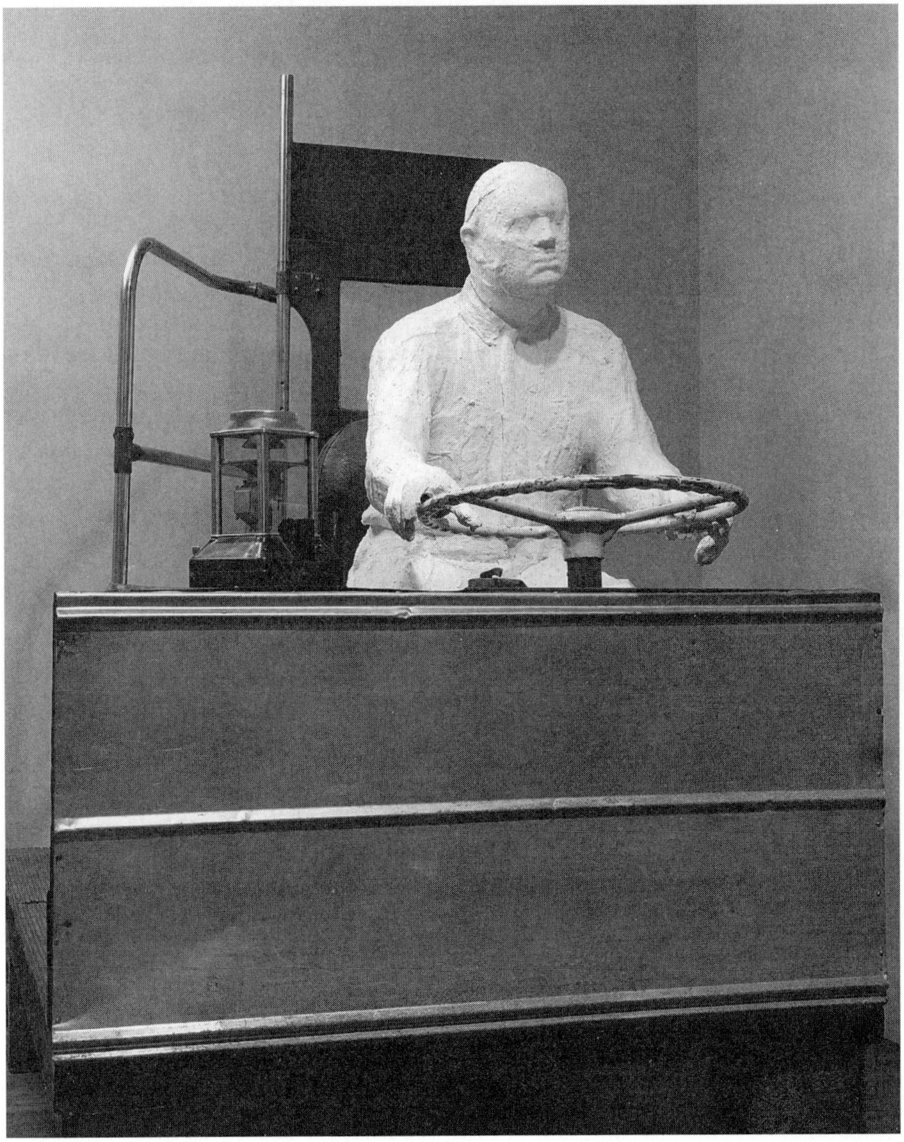

FIGURE 5-23
George Segal, *The Bus Driver*. 1962. Figure of plaster over cheesecloth with bus parts, including coin box, steering wheel, driver's seat, railing, dashboard, etc. Figure 53½ × 26⅞ × 45 inches; overall 7 feet 5 inches × 6 feet 4¾ inches. The Museum of Modern Art, New York. Philip Johnson Fund. (Photograph © 1996 The Museum of Modern Art, New York; Art © 1997 George Segal/Licensed by VAGA, New York)

FIGURE 5-24
Alberto Giacometti, *City Square (La Place)*. 1948. Bronze, 8½ × 25⅜ × 17¼ inches. The Museum of Modern Art. Purchase. (Photograph © 1996 The Museum of Modern Art, New York; Art © 1997 Artists Rights Society [ARS], NY/ADAGP, Paris)

ACCOMMODATION WITH TECHNOLOGY

Many contemporary sculptors see in technology blessings for humankind. It is true that sculpture can be accomplished with the most primitive tools (that, incidentally, is one of the basic reasons sculpture in primitive cultures apparently not only precedes painting but also usually dominates both qualitatively and quantitatively). Nevertheless, sculpture in our day, far more than painting, can take advantage of some of the most sophisticated advances of technology, surpassed in this respect only by architecture. Many sculptors today interpret the positive rather than the negative aspects of technology. This respect for technology is expressed by (1) truth to its materials or (2) care for its products or (3) showing forth its methodology.

David Smith's *Cubi X* (Figure 5-25), like Chryssa's *Times Square Sky* (Figure 5-4), illustrates truth to technological materials. But unlike Chryssa, Smith usually accomplishes this by wedding these materials to nature. The stainless steel cylinders of the *Cubi* support a juggling act of hollow rectangular and square cubes that barely touch one another as they cantilever out into space. Delicate buffing modulates the bright planes of steel, giving the illusion of several atmospheric depths and reflecting light like rippling water. Occasionally, when the light is just right, the effect is like the cascading streams of fountains, recalling the Arabic inscription on the *Fountain of the Lions* in the Alhambra, Granada: "Liquid and solid things are so closely related that none who sees them is able to distinguish which is motionless and which is flowing." Usually, however, the steel reflects with more constancy the colorings of its environment. Smith writes,

> I like outdoor sculpture and the most practical thing for outdoor sculpture is stainless steel, and I make them and I polish them in such a way that on a dull day, they take on the dull blue, or the color of the sky in late afternoon sun, the glow, golden like the rays, the colors of nature. And in a particular sense, I have

FIGURE 5-25
David Smith, *Cubi X*. 1963. Stainless steel; 10 feet 1⅜ inches × 6 feet 6¾ inches × 24 inches, including steel base 2⅞ × 25 × 33 inches. The Museum of Modern Art, New York. Robert O. Lord Fund. (Photograph © 1996 The Museum of Modern Art, New York; Art © 1997 David Smith/Licensed by VAGA, New York)

> used atmosphere in a reflective way on the surfaces. They are colored by the sky and the surroundings, the green or blue of water. Some are down by the water and some are by the mountains. They reflect the colors. They are designed for outdoors.[10]

But Smith's steel is not just a mirror, for in the reflections the fluid surfaces and tensile strength of the steel emerge in a structure that, as Smith puts it, "can face the sun and hold its own."

[10]David Smith in Cleve Gray (ed.), *David Smith*, Holt, Rinehart and Winston, New York, 1968, p. 123.

FIGURE 5-26
Kurt Schwitters, *Merz Konstruktion*. 1921. Painted wood, wire, and paper; 14½ × 8½ inches. Philadelphia Museum of Art. A. E. Gallatin Collection. (Art © 1997 Artists Rights Society [ARS], NY/VG Bild-Kunst, Bonn)

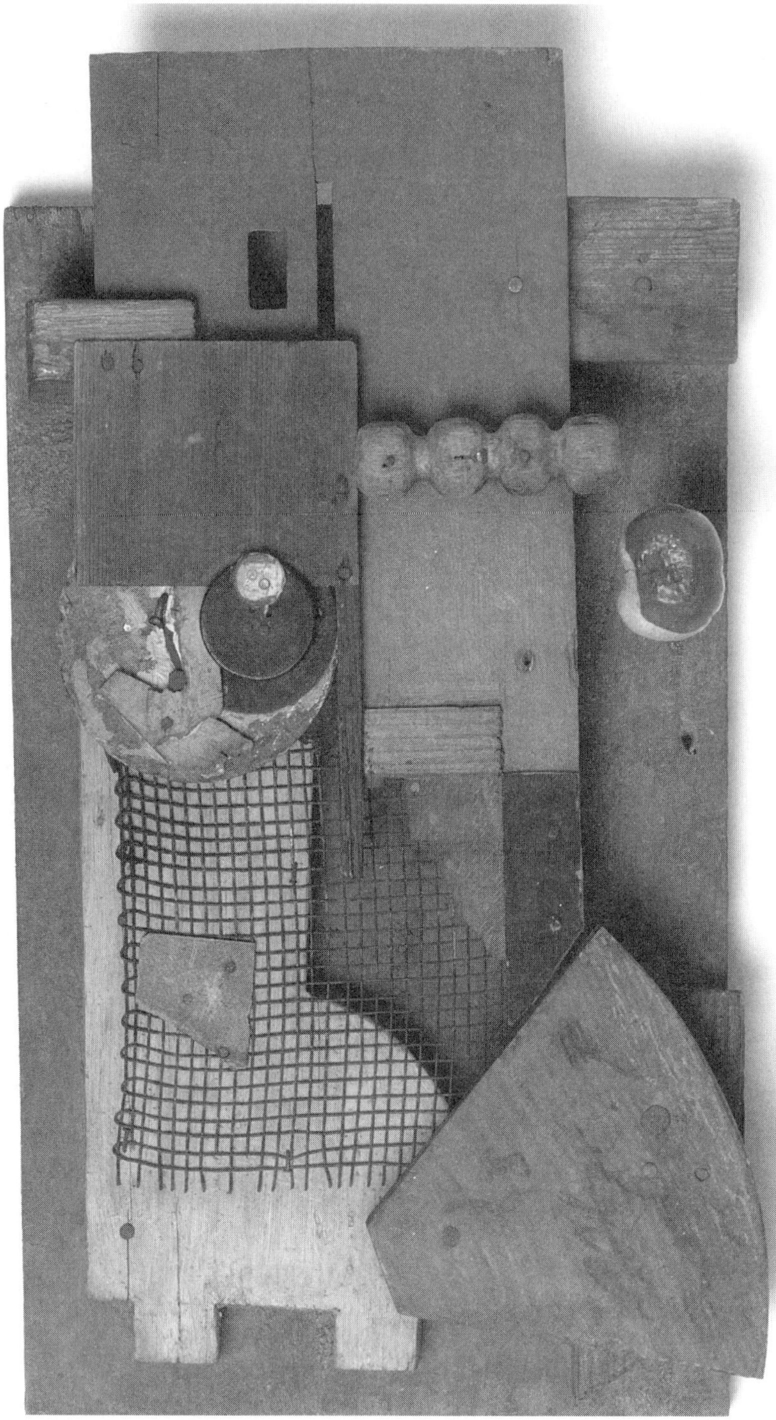

FIGURE 5-27
Marcel Duchamp, *Bottle Rack*. 1914. Galvanized iron, 23¼ inches high. (Art © 1997 Artists Rights Society [ARS], NY/ADAGP, Paris)

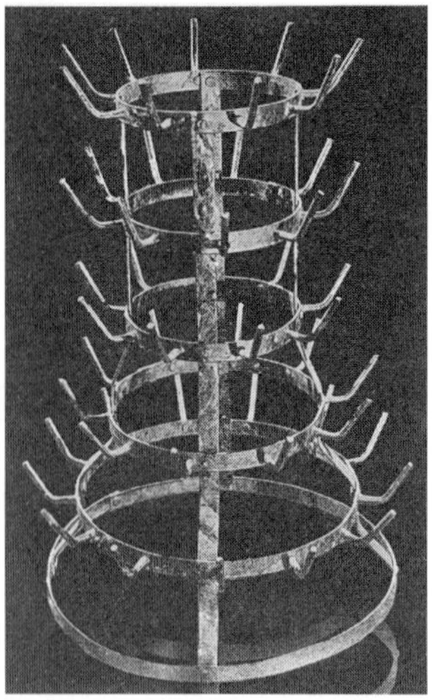

Kurt Schwitters' *Merz Konstruktion* (Figure 5-26) is—except for the old wood—an assemblage of worn-out, discarded, and despised manufactured materials such as cardboard, wire mesh, paper, and nails. The waste of our world is brought to our attention. With sensitive ordering with respect to shape, texture, color, and density, these rejects are rehabilitated. We see and feel them, perhaps for the first time, as things in themselves, a little like returning to an old abandoned house we once lived in but ignored except for practical purposes. We made and used these things, Schwitters is informing us, and we should recognize that, despite their lowly status, they have a dignity, over and above their utility, that demands respect.

Pop sculpture respects the products of technology as well as its materials. Duchamp's *Bottle Rack* (Figure 5-27) of 1914 was probably not so intended. Duchamp at that time was poking fun at overblown artistic pretensions. One of his more hilarious inventions, for example, was a urinal placed on a pedestal and signed R. Mutt, the name of the manufacturer. Nevertheless, *Bottle Rack* and works like it, such as Jim Dine's *Shovel* (Figure 2-1) became prototypes for Pop sculpture. By separating an industrial product from its utilitarian context and isolating it for our contemplation, the sculptor gives us an opportunity to appreciate its intrinsic values. *Bottle Rack* is a "ready-made," for Duchamp had nothing to do with its making. But Duchamp recognized the artistic qualities of what was then a very familiar object. The contrast of the diminishing rings with their spikey "branches" makes an interesting spatial pattern, especially if, as in Man Ray's photograph, light is played rhythmically on the rough surfaces of galvanized iron. Duchamp saw this possibility, for rarely are bottle racks—or any other industrial products, for that matter—so effectively displayed.

Pop sculpture does not always incorporate "ready-mades." By using material different from the original, attention often can be drawn more strongly to the product itself. For example, Oldenburg's *Giant Soft Fan* (Figure 5-28) is made in the functionally impossible materials of vinyl, wood, and foam rubber. Someone might be tempted to use *Bottle Rack* for practical purposes, but *Giant Soft Fan* completely frustrates such temptation. The scale and character of the fans of the marketplace, the ones we usually see only dimly, are completely changed. This ten-foot shining giant opens our eyes to the existence of all those everyday fans. As Oldenburg comments: "I want people to get accustomed to recognize the power of objects. . . . I alter to unfold the object and to add to it other object qualities."[11] This kind of sculpture is concerned not so much with the materials of our consumer world but with its products.

FIGURE 5-28
Claes Oldenburg, *Giant Soft Fan*. 1966–1967. Construction of vinyl filled with foam rubber, wood, metal, and plastic tubing, fan; 10 feet × $58\frac{7}{8}$ inches × $61\frac{7}{8}$ inches, variable; plus cord and plug, 24 feet $3\frac{1}{4}$ inches. The Museum of Modern Art, New York. The Sidney and Harriet Janis Collection. (Photograph © 1996 The Museum of Modern Art, New York)

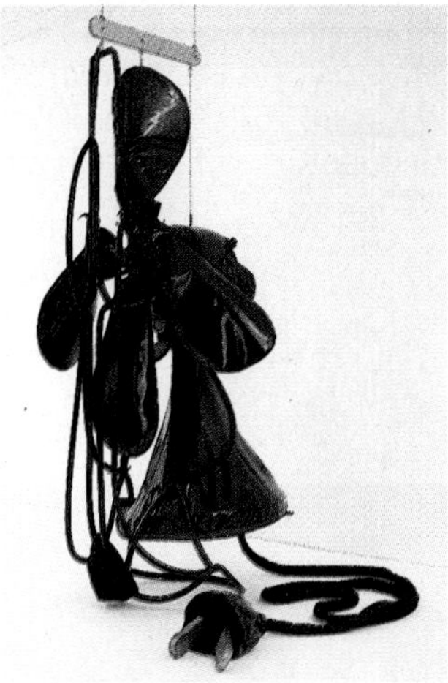

MACHINE SCULPTURE

Some avant-garde sculptors are interested not so much in the materials and products of technology but rather in revealing the machine and its powers: their works are known as "machine sculpture." As in Calder's *Antennae with*

[11]Quoted by Robert Goldwater in *What Is Modern Sculpture?* The Museum of Modern Art, New York, n.d., p. 113.

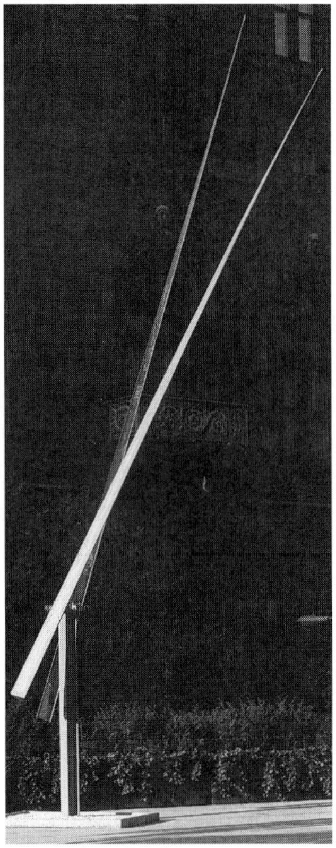

FIGURE 5-29
George Rickey, *Two Lines—Temporal I.* 1964–1977. Two stainless steel mobile blades on a stainless steel base, overall height 35 feet 4⅝ inches high. The Museum of Modern Art, New York. Mrs. Simon Guggenheim Fund. (Photograph © 1996 The Museum of Modern Art, New York; Art © 1997 George Rickey/Licensed by VAGA, New York)

Red and Blue Dots (Figure 5-15) and George Rickey's *Two Lines—Temporal I* (Figure 5-29), machine sculpture usually is "kinetic" or moving sculpture; but the motion of machine sculpture, unlike these works, is primarily a result of mechanical rather than natural forces. Sculptors in this tradition, going back to the ideas and work of László Moholy-Nagy after World War I, welcome the machine and its sculptural possibilities. Rivera hides his machine under *Brussels Construction* (Figure 5-19), but many machine sculptors expose their machines. They are interested not only in the power of the machine but also in the mechanisms that make that power possible. George Rickey, the literary prophet of machine sculpture, writes that "A machine *is* not a projection of anything. The crank-shaft exists in its own right; it is the image. . . . The concreteness of machines is heartening."[12]

Perception Key

TWO LINES—TEMPORAL I AND *HOMAGE TO NEW YORK*

1. Although depending upon air currents for its motion, Rickey's *Two-Lines—Temporal I* (Figure 5-29) is basically a machine—two thirty-five-foot stainless steel "needles" balanced on knife-edge fulcrums. Is this work just an image of a machine? Or does it suggest other images? Does its subject matter include more than just machinery? As you reflect about this, can you imagine perhaps more appropriate places than the Museum of Modern Art for this work?
2. Is Jean Tinguely's *Homage to New York* (Figure 5-30) an image of a machine? Does its subject matter include more than just machinery?

A good case can be made, we believe, for placing *Two Lines—Temporal I* in a grove of tall trees. Despite its mechanical character this work belongs, like Calder's *Antennae with Red and Blue Dots* (Figure 5-15) and Smith's *Cubi X* (Figure 5-25), in nature. Otherwise the lyrical poetry of its gentle swaying is reduced to a metronome. But even in its location in New York, it is much more than just an image of machinery. *Two Lines—Temporal I* suggests something of the skeletal structure and vertical stretch of New York's buildings as well as something of the sway of the skyscrapers as we see them against the sky.

Tinguely is dedicated to humanizing the machine. His *Homage to New York* (Figure 5-30), exhibited at the Museum of Modern Art in 1960, is a better example than *Two Lines—Temporal I* of the image of the machine in its own right. The mechanical parts, collected from junk heaps and dismembered from their original machines, apparently stood out sharply, and yet they were linked together by their spatial locations, shapes, and textures, and sometimes by nervelike wires. Only the old player piano was intact. As the piano played, it was accompanied by howls and other weird sounds in irregular patterns that seemed to be issuing from the wheels, gears, and rods, as if they were painfully communicating with each other in some form of mechanical speech. Some of the machinery that runs New

[12]George Rickey, *Art and Artist,* University of California Press, Berkeley and Los Angeles, 1956, p. 172.

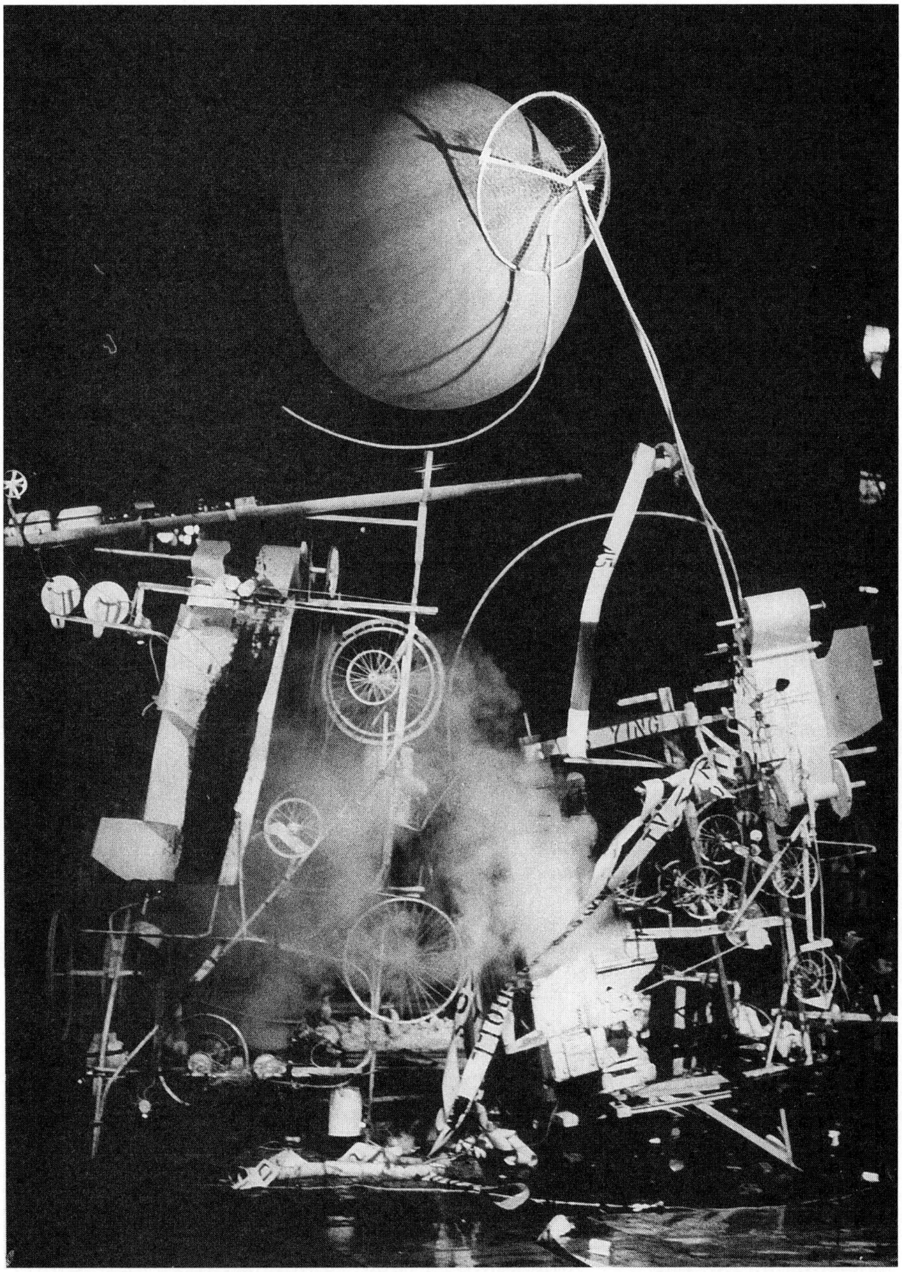

FIGURE 5-30
Jean Tinguely, *Homage to New York*. 1960. Exhibited at the Museum of Modern Art, New York. (Photograph David Gahr; Art © 1997 Artists Rights Society [ARS], NY/ADAGP, Paris)

York City was exposed as vulnerable, pathetic, and comic, but Tinguely humanized this machinery as he exposed it. Even death was suggested, for *Homage to New York* was self-destructing: the piano was electronically wired for burning and, in turn, the whole structure collapsed.

Rather than exposing the machine, sculptors such as Len Lye are more interested in manifesting its powers. Works of this type are usually highly expensive and, up to the present time, rarely exhibited. Unfortunately, it is also very difficult to appreciate their effectiveness except by direct parti-

FIGURE 5-31
Len Lye, *The Loop*. 1963. Stainless steel, 60 × 6 inches. The Art Institute of Chicago. Barbara Ness Smith and Solomon Byron Smith Purchase Fund. (Photograph © 1997 The Art Institute of Chicago)

cipation. One hopes, however, that more of this kind of sculpture will be made available. Lye's *The Loop* (Figure 5-31) was first exhibited in Buffalo in 1965, and he provided the following description in the exhibition catalog:

> The Loop, a twenty-two foot strip of polished steel, is formed into a band, which rests on its back on a magnetized bed. The action starts when the charged magnets pull the loop of steel downwards, and then release it suddenly. As it struggles to resume its natural shape, the steel band bounds upwards and lurches from end to end with simultaneous leaping and rocking motions, orbiting powerful reflections at the viewer and emitting fanciful musical tones which pulsate in rhythm with The Loop. Occasionally, as the boundless Loop reaches its greatest height, it strikes a suspended ball, causing it to emit a different yet harmonious musical note, and so it dances to a weird quavering composition of its own making.[13]

In works such as *The Loop,* the machine is programmed independently of the environment. In "cyborg [cybernetic organism] sculpture," the machine, by means of feedback, is integrated with its environment, often including the participant. Thus the sixteen pivoting polychromed plates of Nicolas Schöffer's aluminum and steel frame *CYSP I* (Figure 5-32)—a name composed of the first two letters of "cybernetics" and "spatio-dynamics"—are operated by small motors located under their axis. Built into the structure are photoelectric cells and microphones sensitive to a wide range of variations in the fields of color, light, and sound. These changes feed into an electronic brain (housed in the base of the sculpture), which, in turn, activates four sets of motor-powered wheels. Depending on the stimuli, the sculpture will move more or less rapidly about the floor, turning more or less sharp angles. Blue, for example, excites rapid movement and makes the plates turn quickly. Darkness and silence are also exciting, whereas intense light and noise are calming. Complex stimuli produce, as in human beings, unpredictable behavior. Moreover, the participant takes part in making the sculpture "come alive." In such work, technical methodology is extended not only to the sculpture but also to ourselves.

Machine sculptures are being developed in many forms. For example, there are water-driven sculptures, works suspended in midair by magnets or by jets of air or water, synthetic membranes stretched like sails by mechanical forces, color and motion produced by polarized light, and mechanically powered environmental sculpture (although such power is absent in *The Bus Driver,* Figure 5-23). Many of these developments are more experimental than artistic—the engineer often dominates the artist. But the story is just beginning, and it will be fascinating to watch its unfolding. At the very least, machine sculpture has had considerable stimulating effect upon the more conventional species of sculpture. No machinery, for instance, is involved in Barbara Hepworth's *Pelagos* (Figure 5-18). The structure was based on carved wood and then the interior was painted. But like

[13]*Len Lye's Bounding Steel Sculptures,* Howard Wise Gallery, New York, 1965.

FIGURE 5-32
Nicholas Schöffer, *CYSP I*. 1956. Aluminum and steel. (Courtesy Nicholas Schöffer)

much of the work of Rickey (Figure 5-29) and Schöffer (Figure 5-32), Hepworth calls on the environment—in this case the landscape and the inspiration of water and wind—for assistance. And, of course, the right kind of landscape is all-important for the full realization of this graceful structure.

EARTH SCULPTURE

Finally, another avant-garde sculpture—"earth sculpture"—even goes so far as to make the earth itself the medium, the site, and the subject matter. The proper spatial selection becomes absolutely essential, for the earth usually must be taken where it is found. Structures are traced in plains, meadows, sand, snow, etc., in order to help make us stop and perceive and enjoy the "form site"—the earth transformed to be more meaningful. Usually nature rapidly breaks up the form and returns the site to its less ordered state. Accordingly, many earth sculptors have a special need for the photographer to preserve their art.

PERCEPTION KEY
EARTH SCULPTURE

Study Michael Heizer's *Circumflex* (Figure 5-33), a 120-foot-long design "carved" out of the bed of a dry lake in Nevada.

1. Does the fact that *Circumflex* is now silted up disqualify this work of art? As you reflect about this, does the fact that the work has been elegantly photographed become relevant?
2. Does *Circumflex* help bring out and make you notice the "earthiness" of the earth? The line of the mountain in the distance? The relation of the plain to the mountain?
3. Does *Circumflex* appear too large, too small, or just right in relation to the landscape?
4. Why do you think Heizer used such a long, free-flowing line juxtaposed against an almost geometrical oval?
5. Suppose works like this were found abundantly throughout the United States. Would you find this objectionable?

FIGURE 5-33
Michael Heizer, *Circumflex*. 1968. Massacre Creek Dry Lake, 120 feet long.

FIGURE 5-34
Louise Nevelson, *City on the High Mountain*. 1983. Steel (painted black), 20 feet 6 inches × 23 inches × 13 feet 6 inches. Storm King Art Center, Mountainville, New York. Purchase.

SCULPTURE IN THE OPEN: "FIELD COMPLEX"

Sculpture in open spaces is by no means a new idea, but the modern practice of placing monumental steel constructions in open natural settings is owing to David Smith's decision to permit some of his work to weather in the open. (See his *Cubi X,* Figure 5-25.) His legendary worksite at Bolton Landing, New York, where he stored many of his pieces, began to attract visitors in the late 1950s. By the early 1960s, he was placing his work carefully to match the setting and he inspired others to create open spaces for large sculpture. Smith said he did not begin placing his work outside with a preconceived "field complex," but one developed as he worked.

One of the most dramatic of such spaces is the Storm King Art Center in Mountainville, New York. Louise Nevelson, whose work in wood often employs findings and remnants, set *City on the High Mountain* (Figure 5-34) near a grove of tall trees at Storm King Art Center. The siting permits the viewer to walk completely around the work, observing the play of light and shadow as it changes from moment to moment and season to season. Like many of her wood pieces, this steel construction is painted uniformly black. The variety of shapes and visual textures creates a dynamic that leads the viewer's eye from level to level, left and right, up and down, without and within.

FIGURE 5-35
Alexander Liberman, *Iliad*. 1974–1976. Steel (painted orange), 36 feet × 54 feet 7 inches × 19 feet 7 inches. Storm King Art Center, Mountainville, New York. Gift of Ralph E. Ogden Foundation.

Alexander Liberman, who, like Nevelson, was born in Kiev, Russia, worked with gas storage tanks, full size, cutting them and balancing them against one another in various configurations. His *Iliad* (Figure 5-35) is one of his several gigantic works at the Storm King Art Center. It appears to be bright red (officially, it is orange) and shows up dramatically against the grass and sky. The high finish glistens, absorbs shadows, and looms over the viewer. The title implies a heroic quality, a martial subject matter, and if one examines the work, one can imagine shields, perhaps weapons of various sorts. But the work most essentially organizes visual space, color, and mass. Yet, as one approaches the work there is a playfulness about it that invites the viewer to participate by walking around close to it, then back to absorb its siting in relation to rolling lawn, trees, and mountain. This work might suffer from compression were it to be sited in a small city park or in an urban plaza. In its present setting, the subtle interrelation of shapes unveils slowly to the peripatetic viewer walking in response to the light and shifting visual elements.

Perception Key

CITY ON THE HIGH MOUNTAIN AND *ILIAD*

1. Compare these two works for their respect of their materials. Is there a sense of "truth to materials" in these works? Is it more in one than the other?
2. These works by design are in a natural setting, but by virtue of their coloration

and structure, they are clearly not natural. Why would such a contrast be desirable for a monumental work of sculpture? Would they be better works if they resembled natural objects?
3. What organizes the shapes of each of these works? Do you see a principle of organization? Do they appear haphazard or carefully planned?
4. How would you talk about the content of these two works? Would their placement be important in a discussion of their content?

SCULPTURE IN PUBLIC PLACES

Sculpture has traditionally shared its location with major buildings, sometimes acting as decoration on the building, as in many churches, or acting as a center point of interest, as in the original placement of Michelangelo's *David,* which was positioned carefully in front of the Palazzo Vecchio, where Florence used to receive foreign envoys. It stood as a warning not to underestimate the Florentines. Many small towns throughout the world have public sculpture that commemorates wars or other important events.

With the rise of shopping malls across the United States and much of the rest of the world, monumental sculpture has often been used as decoration and as a focal point for defining both interior and exterior space. One interesting example is Naum Gabo's *Rotterdam Construction* (Figure 5-36) in front of De Bijenkorf, a large store in Rotterdam designed by Marcel Breuer, a monumentally successful solution to what might seem to have been an impossible commission. The open vertical construction, rooted like a tree but branching out more like the cranes and bridges of Rotterdam, brings out with striking clarity the compact horizontal mass of the building. Rarely have sculpture and architecture achieved such powerful synthesis.

Gabo's work was accepted by the public. However, a more intense display of public alarm was raised when the U.S. government installed Richard Serra's *Tilted Arc* (Figure 5-37) in Federal Plaza in lower Manhattan. People complained that they could not see over it, that it impeded their traffic patterns and forced them to walk out of their way around it, and that it was simply ugly. Serra is a modern sculptor whose work often consists of large panels of steel or lead balanced against one another. Serra was commissioned to place his work on this site—for which it was designed—and a panel of experts selected by the government approved the design before it was installed. When the public outcry grew strong the government relented and asked Serra to remove the work. He would not do so. Finally the government removed it, and what remains are the photographs.

On the other hand, one of the most successful of contemporary public sculptures has been Maya Ying Lin's *Vietnam Veterans Memorial* (Figure 5-38) in Washington, D.C. Since the Vietnam war was both unpopular and a major defeat, fears were that the memorial might stir public antagonism. However, the result has been quite the opposite. The piece is a sloping black granite wall, V-shaped, which descends from grade to ten feet below grade,

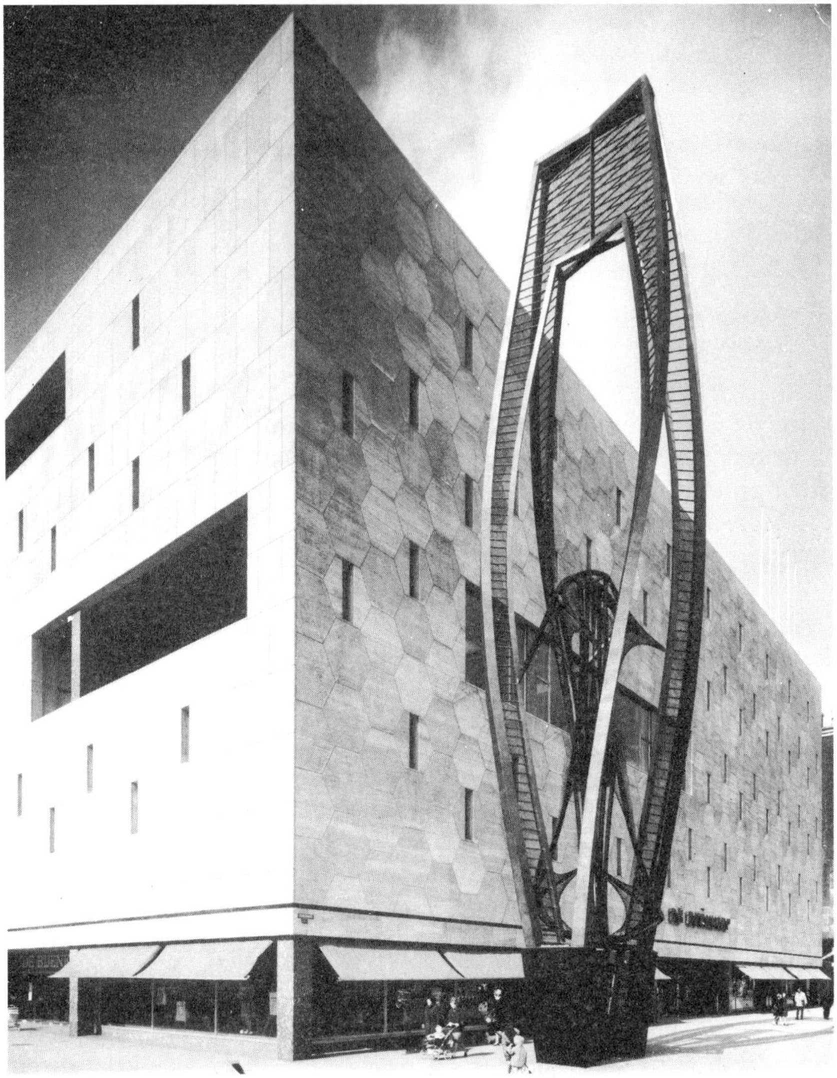

FIGURE 5-36
Naum Gabo, *Rotterdam Construction*. 1954–1957. Steel, bronze wire, free stone substructure, 85 feet high. Copyright, Tom Kroeze, Rotterdam.

FIGURE 5-37
Richard Serra, *Tilted Arc*. 1981. Corten steel; 12 × 120 feet × 2½ inches. Installed Federal Plaza, New York City. Destroyed by the U.S. government March 15, 1989. (Photograph courtesy Gagosian Gallery, New York; Art © 1997 Richard Serra/Artists Rights Society [ARS], New York)

FIGURE 5-38
Maya Ying Lin, *The Vietnam Veterans Memorial*. 1982. Black granite, V-shaped, 493 feet long, 10 feet high on center. Washington, D.C. (David Noble/FPG, International)

incised with more than 58,000 names of dead Americans, embedded in a gently sloping piece of land with other memorial sculptures. Those who visit walk along its length, absorbing the endless list of names as they walk. The impact of the memorial grows in part because the list of names grows with each step down the slope. Visitors respond to the memorial by touching the names, sometimes taking rubbings away with them, sometimes simply touching and weeping. Glenna Goodacre's *Vietnam Women's Memorial* (Figure 5-39) has been installed nearby. It is radically different from Maya Ying Lin's piece and celebrates the efforts of over 265,000 women who served in Vietnam. Goodacre presents the figures of three nurses and a wounded soldier in a manner similar to George Segal's bus driver, although the patinaed bronze of Goodacre's sculpture is less startling than Segal's white plaster. The two pieces, Lin's and Goodacre's, offer unusual contrast in a memorial setting.

FIGURE 5-39
Glenna Goodacre, *Vietnam Women's Memorial: Three Nurses and a Wounded Soldier*. Bronze. 1993. Washington, D.C. (Jerry Sieve/FPG, International)

PERCEPTION KEY

TILTED ARC, THE *VIETNAM VETERANS MEMORIAL*, AND THE *VIETNAM WOMEN'S MEMORIAL*

1. Richard Serra's *Tilted Arc* (Figure 5-37)—a 12-foot-high, 112-foot-long wall of steel—swept across the Federal Plaza in downtown Manhattan, New York City, provoking a storm of controversy that even reached the courts. The majority of the people—apparently the great majority—who work in the buildings around the Plaza as well as nearby dwellers charged that the Arc obstructed

the views; prevented comfortable access across the Plaza and to the entrance of the Jacob K. Javits Building (the main building); made large social and cultural gatherings impossible; was ugly in appearance; and attracted obnoxious graffiti. They wanted the General Services Administration, who commissioned the work, to have the sculpture removed. Serra argued that the work was "site-specific"—integrally related to the structures that compose the architectural environment wherein the Arc is placed— and that to remove it was to destroy it. A committee of distinguished critics unanimously backed Serra. Nevertheless, the General Services Administration had the sculpture removed. Do you agree with their decision? What is at stake in a confrontation of this sort? Is it appropriate for a public sculpture to stir controversy?

2. What effect does public acceptance have on your attitude toward the relative success as works of sculpture of *Tilted Arc* or the *Vietnam Veterans Memorial?* What structural qualities does the *Veterans Memorial* possess in its siting that are not possessed by *Tilted Arc?* What shapes do the two works share? Do you think that the New York public would have been more accepting of *Tilted Arc* if it had been incised with the 58,000 names of the American dead in Vietnam? How would such a change have altered its value as sculpture?
3. Which of these three works would you think is most popular with the viewing public? Which of the three would be most instantly recognizable as sculpture? Why? Is "recognizability" an important factor in evaluating sculpture?
4. Lin's piece has been described as a "national tombstone," while Goodacre's piece has been described as "memorial statuary," similar to the angels often placed over people's graves. Are these descriptions fair? Are they in any way accurate?

SUMMARY

Sculpture is perceived differently from painting, engaging more acutely our sense of touch and the motion of our body. Whereas painting is more about the visual appearance of things, sculpture is more about things as three-dimensional masses. Whereas painting only *represents* voluminosity and density, sculpture presents these qualities. Sculpture in the round, especially, brings out the three-dimensionality of objects. No object is more important to us than our body, and its "strange thickness" is always "with" us. When the human body is the subject matter, sculpture more than any other art reveals a material counterpoint for our mental images of our bodies. Traditional sculpture is made either by modeling or carving. Many contemporary sculptures, however, are made by assembling preformed pieces of material. New sculptural techniques and materials have opened up developments in avant-garde sculpture that defy classification. Nonetheless, contemporary sculptors, generally, have emphasized "truth to materials," respect for the medium that is organized by their forms. They have also had to come to grips with modern technology, either protesting its misuses or interpreting its positive aspects.

CHAPTER 5 BIBLIOGRAPHY

Anderson, Wayne. *American Sculpture in Process: 1930/1970.* Boston: New York Graphic Society, 1975.

Beardsley, John. *A Landscape for Modern Sculpture: Storm King Art Center.* New York: Abbeville, 1985.

Burnham, Jack. *Beyond Modern Sculpture.* New York: George Braziller, 1967.

Elsen, Albert E. *Origins of Modern Sculpture.* New York: George Braziller, 1974.

Giedion-Welcker, Carola. *Contemporary Sculpture: An Evolution in Volume and Space.* New York: George Wittenborn, 1960.

Hammacher, A. M. *The Evolution of Modern Sculpture.* London: Thames & Hudson, 1969.

James, Phillip (ed.). *Henry Moore on Sculpture.* London: Macdonald, 1966.

Kelly, James J. *The Sculptural Idea,* 3rd ed. Minneapolis: Burgess, 1981.

Krauss, Rosalind E. *Passages in Modern Sculpture.* New York: Viking, 1977.

Licht, Fred. *Sculpture: 19th & 20th Centuries.* Greenwich, Conn.: New York Graphic Society, 1967.

Martin, F. David. *Sculpture and Enlivened Space: Aesthetics and History.* Lexington, Ky.: University Press of Kentucky, 1981.

Read, Herbert E. *Modern Sculpture.* New York: Thames & Hudson, 1985.

Rodin, Auguste. *Art.* London: Hodder & Stoughton, 1912.

Sieber, Roy, and Roslyn Adele Walker. *African Art in the Cycle of Life.* Washington, D.C.: National Museum of African Art, 1987.

Trier, Edvard. *Form and Space,* rev. ed. New York: Frederick A. Praeger, 1968.

Wittkower, Rudolf. *Sculpture: Processes and Principles.* New York: Harper and Row, 1977.

CHAPTER 5 WEBSITES

African Art (aesthetics, culture)

World Wide Web: **http://www.lib.virginia.edu/dic/exhib/93.ray.aa/African**

Classic Art

Anonymous FTP: Address: **banzai.cecm.sfu.ca** Path: **/pub/Art/**

Native American Art Gallery (arts and crafts, culture)

World Wide Web: **http://www.info1.com/Naag/**

Palmer Museum of Art (University of Pennsylvania's museum)

World Wide Web: **http://cac.psu.edu/~mtd120/palmer/**

Resources for Art Students (lists of net sites, CD-ROMs, and other resources)

World Wide Web: **http://www.uky.edu/Artsource/sourcelists/electresources.txt**

Rosen Sculpture Exhibition (outdoor sculpture competition and exhibition)

World Wide Web: **http://xx.acs.appstate.edu/art/rosen/main_menu.html**

CHAPTER 6

ARCHITECTURE

Buildings constantly assault us. Our only temporary escape is to the rarely accessible wilderness. We can close the novel, shut off the music, refuse to go to a play or dance, sleep through a movie, shut our eyes to a painting or a sculpture. But we cannot escape from buildings for very long, even in the wilderness. Fortunately, however, sometimes buildings possess artistic quality—and sometimes they are revelatory, that is, they are architecture—drawing us to them rather than pushing us away or making us ignore them. They make our living space more livable.

CENTERED SPACE

Painters do not command real three-dimensional space: they only feign it. Sculptors can mold out into space, but generally they do not enfold an enclosed or inner space for our movement. The "holes" in the sculpture of Henry Moore (Figure 5-20), for example, are to be walked around, not into, whereas our passage through its inner spaces is one of the conditions under which the solids and voids of a work of architecture have their effect. In a sense, architecture is a great hollowed-out sculpture that we perceive by moving about both outside and inside. Space is the material of the architect, the primeval cutter,[1] who carves apart an inner space from an outer space in such a way that both spaces become more fully perceptible and, in turn, more intrinsically valuable.

Inner and outer space come together to the earth to form a centered and

[1]This meaning is suggested by the Greek *architectón.*

illuminated context or clearing. Centered space is the positioned interrelationships of things organized around some paramount thing as the place to which the other things seem to converge. Sometimes this center is a natural thing, such as a great mountain, river, canyon, or forest. Sometimes the center is a natural site enhanced by a work of architecture. Listen to Martin Heidegger, the great German thinker, describing a bridge:

> The bridge swings over the stream "with ease and power." It does not just connect banks that are already there. The banks emerge as banks only as the bridge crosses the stream. The bridge designedly causes them to lie across from each other. One side is set off against the other by the bridge. Nor do the banks stretch along the stream as indifferent border stripes of the dry land. With the banks, the bridge brings to the stream the one and the other expanse of the landscape lying behind them. It brings stream and bank and land into each other's neighborhood. The bridge gathers the earth as landscape around the stream. Thus, it guides and attends the stream through the meadows. Resting upright in the stream's bed, the bridge piers bear the swing of the arches that leave the stream's waters to their own course. The waters may wander on quiet and gay, the sky's floods from storm or thaw may shoot past the piers in torrential waves—the bridge is ready for the sky's weather and its fickle nature. Even where the bridge covers the stream, it holds its flow up to the sky by taking it for a moment under the vaulted gateway and then setting it free once more.
>
> The bridge lets the stream run its course and at the same time grants their way to mortals so that they may come and go from shore to shore. Bridges lead in many ways. The city bridge leads from the precincts of the castle to the cathedral square; the river bridge near the country town brings wagons and horse teams to the surrounding villages. The old stone bridge's humble brook crossing gives to the harvest wagon its passage from the fields into the villages and carries the lumber cart from the field path to the road. The highway bridge is tied into the network of long-distance traffic, paced as calculated for maximum yield. Always and ever differently the bridge escorts the lingering and hastening ways of men to and fro, so that they may get to other banks and in the end, as mortals, to the other side.[2]

If we are near such bridges we tend to be drawn into their clearing, for centered space has an overpowering dynamism that captures both our attention and our bodies. Centered space is centripetal, insisting upon drawing us in. There is an inrush that is difficult to escape, that overwhelms and makes us acquiescent. We perceive space not as a receptacle containing things but rather as a context energized by the positioned interrelationships of things. Centered space has a pulling power that, even in our most harassed moments, we can hardly help feeling. In such places as the piazza before St. Peter's (Figure 6-1), we walk slowly and speak softly. We find ourselves in the presence of a power that seems beyond our control. We feel the sublimity of space, but, at the same time, the centeredness beckons and welcomes us.

[2]Martin Heidegger, *Poetry, Language, Thought,* Albert Hofstadter (trans.). Copyright © 1971 by Martin Heidegger. By permission of Harper & Row, Publishers, Inc., pp. 152ff.

FIGURE 6-1
Piazza before St. Peter's. (Anderson/Art Resource, New York)

SPACE AND ARCHITECTURE

Architecture—as opposed to mere engineering—is the creative conservation of space. Architects perceive the centers of space in nature, and build to preserve these centers and make them more vital. Architects are confronted by centered spaces that desire to be made, through them, into works. These spaces of nature are not offspring of architects alone but appearances that step up to them, so to speak, and demand protection. If an architect succeeds in carrying through these appeals, the power of the natural space streams forth through that person and the work rises. Architects are the shepherds of space. In turn, the paths around their shelters lead us away from our ordinary preoccupations demanding the use of space. We come to rest. Instead of our using up space, space takes possession of us with a ten-fingered grasp. We have a place to dwell.

CHARTRES

On a hot summer day some years ago, following the path of Henry Adams, who wrote *Mont-Saint-Michel and Chartres,* one of the authors was attempting to drive from Mont-Saint-Michel to Chartres in time to catch the setting sun through the western rose window of Chartres Cathedral. The following is an account of this experience:

> In my rushing anxiety—I had to be in Paris the following day and I had never been to Chartres before—I became oblivious of space except as providing land-

FIGURE 6-2
Chartres Cathedral. (Lucas Abreu/Image Bank)

marks for my time-clocked progress. Thus I have no significant memories of the towns and countrysides I hurried through. Late that afternoon the two spires of Chartres (Figures 6-2 and 6-3), like two strangely woven strands of rope let down from the heavens, gradually came into focus. The blue dome of the sky also became visible for the first time, centering as I approached more and more firmly around the axis of those spires. "In lovely blueness blooms the steeple with metal roof" (Hölderlin). The surrounding fields and then the town, coming out now in all their specificity, grew into tighter unity with the church and sky. Later, I recalled a passage from Aeschylus: "The pure sky desires to penetrate the earth, and the earth is filled with love so that she longs for blissful unity with the sky. The rain falling from the sky impregnates the earth, so that she gives birth to plants and grain for beasts and men." No one rushed in or out or around the church. The space around seemed alive and dense with slow currents all ultimately being pulled to and through the central portal.[3] Inside, the space, although spacious far beyond the scale of practical human needs, seemed strangely compressed, full of forces thrusting and counterthrusting in dynamic interrelations. Slowly, in the cool silence inlaid with stone, I was drawn down the long nave, following the stately rhythms of the bays and piers. But my eyes also followed the

FIGURE 6-3
Chartres Cathedral, the West Front. 1194–1260. (Marburg/Art Resource, New York)

[3]Chartres, like most Gothic churches, is shaped roughly like a recumbent Latin cross:

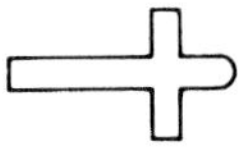

The front (Figure 6-3)—with its large circular window shaped like a rose and the three vertical windows or lancets beneath—faces west. The apse or eastern end of the building contains the high altar. The nave is the central and largest aisle leading from the central portal to the high altar. But before the altar is reached, the transept cuts across the nave. The crossing is the meeting point of the nave and the transept. Both the northern and southern facades of the transept of Chartres contain, like the western facade, glorious rose windows.

vast vertical stretches far up into the shifting shadows of the vaultings. It was as if I were being borne aloft. Yet I continued down the narrowing tunnel of the nave, but more and more slowly as the pull of the space above held back the pull of the space below. At the crossing of the transept, the flaming colors, especially the reds, of the northern and southern roses transfixed my slowing pace, and then I turned back at last to the western rose and the three lancets beneath—a delirium of color, dominantly blue, was pouring through. Earthbound on the crossing, the blaze of the Without was merging with the Within. Radiant space took complete possession of my senses. In the protective grace of this sheltering space, even the outer space which I had dismissed in the traffic of my driving seemed to converge around the center of this crossing. Instead of being alongside things—the church, the town, the fields, the sky, the sun—I was with them, at one with them. This housing of holiness made me feel at home in this strange land.

LIVING SPACE

Living space is the feeling of the positioning of things in the environment, the liberty of movement, and the appeal of paths as directives. Taking possession of space is our first gesture as infants, and sensitivity to the position of other things is a prerequisite of life. Space infiltrates through all our senses, and our sensations of everything influence our perception of space. A breeze broadens the spaciousness of a room that opens on a garden. A sound tells us something about the surfaces and shape of that room. A cozy temperature brings the furniture and walls into more intimate relationships. The smell of books gives that space a personality. Each of our senses helps record the positioning of things, expressed in such terms as "up-down," "left-right," and "near-far." These recordings require a reference system with a center. With abstract space, as when we estimate distances visually, the center is the zero point located between the eyes. With living space, since all the senses are involved, the whole body is a center. Furthermore, when we relate to a place of special value, such as the home, a "configurational center" is formed, a place that is a gathering point around which a field of interest is structured. If we oversimplify, we can say that for Romans, it was the city of Rome to which they most naturally belong, constituting their configurational center—with medieval people it was the church and castle, with Babbitt the office, with Sartre the café, and with de Gaulle the nation. But for most people at almost any time, although probably more so in contemporary times, there are more than a couple of centers. Often these are more or less confused and changing. In living space, nevertheless, places, principal directions, and distances arrange themselves around configurational centers.

FOUR NECESSITIES OF ARCHITECTURE

The architect's professional life is perhaps more difficult than that of any other artist. Architecture is a peculiarly public art because buildings generally have a social function, and many buildings require public funds. More than other artists, the architects must consider the public. If they do not, very few of their plans are likely to materialize. Thus architects must be psychologists, sociologists, economists, businesspeople, politicians, and courtiers. They must also be engineers, for they must be able to construct structurally stable buildings. And then they need luck. Even as famous an architect as Frank Lloyd Wright could not prevent the destruction, for economic reasons, of one of his masterpieces—the Imperial Hotel in Tokyo.

Architects have to take into account four basic and closely interrelated necessities: technical requirements, use, spatial relationships, and content. To succeed, their structures must adjust themselves to these necessities. As for what time will do to their creations, they can only prepare with foresight and hope. Wright's hotel withstood all the earthquakes, but ultimately every building is peculiarly susceptible to the whims of future taste.

TECHNICAL REQUIREMENTS OF ARCHITECTURE

Of the four necessities, the technical requirements of a building are the most obvious. Buildings must stand (and withstand). Architects must know the materials and their potentialities, how to put the materials together, and how the materials will work on a particular site. Stilt construction, for instance, will not withstand earthquakes—and so architects are engineers. But they are something more as well—artists. In solving their technical problems, they must also make their forms revelatory. Their buildings must illuminate something significant that we would otherwise fail to perceive.

Consider, for example, the relationship between the engineering requirements and artistic qualities of the Parthenon, 447–432 B.C. (Figures 6-4 and 6-5). The engineering was superb, but unfortunately the building was almost destroyed in 1687, when it was being used as an ammunition dump

FIGURE 6-4
The Athenian Acropolis with the Parthenon. 447–432 B.C. (Marvin E. Newman/Image Bank)

FIGURE 6-5
The Parthenon. 447–432 B.C. (Marburg/Art Resource, New York)

by the Turks and was hit by a shell from a Venetian gun. Basically the technique used was post-and-lintel (or beam) construction. Set on a base or stylobate, columns (verticals: the posts) support the architrave (horizontals: the lintel) which, in turn, compose, along with the frieze (a running low-relief sculpture on the horizontal surface above the columns), the entablature that supports the pediment and roof.

Perception Key
PARTHENON AND CHARTRES

Study the schematic drawing for the Doric order (Figure 6-6), the order followed in the Parthenon, and Figures 6-4 and 6-5.

1. What visual effect do the narrow vertical grooves or flutes carved into the marble columns of the Parthenon have?
2. The columns bulge or swell slightly. (This curvature is called "entasis.") Can you perceive the bulge in the photograph of the Parthenon?
3. Why are the columns wider at the base than at the top?
4. Why is there a capital between the top of the shaft and the architrave (the plain lintels that span the voids from column to column and compose the lowest member of the entablature)?
5. The capital is made up of three parts: the circular grooves at the bottom (called the necking); the bulging cushionlike molding (called the echinus); and the square block (called the abacus). Why the division of the capital into these three parts?
6. The columns at the corners are a couple of inches thicker than the other columns. Why?
7. The corner and adjacent columns are slightly closer together than the other columns. Is the difference perceptible in the photograph? All the columns except those in the center of each side slant slightly inward. Why?
8. Subtle refinements such as those mentioned above abound throughout the Parthenon. Few if any of them are necessary from a technical standpoint, nor were these irregularities accidental. They are found repeatedly in other Greek

temples of the time. Presumably, then, they are a result of a need to make the form of the temple mean something, to be a form-content. Presumably, then, the Parthenon can still reveal something of the values of the ancient Greeks. What? Compare those values with the values revealed by Chartres. For example, which building seems to reveal a society that places more trust in God? And what kind of God? And in what way are those subtle refinements we have cited above relevant to these questions?

FUNCTIONAL REQUIREMENTS OF ARCHITECTURE

Architects must not only make their buildings stand but also usually stand them in such a way that they reveal their function or use. One contemporary school of architects even goes so far as to claim that form must follow function. If the form succeeds in this, that is all the form should do. In any case, a form that disguises the function of a building seems to irritate almost everyone.

If form follows function in the sense that the form stands "for" the function of its building, then conventional forms or structures are often sufficient. No one is likely to mistake Chartres Cathedral for an office building. We have seen the conventional structures of too many churches and office buildings to be mistaken about this. Nor are we likely to mistake the surrounding office buildings for churches. We recognize the functions of these buildings because they are in the conventional shapes that such buildings so often possess.

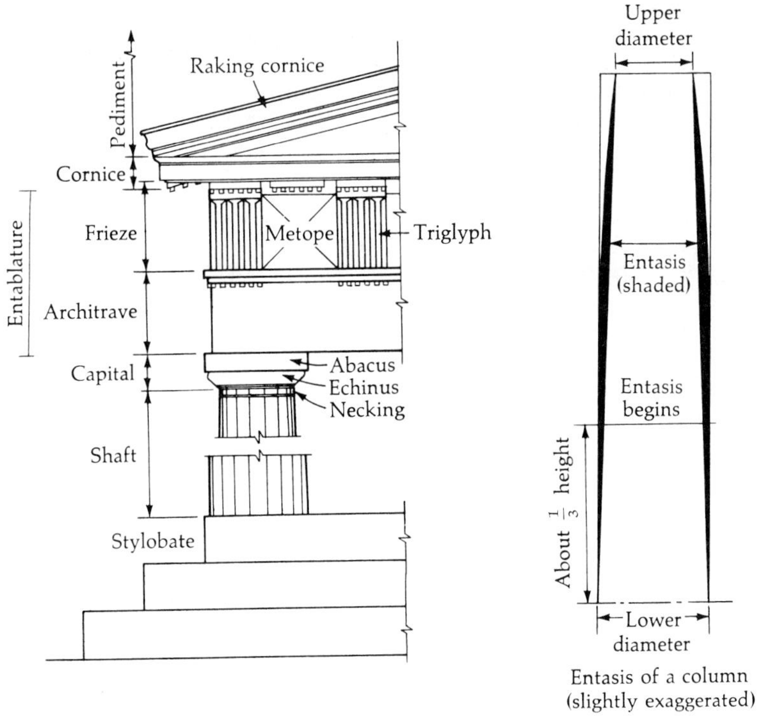

FIGURE 6-6
Elements of the Doric order. Adapted from John Ives Sewell, *A History of Western Art*, rev. ed., Holt, Rinehart and Winston, New York, 1961.

FIGURE 6-7
Robert Smirke, The British Museum. (© British Museum)

Perception Key
FUNCTION AND ARCHITECTURE

1. If the interior of Chartres Cathedral (Figure 6-3) were remodeled into a dental clinic, would you feel dissatisfied with the relationship between the new interior and the old exterior?
2. Study Figure 6-7. What is the function of this building?
3. Are you surprised to learn that this is a museum?
4. Is this building architecture?
5. Would you like to have such a building as a museum in your community? Does this involve you in the question of what architecture is?
6. In your opinion, what must a building be to be a work of architecture?

Perception Key
FORM, FUNCTION, CONTENT, AND SPACE

Study Figures 6-8 and 6-9.

1. What is the basic function of each of these buildings?
2. How do you know what the functions are? How have the respective forms revealed the functions of their buildings? And does it seem appropriate to use the term "reveal" for Figures 6-8 and 6-9? We would argue that Figures 6-8 and 6-9 are architecture because the form of the building in Figure 6-9 is revelatory of the subject matter—of the tension, anguish, striving, and ultimate concern of religious faith; whereas in Figure 6-8 the form of the building is revelatory of the stripped-down, uniform efficiency of an American business corporation. Consider every possible relevant argument against this view.
3. In Figures 6-8 and 6-9 do the buildings center and organize their surrounding space? If so, how is this accomplished?

FIGURE 6-8
Union Carbide Building, New York City. (Public Relations Department, Union Carbide Company)

FIGURE 6-9
Le Corbusier, Notre Dame-du-Haut, Ronchamps, France. (French Government Tourist Office; Art © 1997 Artists Rights Society [ARS], NY/SPADEM, Paris)

Study one of Frank Lloyd Wright's last and most famous works, the Solomon R. Guggenheim Museum in New York City (Figures 6-10 and 6-11), constructed in 1957–1959 but designed in 1943. Wright wrote:

> Here for the first time architecture appears plastic, one floor flowing into another (more like sculpture) instead of the usual superimposition of stratified layers cutting and butting into each other by way of post-and-beam construction. The whole building, cast in concrete, is more like an egg shell—in form a great simplicity—rather than like a crisscross structure. The light concrete flesh is rendered strong enough everywhere to do its work by embedded filaments of steel either separate or in mesh. The structural calculations are thus those of cantilever and continuity rather than the post and beam. The net result of such construction is a greater repose, the atmosphere of the quiet unbroken wave: no meeting of the eye with abrupt changes of form.[4]

The term "cantilever" refers to a structural principle in architecture in which one end of a horizontal form is fixed—usually in a wall—while the other end juts out over space. Steel beam construction makes such forms possible in modern buildings, some of which have, like the Guggenheim Museum, forms extending fluidly into space.

[4]Reprinted from *The Solomon R. Guggenheim Museum,* copyright 1960, by permission of the publishers, The Solomon R. Guggenheim Foundation and Horizon Press, New York, pp. 16ff.

FIGURE 6-10
Frank Lloyd Wright, The Solomon R. Guggenheim Museum, New York City. 1957–1959. (David Heald © The Solomon R. Guggenheim Museum)

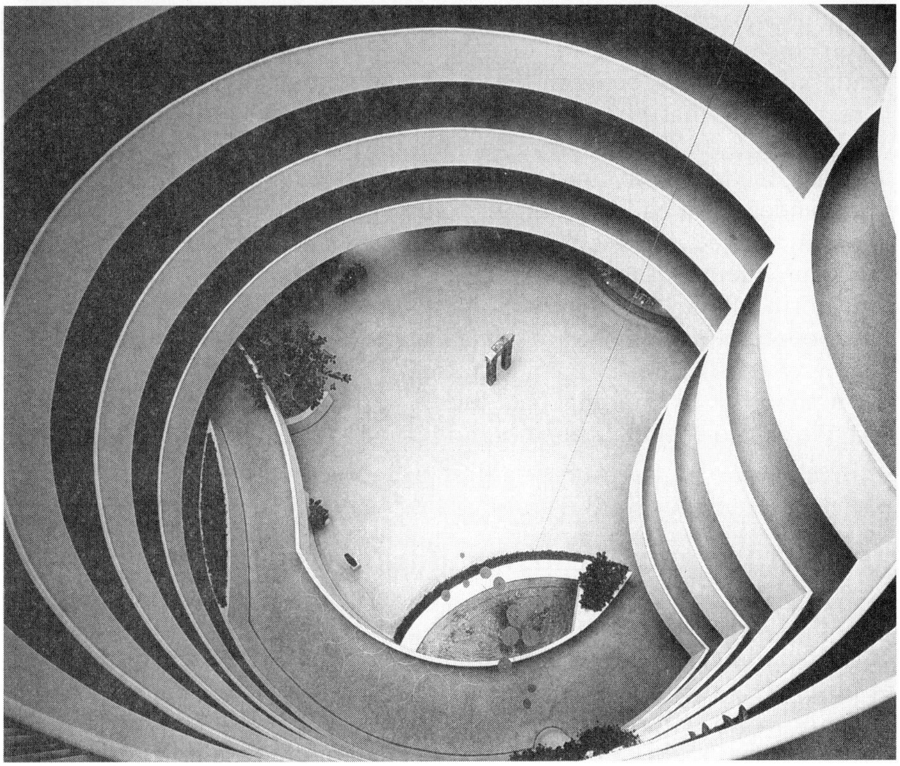

FIGURE 6-11
Frank Lloyd Wright, The Solomon R. Guggenheim Museum, New York City. 1957–1959. Interior. (Robert E. Mates © The Solomon R. Guggenheim Museum)

Perception Key
GUGGENHEIM MUSEUM

1. Does the exterior of this building harmonize with the interior?
2. Does the form reveal the building as an art museum?
3. Elevators take us to the top of the building, and then we participate with the exhibited works of art by walking down the spiraling ramp. This enables us to see each work from many perspectives. Does this seem to you to be an interesting, efficient, and comfortable way of exhibiting works of art?
4. The front of the museum faces Fifth Avenue. The surrounding buildings are tall rectangular solids evenly lined up along the sidewalks. Did Wright succeed in bringing his museum into a harmonious spatial relationship with these other buildings? Or was his purpose perhaps to make his museum stand out in sharp contrast, like a plant among inorganic shapes? But if so, does the museum fit successfully into the spatial context—"the power and embrace of the positioned interrelationships of things"?
5. Originally the museum was to have been situated in Central Park. Do you think that a park site would have been better than its present site?

SPATIAL REQUIREMENTS OF ARCHITECTURE

Wright solved his technical problems (cantilevering, etc.) and his functional problems (efficient and commodious exhibition of works of art) with considerable success. Moreover, the building reveals itself as a museum. But, if you can, check the site for yourself and see if you are satisfied with the spatial relationships between the museum and the surrounding buildings. It seems to us that Wright was not completely successful in this respect, and this, in turn, detracts from some of the "rightness" of the building. In any case, the technical, functional, and spatial necessities are obviously interdependent. If a building is going to be artistically meaningful—that is to say, if it is to be architecture—it must satisfy all four necessities—technical requirements, use, spatial relationships, and content—to some degree or its form will fail to be a form-content. A building that is technically awry with poor lighting or awkward passageways or cramped rooms will distract from any artistic meaning, and so usually will a form that fails to reveal the function of its building, or a form that fails to fit into its spatial context. We will go about our business and ignore those kinds of forms as much as possible.

REVELATORY REQUIREMENTS OF ARCHITECTURE

The function or use of a building is an essential part of the subject matter of that building, what the architect interprets or gives insight into by means of his form. The function of the Union Carbide Building (Figure 6-8) is to house offices. The form of that building reveals that function. But does this function exhaust the subject matter of this building? Is only function revealed? Would we, perhaps, be closer to the truth by claiming that involved with this office function are values closely associated with, but nevertheless distinguishable from, this function? That somehow other values, besides functional ones, are interpreted in architecture? That values from the architect's society somehow impose themselves, and the architect must be sensitive to them? We think that even if architects criticize or react against the values of their time, they must take account of them. Otherwise, the architects' buildings would stand for little more than projections of their personal idiosyncracies.

We are claiming that the essential values of contemporary society are a part of all artists' subject matter, part of what they must interpret in their work, and this—because of the public character of architecture—is especially so with architects. The way architects (and artists generally) are influenced by the values of their society has been given many explanations. According to the art historian Walter Abell, the state of mind of a society influences architects directly. The historical and social circumstances generate psychosocial tensions and latent imagery in the minds of the members of a culture. Architects, among the most sensitive members of a society, release this tension by condensing this imagery in their art. The psyche of the artist, explained by Abell by means of psychoanalytic theory and social psychology, creates the basic forms of art; but this psyche is controlled by the state of mind of the artist's society, which, in turn, is controlled by the historical and social circumstances of which it is a part.

> Art is a symbolical projection of collective psychic tensions. . . . Within the organism of a culture, the artist functions as a kind of preconsciousness, providing a zone of infiltration through which the obscure stirrings of collective intuition can emerge into collective consciousness. The artist is the personal transformer within whose sensitivity a collective psychic charge, latent in society, condenses into a cultural image. He is in short the dreamer . . . of the collective dream.[5]

Whereas Abell stresses the unconscious tensions of the social state of mind that influence the architect's creative process, Erwin Panofsky, another art historian, stresses the artist's mental habits, conscious as well as unconscious, that act as principles to guide the architect. For example:

> We can observe [between about 1130 and 1270] . . . a connection between Gothic art and Scholasticism which is more concrete than a mere "parallelism" and yet more general than those individual (and very important) "influences" which are inevitably exerted on painters, sculptors, or architects by erudite advisors. In contrast to a mere parallelism, the connection which I have in mind is a genuine cause-and-effect relation; but in contrast to an individual influence, this cause-and-effect relation comes about by diffusion rather than by direct impact. It comes about by the spreading of what may be called, for want of a better term, a mental habit—reducing this overworked cliché to its precise Scholastic sense as a "principle that regulates the act." Such mental habits are at work in all and every civilization.[6]

[5]Walter Abell, *The Collective Dream in Art,* Harvard University Press, Cambridge, Mass., 1957, p. 328.
[6]Erwin Panofsky, *Gothic Architecture and Scholasticism,* 2nd Wimmer Lecture, 1948. St. Vincent College. Archabbey Press, Latrobe, Pa., 1951, pp. 20ff. New American Library, New York, 1957, Meridian Books, p. 44.

Whatever the explanation of the architect's relationship to society—and Abell's and Panofsky's are two of the best[7]—the forms of architecture reflect and interpret some of the fundamental values of the society of the architect. Yet even as these forms are settling, society changes. Thus, while keeping the past immanent in the present, architecture takes on more and more the aura of the past, especially if the originating values are no longer viable or easily understandable. Anything that now exists but has a past may refer to, or function as, a sign of the past, but the forms of architecture interpret the past. Not only do the forms of architecture preserve the past more carefully than most things, for most architects build buildings to last, but these structures also enlighten that past. They inform about the values of the artists' society. Architects did the forming, of course, but from beginning to end that forming, insofar as it succeeded artistically, brought forth something of their society's values. Thus architectural forms are weighted with the past—a past, furthermore, that is more public than private. The past is preserved in the forms as part of the content of architecture.

Every stone of the Parthenon, in the way it was cut and fitted, reveals something about the values of the Age of Pericles—for example, the emphasis on moderation and harmony, the importance of mathematical measurement and yet its subordination to human aesthetic needs, the respect for the eminence of humans and their rationality, the immanence rather than the transcendence of the sacred.

Chartres Cathedral is an exceptional example of the preservation of the past. Chartres reveals three principal value areas of that medieval region: the special importance of Mary, to whom the cathedral is dedicated; the doctrines of the cathedral school, one of the most important centers of learning in Europe in the twelfth and thirteenth centuries; and the value preferences of the main patrons—the royal family, the lesser nobility, and the local guilds. The windows of the 175 surviving panels and the sculpture, including more than 2,000 carved figures, were a bible in glass and stone for the illiterate, but they were also a visual encyclopedia for the literate. From these structures the iconographer—the decipherer of the meaning of icons or symbols—can trace almost every fundamental value of the society that created Chartres Cathedral: the conception of human history from Adam and Eve to the Last Judgment; the story of Christ from his ancestors to his Ascension; church history; ancient lore and contemporary history; the latest scientific knowledge; the curriculum of the cathedral school as divided into the trivium and the quadrivium; the hierarchy of the nobility and the guilds; the code of chivalry and manners; and the hopes and fears of the time. Furthermore, the participator also becomes aware of a society that believed God to be transcendent but the Virgin to be both transcendent and immanent, not just a heavenly queen but also a mother. Chartres is Mary's home. For, as Henry Adams insisted: "You had better stop here, once for all, unless you are willing to feel that Chartres was made what it was, not by the artist, but by the Virgin."

[7]For an evaluation of these and other explanations, see F. David Martin, "The Sociological Imperative of Stylistic Development," *Bucknell Review,* vol. XI, no. 4, pp. 54–80, December 1963.

Even if we disagree with Adams, we understand, at least to some extent, Mary's special position within the context of awe aroused by God as "wholly other." The architecture of Chartres does many things, but, above all, its structures preserve that awe. Something of the society of the Chartres that was comes into our present awareness with overwhelming impact. And then we can understand something about the feelings of such medieval men as Abbot Haimon of Normandy who, after visiting Chartres, wrote to his brother monks in Tutbury, England:

> Who has ever heard tell, in times past, that powerful princes of the world, that men brought up in honor and wealth, that nobles, men and women, have bent their proud and haughty necks to the harness of carts, and that, like beasts of burden, they have dragged to the abode of Christ these waggons, loaded with wines, grains, oil, stone, wood, and all that is necessary for the wants of life, or for the construction of the church . . . ? When they have reached the church, they arrange the waggons about it like a spiritual camp, and during the whole night they celebrate the watch by hymns and canticles. On each waggon they light tapers and lamps; they place there the infirm and sick, and bring them the precious relics of the saints for their relief.

Perception Key
VALUES AND ARCHITECTURE

1. Describe other values in addition to the functional that are interpreted by the form of the Union Carbide Building (Figure 6-8).
2. Do the same for Chartres Cathedral (Figures 6-2, 6-3) and Le Corbusier's Notre Dame du Haut (Figure 6-9). Is it easier to describe the values related to Le Corbusier's church? If so, how is this explained?

FIGURE 6-12
Palazzo Vendramin-Calergi, Venice. 1534. (Marburg/Art Resource, New York)

3. Compare the Palazzo Vendramin-Calergi in Venice, completed in 1534 (Figure 6-12), with the Yale Music Building in New Haven, Connecticut, completed in 1926 (Figure 6-13). Which one seems better architecturally? Explain.

To participate with a work of public architecture fully, we must have as complete an understanding as possible of its subject matter—the function of the building and the relevant values of the society which subsidized the building. The more we know about the region of Chartres in medieval times, the more we will appreciate its cathedral. The more we understand our own time, the more we will appreciate the Union Carbide Building. Similarly, the more we understand about the engineering problems involved in a work of architecture, including especially the potentialities of its materials, the better our appreciation. And, of course, the more we know about the stylistic history of architectural details and structures and their possibilities, the deeper will be our appreciation. That tradition is a long and complex one, but you can learn its essentials in any good book on the history of architecture (see the accompanying bibliography).

FIGURE 6-13
Music Building, New Haven, Connecticut, 1926. (Manuscripts and Archives, Yale University Library)

Let us return again to architecture and space, for what most clearly distinguishes architecture from painting and sculpture is the way it works in space. Works of architecture separate an inside space from an outside space. They make that inside space available for human functions. And in interpreting their subject matter (functions and their society's values), architects make space "space." They bring out the power and embrace of the positioned interrelationships of things. Architecture in this respect can be divided into three main types—the earth-rooted, the sky-oriented, and the earth-resting.

EARTH-ROOTED ARCHITECTURE

The earth is the securing agency that grounds the place of our existence, our center. In most primitive cultures it is believed that people are born from the earth. And in many languages people are the "Earth-born." In countless myths, Mother Earth is the bearer of humans from birth to death. Of all things the expansive earth, with its mineral resources and vegetative fecundity, most suggests or is symbolic of security. Moreover, since the solidity of the earth encloses its depth in darkness, the earth is also suggestive of mystery.

No other thing exposes its surface more pervasively and yet hides its depth dimension more completely. The earth is always closure in the midst of disclosure. If we dig below the surface, there is always a further depth in darkness that continues to escape our penetration. Thus the Earth Mother has a mysterious, nocturnal, even funerary aspect—she is also often a goddess of death. But, as the theologian Mircea Eliade points out, "even in respect of these negative aspects, one thing that must never be lost sight of, is that when the Earth becomes a goddess of Death, it is simply because she is felt to be the universal womb, the inexhaustible source of all creation."[8] Nothing in nature is more suggestive or symbolic of security and mystery than the earth. Earth-rooted architecture accentuates this natural symbolism more than any other art.

SITE

Architecture that is earth-rooted discloses the earth by drawing our attention to the site of the building, or to its submission to gravity, or to its raw materials, or to its centrality in outer and inner space. Sites whose surrounding environment can be seen from great distances are especially favorable for helping a building bring out the earth. The site of the Parthenon (Figures 6-4 and 6-5), for example, is superior in this respect to the site of Chartres (Figures 6-2 and 6-3), because the Acropolis is a natural center that stands out prominently within a widespread concave space. Thus the Parthenon is able to emphasize by continuity both the sheer heavy stoni-

[8]Mircea Eliade, *Myths, Dreams and Mysteries,* Philip Mairet (trans.), Harper, New York, 1961, p. 188.

ness of the cliffs of the Acropolis and the gleaming whites of Athens. By contrast, it sets off the deep blue of the Mediterranean sky and sea and the grayish greens of the encompassing mountains that open out toward the weaving blue of the sea like the bent rims of a colossal flower. All these elements of the earth would be present without the Parthenon, of course, but the Parthenon, whose columns from a distance push up like stamens, centers these elements more tightly so that their interrelationships add to the vividness of each. Together they form the ground from which the Parthenon slowly and majestically rises.

GRAVITY

The Parthenon is also exceptional in the way it manifests a gentle surrender to gravity. The horizontal rectangularity of the entablature follows evenly along the plain of the Acropolis with the steady beat of its supporting columns and quiets their upward thrust. Gravity is accepted and accentuated in this serene stability—the hold of the earth is secure.

The site of Mont-Saint-Michel (Figure 6-14) can also be seen from great distances, especially from the sea, and the church, straining far up from the great rock cliffs, organizes a vast scene of sea, sand, shallow hills, and sky. But the spiny, lonely verticality of the church overwhelms the pull of the earth. We are lured to the sky, to the world of light, whereas the Parthenon draws us back into the womb of the earth. Mont-Saint-Michel discloses the earth, for both the earth and a world to be opened up require centering and thus each other, but the defiance of gravity weakens the securing sense of place. Mont-Saint-Michel rapidly moves us around its walls,

FIGURE 6-14
Mont-Saint-Michel. (French Government Tourist Office)

FIGURE 6-15
Rockefeller Center, New York City. 1931–1940. (Courtesy Rockefeller Center © Rockefeller Center Management Corporation)

when the tides permit, with a dizzying effect, whereas the Parthenon moves us around slowly and securely so that our orientation is never in doubt. The significance of the earth is felt much more deeply at the Parthenon than at Mont-Saint-Michel.

The complex of skyscrapers that composes Rockefeller Center (Figure 6-15) in New York City is an exceptional example of an architecture that allows for only a minimal submission to gravity. The surrounding buildings, unless we are high up in one nearby, block out the lower sections of the Center. If we are able to see the lower sections by getting in close, we are blocked from a clear and comprehensive view of the upper sections. The relationships between the lower and upper sections are, therefore, somewhat disintegrated, and there is a sense of these tapering towers, especially the R.C.A. Building (now the G.E. Building in the center of the photograph), not only scraping but being suspended from the sky. The Union Carbide Building (Figure 6-8), not far away, carries this feeling even further by the placement of the shaftlike box on stilts. This apparently weightless building mitigates but does not annihilate our feeling of the earth, for despite its arrowlike soaring, we are aware of its base. Even at night, when the sides of this structure become dark curtains pierced by hundreds of square lights, we feel these lights, as opposed to the light of the stars, as somehow grounded. Architecture in setting up a world always sets forth the earth, and vice versa.

The Mayan Temple of the Sun (Figure 6-16) is part of a gigantic temple complex which is now partly reclaimed by the rain forest. However, its par-

FIGURE 6-16
Temple of the Sun, Chichén Itza, Mexico. Mayan culture, circa 700 A.D. (Lee A. Jacobus)

tial restoration makes us aware of its power to root our attention to its flowing base and stairs. It stands majestically in an open space that must be reached by a passage along densely forested roads so that when we approach it our experience parallels that of approaching St. Peter's Square after having wandered through narrow Roman streets. The temple stands as a brilliant architectural explosion, riveting our attention with a sense of high drama and expectation. The building was used for ceremonial and ritual purposes, with a small dark interior space on its top level from which priests could exit to perform their rites. According to some experts, among those rites were human sacrifices. But whatever they were, for the Mayans, this building had a religious purpose, a platform upon which they served their gods. Around the temple are many more ceremonial buildings and smaller temples, all built of rugged local stone quarried nearby. One of those buildings is a ceremonial sports field in which large teams played a game resembling basketball. The Temple of the Sun was part of a community center in which people prayed, worked, and played.

RAW MATERIALS

When the medium of architecture is made up totally or in large part of unfinished materials furnished by nature, especially when they are from the site, these materials tend to stand forth and help reveal the earthiness of the earth. In this respect stone, wood, and clay in a raw or relatively raw state are much more effective than steel, concrete, and glass. One can appreciate this fact especially on the site of Chichén Itza. If the Parthenon had been made in concrete rather than in native Pentelic marble—the quarries can still be seen in the distance—the building would not grow out of the soil so organically and some of the feeling of the earth would be dissipated. On the other hand, if the paint that originally covered much of the Parthenon had remained, the effect would be considerably less earthy than at present. Wright's Kaufman house (Figure 6-17) is an excellent example of the combined use of manufactured and raw materials that helps set forth the earth. The concrete and glass bring out by contrast the textures of stone and wood taken from the site, while the lacelike flow of the falling water is made even more graceful by its reflection in the smooth clear flow of concrete and glass. Like a wide-spreading plant, drawing the sunlight and rain to its good earth, this home seems to breathe within its homeland.

PERCEPTION KEY
ARCHITECTURE AND MATERIALS

In his *Praise of Architecture*, the great Italian architect Gio Ponti writes: "Beautiful materials do not exist. Only the right material exists. . . . Rough plaster in the right place is the beautiful material for that place. . . . To replace it with a noble material would be vulgar."

1. Do you agree with Ponti?
2. If you agree, refer to examples that corroborate Ponti's point, and discuss.
3. If you disagree, refer to examples that do not corroborate, and discuss.

FIGURE 6-17
Frank Lloyd Wright, Kaufman house (Falling Water), Bear Run, Pennsylvania. 1937–1939. (Scott Frances/Esto)

CENTRALITY

Finally, a building that is strongly centered, both in its outer and inner space, helps disclose the earth. Perhaps no building is more centered in its site than the Parthenon, but the weak centering of its inner space slackens somewhat the significance of the earth. Unlike Chartres, there is no strong pull into the Parthenon, and when we get inside, the inner space, as we reconstruct it, is divided in such a way that no certain center can be felt. There is no place to come to an unequivocal standstill as at Chartres. Even Versailles (Figure 6-18), despite its seemingly never-ending partitions of inner space, brings us eventually to somewhat of a center in the bed of the bedroom of Louis XIV. Yet this centering is made possible primarily by the view from the room that focuses both the pivotal position of the room in the building and the placement of the room on a straight-line axis to Paris in the far distance. Conversely, the inner space of Chartres, most of which from the crossing can be taken in with a sweep of the eye, achieves centrality without this kind of dependence upon outside orientation. Buildings such as the Parthenon and Versailles, which divide the inner space with solid partitions, invariably are weaker in inner centrality than buildings without such divisions. The single interior space of the Temple of the Sun helps center our sense of space, especially after we have climbed the steps to its summit. The experience is similar to climbing a mountain and centering oneself on its peak, emphasizing the earth-centeredness of this building.

Buildings whose inner space not only draws us to a privileged position—that position which gives us the best perception—but whose inner space or

FIGURE 6-18
Palace of Versailles. 1661–1687. (French Government Tourist Office)

FIGURE 6-19
San Vitale, Ravenna, Italy. 526–547. (Scala/Art Resource, New York)

most of it can also be seen from that privileged position evoke a feeling of powerful inner centeredness. This feeling is further enhanced when the expanses of inner space are more or less equidistant from the privileged position. Greek-cross buildings, in which the floor plan resembles a cross whose arms are all equal in length, are likely to center us in inner space more strongly than Latin-cross buildings, such as Chartres (Figure 6-3). If Bramante's and Michelangelo's Greek-cross plan for St. Peter's had been carried out, the centrality of the inner space would have been greatly enhanced. It does not follow, however, that all centrally planned buildings that open up all or almost all of the inner space will be strongly centered internally. San Vitale (Figures 6-19 and 6-20) in Ravenna, for example, is basically an octagon, but the enfolded interior spaces are not clearly outlined and differentiated. There is a floating and welling of space working out and up through the arcaded niches into the outer layers of the ambulatory and gallery that fade into semidarkness. The dazzling colors of the varied marble slabs and the mosaics lining the piers and walls add to our sense of spatial uncertainty. We can easily discover the center of San Vitale if we so desire, but there is no directed movement to it because the indeterminacy of the surrounding spaces makes the feeling of the center insecure and insignificant. The unanchored restlessness of the interior of San Vitale belies its solid weighty exterior.

FIGURE 6-20
San Vitale, Ravenna. Interior. (Hirmer Verlag, Munich)

Buildings in the round, other things being equal, are the most internally centered of all. In the Pantheon (Figure 6-21), almost all the inner space can be seen with a turn of the head, and the grand and clear symmetry of the enclosing shell draws us to the center of the circle, the privileged position, beneath the "eye" of the dome opening to a bit of the sky. Few build-

FIGURE 6-21
Giovanni Paolo Panini, *Interior of the Pantheon, Rome*. Circa 1734. Oil on canvas, 50½ × 39 inches. National Gallery of Art, Washington, D.C. Samuel H. Kress Collection. The Pantheon itself dates from the second century after Christ.

ings root us more firmly in the earth. The massive dome with its stony bluntness seems to be drawn down by the funneled and dimly spreading light falling through the "eye." This is a dome of destiny pressing tightly down. We are driven earthward in this crushing ambience. Even on the outside the Pantheon seems to be forcing down. In the circular interior of Wright's Guggenheim Museum (Figure 6-11) not all of the inner space can be seen from the privileged position, but the smoothly curving ramp that comes down like a whirlpool makes us feel the earth beneath as our only support. Whereas in buildings such as Mont-Saint-Michel and Chartres, mass seems to be overcome, the weight lightened, and the downward motion thwarted, in buildings such as the Pantheon and the Guggenheim Museum, mass comes out heavily and down.

The importance of a center, usually within a circle, as a privileged and even sacred position in relation to the earth is common among the spatial arrangements of ancient cultures—for example, the Stonehenge on the Salisbury Plain of England. And the first city of Rome, according to Plutarch, was laid out by the Etruscans around a circular trench or *mundus*, over which was placed a great capstone. Around the *mundus*, the Etruscans outlined a large circle for the walls which would enclose the city. Following a carefully prescribed ritual, a deep furrow was plowed along the circle and the plow was lifted from the ground wherever a gate was to appear. This circular plan was subdivided by two main cross streets: the *cardo*, running north and south in imitation of the axis of the earth, and the *decumanus*, running east and west, dividing the city into four equal parts. These streets crossed at the site of the *mundus*, believed to be the entrance to the underworld, and the capstone was removed three times each year to allow the spirits passage between the world of the living and the world of the dead. Although such beliefs and customs have long been dead in Western civilization, we still can feel the power of the earth in circular city plans and buildings.

SKY-ORIENTED ARCHITECTURE

Architecture that is sky-oriented suggests or is symbolic of a world as the generating agency that enables us to project our possibilities and realize some of them. A horizon, always a necessary part of a world, is symbolic of the limitations placed upon our possibilities and realizations. The light and heat of the sun are more symbolic than anything else in nature of generative power. Dante declared, "there is no visible thing in the world more worthy to serve as symbol of God than the Sun; which illuminates with visible life itself first and then all the celestial and mundane bodies." The energy of the moving sun brightens the sky which, in turn, opens up for us a spacious context or world within which we attempt to realize our possibilities. In total darkness we may be able to orient ourselves to the earth, but in order to move with direction, as do the blind, we must imagine space as open in some way, as a world enlightened with light even if our imaginations must provide that light. Total darkness, at least until we can envision a world, is terrifying. That is why, as the Preacher of Ecclesiastes proclaims, "the light is sweet, and a pleasant thing it is for the eyes to behold the sun." "The light of the living" is a common Hebrew phrase, and in Greek "to behold light" is synonymous with "to live." The light of the sky reveals space—the positioned interrelationships of things. The dome of the sky, with its limits provided by the horizon, embraces a world within which we find ourselves. But a world is above all the context for activity. A world stirs our imaginations to possibilities. A world, with its suggestion of expectation, turns our faces to the future, just as the smile of the sun lures our eyes. Architecture organizes a world, usually far more tightly than nature, by centering that world on the earth by means of a building. By accentuating the natural symbolism of sunlight, sky, and horizon, sky-oriented architecture opens up a world that is symbolic of our projections into the future.

Such architecture discloses a world by drawing our attention to the sky bounded by a horizon. It accomplishes this by means of making a building appear high and centered within the sky, or defying gravity, or tightly integrating the light of outer with inner space. Negatively, architecture that accents a world de-emphasizes the features that accent the earth. Thus the manufactured materials, such as the steel and glass of the Union Carbide Building (Figure 6-8), help separate this building from the earth. Positively, the most effective means at the disposal of architects for accenting a world is turning their structures toward the sky in such a way that the horizon of the sky forms a spacious context. Architecture is an art of bounding as well as opening.

FIGURE 6-22
Antonio Gaudí, Sagrada Familia (Church of the Holy Family), Barcelona. 1883–1926 and continuing. (Lee A. Jacobus)

Barcelona's Antonio Gaudí created one of the most striking of modern buildings in his Sagrada Familia (Figures 6-22 to 6-24). He had developed a view about the use of natural forms, of fluid lines and fluid spaces. This church is not complete—work is still being done and will continue well into the next century. Gaudí himself never lived to see the erection of the four towers that dominate its facade. The interior space is not yet covered with a roof and the consequence is an emphasis on its sky-orientation. One's eye is lifted upward virtually in any part of the building, although the majority of people know only its exterior (Figure 6-22), whereas the spaces within the church are fluid, rhythmic with their curving surfaces, and currently fascinating because so much of the process of integrating concrete and steel is evident throughout the space. One feels almost part of the growth of the

FIGURE 6-23
Antonio Gaudí, Sagrada Familia, interior detail. (Lee A. Jacobus)

FIGURE 6-24
Antonio Gaudí, Sagrada Familia, exterior detail. (Lee A. Jacobus)

building—because it feels as if it is growing from the ground, like the surrounding trees. Sagrada Familia does not seem as if it is being constructed. Gaudí intended the building to appear organic, with its surfaces defying the architectural rectangles that dominate most modern buildings. One feels a sense of loftiness, of aspiration, height, and limitlessness.

Perception Key
SAGRADA FAMILIA

1. Compare Sagrada Familia with Chartres (Figure 6-3). How do their sky orientations differ? How are they similar? Compare the exterior facade of Sagrada Familia with any church well known to you. What are the differences?
2. Examine the detail over the main entrance (Figure 6-23). How does Gaudí respect the stone out of which the figures and the structure are constructed? Is he concerned with "truth to materials"? How does this entrance compare with the west facade of Chartres?
3. The interior pictured in Figure 6-23 is unfinished, but will look substantially like this when windows are in place and the roof added. What does it share with the exterior of the building? What feelings does it seem to communicate?
4. Do you associate a religious function with this building? What religious values are projected in Sagrada Familia? What does the building reveal?

AXIS MUNDI

Early civilizations often express a need for a world by centering themselves in relation to the sky by means of an *axis mundi*. Mircea Eliade presents many instances, for example, among the nomadic Australians, whose economy is based on gathering food and hunting small game:

> According to the traditions of an Arunta tribe, the Achipla, in mythical times the divine being Numbakula cosmicized their future territory, created their Ancestor, and established their institutions. From the trunk of a gum tree Numbakula fashioned the sacred pole (*kauwa-auwa*) and, after anointing it with blood, climbed it and disappeared into the sky. This pole (the *axis mundi*) represents a cosmic axis, for it is around the sacred pole that territory becomes habitable, hence is transformed into a world. The sacred pole consequently plays an important role ritually. During their wanderings the Achipla always carry it with them and choose the direction they are to take by the direction toward which it bends. This allows them, while being continually on the move, to be always in "their world" and, at the same time, in communication with the sky into which Numbakula vanished. For the pole to be broken denotes catastrophe; it is like "the end of the world," reversion to chaos. Spencer and Gillen report that once, when the pole was broken, "the entire clan were in consternation; they wandered about aimlessly for a time, and finally lay down on the ground together and waited for death to overtake them."[9]

When buildings accent a world, their turning to the sky usually suggests a kind of *axis mundi*. The perpendicularity and centering of the Acropolis (Figure 6-4), for example, make it a kind of natural *axis mundi* that would open up the sky to some extent even if the Parthenon had never been built. But the flat plains around Chartres (Figure 6-2) would rarely turn us to the sky without the spires of the cathedral. Buildings that stretch up far above the land and nearby structures, such as Mont-Saint-Michel (Figure 6-14), Chartres (Figures 6-2 and 6-3), Rockefeller Center (Figure 6-15), the Temple of the Sun (Figure 6-16), and Sagrada Familia (Figure 6-22), not only direct our eye to the sky but also act as a center that orders the sunlight in such a way that a world with a horizon comes into view. The sky both opens up and takes on limits. Such buildings reach up like an *axis mundi*, and the sky reaches down to meet them in mutual embrace. And we are blessed with an orienting center, our motion being given direction and limits.

DEFIANCE OF GRAVITY

The more a building appears to defy gravity, the more it is likely to disclose the sky, for this defiance draws our eyes upward. The thrust against gravity is not simply a question of how high the building goes. Most of the skyscrapers of New York City, like the Woolworth Building (Figure 6-25), seem to stop finally not because they have reached a more or less perfect union with the sky but because the space used up had exhausted them. They hang lifelessly despite their great height. They seem to have just enough strength to stand upright but no power to transcend the rudimentary laws of statics. Gravity wins out after all. The up and down frustrate each other, and their conflict dims the world that might have been.

[9]Mircea Eliade, *The Sacred and the Profane,* Williard R. Trask (trans.), Harcourt Brace Jovanovich, Inc., 1959, pp. 32ff.

FIGURE 6-25
Cass Gilbert, Woolworth Building, New York City. 1913. (Ely-Cruikshank Company, Inc.)

Chartres is not nearly so tall as the Woolworth Building, and yet it appears far taller. The stony logic of the press of the flying buttresses of Chartres and the arched roof, towers, and spires that carry on their upward thrust seem to overcome the binding of the earth, just as the stone birds on the walls seem about to break their bonds and fly out into the world. The reach up is full of vital force and finally comes to rest comfortably and securely in the bosom of the heavens. Mont-Saint-Michel and Durham Cathedral are even more impressive in this respect, mainly because of the advantages of their sites.

But perhaps Brunelleschi's dome of the Cathedral of Florence (Figure 6-26) is the most powerful structure ever built in seeming to defy gravity and achieving height in relation to its site. The eight outside ribs spring up to the cupola with tremendous energy, in part because they repeat the spring

FIGURE 6-26
Filippo Brunelleschi, dome of the Cathedral of Florence. 1420–1436. (Italian Government Travel Office)

of the mountains that encircle Florence. The dome, visible from almost everywhere in and around Florence, appears to be precisely centered in the Arno Valley, precisely as high as it should be in order to organize its sky. The world of Florence begins and ends at the still point of this dome of aspiration (Figure 6-27). On the other hand, Michelangelo's dome of St. Peter's (Figure 6-1), although grander in proportions and over fifty feet higher, fails to organize the sky of Rome as firmly, mainly because the hills of Rome do not lend themselves to centralized organization.

FIGURE 6-27
Filippo Brunelleschi, exterior of the Cathedral of Florence, detail. (Lee A. Jacobus)

INTEGRATION OF LIGHT

When the light of outer space suffuses the light of inner space, especially when the light from the outside seems to dominate or draw the light from the inside, a world is accented. Inside Chartres the light is so majestic that we cannot fail to imagine the light outside that is generating the transfiguration inside. For a medieval man like Abbot Suger the effect was mystical, separating the earth from Heaven:

> When the house of God, many colored as the radiance of precious jewels, called me from the cares of the world, then holy meditation led my mind to thoughts of piety, exalting my soul from the material to the immaterial, and I seemed to find myself, as it were, in some strange part of the universe which was neither wholly of the baseness of the earth, nor wholly of the serenity of heaven, but by the grace of God I seemed lifted in a mystic manner from this lower toward the upper sphere.

On the other hand, for a contemporary person the stained glass is likely to be felt more as integrating rather than separating us from a world. Hagia Sophia in Istanbul (Figure 6-28) has no stained glass, and its glass areas are completely dominated by the walls and dome. Yet the subtle placement of the little windows, especially around the perimeter of the dome, seems to draw the light of the inner space up and out. Unlike the Pantheon (Figure 6-21), the great masses of Hagia Sophia seem to rise. The dome floats gently, despite its diameter of 107 feet, and the great enfolded space beneath is absorbed into the even greater open space outside. We imagine a world.

Sky-oriented architecture reveals the generative activity of a world. The energy of the sun is the ultimate source of all life. The light of the sun enables us to see the physical environment and guides our steps accordingly. "Arise, shine, for thy light is come" (Isaiah 60:1). The sky with its horizon provides a spacious context for our progress. The world of nature vaguely suggests the potentialities of the future. Architecture, however, tightly centers a world on the earth by means of its structures. This unification gives us orientation and security.

FIGURE 6-28
Hagia Sophia, Istanbul, Turkey, interior. 532–537; restored, 558, 975. (Hirmer Verlag, Munich)

EARTH-RESTING ARCHITECTURE

Most architecture accents neither earth nor sky but rests on the earth, using the earth like a platform with the sky as background. Earth-resting buildings may either dominate the earth, as in the case of the Palazzo Farnese (Figures 6-29 and 6-30) in Rome, or relate harmoniously to the earth, as in the case of Mies van der Rohe's residence of Dr. Edith Farnsworth (Figure 6-31) in Plano, Illinois. Generally, earth-resting buildings are not very tall, have flat roofs, and avoid strong vertical extensions such as spires and chimneys. Thus—unlike sky-oriented architecture—the earth-resting type does not strongly organize the sky around itself, as with Chartres (Figure 6-2) or the Cathedral of Florence (Figure 6-26). The sky is involved with earth-resting architecture, of course, but more as a setting.

With earth-resting architecture—unlike earth-rooted architecture—the earth does not appear as an organic part of the building, as in Wright's Kaufman house (Figure 6-17). Rather, the earth appears as a stage. Earth-resting buildings, moreover, are usually cubes that avoid cantilevering structures, as in the Kaufman house, as well as curving lines, as in the Sagrada Familia. Earth-rooted architecture seems to "hug to" the earth, as with the Pantheon (Figure 6-21), or to grow out of the earth, as with the Kaufman house. Earth-resting architecture, on the other hand, seems to "sit on" the earth. Thus, because it does not relate to its environment quite as strongly as earth-rooted and sky-oriented architecture, this kind of architecture usually tends to draw to itself more isolated attention with reference to its shape, articulation of the elements of its walls, lighting, etc.

Earth-resting architecture is usually more appropriate than earth-rooted architecture when the site is severely bounded by other buildings. Perhaps this is a basic deficiency of Wright's Guggenheim Museum (Figure 6-10).

FIGURE 6-29
Antonio da Sangallo and Michelangelo Buonarroti, Palazzo Farnese, Rome. 1534. (Alinari/Art Resource, New York)

FIGURE 6-30
Palazzo Farnese, courtyard. (Alinari/Art Resource, New York)

FIGURE 6-31
Ludwig Mies van der Rohe, Farnsworth residence, Plano, Illinois. 1950. (Jon Miller ©/Hedrich Blessing, Chicago)

In any case, it is obvious that if buildings were constructed close to the Kaufman house (Figure 6-17)—especially earth-resting or sky-oriented types—they would destroy much of the glory of Wright's creation.

PERCEPTION KEY
PALAZZO FARNESE

Study the Palazzo Farnese (Figures 6-29 and 6-30) by Antonio da Sangallo and Michelangelo.

1. The facade of this building is 185 feet by 96½ feet. Is there any particular significance to the large size and proportion of these dimensions? Suppose, for example, that the construction had stopped with the second floor. Would the relationship between width and height be as "right" as it now appears?
2. Does the relationship between the sizes of the three floors have a "rightness"? If so, how is this to be explained?
3. The window pediments of the first floor are all alike. On the second floor, however, there is an a/b rhythm. The windows at the ends of the facade are topped by triangles, and as we move toward the center of the facade, semicircular pediments interrupt the triangular pediments. Why this rhythm? Why not have the same rhythm on the first and third floors? Why do semicircular rather than triangular pediments lead to the central window, with its large family insignia and porch?
4. The cornice—the horizontal molding projecting along the top of the building—is very large, and quoins, or roughly cut stones, accent the ends of the facade. Why?
5. Sangallo designed the first two floors and Michelangelo designed the third. The differences between their two styles are more evident in the courtyard (Figure 6-30). What are these differences? For example, which architect stresses restlessness? How? Why? Did Michelangelo successfully unite his third floor with Sangallo's floors?
6. In answering the above questions are you inevitably led to consider the function of the building? If you were told that this building was a church, for example, would you be both surprised and distressed? Would your answers be different?
7. What function and what values, if any, are revealed in this building? In other words, what is the subject matter that the form informs about? And how does the form achieve its content?

The residence of Dr. Edith Farnsworth (Figure 6-31), designed by Mies van der Rohe, exemplifies his paradoxical doctrine that "less is more." On the Palazzo Farnese much decoration—for example, all the elements around the windows—could be removed and the building would still stand. But with Mies' work, it seems as if nothing is there that is not necessary for the technical solutions of making the building stand.

Study the Wiley House (Figure 6-32) by Philip Johnson, very much in the style of Mies. The functions of this house are explicitly separated—the ground floor contains the "private functions," and the open social functions are reserved for the modular glass pavilion above. Nothing seems to be there that does not work as a practical function.

FIGURE 6-32
Philip Johnson, Wiley house, New Canaan, Connecticut. 1953. (Ezra Stoller © Esto)

PERCEPTION KEY
FARNSWORTH RESIDENCE AND THE PALAZZO FARNESE

1. The simplicity of Mies' house may be misleading. Analyze the placement of the parts and their proportions, and see if you can discover why this work is considered to be a small masterpiece by one of the greatest of modern architects. For instance, why are the posts not out at the corners? Why do the posts meet a projecting line of the roof rather than coming up under the roof?
2. How are light and outer space related differently here than in the Palazzo Farnese?
3. Why is absolute symmetry absent here, whereas in the Palazzo Farnese it is closely approached?
4. What is the content of this home? And how does the form achieve it?
5. Mies' houses have sometimes been criticized as buildings made to be looked at rather than lived in. In the case of the Farnsworth residence, do you agree?
6. Try your hand at designing your ideal home. What form will reveal your values?

The problem of when to use earth-rooted or earth-resting or sky-oriented buildings is usually easily solved: the function of the building generally is the key. Churches and large office buildings, especially in crowded sites, lend themselves to sky orientation. Homes in rural areas lend themselves to earth orientation. Homes in crowded urban areas present special problems. Earth-rooted buildings, such as the Kaufman house (Figure 6-17), normally require relatively large open areas. The most urban dwellings are earth-resting. But as our populations have become increasingly dense, sky-oriented apartment buildings have become a common sight.

FIGURE 6-33
National Gallery of Art, Washington, D.C., Mall entrance. 1941. (National Gallery of Art, photograph by Dennis Brack)

PERCEPTION KEY
WILEY HOUSE

1. Do you think the ground floor and the pavilion relate to one another in a satisfactory way?
2. Are light and air integrated with the structure of the building as gracefully as in Mies' building? Explain.
3. Some critics have remarked of the Wiley House that "less is a bore." Do you agree, or would you like to live in this house?

Consider another earth-resting building, one of the most expensive ever built in this country—the National Gallery of Art (Figure 6-33) in Washington, D.C.

PERCEPTION KEY
THE NATIONAL GALLERY OF ART

1. Would you know the function of this building just by observing it from the outside?
2. Do you find its entrance inviting? Compare St. Peter's (Figure 6-1).
3. Does its form inform you about anything?

Combining the portico of the Temple of Diana and the dome of the Pantheon with vast wings that stretch out to a total length of 785 feet, this monstrous building, despite the very expensive materials and the great engineering skill that went into its making, reveals little except the imitative conservatism of its designers and the wealth and conservatism of its patrons. In the 1930s, when the National Gallery was planned, mainly by John Russell Pope, the United States had risen from its worst depression and was beginning to face, as potentially the most powerful nation in the world, the crisis of the coming Second World War. At the dedication of the gallery in March 1941, President Roosevelt concluded his address:

> Seventy-eight years ago, in the third year of the war between the States, men and women gathered here in the capital of a divided nation, here in Washington, to see the bronze goddess of liberty set upon its top.
>
> It had been an expensive, a laborious business, diverting money and labor from the prosecution of the war and certain critics . . . found much to criticize. . . . But the President of the United States, whose name was Lincoln, when he heard those criticisms, answered: "If people see the Capital going on it is a sign that we intend this Union shall go on."
>
> We may borrow the words for our own. We, too, intend the Union to go on. We intend it shall go on, carrying with it the greatest tradition of the human spirit which created it.
>
> The dedication of this gallery to a living past and to a greater and more richly living future is the measure of the earnestness of our intention that the freedom of the human spirit shall go on too.

Brave words by a brave president. But what living past does the architecture of this building disclose? And in what way does this building bring forth the freedom of the human spirit that shall go on? The gallery reveals rather the taste—derived from Jefferson's belief that the beautiful in architecture had been forever established in Roman masterpieces—that has bound the architecture of Washington to pale imitations of what had once been a living art. Nothing of the thrusting optimism of the United States, its ceaseless and ingenious ferment, its power and pragmatism comes out. Even the superb technology of our country is masked. The engineering excellence of the steel structure is covered up, as if there were something shameful about steel that helped make the United States prosperous. Even the immense dome gets lost in the mass of marble, and so the building spreads out without centering the outer space. Instead, the gallery somewhat awkwardly imposes its huge bulk into the graceful open ensemble of the Mall as planned by L'Enfant. Even the function of the building is hidden. The exterior tells us nothing about the use or even the structuring of the inner space. The building could have been constructed for just about any purpose that requires great inner dimensions. Even a "draw" by the inner into the outer space is lacking, surely an adjunct that a museum of art should provide. Indeed, the forty granite steps of mighty spread which mount up from the Mall to the main entrance, like the terror-inspiring stairways to the Mayan sacrificial platforms, may weaken visitors or drive them away.

PERCEPTION KEY
THE NATIONAL GALLERY AND THE NEW EAST WING

In 1978 the East Wing (Figures 6-34, 6-35)—designed by I.M. Pei and Partners—was completed, supplementing the old or West Wing of the National Gallery. Visit, if possible, both the old and new buildings and study their structures carefully.

1. Does the exterior of the East Wing—a trapezoid divided into two triangular sections—reveal the function of the building as a museum? Compare with the West Wing.
2. Both buildings utilize Tennessee pink marble from the same quarries. Does either succeed in bringing out the marbleness of this marble?
3. Is the technology that underlies the structure of the East Wing as hidden as in the West Wing? When you consider this question, refer again to Figure 3-15, the Georges Pompidou Center for the Arts in Paris, and compare their exteriors.
4. Is there a "draw" into the entrance of the East Wing, inviting one to enter? Compare with the Mall entrance of the West Wing.
5. Do you think that architecturally the East Wing is better or worse than the West Wing? Why? Do you think that our negative evaluations of the West Wing are unjustified? Clarify your position.

URBAN PLANNING

No use of space has become more critical in our time than in the city. In conclusion, therefore, the issues we have been discussing about space and architecture take on special relevance with respect to city planning.

Suppose spacious parking lots were located around the fringes of the city, rapid public transportation were readily available from those lots into the city, and in the city only public and emergency transportation—most of it underground—were permitted. In place of poisonous fumes, screeching noises, and jammed streets, fresh air, fountains, flowers, and sculpture, talk and music, and wide open spaces to walk and enjoy would be possible. Buildings could be participated with. All the diversified character of a city—its theaters, opera, concert halls, museums, shops, stores, offices, restaurants, markets, parks, lakes, squares, outdoor cafes—would take on some spatial unity. Furthermore, we could get to those various places without nervous prostration and the risk of life and limb. How would such a proposal change your attitude toward cities?

Most cities are planned either sporadically in segments or not at all. Natural features, such as rivers and hills, often define living spaces from working spaces. In older cities churches often dominate high ground. Man-made divisions, such as aqueducts, railroad tracks and trestles, bridges, and highways now define neighborhoods, sections, and functional spaces. The invasion of the urban and suburban mall in virtually every community has threatened the old downtown business sections in most cities, and in order to preserve those spaces from blight, imaginative schemes have been

FIGURE 6-34
I. M. Pei, East Wing of the National Gallery of Art, exterior. (Ezra Stoller © Esto)

FIGURE 6-35
I. M. Pei, East Wing of the National Gallery of Art, interior. (Ezra Stoller © Esto)

developed in some cities. San Antonio, Texas, has a waterway that slowly takes residents along a canal lined with shops and restaurants. Providence, Rhode Island, has closed certain areas to automobiles and made them inviting for shoppers, especially those with strollers and children. Many cities have remodeled their inner shopping areas and made planning efforts to keep them lively and attractive. Street music is now common in many downtown areas, such as Canterbury, England; Paris; London; and New York. Architectural decisions can help or hinder such efforts.

Perception Key
CITY PLANNING

1. Do you think the city ought to be saved? What advantages does only the city have? What still gives glamour to such cities as Florence, Venice, Rome, Paris, Vienna, and London?
2. Suppose you agree that New York City is worth saving. Suppose further that you are a city planner for New York City, and assume that funds are available to implement your plans. What would you propose? For example, would you destroy all the old buildings? Joseph Hudnut has written, "There is in buildings that have withstood the siege of centuries a magic which is irrespective of form and technical excellence. . . . the wreckage of distant worlds are radioactive with a long-gathered energy."[10] Do you agree? Would you be satisfied with the cluster of apartment buildings of Stuyvesant Town (Figure 6-36) in Manhattan? What would you do with the Manhattan area in Figure 6-37? Would you separate areas by function? The Wall Street area, for example, contains the financial interests. Is this a good idea? Would you allow factories within the city limits? Or do you think factories are cancers within the city? How would you handle transportation to and within the city? For instance, would you allow expressways to slice through the city, as in Detroit and Los Angeles? If you outlawed the private car from the city, what would you do with the streets? Could the streets become a unifier of the city?

The conglomerate architecture visible in Figure 6-37, a large church on Park Avenue, makes us aware that the setting of many interesting buildings so completely overwhelms them that we hardly know how to respond to them. An urban planner might decide to unify styles of buildings, or to separate buildings so as to permit us to participate with them as they were meant to be seen. Somehow we feel in looking at Figure 6-37 that there has been little or no planning. Of course, some people would consider that such a conglomeration is part of the charm of urban centers. One might feel, for example, that part of the pleasure of looking at the church in Figure 6-37 is responding to its contrast with its surroundings. For some people there is a special energy achieved in such a grouping.

Consider the MetLife Building in Figure 6-38. It would be possible to control the height of buildings (as they did in ancient Rome) so that truly noble buildings would stand out. Some sections of New York actually have

[10]Joseph Hudnut, *Architecture and the Spirit of Man,* Harvard University Press, Cambridge, Mass., 1949, pp. 15ff.

FIGURE 6-36
Stuyvesant Town, New York. (Photograph from *Matrix of Man*, 1968, Sibyl Moholy-Nagy, Praeger Publishers. Courtesy Hattula Moholy-Nagy Hug)

FIGURE 6-37
St. Bartholomew's Church on Park Avenue, New York City. (Lee A. Jacobus)

FIGURE 6-38 *(left)*
The MetLife Building, New York City. (Courtesy MetLife Media & Public Relations)

FIGURE 6-39 *(right)*
Stores and residence, Greenwich Village, New York City. (Lee A. Jacobus)

height restrictions and in some cases top stories have been removed from buildings in construction. In certain areas the buildings on both sides of the avenue create a darkness in the middle of the day. The jam of taxis is only one symptom of the narrowness of avenues in New York City. The architecture along this section of Park Avenue has created a negative space dominated by darkness, making the looming buildings more threatening than pleasurable. Consider the contrast in Figure 6-39, a building in Greenwich Village, New York, where most of the nearby buildings are about as tall as this one. Even though the building is by no means as sleek and mechanically elegant as the MetLife Building or the Union Carbide Building, it has a human scale and a humble brightness.

PERCEPTION KEY
THREE URBAN VIEWS

1. Would you prefer to live in a humble building, such as that in Figure 6-39, or in one of the buildings that create the shadows in the vicinity of the MetLife Building in Figure 6-38?
2. Which of the three buildings in Figures 6-37 to 6-39 is most attractive visually?
3. Which is most revelatory?

If we have been near the truth, then architects are the shepherds of space. And to be sensitive to their buildings is to help, in our humble way, to preserve their preservation. Architects make space a gracious place. Such places, like a home, give us a center from which we can orient ourselves to other places. And then we can be at home in the homeland.

SUMMARY

Architecture is the creative conservation of space—the power of the positioned interrelationships of things. The spatial centers of nature organize things around them, and architecture enhances these centers. Architects carve apart an inner space from an outer space in such a way that both spaces become more fully perceptible and the inner space is made useful. A work of architecture is a configurational center, a place of special value, a place to dwell. Architects must account for four basic and closely interrelated necessities: technical requirements, use, spatial relationships, and content. To succeed, their forms must adjust to these necessities. Because of the public character of architecture, moreover, the common or shared values of contemporary society usually are in a very direct way a part of architects' subject matter. Finally, architecture can be classified into three main types. Earth-rooted architecture brings out with special force the earth and its symbolisms. Such architecture appears organically related to the earth, the site and its materials, and gravity. Sky-oriented architecture brings out with special force the sky and its symbolisms. Such architecture discloses a world by drawing our attention to the sky bounded by a horizon. It accomplishes this by means of making a building high and centered within the sky, or defying gravity, or tightly integrating the light of outer and inner space. Negatively, this kind of architecture de-emphasizes the features that accent the earth. Earth-resting architecture accents neither earth nor sky but rests on the earth, using the earth as a platform with the sky as background. These distinctions should help us solve one of our most pressing problems—making the city civilized. Is it possible to make the city a place to dwell?

CHAPTER 6 BIBLIOGRAPHY

Arnheim, Rudolf. *The Dynamics of Architectural Form.* Berkeley: University of California Press, 1977.

Burchard, John. *The Architecture of America.* Boston: Little, Brown, 1966.

Coles, William A., and Henry Hope Reed, Jr. *Architecture in America: A Battle of Styles.* New York: Appleton-Century-Crofts, 1961.

Coppleston, Trewin (ed.). *World Architecture.* London: The Hamlyn Publishing Group, 1973.

Davern, Jeanne M. (ed.). *Places for People.* New York: McGraw-Hill, 1976.

Fletcher, Banister. *A History of Architecture on the Comparative Method,* 17th ed. New York: Scribner's, 1967.

Frampton, Kenneth. *The Poetics of Construction in Nineteenth and Twentieth Century Architecture.* John Cava (ed.). Cambridge, Mass.: MIT Press, 1996.

Giedion, Sigfried. *Space, Time and Architecture,* 5th ed., rev. and enl. Cambridge, Mass.: Harvard University Press, 1982.

Gloag, John. *The Architectural Interpretation of History.* New York: St. Martin's 1977.

Greene, Herb. *Mind and Image.* Lexington, Ky.: University Press of Kentucky, 1976.

Gropius, Walter. *The New Architecture and the Bauhaus.* London: Faber & Faber, 1965.

———. *The Scope of Total Architecture.* New York: Harper & Row, 1955.

Heyer, Paul. *Architects on Architecture.* New York: Walker, 1966.

Jacobs, Jane. *The Death and Life of Great American Cities.* Harmondsworth: Penguin, 1972.

Jordan, R. Furneaux. *A Concise History of Western Architecture.* New York: Harcourt Brace, 1978.

Le Corbusier. *Towards a New Architecture.* London: Architectural Press, 1987.

Mumford, Lewis. *The City in History.* New York: Harcourt Brace and World, 1969.

———. *The Roots of Contemporary American Architecture.* New York: Dover, 1972.

Nervi, Pier Luigi. *Aesthetics and Technology in Building.* London: Oxford University Press, 1966.

Oliver, Paul (ed.). *Shelter and Society.* London: Barrie and Jenkins, 1976.

Pevsner, Nikolaus. *An Outline of European Architecture*, 7th ed. Baltimore: Penguin, 1974.

Rudofsky, Bernard. *Architecture without Architects.* New York: Museum of Modern Art; distributed by Doubleday, 1965.

Scott, Geoffrey. *The Architecture of Humanism.* London: Norton, 1974.

Scruton, Roger. *The Aesthetics of Architecture.* Princeton, N.J.: Princeton University Press, 1979.

Soleri, Paolo. *The City in the Image of Man.* Cambridge, Mass.: MIT Press, 1973.

Wittkower, Rudolf. *Architecture Principles in the Age of Humanism.* New York: Columbia University Press, 1965.

Wright, Frank Lloyd. *The Living City.* New York: Horizon, 1958.

———. *Modern Architecture.* Princeton, N.J.: Princeton University Press, 1931.

———. *The Natural House.* New York: Horizon, 1954.

———. *A Testament.* New York: Horizon, 1957.

CHAPTER 6 WEBSITES

Architectural Visualization (computer graphics, visual ideas)

World Wide Web: **http://archproplan.auckland.ac.nz/**

Architecture and Sculpture in Turkey (ancient images, archaeological sites)

World Wide Web: **http://www.ncsa.uiuc.edu/SDG/Experimental/anu-art-history/architecture.images.html**

Architecture of the Tropics (tropical architecture, beach sites)

World Wide Web: **http://rossi.arc.miami.edu/**

Architecture Resource Center (general information on architecture)

World Wide Web: **http://www.u-net.com/~birchall/arch.htm**

Christo and Jeanne-Claude (wrapped buildings, Reichstag Castle project)

World Wide Web: **http://www.nbn.com/youcan/christo/**

Classical Architecture of the Mediterranean (great collection of Mediterranean images)

World Wide Web: **http://rubens.anu.edu.au/architecture_form.html**

Contemporary Architecture in Hong Kong (architectural overview of present-day Hong Kong)

World Wide Web: **http://www.ncsa.uiuc.edu/SDG/Experimental/anu-art-history/hongkong.html**

Design in Art and Architecture (mailing list)

List name: **design-1** Address: **listserv@psuvm.psu.edu**

Renaissance and Baroque Architecture (period designs and images)

World Wide Web: **http://www.lib.virginia.edu/dic/colls/arh102/**

C H A P T E R 7

LITERATURE

Literature is an art whose medium is language used to affect the imagination. Words themselves can evoke a response even when they are spoken independently of a grammatical setting, such as a sentence. The word "tintinnabulation," which Edgar Allan Poe uses in one of his poems, has a beautiful sound in itself. Poe also thought that "cellar door" was a beautiful phrase when regarding its sound qualities. However, these sounds are not just musical: they possess meaning, and the sound and the meaning combine to give them a special quality. One would only need to hear some words in an unintelligible foreign language to understand that word sounds, or "musicality," alone only partly qualify as beautiful. Thus, meaning and significance—which is to say the revelation possible in literature—are essential elements of literature and the literary experience.

Fiction writers and poets share many of the techniques of literature because their effects depend on universal language art. For example, a short story writer will use images to clarify a description just as often as a poet may. In "The Pot of Basil," which follows below, Boccaccio describes the return of Lorenzo in a dream using imagery with a direct appeal to the senses: "He appeared to her in a dream, pallid-looking and all disheveled, his clothes tattered and decaying." The poet often mixes metaphor or simile with imagery, as does T. S. Eliot in "The Love Song of J. Alfred Prufrock": "Shall I say, I have gone at dusk through narrow streets / And watched the smoke that rises from the pipes / Of lonely men in shirt-sleeves, leaning out of windows?" In both cases, our sense of participation with the moment of description is enhanced by the imagery that makes it vivid. The fiction writer may depend more heavily on point of view—that position from which the story is told—than the poet, but poets use invented narrators and first-person, third-person, and even second-person narration to tell their poems.

Poets will certainly use rhyme and meter more often than fiction writers, but you will find metrical passages in stories, just as you will find occasional rhyme. Most of what we observe as part of the language art of fiction writers will also be true of poets because both rely on the inherent resources of language.

No matter what specific form literature will take, we wish to emphasize the sound of its language and therefore we wish to revive the tradition of reading aloud. True, most of us are taught to read silently, and most of us have little chance to hear poems or stories recited, but even today such an experience is vital to responding thoroughly to literature. One reason for the sudden rise of rap music is that people really enjoy hearing rhyme and meter in action. Rap lyrics are among the simplest forms of poetry—simple rhyme-schemes, simple metrical patterns—but even though they are simple, they are effective and entertaining. Contemporary poets have largely abandoned rhyme and meter for the better part of two generations, and ironically the need to hear metrical language has surfaced in the popular poetry of the streets and recording studios. The fact that people do not read rap lyrics, but listen to them, reminds us that part of the power of literature is in the aural experience. Part of the fun of poetry is hearing its sensuous surface and connecting it to the significance that lies beneath it.

Geoffrey Chaucer wrote down *The Canterbury Tales* for convenience, more than a century before the invention of the printing press. But he read his tales out loud to an eager audience of courtly listeners who were much more attuned to hearing a good story than to reading it. Today, people interested in literature are usually described as readers, which underscores the dependence we have developed on the printed word for our literary experiences. However, since words "sound" even when read silently and the "sound" is an essential part of the "sense" or meaning of the words, we need to re-emphasize the tradition.

Interestingly enough, e. e. cummings' poem, "l(a"—which we discussed in Chapter 1—might seem to be an exception. Based upon the arrangement of the letters, the most basic elements of literature, the visual structure may seem more important than the sound structure. If cummings' poem were to be recited aloud, it would take at least two people to recite it, since one word—"loneliness"—has to be sustained while the other three words—"a leaf falls"—are spoken. There are many possible ways of reciting the poem, especially if there are several people available to speak various segments.

PERCEPTION KEY
RECITING CUMMINGS' "L(A"

1. With a group, try to stage a recitation of cummings' "l(a" on page 12. Try different approaches using individuals to be responsible for specific letters or syllables or a given word.
2. Comment on the recitations and evaluate them. Can this poem be effectively recited?
3. What unexpected relationships or significances emerged in the process of recitation? What effect on meaning does recitation by a group develop?

Treating literature as spoken language points up its relationship to other serial arts such as music, dance, and film. Literature happens in time. In order to perceive it, we must be aware of what is happening now, remember what happened before, and anticipate what is to come. This is not so obvious with a short lyric poem such as cummings' "l(a" because we are in the presence of something akin to a painting: it seems to be all there in front of us at once. But this is far from the truth. One word follows another; one sentence another; one line or one stanza another. There is no way to perceive the "all-at-onceness" of a literary work as we sometimes perceive a painting, although cummings' poem comes close.

A work of literature is, in one sense, a construction of separable elements like architecture. The details of a scene, a character or event, or a symbol pattern can be conceived of as the bricks in the wall of a literary structure. If one of these details is imperfectly understood, our understanding of the total structure will be imperfect. The theme (main idea) of a literary work is usually structural, comparable to an architectural decision: is it a house, church, urban mall, airport, or garage? Decisions about the sound of the language, the characters, the events, the setting, are comparable to the decisions regarding the materials, size, shape, and landscape of architecture. Here, perhaps, the analogy ends. But its usefulness will be seen as we proceed in our discussions about the details and structures of literature.

Our structural emphasis in the following pages will be on narrative—both the episodic narrative, in which all or most of the parts are loosely related episodes, and the organic narrative, in which the parts are tightly interrelated. Once we have explored some of the basic structures of literature, we will examine some of the more important details. In everyday language situations, what we say is often what we mean. But in a work of literature language is rarely that simple. Language has *denotation*: a literal level where words mean what they obviously say, and *connotation*: a subtler level at which words mean more than they obviously say. When we are being denotative, we say the rose is sick and mean nothing more than that. But if we are using language connotatively, we might mean any of several things by such a statement. When the poet William Blake says the rose is sick, he is describing a symbolic rose, something very different from a literal rose. He may mean that the rose is morally sick, spiritually defective, and that we are in some ways the rose. The symbol, simile, metaphor, image, and diction (word choices) are the main details of literary language that we will examine. All these details are found in poetry, fiction, drama, and even the essay.

LITERARY STRUCTURES

THE NARRATIVE AND THE NARRATOR

The narrative is a story told to an audience by a teller controlling the order of events and the emphasis those events receive. Most narratives concentrate upon the events. But some narratives have very little action: they reveal depth of character through responses to action. Sometimes the narrator is a character in the fiction; sometimes the narrator pretends an awareness of an audience other than the reader. However, the author controls the narrator and through the narrator really controls the reader. Consider the following narrative poem by D. H. Lawrence:

PIANO

Softly, in the dusk, a woman is singing to me;
Taking me back down the vista of years, till I see
A child sitting under the piano, in the boom of the tingling strings
And pressing the small, poised feet of a mother who smiles as she sings.

In spite of myself, the insidious mastery of song
Betrays me back, till the heart of me weeps to belong
To the old Sunday evenings at home, with winter outside
And hymns in the cozy parlor, the tinkling piano our guide.

So now it is vain for the singer to burst into clamor
With the great black piano appassionato. The glamor
Of childish days is upon me, my manhood is cast
Down by the flood of remembrance, I weep like a child for the past.

Perception Key
"PIANO"

1. What is more fully developed, events or character? Or are they more or less equally important?
2. What do we know about the narrator?
3. Is the narrator D. H. Lawrence? Does it make a significant difference to your understanding of the poem to know that answer? Why or why not?
4. Is the narrator aware of the audience to whom the narrative is addressed? If so, what assumptions does the narrator make about the audience?

Lawrence's poem relates events that are interesting mainly because they reveal something about the character of the narrator, especially his double focus as man and as child, with all the ambiguities that the narrator's memory evokes. If your background information includes something about the life of D. H. Lawrence, you probably will identify Lawrence as the narrator. The poem certainly has autobiographical roots: Lawrence's closeness to his mother evokes a dimension of poignancy to our participation. Yet if we did not have this information, not much would be lost. The revelation of the narrator's character is general in the sense that most of us understand and sympathize with the narrator's feelings, no matter whether the narrator is or is not Lawrence.

Notice that in order to be consistent we must treat the narrator as a character in the literary work. Thus we understand the "I" of "Piano" as a character in the poem just as much as the mother is. But the problem with that is curious. Since we conceive of ourself as "I," we may also accept the "I" of a narrative with no further examination. Lawrence is the "I," and that is all there is to it for some readers. Yet there is no compelling reason for us to think this; it is merely a matter of psychological habit and convenience, and it is part of the natural effect of using first-person point of view in a narrative.

The following poem is a powerful example of the way in which Sylvia Plath uses the first person narrator while creating an "I" character who is not herself. The poem is told by someone in an iron lung:

PARALYTIC

It happens. Will it go on?—
My mind a rock,
No fingers to grip, no tongue,
My god the iron lung

That loves me, pumps
My two
Dust bags in and out,
Will not

Let me relapse
While the day outside glares by like ticker tape
The night brings violets,
Tapestries of eyes,

Lights,
The soft anonymous
Talkers: "You all right?"
The starched, inaccessible breast.

Dead egg, I lie
Whole
On a whole world I cannot touch,
At the white, tight

Drum of my sleeping couch
Photographs visit me—
My wife, dead and flat, in 1920 furs,
Mouth full of pearls,

Two girls
As flat as she, who whisper "We're your daughters."
The still waters
Wrap my lips,

Eyes, nose and ears,
A clear
Cellophane I cannot crack.
On my bare back

I smile, a buddha, all
Wants, desire
Falling from me like rings
Hugging their lights.

The claw
Of the magnolia,
Drunk on its own scents,
Asks nothing of life.

PERCEPTION KEY
"PARALYTIC"

1. Analyze the narrative. What are the limitations of telling a story from the point of view of a person who is paralyzed?
2. What is the role of the magnolia claw—a living but not a moving instrument, as with people's hands—in the poem?
3. Explore some of the implications of the fact that the narrator of the poem is an imaginary character invented by the poet. Is this information crucial to a full understanding of the poem?
4. Sylvia Plath committed suicide not long after writing this poem. Does that information add intensity to your experience of the poem?

NARRATIVE STRUCTURES

The term "episodic narrative" describes one of the oldest kinds of literature, often used in the epic, as in Homer's *Odyssey.* We are aware of the overall structure of the story centering on the adventures of Odysseus, but each adventure is almost a complete structure in itself. We develop a clear sense of the character of Odysseus as we follow him in his adventures, but this does not always happen in episodic literature. Often the adventures are completely disconnected from one another, and the thread that is intended to connect everything—the personality of the main character (protagonist)—is not strong enough to keep things together. Sometimes the character may even seem to be a different person from one episode to the next. This is often the case in oral literature, compositions by tellers or singers of stories rather than by persons who wrote their narratives down. In the former cases, the tellers or singers gathered adventures from many sources and joined them in one long narrative. The chances of disconnectedness, then, are quite likely. But disconnectedness is sometimes not undesirable. It may gain several things: compression, speed of pacing, and variety of action that sustains attention. Some of the most famous episodic narratives are novels: Fielding's *Tom Jones,* Cervantes' *Don Quixote,* and Defoe's *Moll Flanders.*

The organic narrative connects every action and every character in subtle ways so that as the narrative unfolds, the reader is given more and more information about all the events of the story. If there are separable high points to the story, the narrative provides clear motivation and opportunity for the events to cohere in a dramatic and reasonable way. In an organically organized narrative emphasis on individual moments of action is lessened and emphasis on character is heightened. When such emphasis is done well, the narrative seems to derive from character and reveals character at each opportunity. The action is still important, but not in and of itself. Rather, the action is important as it proceeds naturally from character and circumstance.

The following narrative, "The Pot of Basil," is a single story that qualifies as organic. However, it is in a larger book, *The Decameron,* by Giovanni Boccaccio, which is itself episodic. *The Decameron* is a collection of stories told by several young people who hide themselves away during the Great Plague in Florence in 1348. To while away the time, they tell stories. Boccaccio is clever in that he reveals the character of the teller of the story while the narrative itself reveals the characters who act in it. Much more is revealed, of course, but the neat trick is that each of the narratives is complete and organic in itself, while the overall book is episodic. This story is told by a young woman named Filomena, who begins by explaining that she does not think her story will be as moving as the story she just heard Elissa tell.

THE POT OF BASIL

This story of mine, fair ladies, will not be about people of so lofty a rank as those of whom Elissa has been speaking, but possibly it will prove to be no less touching, and I was reminded of it by the mention that has just been made of Messina, which was where it all happened.

In Messina, there once lived three brothers, all of them merchants who had been left very rich after the death of their father, whose native town was San Gemignano. They had a sister called Lisabetta, but for some reason or other they had failed to bestow her in marriage, despite the fact that she was uncommonly gracious and beautiful.

In one of their trading establishments, the three brothers employed a young Pisan named Lorenzo, who planned and directed all their operations, and who, being rather dashing and handsomely proportioned, had often attracted the gaze of Lisabetta. Having noticed more than once that she had grown exceedingly fond of him, Lorenzo abandoned all his other amours and began in like fashion to set his own heart on winning Lisabetta. And since they were equally in love with each other, before very long they gratified their dearest wishes, taking care not to be discovered.

In this way, their love continued to prosper, much to their common enjoyment and pleasure. They did everything they could to keep the affair a secret, but one night, as Lisabetta was making her way to Lorenzo's sleeping-quarters, she was observed, without knowing it, by her eldest brother. The discovery greatly distressed him, but being a young man of some intelligence, and not wishing to do anything that would bring discredit upon his family, he neither spoke nor made a move, but spent the whole of the night applying his mind to various sides of the matter.

Next morning he described to his brothers what he had seen of Lisabetta and

Lorenzo the night before, and the three of them talked the whole thing over at considerable length. Being determined that the affair should leave no stain upon the reputation either of themselves or of their sister, he decided that they must pass it over in silence and pretend to have neither seen nor heard anything until such time as it was safe and convenient for them to rid themselves of this ignominy before it got out of hand.

Abiding by this decision, the three brothers jested and chatted with Lorenzo in their usual manner, until one day they pretended they were all going off on a pleasure-trip to the country, and took Lorenzo with them. They bided their time, and on reaching a very remote and lonely spot, they took Lorenzo off his guard, murdered him, and buried his corpse. No one had witnessed the deed, and on their return to Messina they put it about that they had sent Lorenzo away on a trading assignment, being all the more readily believed as they had done this so often before.

Lorenzo's continued absence weighed heavily upon Lisabetta, who kept asking her brothers, in anxious tones, what had become of him, and eventually her questioning became so persistent that one of her brothers rounded on her, and said:

"What is the meaning of this? What business do you have with Lorenzo, that you should be asking so many questions about him? If you go on pestering us, we shall give you the answer you deserve."

From then on, the young woman, who was sad and miserable and full of strange forebodings, refrained from asking questions. But at night she would repeatedly utter his name in a heart-rending voice and beseech him to come to her, and from time to time she would burst into tears because of his failure to return. Nothing would restore her spirits, and meanwhile she simply went on waiting.

One night, however, after crying so much over Lorenzo's absence that she eventually cried herself off to sleep, he appeared to her in a dream, pallid-looking and all disheveled, his clothes tattered and decaying, and it seemed to her that he said:

"Ah, Lisabetta, you do nothing but call to me and bemoan my long absence, and you cruelly reprove me with your tears. Hence I must tell you that I can never return, because on the day that you saw me for the last time, I was murdered by your brothers."

He then described the place where they had buried him, told her not to call to him or wait for him any longer, and disappeared.

Having woken up, believing that what she had seen was true, the young woman wept bitterly. And when she arose next morning, she resolved to go to the place and seek confirmation of what she had seen in her sleep. She dared not mention the apparition to her brothers, but obtained their permission to make a brief trip to the country for pleasure taking with her a maidservant who had once acted as her go-between and was privy to all her affairs. She immediately set out, and on reaching the spot, swept aside some dead leaves and started to excavate a section of the ground that appeared to have been disturbed. Nor did she have to dig very deep before she uncovered her poor lover's body, which, showing no sign as yet of decomposition or decay, proved all too clearly that her vision had been true. She was the saddest woman alive, but knowing that this was not time for weeping, and seeing that it was impossible for her to take away his whole body (as she would dearly have wished), she laid it to rest in a more appropriate spot, then severed the head from the shoulders as best she could and enveloped it in a towel. This she handed into her maidservant's keeping whilst she covered over the remainder of the corpse with soil, and then they returned home, having completed the whole of their task unobserved.

Taking the head to her room, she locked herself in and cried bitterly, weeping so profusely that she saturated it with her tears, at the same time implanting a thousand kisses upon it. Then she wrapped the head in a piece of rich cloth, and laid it in a large and elegant pot, of the sort in which basil or marjoram is grown. She next covered it with soil, in which she planted several sprigs of the finest Salernitan basil, and never watered them except with essence of roses or orange-blossom, or with her own teardrops. She took to sitting permanently beside this pot and gazing lovingly at it, concentrating the whole of her desire upon it because it was where her beloved Lorenzo lay concealed. And after gazing raptly for a long while upon it, she would bend over it and begin to cry, and her weeping never ceased until the whole of the basil was wet with her tears.

Because of the long and unceasing care that was lavished upon it, and also because the soil was enriched by the decomposing head inside the pot, the basil grew very thick and exceedingly fragrant. The young woman constantly followed this same routine, and from time to time she attracted the attention of her neighbors. And as they had heard her brothers expressing their concern at the decline in her good looks and the way in which her eyes appeared to have sunk into their sockets, they told them what they had seen, adding:

"We have noticed that she follows the same routine every day."

The brothers discovered for themselves that this was so, and having reproached her once or twice without the slightest effect, they caused the pot to be secretly removed from her room. When she found that it was missing, she kept asking for it over and over again, and because they would not restore it to her she sobbed and cried without a pause until eventually she fell seriously ill. And from her bed of sickness she would call for nothing else except her pot of basil.

The young men were astonished by the persistence of her entreaties, and decided to examine its contents. Having shaken out the soil, they saw the cloth and found the decomposing head inside it, still sufficiently intact for them to recognize it as Lorenzo's from the curls of his hair. This discovery greatly amazed them, and they were afraid lest people should come to know what had happened. So they buried the head, and without breathing a word to anyone, having wound up their affairs in Messina, they left the city and went to live in Naples.

The girl went on weeping and demanding her pot of basil, until eventually she cried herself to death, thus bringing her ill-fated love to an end. But after due process of time, many people came to know of the affair, and one of them composed the song which can still be heard to this day:

> Whoever it was,
> Whoever the villain
> That stole my pot of herbs, etc.

This story has long fascinated writers, many of whom have told it again in various ways. The narrative reveals a great deal about the pride of families and the power men in the family have over women and their wishes. It also builds a great deal of sympathy for women. The narrator of the story is Filomena, a woman, telling the story to other young women. We can presume that all of them are interested in romance and that all of them belong to wealthy families similar to the one described in the tale. The question of snobbery is always relevant in a society with a class system, such as the one Boccaccio describes. Thus, when the brothers decide that Lorenzo is not good enough for their sister, they act out of their sense of social propriety. They reject Lorenzo even though he is unusually capable in their company and is, by our standards, a distinct success. Further, when they learn that Lorenzo has been sleeping with Lisabetta, they decide to avenge the family honor—all without bothering to discuss the matter with Lisabetta. The brothers act in a fashion they feel is time-honored and reasonable.

PERCEPTION KEY
"THE POT OF BASIL"

1. What are the events of the narrative? Which actions are the most important?
2. Who is the most sympathetic character? Is that the main character of the narrative? Which character do you learn most about?
3. Which character is least sympathetic?
4. Is Lorenzo a good person? Did Lisabetta behave well?
5. To what extent does the story imply that love and madness are related?
6. Look up basil in a good dictionary; look it up in a dictionary of herbs. What associations does it have that relate to the story?

The imagery of the story, especially centering on the basil, a plant that is not only a seasoning herb, but also an herb associated with medicinal practices and funerary ceremonies, is dark and consistently foreboding. Lisabetta's are tears of mourning, watering the grave of her beloved with the grief of a love destroyed by pride. By cutting off her lover's head, she also suggests a kind of madness, because it would take an unbalanced mind to bury Lorenzo's head in a pot and water the plant its decomposing flesh fed. But this motif—burial—is partly at the center of the story. The father of the family has been buried, but patriarchy is resurrected in the brothers. Lisabetta is not married, but buried within the family. Lorenzo is murdered and buried, but his ghost walks and his body is dug up again. Then, his head is buried in the pot of basil only to be disinterred once more and discarded. Lisabetta's love for him was buried (or hidden) while Lorenzo lived; the brothers' love for Lisabetta was buried under their sense of social responsibility; finally, her sanity is buried within her and her own death joins her beneath the ground with Lorenzo. These images of burial help make the narrative organic and complete. The darkness of the setting, which is dominated by images of night, also contributes to the unity of the narrative. The tears that dominate the story evoke enormous grief and Lisabetta can be said to have "cried herself to death."

Certainly the teller of the story—Filomena—is sympathetic to Lisabetta. She also seems pleased by Lorenzo, since she describes him as dashing and capable. She has little sympathy with the brothers, describing the only one who speaks to Lisabetta as a tyrant, a threatening ogre. Filomena does not imply any disgrace for Lisabetta's behavior, nor does she imply that Filomena did anything for which she should feel regret. The point of view of the story is carefully controlled and the narrative is organically structured so that each detail fits into the entirety in a way that helps us to interpret the action and the characters in relation to the action.

THE QUEST NARRATIVE

The quest narrative is simple enough on the surface: a hero sets out in search of a valuable treasure that must be found and rescued at all cost. Such, in simple terms, is the plot of almost every adventure yarn and adventure film ever written. However, where most such yarns and films content themselves with erecting impossible obstacles which the heroes overcome with guts, imagination, and skill, the quest narrative has other virtues. Herman Melville's *Moby Dick,* the story of Ahab's determination to find and kill the white whale that took his leg from him, is also a quest narrative. It achieves unity by focusing all its attention on the quest and its object. But at the same time it explores in great depth the psychology of all those who take part in the adventure. Ahab becomes a type of monomaniac, a man who can see only one side of things. The narrator, Ishmael, is like an Old Testament prophet in that he has lived the experience, has looked into the face of evil, and has come back to tell the story to anyone who will listen, hoping to impart wisdom and sensibility to those who were not there. The heart of this novel is centered on the question of good and evil. When the novel begins, those values seem fairly clear and fairly well defined. But as the novel progresses, the question becomes murkier and murkier because the actions of the novel begin a reversal of values that is often a hallmark of the quest narrative.

Because most humans feel uncertain about their own nature—where they have come from, who they are, where they are going—it is natural that writers from all cultures should invent fictions that string adventures and character development on the thread of the quest for self-understanding. This quest is so attractive to our imaginations that we find it sustains our attention almost all the time. And while our attention is arrested by the narrative, the author can broaden and deepen the meaning of the quest until it engages our conceptions of ourselves. Such a search usually reveals some identity of the reader with the protagonist.

The quest structure in Ralph Ellison's *Invisible Man* is so deeply rooted in the novel that the protagonist has no name. We know a great deal about him because he narrates the story and tells us about himself. He is black, southern, and, as a young college student, ambitious. His earliest heroes are George Washington Carver and Booker T. Washington. He craves the dignity and the opportunity he associates with their lives. But things go wrong. He is dismissed unjustly from his college in the South and must, like Odysseus, leave home to seek his fortune. He imagines himself destined for better things and eagerly pursues his fate, finding a place to live and work up North, beginning to find his identity as a black man. He discovers the sophisticated urban society of New York City, the political subtleties of communism, the pains of black nationalism, and the realities of his relationship to white people, to whom he is an invisible man. Yet he does not hate the whites, and in his own image of himself he remains an invisible man. The novel ends with the protagonist in an underground place he has found and which he has lighted, by tapping the lines of the electric company, with almost 200 electric light bulbs. Despite this colossal illumination, he still cannot think of himself as visible. He ends his quest without discovering who he is beyond this fundamental fact: he is invisible. Black or white, we can identify in many ways with this quest, for Ellison is showing us that invisibility is in all of us.

PERCEPTION KEY
THE QUEST NARRATIVE

Read a quest narrative. Some suggestions: Ralph Ellison, *Invisible Man*; Mark Twain, *The Adventures of Huckleberry Finn*; Herman Melville, *Moby Dick*; J. D. Salinger, *The Catcher in the Rye*; Graham Greene, *The Third Man*; Franz Kafka, *The Castle*; Albert Camus, *The Stranger*; and Toni Morrison, *Beloved*. How does the quest help the protagonist get to know himself or herself better? Does the quest help you understand yourself better? Is the quest novel basically episodic or organic in structure?

The quest narrative is native to American culture. Mark Twain's *Huckleberry Finn* is one of the most important examples in American literature. But whereas *Invisible Man* is an organic quest narrative, because the details of the novel are closely interwoven, *Huckleberry Finn* is an episodic quest narrative. Huck's travels along the great Mississippi River qualify as episodic in the same sense that *Don Quixote,* to which this novel is closely related, is episodic. Huck is questing for freedom for Jim, but also for freedom from his own father. Like Don Quixote, Huck comes back from his quest rich in the knowledge of who he is. One might say Don Quixote's quest is for the truth about who he is and was, since he is an old man when he begins. But Huck is an adolescent, and his quest is for knowledge of who he is and can be.

THE LYRIC

The lyric structure, virtually always a poem, primarily reveals a limited but deep feeling about some thing or event. The lyric is often associated with the feelings of the poet, although we have already seen that it is not difficult for poets to create narrators distinct from themselves and to explore hypothetical feelings.

If we participate we find ourselves caught up in the emotional situation of the lyric. It is usually revealed to us through a recounting of the circumstances the poet reflects on. T. S. Eliot speaks of an "objective correlative": an object that correlates with the poet's feeling and helps express that feeling. Eliot has said that poets must find the image, situation, object, event, or person that "shall be the formula for that *particular* emotion" so that readers can comprehend it. This may be too narrow a view of the poet's creative process, because poets can understand and interpret emotions without necessarily undergoing them. Otherwise, it would seem that Shakespeare, for example, and even Eliot would have blown up like overcompressed boilers if they had had to experience directly all the feelings they interpreted in their poems. But in any case, it seems clear that the lyric has feeling—emotion, passion, or mood—as basic in its subject matter.

The word "lyric" implies a personal statement by an involved writer who feels deeply. In one limited sense, lyrics are poems to be sung to music. Most lyrics before the seventeenth century were set to music—in fact, most medieval and Renaissance lyrics were written to be sung with musical accompaniment. And the writers who composed the words were usually the composers of the music—at least until the seventeenth century, when specialization began to separate those functions.

John Keats (1795–1821), an English poet of the romantic period, died of tuberculosis. The following sonnet, written in 1818, is grounded in his awareness of early death:

When I have fears that I may cease to be
Before my pen has glean'd my teeming brain,
Before high-piled books, in charact'ry,
Hold like rich garners the full-ripen'd grain;
When I behold, upon the night's starr'd face,
Huge cloudy symbols of a high romance,
And think that I may never live to trace
Their shadows, with the magic hand of chance;
And when I feel, fair creature of an hour!
That I shall never look upon thee more,
Never have relish in the faery power
Of unreflecting love! then on the shore
Of the wide world I stand alone, and think
Till love and fame to nothingness do sink.

Perception Key
"WHEN I HAVE FEARS . . ."

1. This poem has no setting (environmental context), yet it establishes an atmosphere of uncertainty and, possibly, of terror. How does Keats create this atmosphere?
2. The poet is dying and knows he is dying—why does he then labor over the rhyme and meter of this poem? What does the poem do for the dying narrator?
3. What does the narrator wish to reveal about himself? What does he reveal about himself that may not be intentional?

Keats interprets a terrible personal feeling. He realizes he may die before he can write his best poems. The epitaph Keats chose for his headstone just before he died is: "Here lies one whose name was writ on water." He was wrong in believing that his poems would not be read by posterity. Moreover, his work is so brilliant that we cannot help wondering what else he might have done. Had Chaucer, Shakespeare, Milton, or Joyce died at twenty-six, we might not know their names, for their important work was yet to come.

It is not difficult for us to imagine how Keats must have felt. The lyric mode does not usually rely on narrative, but on our ability to respond to the circumstances described. In this poem, Keats has important resources. One is the fact that since we all will die, we can sympathize with the thought of death cutting a life's work short. The tone Keats establishes in the poem—one of direct speech, honestly said, not overdone or melodramatic—helps him communicate his emotions. It gives the poem an immediacy: one human being telling something straight from the heart to another. Keats modulates the tone slightly, slowing things down enough at the end of the poem for us to sense and share the despairing contemplative mood "to nothingness do sink."

An entirely different mood established by quite different means characterizes the next poem. It was written in the second half of the nineteenth century by a Jesuit priest. It is very personal but also, like the psalms of the Bible, something of a prayer or hymn of praise.

PIED BEAUTY

Glory be to God for dappled things—
For skies of couple-colour as a brinded cow;
or rose-moles all in stipple upon trout that swim;
Fresh-firecoal chestnut-falls; finches' wings;
Landscape plotted and pieced—fold, fallow, and plough;
And all trades, their gear and tackle and trim.

All things counter, original, spare, strange;
Whatever is fickle, freckled (who knows how?)
With swift, slow; sweet, sour; adazzle, dim;

He fathers-forth whose beauty is past change:
Praise him.[1]

Gerard Manley Hopkins

PERCEPTION KEY
"PIED BEAUTY"

1. Hopkins reveals joy in this poem. How? Are there details inconsistent with joyousness?
2. Is the awareness of the sensory essential in our experience of the poem? How many senses does Hopkins make reference to?

[1]*Pied*: spotted, like "dappled" and "couple-colour." *Brinded*: spots or streaks on a buff-colored background. *Chestnut falls*: the skin of the hot chestnut, stripped off. *Plotted and pieced*: fields of different shaped rectangles. *Fold, fallow,* and *plough*: fields used for different purposes and that look different to the eye.

3. Query people who have read the poem under circumstances similar to yours, then query people who come to it "cold." How different is their understanding of the poem?
4. God is referred to as him rather than Him in the last line. Is this simply a printer's convention? What does it mean to call this poem a religious lyric?

The usefulness of the lyric for bringing out the significance of things as felt meditatively—"emotion recollected in tranquility," Wordsworth—is so great that perhaps this is its most important purpose. It is a mode that in its self-awareness can explore leisurely those aspects of things that help clarify feelings. Without necessarily having a story to tell, the poet need not rush off into anything that is not central to the meditation itself. One famous meditative poem is Walt Whitman's "A Noiseless Patient Spider," a poem that is perhaps as much a tribute to the patience of Walt Whitman as it is to the spider. Out of Whitman's contemplation of the spider comes insight into the human soul.

A NOISELESS PATIENT SPIDER

A noiseless patient spider,
I mark'd where on a little promontory it stood isolated,
Mark'd how to explore the vacant vast surrounding,
It launch'd forth filament, filament, filament, out of itself,
Ever unreeling them, ever tirelessly speeding them.

And you O my soul where you stand,
Surrounded, detached, in measureless oceans of space,
Ceaselessly musing, venturing, throwing, seeking the spheres to connect them,
Till the bridge you will need be form'd, till the ductile anchor hold,
Till the gossamer thread you fling catch somewhere, O my soul.

PERCEPTION KEY
"A NOISELESS PATIENT SPIDER"

1. Whitman sees a connection between the spider and the human soul. What, exactly, is that connection? How reasonable does it seem to you? How illuminating?
2. In what sense does Whitman connect people with nature in this poem? What is the meaning of such a connection?

Five lyrics follow. They are very different in nature, although each one focuses on strong feelings. Symbols, metaphors, and images interpret those feelings for the attentive reader. Marvell's "To His Coy Mistress" is a *carpe diem* lyric. *Carpe diem* is Latin for "seize the day," meaning to do now what you will not be able to do later, when you get older. It is a special form of the lyric of sexual seduction. Marvell's images of "time's winged chariot" and the grave as "a fine and private place" are memorable and intense. Blake's "Tyger" seems to be about many things, especially the nature of evil and the nature of nature. The tiger is a powerful symbol in the poem, but it is not easy to say precisely what it symbolizes. It is a poem that, of the five, has most frequently been set to music. Matthew Arnold's "Dover Beach" has been set to music as well. It focuses on the isolation of two people who contemplate the uncertainties and terror of the future. For the modern reader, this is a particularly timely poem, since "the armies of the night"—to use Norman Mailer's paraphrase of Arnold—have been more highly visible in this century than in any other. Emily Dickinson describes a moment that some have interpreted as near-death. Her imagery is memorable, concrete, and convincing. Audre Lorde's "Coal" meditates on values and feelings. Her imagery and metaphors are accessible and touching. In these selections we study the rich varieties of the lyric.

TO HIS COY MISTRESS

Had we but world enough, and time,
This coyness, lady, were no crime.
We would sit down, and think which way
To walk, and pass our long love's day.
Thou by the Indian Ganges' side
Shouldst rubies find; I by the tide
Of Humber would complain. I would
Love you ten years before the Flood;
And you should, if you please, refuse
Till the Conversion of the Jews.
My vegetable love should grow
Vaster than empires, and more slow.
An hundred years should go to praise
Thine eyes, and on thy forehead gaze;
Two hundred to adore each breast,
But thirty thousand to the rest.
An age at least to every part,
And the last age should show your heart.
For, Lady, you deserve this state,
Nor would I love at lower rate.

But at my back I always hear
Time's winged chariot hurrying near;
And yonder all before us lie
Deserts of vast eternity.
Thy beauty shall no more be found,
Nor, in thy marble vault, shall sound
My echoing song: then worms shall try
That long preserved virginity:
And your quaint honor turn to dust,
And into ashes all my lust:
The grave's a fine and private place,
But none, I think, do there embrace.

Now, therefore, while the youthful hue
Sits on thy skin like morning dew,
And while thy willing soul transpires

At every pore with instant fires,
Now let us sport us while we may;
And now, like amorous birds of prey,
Rather at once our time devour,
Than languish in his slow-chapped power.
Let us roll all our strength, and all
Our sweetness, up into one ball:
And tear our pleasures with rough strife
Thorough the iron gates of life.
Thus, though we cannot make our sun
Stand still, yet we will make him run.

Andrew Marvell

THE TYGER

Tyger! Tyger! burning bright
In the forests of the night,
What immortal hand or eye
Could frame thy fearful symmetry?

In what distant deeps or skies
Burnt the fire of thine eyes?
On what wings dare he aspire?
What the hand dare seize the fire?

And what shoulder, and what art,
Could twist the sinews of thy heart?
And when thy heart began to beat,
What dread hand? and what dread feet?

What the hammer? what the chain?
In what furnace was thy brain?
What the anvil? what dread grasp
Dare its deadly terrors clasp?

When the stars threw down their spears,
And water'd heaven with their tears,
Did he smile his work to see?
Did he who made the Lamb make thee?

Tyger! Tyger! burning bright
In the forests of the night,
What immortal hand or eye
Dare frame thy fearful symmetry?

William Blake

DOVER BEACH

The sea is calm to-night.
The tide is full, the moon lies fair
Upon the straits;—on the French coast, the light
Gleams and is gone; the cliffs of England stand,
Glimmering and vast, out in the tranquil bay.
Come to the window, sweet is the night air!
Only, from the long line of spray
Where the sea meets the moon-blanch'd land,
Listen, you hear the grating roar
Of pebbles which the waves draw back, and fling,
At their return, up the high strand,
Begin, and cease, and then again begin,
With tremulous cadence slow, and bring
The eternal note of sadness in.

Sophocles long ago
Heard it on the Ægæan, and it brought
Into his mind the turbid ebb and flow
Of human misery; we
Find also in the sound a thought,
Hearing it by this distant northern sea.

The Sea of Faith
Was once, too, at the full, and round earth's shore
Lay like the folds of a bright girdle furl'd.
But now I only hear
Its melancholy, long, withdrawing roar,
Retreating, to the breath
Of the night-wind, down the vast edges drear
And naked shingles of the world.

Ah, love, let us be true
To one another! for the world, which seems
To lie before us like a land of dreams,
So various, so beautiful, so new,
Hath really neither joy, nor love, nor light,
Nor certitude, nor peace, nor help for pain;
And we are here as on a darkling plain
Swept with confused alarms of struggle and flight,
Where ignorant armies clash by night.

Matthew Arnold

AFTER GREAT PAIN, A FORMAL FEELING COMES

After great pain, a formal feeling comes—
The Nerves sit ceremonious, like Tombs—
The stiff Heart questions was it He, that bore,
And Yesterday, or Centuries before?

The Feet, mechanical, go round—
Of Ground, or Air, or Ought—
A Wooden way
Regardless grown,
A Quartz contentment, like a stone—

This is the Hour of Lead—
Remembered, if outlived,
As Freezing persons, recollect the Snow—
First—Chill—then Stupor—then the letting go—

Emily Dickinson

COAL

is the total black, being spoken
from the earth's inside.
There are many kinds of open
how a diamond comes into a knot of flame
how sound comes into words, coloured
by who pays what for speaking.

Some words are open like a diamond
on glass windows
singing out within the crash of sun
Then there are words like stapled wagers
in a perforated book—buy and sign and tear apart—
and come whatever wills all chances
the stub remains
an ill-pulled tooth with a ragged edge.
Some words live in my throat
breeding like adders. Others know sun
seeking like gypsies over my tongue
to explode through my lips
like young sparrows bursting from shell.
Some words
bedevil me.

Love is a word, another kind of open.
As the diamond comes into a knot of flame
I am Black because I come from the earth's inside
Now take my word for jewel in the open light.

Audre Lorde

Perception Key
VARIETIES OF LYRIC

1. Begin by establishing a *taxonomy* of the lyric, drawing up a list of the qualities the lyric possesses. Decide which qualities are most and least important.
2. Describe the emotional issues raised in each poem.

3. Which of these poems evokes the strongest emotion in you? Do you think your response is specific to you, or would most readers respond as you do?
4. Select a favorite song lyric. What does it have in common with the lyrics of Marvell, Blake, Arnold, Dickinson, and Lorde? What different qualities does it have?
5. If possible, listen to Ralph Vaughn-Williams' musical setting of Blake's "Tyger." Does this music make the poem more interesting? More understandable? If you cannot obtain a recording of the Vaughn-Williams piece, experiment with some song lyrics you can find more easily. What is the relative importance of the words to the music? Are the words or the music more important? Why?
6. Try your hand at writing a lyric. Decide before you write something what you are trying to say. Do not be surprised or disappointed if you modify your objective as you proceed. Keep refining your lines in order to achieve what you want. Give your lyric to someone and find out what he or she thinks you have accomplished.

LITERARY DETAILS

So far we have been analyzing literature with reference to structure, the overall order. But within every structure are details that need close examination in order to properly perceive the structure.

Language is used in literature in ways that differ from everyday uses. This is not to say that literature is artificial and unrelated to the language we speak but, rather, that we sometimes do not see the fullest implications of our speech and rarely take full advantage of the opportunities language affords us. Literature uses language to reveal meanings that are usually absent from daily speech.

Our emphasis here in treating matters of detail will be upon the image, metaphor, and symbol. There are other, often subtler, details of language also worthy of attention, but the image, metaphor, and symbol are so central to literature of all genres that they will stand as introduction enough for our purposes. To those details we will add one further: "diction," meaning the choice of words for a given situation.

THE IMAGE

An image in language asks us to imagine or "picture" what is referred to or being described. Most images appeal to our sense of sight, but sound, taste, odor, and touch are often involved. One of the most striking resources of language is its capacity to help us reconstruct in our imagination the "reality" of perceptions. This resource is sometimes as important in prose as in poetry. Consider, for example, the opening passage from Virginia Woolf's story, "Kew Gardens":

> From the oval-shaped flower-bed there rose perhaps a hundred stalks spreading into heart-shaped or tongue-shaped leaves half way up and unfurling at the tip red or blue or yellow petals marked with spots of color raised upon the surface;

> and from the red, blue, or yellow gloom of the throat emerged a straight bar, rough with gold dust and slightly clubbed at the end. The petals were voluminous enough to be stirred by the summer breeze, and when they moved, the red, blue, and yellow lights passed one over the other, staining an inch of the brown earth beneath with a spot of the most intricate color. The light fell either upon the smooth gray back of a pebble, or the shell of a snail with its brown circular veins, or, falling into a raindrop, it expanded with such intensity of red, blue, and yellow the thin walls of water that one expected them to burst and disappear. Instead, the drop was left in a second silver gray once more, and the light now settled upon the flesh of a leaf, revealing the branching thread of fiber beneath the surface, and again it moved on and spread its illumination in the vast green spaces beneath the dome of the heart-shaped and tongue-shaped leaves. Then the breeze stirred rather more briskly overhead and the color was flashed into the air above, into the eyes of the men and women who walk in Kew Gardens in July.

Woolf takes great pains in the opening of this story to appeal to the visual sensibilities of the reader by presenting an intense image of flowers and the light passing through them "staining" the ground. Colors and perceptible shapes: "Tongue-shaped," "heart-shaped," "slightly clubbed at the end" all make appeal to the visual sense, and the imagery promises a sensuous experience in the story. As you read you participate with the imagery first, then with the entire story.

In a short story, such moments are sometimes fleeting, perhaps just an instant in the total structure. But Woolf's entire story is composed of such details, helping to engage the reader's participation. For a poet such as Ezra Pound, the image is almost all there is. Pound and several other writers of the early twentieth century grouped together and became known as Imagist poets. One classic example of this school is Pound's famous poem:

IN A STATION OF THE METRO

The apparition of these faces in the crowd.
Petals on a wet, black bough.

The Metro is the Paris subway. The poem makes no comment about the character of these faces. The poem simply asks us to "image" the scene; we must reconstruct it in our imagination. And in doing so we visualize with clarity one aspect of the appearance of these faces: They are like petals on a wet, black bough. Such comparisons are metaphoric.

Archibald MacLeish, poet and critic, points out in *Poetry and Experience* that not all images in poetry work metaphorically, i.e., as a comparison of two things. This may be the case even when the images are placed side beside. Thus in a grave in John Donne's "The Relic" "a loving couple lies," and there is this marvelous line: "A bracelet of bright hair about the bone. . . ." The image of a bracelet of bright hair is coupled with an image of a bone. The images lie side by side, tied by the "b" sounds. Their coupling is startling because of the immediacy of their contrasting associations: vital life and inevitable death. There is no metaphor here (something is like something else in some significant way). There is simply one image juxtaposed beside another. We hear or read through the sounds—but never leave them—into their references, through the references to the images they create, through the images to their relationship, and finally to the poignant meaning: even young girls with golden hair die. We all know that, of course, but now we face it, and feel it, because of the meaning generated by those images lying side by side: life, death, beauty, devotion, and sorrow bound together in that unforgettable grave.

PERCEPTION KEY
JOHN DONNE

1. Suppose the word "blonde" were substituted for "bright." Would the meaning of the line be enhanced or diminished? Why?
2. Suppose the word "white" were placed in front of "bone." Would the meaning of the line be enhanced or diminished? Why?

In his use of imagery, Pound was influenced by Chinese and Japanese poets. The following poem is by the Chinese poet Tu Mu (803–852):

THE RETIRED OFFICIAL YÜAN'S HIGH PAVILION

The West River's watershed sounds beyond the sky.
Shadows of pines in front of the studio sweep the clouds flat.
Who shall coax me to blow the long flute
Leaning together on the spring wind with the moonbeams for our toys?

PERCEPTION KEY
"THE RETIRED OFFICIAL YÜAN'S HIGH PAVILION"

1. Do the images enhance the meaning of the poem? How?
2. Do these images work more like the images of Donne's poem or those of Pound's? Explain.
3. Are such images present in Emily Dickinson's lyric? Are they present in Andrew Marvell's lyric?

THE METAPHOR

Metaphor helps writers intensify language. Metaphor is a comparison designed to heighten our perception of the things compared and to invoke meditation on the comparison. Poets or writers will usually let us know which of the things compared is the main object of their attention. For example, in the following poem Shakespeare compares his age to the autumn of the year and himself to a glowing fire that consumes itself with vitality. The structure of this sonnet is marked by developing one metaphor in each of three quatrains (a group of four rhyming lines) and a couplet that offers a kind of summation of the entire poem.

SONNET 73

That time of year thou mayst in me behold
When yellow leaves, or none, or few, do hang
Upon those boughs which shake against the cold,
Bare ruined choirs, where late the sweet birds sang.
In me thou see'st the twilight of such day
As after sunset fadeth in the west,
Which by and by black night doth take away,
Death's second self, that seals up all in rest.
In me thou see'st the glowing of such fire
That on the ashes of his youth doth lie,
As the death-bed whereon it must expire,
Consumed with that which it was nourished by.
    This thou perceiv'st, which makes thy love more strong,
    To love that well which thou must leave ere long.

William Shakespeare

Perception Key
SHAKESPEARE'S 73RD SONNET

1. The first metaphor compares the narrator's age with autumn. How are "yellow leaves, or none" appropriate to be compared with a man's age? What is implied by the comparison? The "bare ruined choirs" are the high place in the church—what place, physically, would they compare with in a man's body?
2. The second metaphor is the "sunset" fading "in the west." What is this compared with in a man's life? Why is the imagery of the second quatrain effective?
3. The third metaphor is the "glowing" fire. What is the point of this metaphor? What is meant by the fire's consuming "that which it was nourished by"? What is being consumed here?
4. Why does the conclusion of the poem follow logically from the metaphors developed in the first three quatrains?
5. Since the message of the poem is "complete" in the ending couplet, what do the metaphors add to the experience of reading the poem? Would the poem reveal any less about the plight of the aging lover if the first twelve lines were simply left out?

The standard definition of the metaphor is that it is a comparison made without any explicit words to tell us a comparison is being made. The simile is the kind of comparison that has explicit words: "like," "as," "than," "as if," and a few others. We have no trouble recognizing the simile, and we may get so used to reading similes in literature that we recognize them without any special degree of awareness.

Some people make a fuss over the difference between a metaphor and a simile. We will not do so because basically both are forms of comparison for effect. Our discussion, then, will use the general term "metaphor" and use the more special term "simile" only when necessary. On the other hand, the term "symbol," which is also metaphoric, will be treated separately, since its effect is usually much more specialized than the nonsymbolic metaphor.

The use of metaphor pervades all cultures. Daily conversation—usually none too literary in character—is full of metaphoric language used to emphasize our points and give color and feeling to our speech (check this for yourself). The Chinese poet Li Ho (791–817) shows us the power of the metaphor in a poetic tradition very different from that of the West.

THE GRAVE OF LITTLE SU

I ride a coach with lacquered sides,
My love rides a dark piebald horse.
Where shall we bind our hearts as one?
On West Mound, beneath the pines and cypresses.
(Ballad ascribed to the singing girl Little Su, circa 500 A.D.).

Dew on the secret orchid
No thing to bind the heart to.
Misted flowers I cannot bear to cut.
Grass like a cushion,
The pine like a parasol:
The wind is a skirt,
The waters are tinkling pendants.
A coach with lacquered sides
Waits for someone in the evening.
Cold blue candle-flames
Strain to shine bright.
Beneath West Mound
The wind puffs the rain.

Little Su was important to the narrator, but the portrayal of his feeling for her is oblique—which is, perhaps, why so many metaphors appear in such a short poem. Instead of striking bluntly and immediately, the metaphoric language resounds with nuances, so that we are aware of its cumulative impact only after the reading.

PERCEPTION KEY
"THE GRAVE OF LITTLE SU"

Enumerate the uses of metaphor in the poem. Compare what you find with the findings of other readers. Are you in disagreement? If so, what does this mean? How does the metaphor in this poem differ from metaphor in Sonnet 73? How is it similar?

Metaphor pervades poetry, but we do not always realize how extensive the device is in other kinds of literature. Prose fiction, drama, or literature meant for the stage, essays, and almost every form of writing use metaphors. Poetry in general, however, tends to have a higher metaphoric density than other forms of writing, partly because poetry is somewhat distilled and condensed to begin with. Rarely, however, is the density of metaphor quite as thick as in "The Grave of Little Su."

Since literature depends so heavily on metaphor, it is essential that we reflect on its use. One kind of metaphor tends to evoke an image and involves us mainly on a perceptual level—because we perceive in our imagination something of what we would perceive were we there. This kind we shall call a "perceptual metaphor." Another kind of metaphor tends to evoke ideas, gives us information that is mainly conceptual. This kind of metaphor we shall call a "conceptual metaphor." To tell us the pine is like a parasol is basically perceptual: were we there, we would see that the cone shape of the pine resembles that of a parasol. But to tell us the wind is a skirt is to go far beyond perception and simple "likeness." The metaphor lures us to reflect upon the suggestion that the wind resembles a skirt, and we begin to think about the ways in which this might be true. Then we are lured further—this is an enticing metaphor—to explore the implications of this truth. If the wind is like a skirt, what then is its significance in the poem? In what ways does this conceptual metaphor help us to understand the poet's insights at the grave of Little Su? In what ways does the perceptual metaphor of the pine and parasol help us?

The answer to how the wind is a skirt is by no means simple. Its complexity is one of the precious qualities of this poem. It is also one of the most precious possibilities of strong conceptual metaphors generally, for then one goes beyond the relatively simple perceptual comparison into the more suggestive and significant acts of understanding. We suggest, for instance, that if the wind is like a skirt, it clothes a girl: Little Su. But Little Su is dead, so perhaps it clothes her spirit. The comparison then is between the wind and the spirit. Both are impossible to see, but the relationships between their meanings can be understood and felt.

The same kind of complexity is present in Tu Mu's poem, "The Retired Official Yüan's High Pavilion." The last line suggests that the moonbeams are toys. The metaphor is quiet, restrained, but as direct as the wind–skirt metaphor. Moreover, the last line suggests that the wind is something that can be leaned against. Turn back to that poem to see just how these metaphors expand the mysterious quality of the poem.

THE SYMBOL

The symbol is a further use of metaphor. Being a metaphor, it is a comparison between two things; but unlike most perceptual and conceptual metaphors, only one of the things compared is clearly stated. The symbol is clearly stated, but what it is compared with (sometimes a very broad range of meanings) is only hinted at. For instance, the white whale in Herman Melville's novel, *Moby Dick,* is a symbol both in the novel and in the mind of Captain Ahab, who sees the whale as a symbol of all the malevolence and evil in a world committed to evil. But we may not necessarily share Ahab's views. We may believe that the whale is simply a beast and not a symbol at all. Or, we may believe that the whale is a symbol for nature, which is constantly being threatened by human misunderstanding. Such a symbol can mean more than one thing. It is the peculiar quality of most symbols that they do not sit still; even their basic meanings keep changing. Symbols are usually vague and ambiguous. It is said that many symbols are a product of the subconscious, which is always treating things symbolically and always searching for implicit meanings. If this is so, it helps account for the persistence of symbols in even the oldest literature.

Perhaps the most important thing to remember about the symbol is that it implies rather than explicitly states meaning. We sense that we are dealing with a symbol in those linguistic situations in which we feel there is more being said than meets the eye. Most writers are quite open about their symbols, as in William Blake's poetry. He saw God's handiwork everywhere, but he also saw forces of destruction everywhere. Thus his poetry discovers symbols in almost every situation and thing, not just in those situations and things that are usually accepted as meaningful. The following poem is an example of his technique. At first the poem may seem needlessly confusing, because we do not know how to interpret the symbols. But a second reading begins to clarify the meaning of the symbols.

THE SICK ROSE

O rose, thou art sick!
        The invisible worm,
That flies in the night,
        In the howling storm,
Has found out thy bed
        Of crimson joy;
And his dark secret love
        Does thy life destroy.

William Blake

Perception Key
"THE SICK ROSE"

1. The rose and the worm stand as opposites in this poem, symbolically antagonistic. In discussion with other readers, explore possible meanings for the rose and the worm.
2. The bed of crimson joy and the dark secret love are also symbols. What are their meanings? Consider them closely in relation to the rose and the worm.
3. What is not a symbol in this poem?

Blake used such symbols because he saw a richness of implication in them that linked him to God. He thus shared in a minor way the creative act with God and helped others understand the world in terms of symbolic meaningfulness. For most other writers, the symbol is used more modestly to expand meaning, encompassing deep ranges of suggestion. The symbol has been compared with a stone dropped into the still waters of a lake: the stone itself is very small, but the effects radiate from its center to the edges of the lake. The symbol is dropped into our imagination, and it, too, radiates with meaning. But the marvelous thing about the symbol is that it tends to be permanently expansive: who knows where the meaningfulness of Blake's rose ends?

Prose fiction has made extensive use of the symbol. In Melville's *Moby Dick*, the white whale is a symbol, but so, too, is Ahab and the entire journey they undertake. The quest for Moby Dick is itself a symbolic quest. The albatross in Samuel Coleridge's "The Ancient Mariner" is a symbol, and so is the Ancient Mariner's stopping one of the wedding guests to make him hear the entire narrative. In these cases the symbols operate both structurally, in the entire narrative, and in the narrative's details.

In Dostoevsky's *Crime and Punishment*, the murderer-to-be, Raskolnikov, has a symbolic dream shortly before he kills the old woman, Alena. In the dream Raskolnikov is a child again, walking through city streets with his father:

> Suddenly there was a great explosion of laughter that drowned everything else: the old mare had rebelled against the hail of blows and was lashing out feebly with her hoofs. Even the old man could not help laughing. Indeed, it was ludicrous that such a decrepit old mare could still have a kick left in her.
>
> Two men in the crowd got whips, ran to the horse, one on each side, and began to lash at her ribs.
>
> "Hit her on the nose and across the eyes, beat her across the eyes!" yelled Mikolka.
>
> "Let's have a song, lads!" someone called from the wagon, and the others joined in. Somebody struck up a coarse song, a tambourine rattled, somebody else whistled the chorus. The fat young woman went on cracking nuts and giggling.
>
> . . . The boy ran towards the horse, then round in front, and saw them lashing her across the eyes, and actually striking her very eyeballs. He was weeping. His heart seemed to rise into his throat, and tears rained from his eyes. One of the whips stung his face, but he did not feel it; he was wringing his hands and crying aloud. He ran to a grey-haired, grey-bearded old man, who was shaking his head in reproof. A peasant-woman took him by the hand and tried to lead him away, but he tore himself loose and ran back to the mare. She was almost at her last gasp, but she began kicking again.
>
> "The devil fly away with you!" shrieked Mikolka in a fury.
>
> He flung away his whip, stooped down and dragged up from the floor of the cart a long thick wooden shaft, grasped one end with both hands, and swung it with an effort over the wretched animal.
>
> Cries rose: "He'll crush her!" "He'll kill her!"
>
> "She's my property," yelled Mikolka, and with a mighty swing let the shaft fall. There was a heavy thud.[2]

The symbolism of this passage becomes clearer in the context of the entire

[2]From Dostoevsky's *Crime and Punishment,* translated by J. L. Coulson, published by Oxford University Press, 1953. Reprinted by permission of the publisher.

novel. Raskolnikov is planning a brutal murder of an aged shopkeeper. Only a couple of pages later, Raskolnikov reflects on his dream:

> "God!" he exclaimed, "is it possible, is it possible, that I really shall take an axe and strike her on the head, smash open her skull . . . that my feet will slip in warm, sticky blood, and that I shall break the lock, and steal, and tremble, and hide, all covered in blood . . . with the axe . . . ? God, is it possible?"[3]

PERCEPTION KEY
CRIME AND PUNISHMENT

1. What does the old mare symbolize in Raskolnikov's dream? What does the entire situation symbolize?
2. Sample opinion from others and explore the effectiveness of having the beating of the horse revealed in a dream. Is this weaker or stronger in symbolic value than if the scene had actually taken place on the streets in front of Raskolnikov? Why?
3. How much does this symbolic action reveal about Raskolnikov? Does he seem—considering what he is actually about to do—different as a boy than as an adult? How would you characterize his sensitiveness and his compassion?
4. Dostoevsky uses the dream as a symbol. Are your dreams symbolic?

DICTION

Diction refers to the choice of words. But because the entire act of writing involves the choice of words, the term "diction" is usually reserved for literary acts (speech as well as the written word) that use words chosen especially carefully for their impact. The diction of a work of literature will sometimes make that work seem "inevitable," as if there were no other way of saying the same thing, as in Shakespeare's: "To be, or not to be." Try saying that in other words.

Inevitability sometimes results from our having heard a passage expressed the same way again and again. We get used to it, and want no variations. But that is also often because, among the choices we have, we recognize the best and choose it over others whose meanings may be essentially the same. That is almost surely the case with Psalm 23. One of the three translations that follow has been so popular that to the ears of those who have often heard the psalm read, the other two would seem to be completely defective. As you compare the following versions, consider that although two were popular in their own time, only one is truly popular today. Which one do you think it is?

My shepherd is the living Lord; nothing, therefore, I need.
In pastures fair, with waters calm, he set me for to feed.
He did convert and glad my soul, and brought my mind in frame
To walk in paths of righteousness for his most holy name.

[3]Ibid.

Yea, though I walk in the vale of death, yet will I fear none ill;
Thy rod, thy staff doth comfort me, and thou art with me still.
And in the presence of my foes, my table thou has spread;
Thou shalt, O Lord, fill full my cup and eke anoint my head.
Through all my life thy favor is so frankly showed to me
That in thy house forevermore my dwelling place shall be.

Sternhold and Hopkins, 1567

The Lord is my shepherd, I shall not want.
He maketh me to lie down in green pastures: he leadeth me beside the still waters.
He restoreth my soul: he leadeth me in the paths of righteousness for his name's sake.
Yea, though I walk through the valley of the shadow of death,
I will fear no evil: for thou art with me; thy rod and thy staff they comfort me.
Thou preparest a table before me in the presence of mine enemies: thou anointest my head with oil; my cup runneth over.
Surely goodness and mercy shall follow me all the days of my life: and I will dwell in the house of the Lord forever.

King James Version, 1611

Because the Lord acts as my shepherd, I don't need anything.
He lets me lie down in green pastureland and walk near quiet rivers.
He restores my soul and leads me on the right path in his name.
Yes, even though I walk through some tough neighborhoods,
I'm not afraid of anyone because God is with me.
He makes a table ready for me in front of those who despise me.
God anoints me with oil and gives me more than enough of everything.
I expect God will look after me through all the days of my life
And when I die, I will live with God forever.

Andre James, 1995

PERCEPTION KEY
PSALM 23

1. Compare the Sternhold–Hopkins version with the King James version. What word choices are particularly strong or weak in either version? Does the lack of rhyme in the King James version weaken or strengthen the meaning? Explain.
2. Compare the rhythms of the three versions. Which is more effective? Why? Which is most poetic in feel? Which most prosaic?
3. As an experiment, read the Sternhold–Hopkins version to friends and ask them what the name of the piece is. Does it come as a surprise when they realize which psalm it is?
4. Try your hand at revising the Sternhold–Hopkins version. "Translate" it into contemporary English. Ask others to do the same. Compare the best translation with the King James version.
5. What is it about the diction of the King James version that apparently makes it so effective? Be specific.

The careful use of diction can sometimes aid a satirist, whose intention is to say one thing and mean another. One classic example of this is Jonathan Swift's essay, "A Modest Proposal," in which he most decorously suggests that the solution to the poverty-stricken Irish farmer's desperation was the sale of his infant children—for the purpose of serving them up as plump, tender roasts for Christmas dinners in England. The diction is so subtly ironic that it is with some difficulty that many readers finally realize Swift is writing satire. By the time one reaches the following passage, one should surely understand the irony:

> I have been assured by a very knowing American of my acquaintance in London, that a young healthy child well nursed is at a year old a most delicious, nourishing, and wholesome food, whether stewed, roasted, baked, or boiled; and I make no doubt that it will equally serve in a fricasee or a ragout.

Examine the following poem for its narrative qualities and for the details of imagery, metaphor, symbol, and diction. The poem is a monologue in which the Duke of Ferrara speaks to a distinguished visitor about his late wife, the last duchess. The visitor has come to help broker a marriage between the duke and the daughter of the count, for whom the listener is a retainer. The reader can be imagined as overhearing the one-sided conversation.

MY LAST DUCHESS

Ferrara

That's my last Duchess painted on the wall,
Looking as if she were alive. I call
That piece a wonder, now: Frà Pandolf's hands
Worked busily a day, and there she stands.
Will't please you sit and look at her? I said
"Frà Pandolf" by design, for never read
Strangers like you that pictured countenance,
The depth and passion of its earnest glance,
But to myself they turned (since none puts by
the curtain I have drawn for you, but I)
And seemed as they would ask me, if they durst,
How such a glance came there; so, not the first
Are you to turn and ask thus. Sir, 'twas not
Her husband's presence only, called that spot
Of joy into the Duchess' cheek: perhaps
Frà Pandolf chanced to say, "Her mantle laps
Over my lady's wrist too much," or "Paint
Must never hope to reproduce the faint
Half-flush that dies along her throat": such stuff
Was courtesy, she thought, and cause enough
For calling up that spot of joy. She had
A heart—how shall I say?—too soon made glad,
Too easily impressed; she liked whate'er
She looked on, and her looks went everywhere.
Sir, 'twas all one! My favor at her breast.

The dropping of the daylight in the West,
The bough of cherries some officious fool
Broke in the orchard for her, the white mule
She rode with round the terrace—all and each
Would draw from her alike the approving speech,
Or blush, at least. She thanked men—good! But thanked
Somehow—I know not how—as if she ranked
My gift of a nine-hundred-years-old name
With anybody's gift. Who'd stoop to blame
This sort of trifling? Even had you skill
In speech—(which I have not)—to make your will
Quite clear to such an one, and say, "Just this
Or that in you disgusts me; here you miss,
Or there exceed the mark"—and if she let
Herself be lessoned so, nor plainly set
Her wits to yours, forsooth, and made excuse
—E'en then would be some stooping; and I choose
Never to stoop. Oh sir, she smiled, no doubt,
Whene'r I passed her; but who passed without
Much the same smile? This grew; I gave commands;
Then all smiles stopped together. There she stands
As if alive. Will't please you rise? We'll meet
The company below, then. I repeat,
The Count your master's known munificence
Is ample warrant that no just pretense
Of mine for dowry will be disallowed;
Though his fair daughter's self, as I avowed
At starting, is my object. Nay, we'll go
Together down, sir. Notice Neptune, though,
Taming a sea horse, thought a rarity,
Which Clause of Innsbruck cast in bronze for me!

Robert Browning

Perception Key
"MY LAST DUCHESS"

1. The poem offers two portraits: one of the duke, as he converses with his guest, and the other of the duchess, both as she was painted, and as the duke remembered her. How would you characterize the duke and the duchess?
2. Explain what makes this a lyric poem or a narrative poem.
3. Comment on the imagery of the poem. Which images are most sensuous, and which are the most intense?
4. Identify the metaphors and symbols in the poem.
5. Comment on the diction. Which verbal expressions most clearly "give away" the duke in his efforts to impress his guest? Why does the duke "drop names" of famous artists? Do you think the listener is impressed?
6. What is revealed in this poem?

SUMMARY

Our emphasis throughout this chapter has been on literature as spoken language, and the wedding of sound and sense. Literature is not passive; it does not sit on the page; it is engaged actively in the lives of those who give it a chance. Reading the literary samples in this chapter aloud clarifies this point.

We have been especially interested in two aspects of literature: its structure and its details. Any artifact is composed of an overall organization that gathers details and parts into unity. It is the same in literature, and one of the prerequisites of coming to an understanding of how writers can reveal to us the visions they have of their subject matter is the awareness of how details are combined into structures. The use of image, metaphor, symbol, diction, as well as other details determines in an essential sense the content of a work of literature.

Structural strategies, such as the choice between a narrative or a lyric, will determine to a large extent how details are used. There are many kinds of structures besides the narrative and the lyric, although these two offer convenient polarities that help indicate the nature of literary structure. It would be useful for any student of literature—in addition to the already discussed episodic, organic, and quest structures—to discover how many other kinds of structures can be used. And it also would be useful to determine how the different structural strategies tend toward the selection of different subject matters. We have made some suggestions as starters: pointing out the capacity of the narrative for reaching into a vast range of experience, especially its psychological truths, whereas the lyric is best adapted to revealing feeling.

CHAPTER 7 BIBLIOGRAPHY

Auerbach, Erich. *Mimesis.* Princeton, N.J.: Princeton University Press, 1973.

Bodkin, Maud. *Archetypal Patterns in Poetry.* New York: AMS Press, 1978.

Booth, Wayne. *The Rhetoric of Fiction,* 2d ed. Harmondsworth: Penguin, 1987.

Brooks, Cleanth. *The Well-Wrought Urn.* London: Reynal and Hitchcock, 1947.

Burke, Kenneth. *The Philosophy of Literary Form.* Baton Rouge: Louisiana University Press, 1941.

Eagleton, Terry. *Literary Theory: An Introduction.* Oxford, England: Oxford University Press, 1983.

Eco, Umberto. *Interpretation and Overinterpretation.* Cambridge, England: Cambridge University Press, 1992.

Eliot, T. S. *Selected Essays: New Edition.* New York: Harcourt Brace & World, 1978.

Fish, Stanley. *Is There a Text in This Class?* Cambridge, Mass.: Harvard University Press, 1980.

Forster, E. M. *Aspects of the Novel.* New York: Harcourt Brace & World, 1973.

Frye, Northrop. *Anatomy of Criticism.* Princeton, N.J.: Princeton University Press, 1990.

Groden, Michael, and Martin Kreisworth. *The Johns Hopkins Guide to Literary Theory & Criticism.* Balti-

more: The Johns Hopkins University Press, 1994.
Hirsch, E. D. *The Aims of Interpretation.* Chicago: University of Chicago Press, 1978.
James, Henry. *The Art of the Novel.* New York: Scribner's, 1978.
Leavis, F. R. *The Great Tradition.* New York: NYU Press, 1973.
Lentricchia, Frank. *After the New Criticism.* Chicago: Chicago University Press, 1980.
———. *Criticism and Social Change.* Chicago: University of Chicago Press, 1983.
Møller, Lis. *The Freudian Reading.* Philadelphia: University of Pennsylvania Press, 1991.
Newton, K. M. *Twentieth-Century Literary Theory.* London: Macmillan, 1988.
Scholes, Robert. *Textual Power.* New Haven: Yale University Press, 1985.
Stoll, E. E. *From Shakespeare to Joyce.* New York: Doubleday, 1944.
Wellek, Rene, and Austin Warren. *Theory of Literature,* 3rd ed. New York: Harcourt Brace Jovanovich, 1984.
Wimsatt, William K., and Cleanth Brooks. *Literary Criticism: A Short History.* Chicago: University of Chicago Press, 1983.

CHAPTER 7 WEBSITES

Author Homepages (information resource for various authors; homepages exist for many individual authors)

World Wide Web: **http://www.li.net/~scharf/author.html**

Book of Kells (artwork and text from the eighth-century Irish illuminated book)

World Wide Web: **http://www.tcd.ie/kells.html**

Electronic Texts Archive (literature, electronic books, and journals)

Gopher: Name: **Rice University** Address: **riceinfo.rice.edu** Select: **Information by subject area**

Irish Poetry (Irish poems—some set to music)

World Wide Web: **http://www.spinfo.uni-koeln.de/~dm/eire.html**

Literature Servers (direct links to various projects and Usenet groups)

World Wide Web: **http://www.cs.fsu.edu/projects/group4/litpage.html**

Native American Literature (mailing list)

List name: **nativelit-1** Address: **listserve@cornell.edu**

Poems and Prose (links to Keats, Burns, and others; links to newer poets)

World Wide Web: **http://www.hooked.net/users/sven/poets.corner.html**

Poetry Archives (international poetry)

World Wide Web: **http://sunsite.unc.edu/dykki/poetry/home.html** or **http://english-server.hss.cmu.edu/Poetry.html** or **http://www.cs.brown.edu:80/fun/bawp/**

Project Gutenberg (source for classic literature online)

World Wide Web: **http://jg.cso.uiuc.edu/PG** or **http://med.amsa.bu.edu/Gutenbert/Welcome.html**

Shakespeare (complete texts—poems, plays, and sonnets)

World Wide Web: **http://the-tech.mit.edu/Shakespeare.html**

Women and Literature (works by Sylvia Plath, Jane Austen, and others)

World Wide Web: **http://sunsite.unc.edu/cherylb/women/wlit.html**

Women Authors (writers' works, pictures, and biographies)

World Wide Web: **http://www.cs.cmu.edu/afs/cs.cmu.edu/user/mmbt/www/women/writers.html**

CHAPTER 8

DRAMA

Drama is a species of literature whose basic medium is spoken language. Moreover, drama can be read, somewhat like a poem or a novel. But the word "drama" comes from the Greek word meaning "act." Drama is spoken language acted, to be produced for public exhibition, usually upon a stage. To read a play is not only quite unlike seeing it in a theater but also unlike reading other kinds of literature. Novels, for example, are usually read silently. Poetry is performed, but it, too, is most often read silently. The script of a play, on the other hand, like the score of music, is designed for performance. From that script must be developed a synthesis of related arts—acting, scenery, lighting, perhaps music, dance, and even film. Drama as a complete work of art exists in the presentation. Its success depends on interpreters, such as directors and actors, who intervene between the dramatist and the audience. Moreover, for most of us the stage is not easily available, as are books or records or film. Rarely can we choose a play, as one may choose a poem, to suit our immediate preference. We have to take what is offered. Thus much of the time we have to read the drama and re-create in our imaginations something of what the play on the stage would be like. This requires considerable initiation. We learn both from our theater experiences and, we hope, from a text such as this.

ARISTOTLE AND THE ELEMENTS OF DRAMA

Much of what modern commentators say about drama goes back to theories Aristotle put forth in his *Poetics*. Eighteenth-century commentators tended to interpret his ideas in such a way as to present them as rules. For example, they interpreted tragedy as a serious action whose consequences reached sometimes as far as the gods. The *tragic hero* was always an aristocrat or ruler. Aristotle's *hamartia* was interpreted as a *tragic flaw* in character that produced the tragic fall. The tragic hero is the victim of *fate,* a force that can be resisted, but not overcome. The rules devised in the eighteenth century (and earlier) insisted on the "unities": that there be only one plot in a tragedy, that the action should take place in one locale, that it should be completed in one day, and that the main character should display a unity of behavior. Aristotle felt that tragedy evoked or ought to evoke two emotions from the audience: pity and fear. Pity was sympathy for the tragic hero; fear was the awareness that such a fate could befall anyone. The experience of tragedy produced a *catharsis* in the audience, a purging of emotions, especially those relating to violence and anger.

Aristotle felt that the tragic hero was in search of understanding and that the most intense moment in the drama came when the hero perceived the truth. He called that moment *anagnorisis,* or recognition. When the tragic hero's fortunes reversed—the *peripeteia*—we see there is no hope for the hero. Aristotle felt it was most powerful when the recognition and reversal of fortune occurred at the same moment in the drama. In the *Poetics* Aristotle determined six elements essential to drama: plot, character, diction, thought, spectacle, and song. He discusses each of these insofar as they aid the dramatist in imitating an action and thus producing drama.

THE IMITATION OF LIFE

Dramatic narrative depends on showing rather than telling. Drama exhibits events at the moment of their occurring, vividly, with immediate impact. No other art comes closer to life, and hence drama, more than any other art, led Aristotle to his theory of art as the imitation of nature—nature being life in general, not just the outdoors. In his analysis of Sophocles' *Oedipus Rex,* for example, Aristotle claimed that tragedy is the imitation of human action. From other comments he made, we can safely assume he meant to include comedy and other forms of drama. Some ways in which this conception can be applied to the dramatic arts are fairly obvious. For instance, certain kinds of drama imitate an action by allusion. The modern musical dramas *Godspell* and *Jesus Christ Superstar* allude to the story of Christ. They do not, however, aim at representing the gospels with accuracy. Historical plays, such as Shakespeare's *Henry V,* strive for enough accuracy to reasonably resemble what happened. Hal Holbrook's imitation of Mark Twain, Julie Harris' imitation of Emily Dickinson, Keith Carradine's imitation of Will Rogers, and James Whitmore's Harry Truman attempt to present a recognizable likeness in appearance and action of the original. Anna Deavere Smith (Figure 8-1) in two extraordinary one-woman performances, *Fires in the Mirror: Crown Heights, Brooklyn, and Other Identities* and *Twilight: Los Angeles, 1992,* takes the roles of dozens of ordinary people, male and female, of various ages and races, and convinces her audiences that she speaks with their authority. Her focus was on racial and religious violence in Brooklyn, centering on the death of a black child and

FIGURE 8-1
Anna Deavere Smith. (Courtesy Berkeley Repertory Theatre, California; photograph by Ken Friedman 1996)

the killing of a Jewish rabbinical student in the ensuing riots. The Los Angeles riots of 1992, following the failure to convict the policemen who beat Rodney King after he was stopped in his car, produced another victim in Reginald Denny, hauled from his truck and beaten. Both events produced intense emotional responses from the entire nation, and Anna Deavere Smith explored them from a variety of points of view.

PERCEPTION KEY
VARIETIES OF IMITATION

1. What recent imitations of famous persons or historical events have you witnessed? What is their appeal? Is the accuracy of the portrayals an important source of your pleasure in witnessing these imitations?
2. Two kinds of imitation have been noted: allusion and retelling. What other kinds of imitation can you recall from your experience of drama?

Realism is not a very useful standard for evaluating drama. If absolute realism were achieved in drama, we would abominate it. If characters really went to sleep onstage, or really got drunk and forced us to wait for them to sober up, we would have much more realism, but the drama would be much less interesting. Drama—or any other art, for that matter—should be only realistic enough to allow a meaningful revelation of reality.

The history of drama is filled with amusing anecdotes about the extent to which a drama has been realistic enough to cause an audience to mistake drama for real life. For instance, when Arthur Miller's *Death of a Salesman* (1949) played to early audiences that included salesmen at New York conventions, stories have circulated that several salesmen rose in anguish to help the hero, Willy Loman, by offering good business advice to help him from losing his "territory." These are breakdowns of a "distance" that we ought to maintain with all art, and they help explain why realism has limits. Our awareness of the difference between life and art is sometimes described as "aesthetic distance." Maintaining that distance implies the possibility of truly participating with the drama, since it implies the loss of self that participation demands. When spectators leap onstage to right the wrongs of drama, they show that there has been no loss of self. Indeed, because they see themselves as capable of changing the action, they are projecting their own ego into—rather than participating with—the dramatic action unfolding before them.

ELEMENTS OF DRAMA

Drama uses the resources of the theater to show human action in such a way that we gain deeper understanding of human experience. Because a play is limited by the capacity of an average audience for sustained concentration, most plays run for approximately two hours, with intermissions as concessions to the need for mental and physical relaxation. Thus a drama must unfold rapidly and be interesting at all times. Perhaps a novel may occasionally make us nod. We can take a break. But if a drama nods, we leave. Furthermore, the drama must be comprehensible, independent of extended explanations, and this must be accomplished mainly through the conduct and speech of the actors. Dramatists must leave the significance of what is happening largely to inference, whereas novelists, for example, have many leisurely ways of reflecting about the significance of the action. Nevertheless, there are conventions, such as the soliloquy—an extended speech by a character alone with the audience—which allow for extended reflection and explanation in the drama.

The basic elements of drama are action, character, setting, and ideas. Action is the plot or ongoing business of the characters—what they strive for, what they expect to see happen. Character is either developed or flat, either individuated or typed, either psychological or symbolic. Setting is either established explicitly and reproduced on stage with realistic or expressionist sets, or it is hinted at and suggested. Sometimes the setting is geographic and identified concretely, and sometimes it is left purposely vague. Ideas are similar to the themes of literature, the concepts that are introduced—either specified or merely insinuated—throughout the drama.

The setting is articulated through the manipulation of lights and scenery as well as through reference and local color. But action, character, and ideas are articulated through dialogue, which is normally the interaction of characters speaking to one another. Dialogue, the spoken word of actors personating the characters of the drama, carries the burden of making the dramatist's point clear. It, more than any other technique, distinguishes drama from the novel or the poem, both of which may also contain dialogue.

Soliloquies are a form of dialogue in which a character delivers a brief speech to the audience—or into "space" as a mode of reflective discourse. The soliloquy has taken on a special force because it has been assumed that since no other characters are nearby, the character delivering the soliloquy can be trusted to tell the truth. *Hamlet* is especially noted for its soliloquies. His most famous speech is a soliloquy beginning:

> To be, or not to be, that is the question:
> Whether 'tis nobler in the mind to suffer
> The slings and arrows of outrageous fortune,
> Or to take arms against a sea of troubles,
> And by opposing end them. To die, to sleep—
> No more—and by a sleep to say we end
> The heart-ache and the thousand natural shocks
> That flesh is heir to. To die, to sleep;
> To sleep, perchance to dream. Ay, there's the rub,
> For in that sleep of death what dreams may come
> When we have shuffled off this mortal coil,
> Must give us pause. [3.1.57–69]

Monologues differ from soliloquies in that one character speaks at great length, perhaps taking up an entire act, or even an entire play. Brian Friel's *The Faith Healer* is exceptional for its three long monologues by three different characters, none of whom appears on stage with anyone else. On the other hand, the soliloquy, which is also a piece of dialogue delivered by one character, differs in that it is usually an interruption of an action that consists of dialogue among characters. Dialogue can be brisk and snappy, with short speeches delivered in rapid fire, or it can be marked by expansive passages that give the character an opportunity to speak extensively and then listen to an extensive response.

PERCEPTION KEY
THE SOLILOQUY

A soliloquy occurs when a character in a drama reveals his or her thoughts to the audience but not to the other characters. Study the use of the soliloquy in a couple of plays—for example, Shakespeare's *Hamlet* (3.3.73–96; 4.4.32–66) and Tennessee Williams' *The Glass Menagerie* (Tom's opening speech; Tom's long speech in scene 5; his opening speech in scene 6). What does the soliloquy accomplish? Suppose their use was greatly expanded: would it enliven the drama?

Dramatists must get to their subject matter rapidly, and interpret that subject matter by forming act, character, setting, and ideas in such a way that the subject matter is better understood. As Aristotle pointed out long ago, drama is most convincing when it shows not the historically accurate but that which is humanly probable or plausible. The basic medium of drama is spoken language acted. The form of a drama organizes that medium in order to reveal (the content) of some human experience (subject matter). Because of the limitations of time and space, the subject matter of drama is rarely as broad as that of the epic or the novel. On the other hand, the intensity of drama tends to evoke a level of participation that the other literary arts rarely achieve.

ARCHETYPAL PATTERNS

Certain structural principles tend to govern the shape of dramatic narrative, just as they do the narrative of fiction. The discussion of episodic and organic structures in the previous chapter have relevance for drama as well. However, drama originated from ancient rituals (as far as we know) and seems to maintain some of its shape from a reference to those rituals. For example, the ritual of sacrifice—which implies that the individual must be sacrificed for the commonweal of society—seems to find its way into a great many dramas, both old and new. Such a pattern is archetypal, which is to say, it is a basic psychological pattern that people apparently react to on a subconscious level. These patterns are deep in the myths that we have absorbed into our culture. We "feel" their importance even if we do not recognize them consciously.

Archetypal drama aims at symbolic or mythic interpretations of experience. For instance, one's search for personal identity, since it seems to be a pattern repeated in all ages, can serve as a primary archetypal structure for drama. This particular archetype is the driving force in Sophocles' *Oedipus Rex,* Shakespeare's *Hamlet,* August Wilson's *The Piano Lesson,* and many more plays—notably, but by no means exclusively, in tragedies. (As we shall see, comedy also has appropriate archetypes.) One reason this archetype is so powerful is that it takes enormous risks. Most of us are content to watch other people discover their own identities, since there is an implied terror in finding that we may not be the delightful, humane, and wonderful people we want others to think we are.

The power of the archetype derives, in part, from our recognition of a pattern that has been repeated by the human race throughout history. The psychologist Carl Jung, whose work spurred critical awareness of archetypal patterns in all the arts, believed that the greatest power of the archetype lies in its capacity to reveal through art the "imprinting" of human experience. Maud Bodkin, a critic who developed Jung's views, explains them this way:

> The special emotional significance going beyond any definite meaning conveyed—[Jung] attributes to the stirring in the reader's mind, within or beneath his conscious response, of unconscious forces which he terms "primordial images" or archetypes. These archetypes he describes as "psychic residua of numberless experiences of the same type," experiences which have happened not to the individual but to his ancestors, and of which the results are inherited in the structure of the brain.[1]

The quest narrative discussed in Chapter 7 sometimes is an example of an archetypal structure, one that recurs in drama frequently. For instance, Hamlet is seeking the truth about his father's death, but in doing so he is also trying to discover his own identity as it relates to his mother. Sophocles' Oedipus tells about a man who kills his father, marries his mother, suffers a plague on his lands, and is ultimately blinded and ostracized. Freud

[1]Maud Bodkin, *Archetypal Patterns in Poetry,* Oxford University Press, New York, 1934, p. 1.

thought the play so archetypal that he saw in it a profound human psychological pattern, which he called the Oedipus complex: the desire of a child to "get rid of" the same-sex parent and to have a sexual union with the parent of the opposite sex. Not all archetypal patterns are so thrilling, but most reveal an aspect of basic human desires. Drama—because of its immediacy and compression of presentation—is, perhaps, the most powerful means of expression for such archetypes.

Some of the more important archetypes include those of an older man, usually a king, who is betrayed by a younger man, his trusted lieutenant, in regard to a woman. This is the theme of Lady Gregory's *Diarmuid and Grania.* The loss of innocence, a variation on the Garden of Eden theme, is another favorite, as in Strindberg's *Miss Julie* and Ibsen's *Ghosts* or *The Wild Duck.* The archetypal quest for self-identity is so common in all literature that it is even sometimes parodied, as in Oscar Wilde's *The Importance of Being Earnest.* Tom Stoppard's *Arcadia* combines both archetypes: innocence and the quest for knowledge. In that play, the quest for knowledge extends to the universe of mathematics on one level and to the immediate arcadian environment of the heroine, a young girl who dies tragically in an idyllic setting in the early nineteenth century.

The four seasons set temporal dimensions for the development of archetypes because the seasons are intertwined with patterns of growth and decay. The origins of drama, which are obscure beyond recall, may have been linked with rituals associated with the planting of seed, the reaping of crops, and the entire complex issue of fertility and death. In *Anatomy of Criticism,* Northrop Frye associates comedy with spring, romance with summer, tragedy with autumn, irony and satire with winter. His associations suggest that some archetypal drama may be rooted in connections between human destiny and the rhythms of nature. Such origins may account for part of the power that archetypal drama has on our imaginations, for the influences that derive from such origins presumably are deeply pervasive in all of us. These influences may also help explain why tragedy usually involves the death of a hero—although sometimes, as in the case of Oedipus, death is withheld—and why comedy frequently ends with one or more marriages, as in Shakespeare's *As You Like It, Much Ado About Nothing,* and *A Midsummer Night's Dream,* with their suggestions of fertility. Such drama seems to thrive on seasonal patterns and on the capacity to excite in us a recognition of events that on the surface may not seem important, but that underneath have profound meaning.

Perception Key
ARCHETYPES

1. You may wish to supplement the comments above by reading the third chapter of Northrop Frye's *Anatomy of Criticism* or the *Hamlet* chapter in Francis Fergusson's *The Idea of a Theater.* Discuss archetypes with friends interested in the concept.
2. Whether or not you do additional reading, consider the recurrent patterns you have observed in dramas—include television dramas or television adaptations

of drama. Can you find any of the patterns we have described? Do you see other patterns showing up? Do the patterns you have observed seem basic to human experience? For example, do you associate gaiety with spring, love with summer, death with fall, and bitterness with winter? If so, what are the origins of these associations for you? Do you believe these origins are shared by most or all people?

3. Archetypes are often very closely connected with myths and fairy tales. Can you think of any famous myths or fairy tales that have been used in dramas? Consider myths of creation such as the Greek, Christian, and the American Indians, or fairy tales such as Cinderella, Hansel and Gretel, and Pinocchio.

GENRES OF DRAMA: TRAGEDY

Carefully structured plots were favored by Aristotle, and are usually essential in tragedies. This is particularly true of those Greek and Shakespearian tragedies in which fate plays a dominant role. But for the best tragedies, according to Aristotle, the action must also arise from the searchings of a noble character. The strengths and flaws of the protagonist (the leading character) must be factors contributing to the dramatic outcome. Aristotle may not have been fully convinced of this, however, since he tells us in the *Poetics* that "without action there could be no tragedy, whereas a tragedy without characterization is possible." Such action dramas have often been produced by dramatists for the popular stage and by writers for television. But when we turn to the great tragedies that most define the genre, we think immediately of great characters: Oedipus; Agamemnon; Prometheus; Hamlet; Macbeth; King Lear; Julius Caesar; Samson. In most modern tragedies, such as O'Neill's *Desire Under the Elms* and Miller's *Death of a Salesman,* the characters still remain at the center of the drama.

Modern drama tends to avoid traditional tragic structures because modern concepts of character, sin, guilt, death, and fate have been greatly altered. Modern psychology "explains" character in ways the ancients either would not have understood or would have disputed. It has been said that there is no modern tragedy because there can be no character noble enough to be tragic. Moreover, the acceptance of chance as a force equal to fate in our lives has also reduced the power of tragedy in modern times. Even myth—which some modern playwrights still understand as valid—has a diminished vitality in modern tragedy. It may be that the return of a strong integrating myth—a world vision that sees the actions of humanity as tied into a large scheme of cosmic or religious events—is a prerequisite for producing a new dramatic structure that we can recognize as tragic.

TRAGIC RHYTHM

For Aristotle the tragic rhythm is marked by three critical moments in the action of the drama: reversal, when events turn from good to bad; recognition, the awareness by the protagonists of the reversal; pathos, the suffering that follows the reversal. In the best tragedies, according to Aristo-

FIGURE 8-2
Greek Amphitheater. Athens Festival, Herod Atticus Theatre. (Courtesy Greek National Tourist Organization)

tle, recognition occurs simultaneously with the reversal, as in *Oedipus Rex,* when Oedipus discovers the identity of the killer of Laius is none other than himself. Most tragedies follow this pattern, more or less. Modern tragedies may seem less powerful because more democratic attitudes make it difficult for us to take high-born characters seriously. But cannot ordinary characters be tragic? Arthur Miller's *Death of a Salesman* proved they can. The fall of Willy Loman, a very ordinary man, seems profoundly tragic. If Aristotle were analyzing tragedy now, he might revise some of his assertions about the character of the tragic protagonist.

THE TRAGIC STAGE

The great ages of tragedy have been Greek and Elizabethan. These two historical periods have shared certain basic ideas: for instance, that there is a "divine providence that shapes our ends," as Hamlet says, and that fate is immutable, as the Greek tragedies tell us. Both periods were marked by considerable prosperity and public power, and both ages were deeply aware that sudden reversals in prosperity could change everything. In addition both ages had somewhat similar ideas about the way a stage should be constructed. The relatively temperate climate of Greece permitted an open amphitheater, with seating on three sides of the stage. The Greek architects often had the seats carved out of hillside rock, and their attention to acoustics was so remarkable that even today in some of the surviving Greek theaters a whisper on the stage can be heard throughout the audience. The Elizabethan stages were roofed wooden structures jutting into open space enclosed by stalls in which the well-to-do sat (the not so well-to-do stood around the stage), providing for sight lines from three sides. Each kind of theater was similar to a modified theater-in-the-round, such as is used occasionally today. A glance at Figures 8-2, 8-3, and 8-4 will show that these theaters are very different from the standard theater of our time—the proscenium theater.

The proscenium acts as a "frame" to separate the action taking place on stage from the audience. The Greek and Elizabethan stages are not so explicitly framed, thus involving the audience more directly spatially and, in turn, perhaps, emotionally. The Greek theater illustrated in Figure 8-2 has been slightly modified, with a staging area elevated at the base of the seats. In the original Greek theater, the area on which the action took place was a circle, called the orchestra, which gave the actors space in which to move. The absence of a separate stage put the actors on the same level as those seated at the lowest level of the audience.

FIGURE 8-3
Modern rendering of DeWitt's 1596 drawing of the interior of an Elizabethan theater. (Courtesy University of Utrecht)

Perception Key
THE PROSCENIUM STAGE

Test the preceding observations by examining your own experience in the theater. What is the effect of setting apart the dramatic action of a play by framing it with a proscenium? Do you know of any plays that are weakened because of the proscenium frame? Explain.

FIGURE 8-4
Auditorium and proscenium, Royal Opera House, Covent Garden, London. (Woodmansterne Publications, England)

FIGURE 8-5
Romeo and Juliet. Olivia Hussey as Juliet in Zefferelli's film. (Paramount Pictures/The Kobol Collection)

SHAKESPEARE'S *ROMEO AND JULIET*

For a contemporary audience, *Romeo and Juliet* is probably easier to participate with than most Greek tragedies because, among other reasons, its tragic hero and heroine, although aristocratic, are not a king and queen. Their youth and innocence add to their remarkable appeal. The play presents the archetypal story of star-crossed lovers whose fate—mainly because of the hatred their families bear one another—is sealed from the first. The archetype of lovers who are not permitted to love refers to a basic struggle among forces that lie so deep in our psyche that we need a drama such as this to help reveal them. It is the struggle between light and dark, between the world in which we live on the surface of the earth with its light and openness, and the world of darkness, the underworld of the Greeks and the hell of the Christians. Young lovers represent life, the promise of fertility, and the continuity of the human race. Most of us who are no longer in the bloom of youth were once such people, and we can both sympathize with and understand their situation. Few subject matters could be more potentially tragic than that of young lovers whose promise is plucked by death. This theme was developed by Boccaccio in "The Pot of Basil," discussed in the previous chapter.

The play begins with some ominous observations by Montague, Romeo's father. He points out that when Romeo, through love of a girl named Rosaline (who does not appear in the play), comes home just before dawn, he locks "fair daylight out," making for himself an "artificial night." In other words, Montague tells us that Romeo stays up all night, comes home, pulls down the shades, and converts day into night. These observations seem innocent enough unless one is already familiar with the plot; then it seems a clear and tragic irony: that Romeo, by making his day a night, is already foreshadowing his fate. After Juliet has been introduced, her nurse wafts her offstage with an odd bit of advice aimed at persuading her of the wisdom of marrying Count Paris, the man her mother has chosen. "Go, girl, seek happy nights to happy days." At first glance, the advice seems innocent. But with knowledge of the entire play, it is prophetic. Shakespeare's details invariably tie in closely with the structure. Everything becomes relevant.

Much of the play takes place at night, and one film version (Figure 8-5) by Franco Zefferelli was particularly impressive for exploiting dramatic lighting, part of Aristotle's "spectacle," one of the basic elements of tragedy. Spectacle includes all the visual elements of a production, which, in their richness or starkness, can combine to intensify the dramatic values of the play. Zefferelli's spectacle was also intensified by the costuming, the simplicity of which broke with tradition, helping make this production one of the most successful and influential.

PERCEPTION KEY
ARISTOTLE'S ELEMENTS

Aristotle's elements in his order of importance are plot, character, diction, thought, spectacle, and music.

1. Do you think that tragedy can exist without one or more of these elements? If so, which one or ones?
2. Is music in a film production likely to be a more important element than in a stage production? Why or why not?
3. If you are able to see Zefferelli's film of *Romeo and Juliet,* judge the effectiveness of the music.

When Romeo first speaks with Juliet, it is not only night but also in Capulet's orchard: symbolically a place of fruitfulness and fulfillment. Romeo sees her and imagines her not as chaste Diana of the moon, but as his own luminary sun: "But soft! What light through yonder window breaks?/ It is the East, and Juliet is the sun!" He sees her as his "bright angel." When she, unaware he is listening below, asks, "O Romeo, Romeo! Wherefore art thou Romeo?/ Deny thy father and refuse thy name," she is touching on profound things. She is, without fully realizing it, asking the impossible: that he not be himself. The denial of identity often brings great pain, as witness Oedipus who at first refused to believe he was his father's child. When Juliet asks innocently, "What's in a name? That which we call a rose / By any other name would smell as sweet," she is asking that he ignore his identity. The mythic implications of this are serious, and in this play fatal. Denying one's heritage is rather like Romeo's attempting to deny day its sovereignty.

When they finally speak, Juliet explains ironically that she has "night's cloak to hide me" and that the "mask of night is upon my face." We know, as she speaks, that eternal night will be on that face, and all too soon. Their marriage, which occurs offstage as Act Two ends, is also performed at night in Friar Lawrence's cell, with his hoping that the heavens will smile upon "this holy act." But he is none too sure. And before Act Three is well under way the reversals begin. Mercutio, Romeo's friend, is slain because of Romeo's intervention. Then Romeo slays Tybalt, Juliet's cousin, and finds himself doomed to exile from both Verona and Juliet. Grieving for the dead Tybalt and the banished Romeo, Juliet misleads her father into thinking the only cure for her condition is a quick marriage to Paris, and Romeo comes to spend their one night of love together before he leaves Verona. Naturally they want the night to last and last—again an irony we are prepared for—and when daylight springs, Romeo and Juliet have a playful argument over whether it is the nightingale or the lark that sings. Juliet wants him to stay, so she defends the nightingale; he knows he must go, so he points to the lark and the coming light. Then both, finally, admit the truth. His line is, "More light and light—more dark and dark our woes."

Another strange archetypal pattern, part of the complexity of the subject matter, has begun here: the union of sex and death as if they were aspects of the same thing. In Shakespeare's time death was a metaphor for making love and when a singer of a love song protested that he was dying, he expected everyone to understand that he was talking about the sexual act. In *Romeo and Juliet* sex and death go together, both literally and symbolically. The first most profound sense of this appears in Juliet's pretending death in order to avoid marrying Paris. She takes a potion from Friar Lawrence—who is himself afraid of a second marriage because of possible bigamy charges—and appears, despite all efforts of investigation, quite dead. (See Figure 8-6.)

When Romeo hears that she has been placed in the Capulet tomb, he determines to join her in death as he was unable to in life. The message Friar

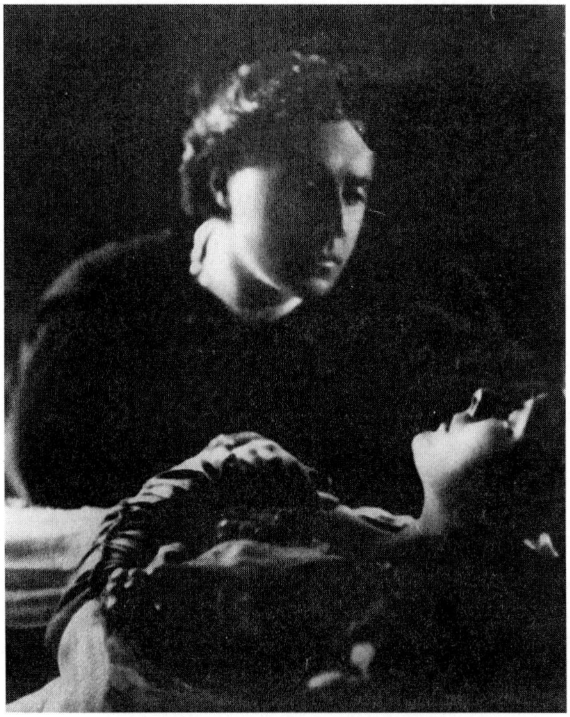

FIGURE 8-6
Romeo and Juliet. E. H. Sothern and Julia Marlow. (Theatre Collection, The New York Public Library for the Performing Arts, Lincoln Center)

Lawrence had sent by way of another friar explaining the counterfeit death did not get through to Romeo. And it did not get through because genuine death, in the form of plague, had closed the roads to Friar John, another kind of reversal that Aristotle would have approved. When Romeo descends underground into the tomb he must ultimately fight Paris, although he does not wish to. After killing Paris, Romeo sees the immobile Juliet. He fills his cup (a female symbol) with poison, and drinks. When Juliet awakes from her potion and sees both Paris and Romeo dead, she can get no satisfactory answer for these happenings from Friar Lawrence. His fear is so great that he runs off as the authorities bear down on the tomb. This leaves Juliet to give Romeo one last kiss on his still warm lips, then plunge his dagger (a male symbol) into her heart and die.

Earlier, when Capulet thought his daughter was dead, he exclaimed to Paris: "O son, the night before thy wedding day / Hath Death lain with thy wife. There she lies, / Flower as she was, deflowered by him. / Death is my son-in-law, Death is my heir." At the end of the play, both Juliet and his real son-in-law, Romeo, are indeed married in death. The linkage of death and sex is ironically enacted in their final moments, which include the awful misunderstandings that the audience beholds in sorrow, that make Romeo and Juliet take their own lives for love of one another. And among the last lines is one that helps clarify one of the main themes: "A glooming peace this morning with it brings. / The sun for sorrow will not show his head." Theatergoers have mourned these deaths for generations, and the promise that these two families will now finally try to get along together in a peaceful manner does not seem strong enough to brighten the ending of the play.

Perception Key
TRAGEDY

1. If you have been fortunate enough to see a production of *Romeo and Juliet,* either live or on film, examine your experience. Did you perceive any of the archetypal patterns that we have mentioned? How fully were they developed? What about the struggle between day and night or light and dark? Was it dramatized in the spectacle of the play? Our discussion of the play did not treat the question of the tragic flaw: the weakness of character that permits the tragedy to befall the main characters. One of Romeo's flaws may be rashness—the rashness that led him to kill Tybalt and thus be banished. But he may have other flaws as well. What might they be? What are Juliet's tragic flaws, if any?
2. You may not have been able to see *Romeo and Juliet,* but perhaps other tragedies are available. Try to see any of the tragedies by Aeschylus, Sophocles, Shakespeare, Ibsen's *Ghosts,* John Millington Synge's *Riders to the Sea,* or Arthur Miller's *Death of a Salesman.* Analyze the issues of tragedy we have raised. For example, decide whether the play is archetypal. Are there reversals and recognitions of the sort Aristotle analyzed? Did the reversal and recognition occur simultaneously? Are the characters important enough—if not noble enough—to excite your sympathy?
3. If you were to write a tragedy, what kind of tragic protagonist (hero) would you choose? What kind of plot? Why?

COMEDY: OLD AND NEW

Ancient Western comedies were performed at a time associated with wine making, thus linking the genre with the wine god, Bacchus, and his relative, Comus—from which the word "comedy" comes. Comedy first achieved institutional status in ancient Greece. Some of the earliest comedies, along with satyr plays, were frankly phallic in nature, and many of the plays of Aristophanes, the master of Old Comedy, were raucous and coarse. Plutarch was offended by plays like *The Clouds, The Frogs, The Wasps,* and especially *Lysistrata,* the world's most well-known phallic play, concerning a situation in which the women of a community withhold sex until the men decide not to wage any more war. At one point in the play, the humor centers on the men walking around with enormous erections under their togas. Obviously Old Comedy is old in name only, since it is still present in the routines of nightclub comedians and the bawdy entertainment halls of the world.

By contrast, the New Comedy of Menander, with titles such as *The Flatterer, The Lady from Andros, The Suspicious Man,* and *The Grouch,* his only surviving complete play, concentrated on the more common situations in the everyday life of the Athenian. It also avoided the brutal attacks on individuals, such as Socrates, which characterize much Old Comedy. Menander's critics credit him with having helped develop the comedy of manners, the type of drama that uses the manners of a society as a basic part of its subject matter.

Old Comedy is associated with our modern farce, burlesque, and the broad humor and make-believe violence of slapstick. New Comedy is suave and subtle. Concentrating on manners, New Comedy developed type characters, for they helped focus upon the foibles of social behavior. Type characters, such as the gruff and difficult man who turns out to have a heart of gold, the good cop, the bad cop, the ingenue, the finicky person, or the sloppy person—all these work well in comedies. Such characters can become stereotypes—with totally predictable behavior patterns—although the best dramatists make them complex enough so that they are not completely predictable.

PERCEPTION KEY
TYPE CHARACTERS

1. Television series comedies thrive on type characters. If you have seen some of the characters from the following series you may be able to describe their type: Sam, Woody, Norm, or Carla in *Cheers;* Oscar and Felix in *The Odd Couple;* George or Kramer in *Seinfeld* (Figure 8-7); Murphy Brown or Miles in *Murphy Brown.* What other type characters can you identify from television comedies? What makes them interesting or successful as types?
2. New Comedy usually uses type characters to make a socially useful point. Do series such as *Friends, Cheers,* or *Seinfeld* make socially useful observations about modern life?

Both Old and New Comedy, despite or rather because of their humor, can have serious meaning. Not only is laughter pleasurable, but through laugh-

FIGURE 8-7
A still from *Seinfeld*. (Courtesy Castle Rock Entertainment, Beverly Hills, California, photograph by Byron Cohen)

ter the dramatist can reveal the weaknesses and stupidities of human behavior, especially social behavior. Comedy is a powerful reformer of society, as Henri Bergson has demonstrated in *Laughter*, which is one of the reasons dictators are so quick to censor the comic dramatist. We love to be laughed with, but hate to be laughed at. No normal person likes to be seen as ridiculous. When comedy reveals aspects of ourselves that are laughable, we mend our ways.

Just as tragedy can make use of archetypal patterns, comedy—and especially New Comedy—often has archetypal patterns of its own. For example, there is the pattern pointing toward marriage and the new life made possible by the hoped-for fruitfulness of such a union. The forces of society, personified often by a parent or controlling older person, are usually pitted against the younger characters who wish to be married. Thus one of the most powerful archetypal patterns of comedy is a variant of the "generation gap." The "parent" can be any older person who blocks the younger people, usually by virtue of controlling their inheritance or their wealth. When the older person wishes to stop a marriage, he or she becomes the "blocking character." This character, for reasons that are usually social or simply mercenary, does everything possible to stop the young people from getting together.

Naturally, the blocking character fails. But the younger characters do not merely win their own struggle. They usually go on to demonstrate the superiority of their views over those of the blocking character. For example, they may demonstrate that true love is a better reason for marrying than merging two neighboring estates. One common pattern is for two lovers to decide to marry regardless of their social classes. The male, for instance, may be a soldier or a student but not belong to the upper class to which the female belongs. But usually at the last minute through the means of a birthmark or the admission of another character who knew all along, the lower-class character will be shown to be a member of the upper class in disguise. Often the character himself will not know the truth until the last minute in the drama. This is a variant of Aristotle's recognition, although it does not have unhappy consequences. In all of this, New Comedy is usually in tacit agreement with the standards of the society it entertains. It stretches the social standards and is thus evolutionary rather than revolutionary.

Blocking characters are often eccentrics whose behavior is marked by an extreme commitment to a limited perspective. They may be misers, for example, whose entire lives are devoted to mercenary goals, although they may not be able to enjoy the money they heap up; or malcontents, forever looking on the dark side of humanity; or hypochondriacs, whose every move is dictated by their imaginary illnesses. Such characters are so rigid that their behavior is a form of a vice. The effort of the younger characters is often to reform the older characters, educating them away from their entrenched and narrow values toward accepting the idealism and hopefulness of the young people who, after all, are in line to inherit the world that the older people are reluctant to turn over. Few generations give way without a struggle, and this archetypal struggle on the comic stage may serve to give hope to the young when they most need it, as well as possibly help to educate the old so as to make the real struggle less terrible.

Perception Key
OLD AND NEW COMEDY

Studying comedy in the abstract is difficult. It is best for you to test what has been discussed above by comparing our descriptions and interpretations with your own observations. If you have a chance to see some live comedy on stage, use that experience, but if that is impossible, watch some television comedy.

1. Is there criticism of society? Is it savage as in Old Comedy or relatively gentle as in New Comedy?
2. Are there blocking characters? Do they function somewhat in the ways described above? Are there any new twists?
3. Do you find examples of the generation gap? Are they similar to the archetypal pattern of the blocking character opposing the marriage of younger people? Do you observe any modern variations of this archetype?
4. See or read at least two comedies. How many type characters can you identify? Is there an example of the dumb blonde? The braggart tough guy? The big lover? The poor but honest fellow? The dumb cop? Do you find examples of stereotypes? Do stereotypes or types dominate? Which do you find more interesting? Why?

TRAGICOMEDY: THE MIXED GENRE

On the walls beside many stages we find two masks: the tragic mask with a downturned mouth, and the comic mask with an upturned mouth. If there were a third mask, it would probably have an expression of bewilderment, as if someone had just asked a totally unanswerable question. Mixing the genres of tragedy and comedy in a drama may give such a feeling. Modern audiences are often left with many unanswered questions when they leave the theater. They are not always given resolutions that wrap things up neatly. Instead, tragicomedy tends, more than either tragedy or comedy, to reveal the ambiguities of the world. It does not usually end with the finality of death or the promise of a new beginning. It usually ends somewhere in between.

The reason tragicomedy has taken some time to become established as a genre may have had something to do with the fact that Aristotle did not provide an analysis. Thus for a long time tragicomedy was thought of as a mixing of two pure genres and consequently inferior in kind. The mixing of tragedy and comedy is surely justified, if for no other reason than the mixture works so well, as proved by most of the plays of Chekhov among many others. This mixed genre is simply a way of making our drama truer to life. As playwright Sean O'Casey commented to a college student: "As for the blending 'Comedy with Tragedy,' it's no new practice—hundreds have done it, including Shakespeare. . . . And, indeed, Life is always doing it, doing it, doing it. Even when one lies dead, laughter is often heard in the next room. There's no tragedy that isn't tinged with humour, no comedy that hasn't its share of tragedy—if one has eyes to see, ears to hear." Much of our most impressive modern drama is mixed in genre so that, as O'Casey points out, it is rare to find a comedy that has no sadness to it, or a tragedy that is unrelieved by laughter.

One result of the present domination of tragicomedy over tragedy and comedy is that the modern playwright can emphasize irony, one of the most powerful dramatic techniques. Dramatic irony explores the disparity between the outcome of a character's action and the outcome he or she anticipates. In turn, this irony plays against the expectations and sometimes the desires of an audience, thus building tension based on the audience's anticipation of the action. This tension is often built by giving the audience more information about a situation or a character than the characters in the drama have. The audience then can observe the ironic twists of the action. Irony exists in tragedy, as with *Romeo and Juliet,* whose title characters die "ironically" as a result of Friar Lawrence's plan to unite them happily.

Susan Glaspell's *Trifles* (Figure 8-8), which follows, offers us an example of a mixed genre. The central action of the drama is tragic, but we never actually meet the characters who figure in the tragic action. Instead, we focus on a group of self-important men who think they are in possession of the important facts about a murder. These characters give way to another group, this time of women who have come into the house to be of help. Their intention is not to investigate the murder, yet their observations are the ones that give the audience a true vision of what happened in the farmhouse. They observe the trifles that add up to a terrible story. The ultimate story is powerful. Once we leave the theater, we take the play and its problems with us. Its thought is "portable," and if we have participated fully with the drama, we are aware that a transformation has taken place within us.

FIGURE 8-8
A still from a production of *Trifles*. (Theatre Collection, The New York Public Library for the Performing Arts, Lincoln Center)

TRIFLES

by Susan Glaspell

1916

CHARACTERS

GEORGE HENDERSON, *County Attorney*
HENRY PETERS, *Sheriff*
LEWIS HALE, *A Neighboring Farmer*
MRS. PETERS
MRS. HALE

SCENE

The kitchen in the now abandoned farmhouse of **JOHN WRIGHT**, *a gloomy kitchen, and left without having been put in order—unwashed pans under the sink, a loaf of bread outside the breadbox, a dish towel on the table—other signs of incompleted work. At the rear the outer door opens and the* **SHERIFF** *comes in followed by the* **COUNTY ATTORNEY** *and* **HALE**. *The* SHERIFF *and* HALE *are men in middle life, the* COUNTY ATTORNEY *is a young man; all are much bundled up and go at once to the stove. They are followed by two women—the* SHERIFF*'s wife first, she is a slight wiry woman, a thin nervous face.* **MRS. HALE** *is larger and would ordinarily be called more comfortable looking, but she is disturbed now and looks fearfully about as she enters. The women have come in slowly, and stand close together near the door.*

COUNTY ATTORNEY *[rubbing his hands]:* This feels good. Come to the fire, ladies.

MRS. PETERS *[after taking a step forward]:* I'm not—cold.

SHERIFF *[unbuttoning his overcoat and stepping away from the stove as if to mark the beginning of official business]:* Now, Mr. Hale, before we move things about, you explain to Mr. Henderson just what you saw when you came here yesterday morning.

COUNTY ATTORNEY: By the way, has anything been moved? Are things just as you left them yesterday?

SHERIFF *[looking about]:* It's just the same. When it dropped below zero last night I thought I'd better send Frank out this morning to make a fire for us—no use getting pneumonia with a big case on, but I told him not to touch anything except the stove—and you know Frank.

COUNTY ATTORNEY: Somebody should have been left here yesterday.

SHERIFF: Oh—yesterday. When I had to send Frank to Morris Center for that man who went crazy—I want you to know I had my hands full yesterday, I knew you could get back from Omaha by today and as long as I went over everything here myself—

COUNTY ATTORNEY: Well, Mr. Hale, tell just what happened when you came here yesterday morning.

HALE: Harry and I had started to town with a load of potatoes. We came along the road from my place and as I got here I said, "I'm going to see if I can't get John Wright to go in with me on a party telephone." I spoke to Wright about it once before and he put me off, saying folks talked too much anyway, and all he asked was peace and quiet—I guess you know about how much he talked himself; but I thought maybe if I went to the house and talked about it before his wife, though I said to Harry that I didn't know as what his wife wanted made much difference to John—

COUNTY ATTORNEY: Let's talk about that later, Mr. Hale. I do want to talk about that, but tell now just what happened when you got to the house.

HALE: I didn't hear or see anything; I knocked at the door, and still it was all quiet inside. I knew they must be up, it was past eight o'clock. So I knocked again, and I thought I heard somebody say, "Come in." I wasn't sure, I'm not sure yet, but I opened the door—this door *[Indicating the door by which the two women are still standing]* and there in that rocker—*[Pointing to it.]* sat Mrs. Wright.

[They all look at the rocker.]

COUNTY ATTORNEY: What—was she doing?

HALE: She was rockin' back and forth. She had her apron in her hand and was kind of—pleating it.

COUNTY ATTORNEY: And how did she—look?

HALE: Well, she looked queer.

COUNTY ATTORNEY: How do you mean—queer?

HALE: Well, as if she didn't know what she was going to do next. And kind of done up.

COUNTY ATTORNEY: How did she seem to feel about your coming?

HALE: Why, I don't think she minded—one way or other. She didn't pay much attention. I said, "How do, Mrs. Wright, it's cold, ain't it?" And she said, "Is it?"—and went on kind of pleating at her apron. Well, I was surprised; she didn't ask me to come up to the stove, or to set down, but just sat there, not even looking at me, so I said, "I want to see John." And then she—laughed. I guess you would call it a laugh. I thought of Harry and the team outside, so I said a little sharp: "Can't I see John?" "No," she says, kind o'dull like. "Ain't he home?" says I. "Yes," says she, "he's home." "Then why can't I see him?" I asked her, out of patience. "'Cause he's dead," says she. *"Dead?"* says I. She just nodded her head, not getting a bit excited, but rockin' back and forth. "Why—where is he?" says I, not knowing what to say. She just pointed upstairs—like that *[Himself pointing to the room above].* I got up, with the idea of going up there. I walked from there to here—then I says, "Why, what did he die of?" "He died of a rope round his neck," says she, and just went on pleatin' at her apron. Well I went out and called Harry. I thought I might—need help. We went upstairs and there he was lyin'—

COUNTY ATTORNEY: I think I'd rather have you go into that upstairs, where you can point it all out. Just go on now with the rest of the story.

HALE: Well, my first thought was to get that rope off. It looked . . . *[Stops, his face twitches.]* . . . but Harry, he went up to him, and he said, "No, he's dead all right, and we'd better not touch anything." So we went back down stairs. She was still sitting that same way. "Has anybody been notified?" I asked. "No," says she, unconcerned. "Who did this, Mrs. Wright?" said Harry. He said it businesslike—and she stopped pleatin' of her apron. "I don't know," she says. "You don't *know?"* says Harry. "No," says she. "Weren't you sleepin' in the bed with him?" says Harry. "Yes," says she, "but I was on the inside." "Somebody slipped a rope round his neck and strangled him and you didn't wake up?" says Harry. "I didn't wake up," she said after him. We must'a looked as if we didn't see how that could be, for after a minute she said, "I sleep sound." Harry was going to ask her more questions but I said maybe we ought to let her tell her story first to the coroner, or the sheriff, so Harry went fast as he could to Rivers' place, where there's a telephone.

COUNTY ATTORNEY: And what did Mrs. Wright do when she knew that you had gone for the coroner?

HALE: She moved from that chair to this one over here *[Pointing to a small chair in the corner.]* and just sat there with her hands held together and looking down. I got a feeling that I ought to make some conversation, so I said I had come in to see if John wanted to put in a telephone, and at that she started to laugh, and then she stopped and looked at me—scared. *[The* COUNTY ATTORNEY, *who has had his notebook out, makes a note.]* I dunno, maybe it wasn't scared. I wouldn't like to say it was. Soon Harry got back, and then Dr. Lloyd came, and you, Mr. Peters, and so I guess that's all I know that you don't.

COUNTY ATTORNEY *[looking around]:* I guess we'll go upstairs first—and then out to the barn and around there. *[To the* SHERIFF*]* You're convinced that there was nothing important here—nothing that would point to any motive.

SHERIFF: Nothing here but kitchen things.

[The COUNTY ATTORNEY, *after again looking around the kitchen, opens the door of a cupboard closet. He gets up on a chair and looks on a shelf. Pulls his hand away, sticky.]*

COUNTY ATTORNEY: Here's a nice mess.

[The women draw nearer.]

MRS. PETERS *[to the other woman]:* Oh, her fruit; it did freeze. [*To the* COUNTY ATTORNEY] She worried about that when it turned so cold. She said the fire'd go out and her jars would break.

SHERIFF: Well, can you beat the women! Held for murder and worryin' about her preserves.

COUNTY ATTORNEY: I guess before we're through she may have something more serious than preserves to worry about.

HALE: Well, women are used to worrying over trifles.

[The two women move a little closer together.]

COUNTY ATTORNEY *[with the gallantry of a young politician]:* And yet, for all their worries, what would we do without the ladies? *[The women do not unbend. He goes to the sink, takes a dipperful of water from the pail and pouring it into a basin, washes his hands. Starts to wipe them on the roller towel, turns it for a cleaner place.]* Dirty towels! *[Kicks his foot against the pans under the sink.]* Not much of a house-keeper, would you say, ladies?

MRS. HALE *[stiffly]:* There's a great deal of work to be done on a farm.

COUNTY ATTORNEY: To be sure. And yet *[With a little bow to her]* I know there are some Dickson county farmhouses which do not have such roller towels.

[He gives it a pull to expose its full length again.]

MRS. HALE: Those towels get dirty awful quick. Men's hands aren't always clean as they might be.

COUNTY ATTORNEY: Ah, loyal to your sex, I see. But you and Mrs. Wright were neighbors. I suppose you were friends, too.

MRS. HALE *[shaking her head]:* I've not seen much of her of late years. I've not been in this house—it's more than a year.

COUNTY ATTORNEY: And why was that? You didn't like her?

MRS. HALE: I liked her all well enough. Farmers' wives have their hands full, Mr. Henderson. And then—

COUNTY ATTORNEY: Yes—?

MRS. HALE *[looking about]:* It never seemed a very cheerful place.

COUNTY ATTORNEY: No—it's not cheerful. I shouldn't say she had the homemaking instinct.

MRS. HALE: Well, I don't know as Wright had, either.

COUNTY ATTORNEY: You mean that they didn't get on very well?

MRS. HALE: No, I don't mean anything. But I don't think a place'd be any cheerfuller for John Wright's being in it.

COUNTY ATTORNEY: I'd like to talk more of that a little later. I want to get the lay of things upstairs now.

[He goes to the left, where three steps lead to a stair door.]

SHERIFF: I suppose anything Mrs. Peters does'll be all right. She was to take in some clothes for her, you know, and a few little things. We left in such a hurry yesterday.

COUNTY ATTORNEY: Yes, but I would like to see what you take, Mrs. Peters, and keep an eye out for anything that might be of use to us.

MRS. PETERS: Yes, Mr. Henderson.

[The women listen to the men's steps on the stairs, then look about the kitchen.]

MRS. HALE: I'd hate to have men coming into my kitchen, snooping around and criticizing.

[She arranges the pans under sink which the COUNTY ATTORNEY *had shoved out of place.]*

MRS. PETERS: Of course it's no more than their duty.

MRS. HALE: Duty's all right, but I guess that deputy sheriff that came out to make the fire might have got a little of this on. *[Gives the roller towel a pull.]* Wish I'd thought of that sooner. Seems mean to talk about her for not having things slicked up when she had to come away in such a hurry.

MRS. PETERS *[Who has gone to a small table in the left rear corner of the room, and lifted one end of a towel that covers a pan]:* She had bread set.

[Stands still.]

MRS. HALE *[eyes fixed on a loaf of bread beside the breadbox, which is on a low shelf at the other side of the room. Moves slowly toward it]:* She was going to put this in there. *[Picks up loaf, then abruptly drops it. In a manner of returning to familiar things.]* It's a shame about her fruit. I wonder if it's all gone. *[Gets up on the chair and looks.]* I think there's some here that's all right, Mrs. Peters. Yes—here; *[Holding it toward the window.]* this is cherries, too. *[Looking again.]* I declare I believe that's the only one. *[Gets down, bottle in her hand. Goes to the sink and wipes it off on the outside.]* She'll feel awful bad after all her hard work in the hot weather. I remember the afternoon I put up my cherries last summer.

[She puts the bottle on the big kitchen table, center of the room. With a sigh, is about to sit down in the rocking-chair. Before she is seated realizes what chair it is; with a slow look at it, steps back. The chair which she has touched rocks back and forth.]

MRS. PETERS: Well, I must get those things from the front room closet. *[She goes to the door at the right, but after looking into the other room, steps back.]* You coming with me, Mrs. Hale? You could help me carry them.

[They go in the other room; reappear, MRS. PETERS *carrying a dress and skirt,* MRS. HALE *following with a pair of shoes.]*

MRS. PETERS: My, it's cold in there.

[She puts the clothes on the big table, and hurries to the stove.]

MRS. HALE *[examining her skirt]:* Wright was close. I think maybe that's why she kept so much to herself. She didn't even belong to the Ladies Aid. I suppose she felt she couldn't do her part, and then you don't enjoy things when you feel shabby. She used to wear pretty clothes and be lively, when she was Minnie Foster, one of the town girls singing in the choir. But that—oh, that was thirty years ago. This all you want to take in?

MRS. PETERS: She said she wanted an apron. Funny thing to want, for there isn't much to get you dirty in jail, goodness knows. But I suppose just to make her feel more natural. She said they was in the top drawer in this cupboard. Yes, here. And then her little shawl that always hung behind the door. *[Opens stair door and looks.]* Yes, here it is.

[Quickly shuts door leading upstairs.]

MRS. HALE *[abruptly moving toward her]:* Mrs. Peters?

MRS. PETERS: Yes, Mrs. Hale?

MRS. HALE: Do you think she did it?

MRS. PETERS *[in a frightened voice]:* Oh, I don't know.

MRS. HALE: Well, I don't think she did. Asking for an apron and her little shawl. Worrying about her fruit.

MRS. PETERS *[starts to speak, glances up, where footsteps are heard in the room above. In a low voice]:* Mr. Peters says it looks bad for her. Mr. Henderson is awful sarcastic in a speech and he'll make fun of her sayin' she didn't wake up.

MRS. HALE: Well, I guess John Wright didn't wake when they was slipping that rope under his neck.

MRS. PETERS: No, it's strange. It must have been done awful crafty and still. They say it was such a—funny way to kill a man, rigging it all up like that.

MRS. HALE: That's just what Mr. Hale said. There was a gun in the house. He says that's what he can't understand.

MRS. PETERS: Mr. Henderson said coming out that what was needed for the case was a motive; something to show anger, or—sudden feeling.

MRS. HALE *[who is standing by the table]:* Well, I don't see any signs of anger around here. *[She puts her hand on the dish towel which lies on the table, stands looking down at table, one half of which is clean, the other half messy.]* It's wiped to here. *[Makes a move as if to finish work, then turns and looks at loaf of bread outside the breadbox. Drops towel. In that voice of coming back to familiar things.]* Wonder how they are finding things upstairs. I hope she had it a little more red-up° up there. You know, it seems kind of *sneaking.* Locking her up in town and then coming out here and trying to get her own house to turn against her!

MRS. PETERS: But Mrs. Hale, the law is the law.

MRS. HALE: I s'pose 'tis. *[Unbuttoning her coat.]* Better loosen up your things, Mrs. Peters. You won't feel them when you go out.

*[*MRS. PETERS *takes off her fur tippet, goes to hang it on hook at back of room, stands looking at the underpart of the small corner table.]*

MRS. PETERS: She was piecing a quilt.

[She brings the large sewing basket and they look at the bright pieces.]

MRS. HALE: It's log cabin-pattern. Pretty, isn't it? I wonder if she was goin' to quilt it or just knot it?

[Footsteps have been heard coming down the stairs. The SHERIFF *enters followed by* HALE *and the* COUNTY ATTORNEY.]

SHERIFF: They wonder if she was going to quilt it or just knot it!

[The men laugh; the women look abashed.]

COUNTY ATTORNEY *[rubbing his hands over the stove]:* Frank's fire didn't do much up there, did it? Well, let's go out to the barn and get that cleared up.

[The men go outside.]

MRS. HALE *[resentfully]:* I don't know as there's anything so strange, our takin' up our time with little things while we're waiting for them to get the evidence. *[She sits down at the big table smoothing out a block with decision.]* I don't see as it's anything to laugh about.

MRS. PETERS *[apologetically]*: Of course they've got awful important things on their minds.

[Pulls up a chair and joins MRS. HALE *at the table.]*

MRS. HALE *[examining another block]:* Mrs. Peters, look at this one. Here, this is the one she was working on, and look at the sewing! All the rest of it has been so nice and even. And look at this! It's all over the place! Why, it looks as if she didn't know what she was about!

[After she has said this they look at each other, then start to glance back at the door. After an instant MRS. HALE *has pulled at a knot and ripped the sewing.]*

MRS. PETERS: Oh, what are you doing, Mrs. Hale?

MRS. HALE *[mildly]:* Just pulling out a stitch or two that's not sewed very good. *[Threading a needle.]* Bad sewing always made me fidgety.

MRS. PETERS *[nervously]:* I don't think we ought to touch things.

°red-up: ready for company.

MRS. HALE: I'll just finish up this end. *[Suddenly stopping and leaning forward.]* Mrs. Peters?

MRS. PETERS: Yes, Mrs. Hale?

MRS. HALE: What do you suppose she was so nervous about?

MRS. PETERS: Oh—I don't know. I don't know as she was nervous. I sometimes sew awful queer when I'm just tired. [MRS. HALE *starts to say something, looks at* MRS. PETERS, *then goes on sewing.]* Well, I must get these things wrapped up. They may be through sooner than we think. *[Putting apron and other things together.]* I wonder where I can find a piece of paper, and string.

MRS. HALE: In that cupboard, maybe.

MRS. PETERS *[looking in cupboard]:* Why, here's a birdcage. *[Holds it up.]* Did she have a bird. Mrs. Hale?

MRS. HALE: Why, I don't know whether she did or not—I've not been here for so long. There was a man around last year selling canaries cheap, but I don't know as she took one; maybe she did. She used to sing real pretty herself.

MRS. PETERS *[Glancing around]:* Seems funny to think of a bird here. But she must have had one, or why would she have a cage? I wonder what happened to it.

MRS. HALE: I s'pose maybe the cat got it.

MRS. PETERS: No, she didn't have a cat. She's got that feeling some people have about cats—being afraid of them. My cat got in her room and she was real upset and asked me to take it out.

MRS. HALE: My sister Bessie was like that. Queer, ain't it?

MRS. PETERS *[examining the cage]:* Why, look at this door. It's broke. One hinge is pulled apart.

MRS. HALE *[looking too]:* Looks as if someone must have been rough with it.

MRS. PETERS: Why, yes.

[She brings the cage forward and puts it on the table.]

MRS. HALE: I wish if they're going to find any evidence they'd be about it. I don't like this place.

MRS. PETERS: But I'm awful glad you came with me, Mrs. Hale. It would be lonesome for me sitting here alone.

MRS. HALE: It would, wouldn't it? *[Dropping her sewing.]* But I tell you what I do wish, Mrs. Peters. I wish I had come over sometimes when *she* was here. I—*[Looking around the room.]*—wish I had.

MRS. PETERS: But of course you were awful busy, Mrs. Hale—your house and your children.

MRS. HALE: I could've come. I stayed away because it weren't cheerful and that's why I ought to have come. I—I've never liked this place. Maybe because it's down in a hollow and you don't see the road. I dunno what it is but it's a lonesome place and always was. I wish I had come over to see Minnie Foster sometimes. I can see now—

[Shakes her head.]

MRS. PETERS: Well, you mustn't reproach yourself, Mrs. Hale. Somehow we just don't see how it is with other folks until—something comes up.

MRS. HALE: Not having children makes less work—but it makes a quiet house, and Wright out to work all day, and no company when he did come in. Did you know John Wright, Mrs. Peters?

MRS. PETERS: Not to know him; I've seen him in town. They say he was a good man.

MRS. HALE: Yes—good; he didn't drink, and kept his word as well as most, I guess, and paid his debts. But he was a hard man, Mrs. Peters. Just to pass the time of day with him—*[Shivers.]* Like a raw wind that gets to the bone. *[Pauses, her eye falling on the cage.]* I should think she would'a wanted a bird. But what do you suppose went with it?

MRS. PETERS: I don't know, unless it got sick and died.

[She reaches over and swings the broken door, swings it again. Both women watch it.]

MRS. HALE: You weren't raised round here, were you? [MRS. PETERS *shakes her head.]* You didn't know—her?

MRS. PETERS: Not till they brought her yesterday.

MRS. HALE: She—come to think of it, she was kind of like a bird herself real sweet and pretty, but kind of timid and—fluttery. How—she—did change. *[Silence; then as if struck by a happy thought and relieved to get back to everyday things.]* Tell you what, Mrs. Peters, why don't you take the quilt in with you? It might take up her mind.

MRS. PETERS: Why, I think that's a real nice idea, Mrs. Hale. There couldn't possibly be any objection to it, could there? Now, just what would I take? I wonder if her patches are in here—and her things.

[They look in the sewing basket.]

MRS. HALE: Here's some red. I expect this has got sewing things in it. *[Brings out a fancy box.]* What a pretty box. Looks like something somebody would give you. Maybe her scissors are in here. *[Opens box. Suddenly puts her hand to her nose.]* Why—[MRS. PETERS *bends nearer, then turns her face away.]* There's something wrapped up in this piece of silk.

MRS. PETERS: Why, this isn't her scissors.

MRS. HALE *[lifting the silk]:* Oh. Mrs. Peters—it's—

[MRS. PETERS *bends closer.]*

MRS. PETERS: It's the bird.

MRS. HALE *[Jumping up]:* But, Mrs. Peters—look at it! Its neck! Look at its neck! It's all—other side *to.*

MRS. PETERS: Somebody—wrung—its—neck.

[Their eyes meet. A look of growing comprehension, of horror. Steps are heard outside. MRS. HALE *slips box under quilt pieces, and sinks into her chair. Enter* SHERIFF *and* COUNTY ATTORNEY. MRS. PETERS *rises.]*

COUNTY ATTORNEY *[as one turning from serious things to little pleasantries]:* Well, ladies have you decided whether she was going to quilt it or knot it?

MRS. PETERS: We think she was going to—knot it.

COUNTY ATTORNEY: Well, that's interesting, I'm sure. *[Seeing the birdcage.]* Has the bird flown?

MRS. HALE *[putting more quilt pieces over the box]:* We think the—cat got it.

COUNTY ATTORNEY *[Preoccupied]:* Is there a cat?

[MRS. HALE *glances in a quick covert way at* MRS. PETERS.]

MRS. PETERS: Well, not *now.* They're superstitious, you know. They leave.

COUNTY ATTORNEY *[to* SHERIFF PETERS, *continuing an interrupted conversation]:* No sign at all of anyone having come from the outside. Their own rope. Now let's go up again and go over it piece by piece. *[They start upstairs.]* It would have to have been someone who knew just the—

[MRS. PETERS *sits down. The two women sit there not looking at one another, but as if peering into something and at the same time holding back. When they talk now it is in the manner of feeling their way over strange ground, as if afraid of what they are saying, but as if they can not help saying it.]*

MRS. HALE: She liked the bird. She was going to bury it in that pretty box.

MRS. PETERS *[in a whisper]:* When I was a girl—my kitten—there was a boy took a hatchet, and before my eyes—and before I could get there—*[Covers her face an instant.]* If they hadn't held me back I would have—*[Catches herself, looks upstairs where steps are heard, falters weakly.]*—hurt him.

MRS. HALE *[with a slow look around her]:* I wonder how it would seem never to have had any children around. *[Pause.]* No, Wright wouldn't like the bird—a thing that sang. She used to sing. He killed that, too.

MRS. PETERS *[moving uneasily]:* We don't know who killed the bird.

MRS. HALE: I knew John Wright.

MRS. PETERS: It was an awful thing was done in this house that night, Mrs. Hale. Killing a man while he slept, slipping a rope around his neck that choked the life out of him.

MRS. HALE: His neck. Choked the life out of him.

[Her hand goes out and rests on the birdcage.]

MRS. PETERS *[with rising voice]:* We don't know who killed him. We don't *know.*

MRS. HALE *[her own feeling not interrupted]:* If there'd been years and years of nothing, then a bird to sing to you, it would be awful—still, after the bird was still.

MRS. PETERS *[something within her speaking]:* I know what stillness is. When we homesteaded in Dakota, and my first baby died—after he was two years old, and me with no other then—

MRS. HALE *[moving]:* How soon do you suppose they'll be through, looking for the evidence?

MRS. PETERS: I know what stillness is. *[Pulling herself back.]* The law has got to punish crime, Mrs. Hale.

MRS. HALE *[not as if answering that]:* I wish you'd seen Minnie Foster when she wore a white dress with blue ribbons and stood up there in the choir and sang. *[A look around the room.]* Oh, I *wish* I'd come over here once in a while! That was a crime! That was a crime! Who's going to punish that?

MRS. PETERS *[looking upstairs]:* We mustn't—take on.

MRS. HALE: I might have known she needed help! I know how things can be—for women. I tell you, it's queer, Mrs. Peters. We live close together and we live far apart. We all go through the same things—it's all just a different kind of the same thing. *[Brushes her eyes; noticing the bottle of fruit, reaches out for it.]* If I was you I wouldn't tell her her fruit was gone. Tell her it *ain't.* Tell her it's all right. Take this in to prove it to her. She—she may never know whether it was broke or not.

MRS. PETERS *[takes the bottle, looks about for something to wrap it in; takes petticoat from the clothes brought from the other room, very nervously begins winding this around the bottle. In a false voice]:* My, it's a good thing the men couldn't hear us. Wouldn't they just laugh! Getting all stirred up over a little thing like a—dead canary. As if that could have anything to do with—with—wouldn't they *laugh!*

[The men are heard coming down stairs.]

MRS. HALE *[under her breath]:* Maybe they would—maybe they wouldn't.

COUNTY ATTORNEY: No, Peters, it's all perfectly clear except a reason for doing it. But you know juries when it comes to women. If there was some definite thing.

Something to show—something to make a story about—a thing that would connect up with this strange way of doing it—

[The women's eyes meet for an instant. Enter HALE *from outer door.]*

HALE: Well, I've got the team around. Pretty cold out there.

COUNTY ATTORNEY: I'm going to stay here a while by myself. *[To the* SHERIFF.] You can send Frank out for me, can't you? I want to go over everything. I'm not satisfied that we can't do better.

SHERIFF: Do you want to see what Mrs. Peters is going to take in?

[The COUNTY ATTORNEY *goes to the table, picks up the apron, laughs.]*

COUNTY ATTORNEY: Oh, I guess they're not very dangerous things the ladies have picked out. *[Moves a few things about, disturbing the quilt pieces which cover the box. Steps back.]* No, Mrs. Peters doesn't need supervising. For that matter, a sheriff's wife is married to the law. Ever think of it that way, Mrs. Peters?

MRS. PETERS: Not—just that way.

SHERIFF *[Chuckling]:* Married to the law. *[Moves toward the other room.]* I just want you to come in here a minute, George. We ought to take a look at these windows.

COUNTY ATTORNEY *[scoffingly]:* Oh, windows sheriff! We'll be right out, Mr. Hale.

[HALE *goes outside. The* SHERIFF *follows the* COUNTY ATTORNEY *into the other room. Then* MRS. HALE *rises, hands tight together, looking intensely at* MRS. PETERS, *whose eyes make a slow turn, finally meeting* MRS. HALE'S. *A moment* MRS. HALE *holds her, then her own eyes point the way to where the box is concealed. Suddenly* MRS. PETERS *throws back quilt pieces and tries to put the box in the bag she is wearing. It is too big. She opens box, starts to take bird out, cannot touch it, goes to pieces, stands there helpless. Sound of a knob turning in the other room.* MRS. HALE *snatches the box and puts it in the pocket of her big coat. Enter* COUNTY ATTORNEY and SHERIFF.]

COUNTY ATTORNEY *[facetiously]:* Well, Henry, at least we found out that she was not going to quilt it. She was going to—what is it you call it, ladies?

MRS. HALE *[her hand against her pocket]:* We call it—knot it, Mr. Henderson.

Curtain

Perception Key
SUSAN GLASPELL'S *TRIFLES*

1. What is tragic about this play? What is comic? How might this play help define the concept of tragicomedy?
2. What is the significance of the title of the play? It seems intended as an ironic comment. What is the irony?
3. Does Glaspell rely on type characters?
4. Why does Mrs. Wright not appear in the play? How do we learn about her and her circumstances? What seem to be the facts about her life with her husband?
5. How does Glaspell exploit the differences between the perceptions of the men and the perceptions of the women? Which of them is more perceptive?
6. Why is the broken birdcage significant to understanding the deep feelings that Mrs. Wright seems to have had? Is the birdcage a symbol?

7. What do we learn about Mrs. Wright from the discussion of her quilting?
8. Which lines of dialogue seem most revealing of the truth of Mrs. Wright's circumstances?
9. How does the setting contribute to the power of the drama?
10. Comment on the plot. All the main action happens before the play begins. What is the primary action of the drama we witness? What is being sought? What is discovered? Do the men discover what the women discover?
11. Are the circumstances of the drama relevant to the time of its first performance (1916), or would it be relevant to any era?

EXPERIMENTAL DRAMA

The last forty years have seen exceptional experimentation in drama in the Western world. Samuel Beckett wrote plays with no words at all, as in *Acts Without Words*. One of his plays, *Not I,* has an oversized mouth talking with a darkened, hooded figure, thus reducing character to a minimum. In *Waiting for Godot,* plot was reduced in importance. In *Endgame* the characters are immobilized in garbage cans, thereby minimizing spectacle. Beckett's experiments have demonstrated that even when the traditional elements of drama are de-emphasized or removed, it is still possible for drama to evoke intense participative experiences. Beckett has been the master of refining away. He seems to have subscribed to the catch phrase—"less is more"—of the Bauhaus school of architectural design.

Another important thrust of experimental drama has been to assault the audience. Antonin Artaud's "Theater of Cruelty" has regarded audiences as comfortable, pampered groups of privileged people. Peter Weiss' play—*The Persecution and Assassination of Marat as Performed by the Inmates of the Asylum at Charenton under the Direction of the Marquis de Sade* (or *Marat/Sade*)—was influenced by Artaud's thinking. Through a depiction of insane inmates contemplating the audience at a very close range (Figure 8-9), it sought to break down the traditional security associated with the proscenium theater. *Marat/Sade* ideally was performed in a theater-in-the-round with the audience sitting on all sides of the actors, and without the traditional fanfare of lights dimming for the beginning and lighting up for the ending. The audience is deliberately made to feel uneasy throughout the play. As Susan Sontag said:

> While the "cruelty" in *Marat/Sade* is not, ultimately, a moral issue, it is not an aesthetic one either. It is an ontological issue. While those who propose the aesthetic version of "cruelty" interest themselves in the richness of the surface of life, the proponents of the ontological version of "cruelty" want their art to act out the widest possible context for human action, at least a wider context than that provided by realistic art. That wider context is what Sade calls "nature" and what Artaud means when he says that "everything that acts is a cruelty."[2]

[2]Susan Sontag, "Marat/Sade/Artaud," *Against Interpretation,* Farrar, Straus & Giroux, New York, 1965.

FIGURE 8-9
Marat/Sade. The Academy Theatre production, Atlanta, Georgia. (Courtesy Atlanta History Center)

By describing the cruelty in *Marat/Sade* as ontological, Sontag means that the depiction of intense cruelty within the drama is there because cruelty underlies all human events, and the play attempts a revelation of that all-pervasive cruelty. She goes on to explain that the audience's own discomfort is a natural function of this revelation.

Marat/Sade has usually been performed without a proscenium frame, but, nonetheless, on a stage, a space set apart from those watching. Julian Beck and Judith Malina experimented early in the 1960s, in a play by Jack Gelber called *The Connection,* with reducing even further the distance between players and audience. The play was about a group of addicts waiting for their dealer to show up, and it was specifically designed to seem like a non-

FIGURE 8-10
Robert Wilson in *Hamlet: A Monologue* at Alice Tully Hall. (Sara Krulwich/The New York Times Pictures)

play. Gelber was in the audience—clearly identified as the author—complaining about the way the production was distorting his play. In later Beck/Malina plays, such as *Paradise Now,* the distinction between players and audience grew even slighter, with no separation of space between the players and the audience.

Richard Schechner's play *Dionysus in '69* also did away with spatial separation. The space of the theater was the stage space, with a design by Jerry Rojo that made players and audience indistinguishable. The play demanded that everyone become part of the action; in some performances—and in the filmed performance—most of the players and audience ended the drama with a modern-day orgiastic rite. Such experimentation, indeed, seems extreme. But it is analogous with other dramatic events in other cultures, such as formal religious and celebratory rites.

Another significant aspect of the contemporary experimental drama is the tendency to interpret freely the written text. The director tends to become more identified with the play than the author. Andrei Serban, the director of such productions in the 1980s as *The Cherry Orchard* and *Agamemnon,* reinterprets these plays so freely that the authors, Chekhov and Aeschylus, hardly get a notice. When Brecht's *Three-Penny Opera* was performed, Richard Foreman, director of the highly experimental Hysteric-Ontological Theater in New York, dominated the play so much that the original text was almost ignored. Much of the experimental theater of today is in the hands of such directors as Peter Brook of England, Jerzy Grotowski of Poland, George C. Wolfe of New York's Public Theater, and Robert Wilson, as well as a number of writers, actors, and directors in other parts of the world.

Robert Wilson, known for his day-long dramas and extraordinary staging of modern operas, performed *Hamlet* as a monologue in 1995 (Figure 8-10). Dressed in black, alone on stage, he played Hamlet as a man who reviewed his life moment by moment, reenacting the scenes of the play and telling the entire story from his point of view. Wilson depended on intense music and sounds, such as explosions and clanging, as well as on unusual lighting effects. *Hamlet* invites experimentation. Tom Stoppard interpreted the action from the point of view of Rosencrantz and Guildenstern in *Rosencrantz and Guildenstern Are Dead* (1966); Heiner Müller produced a wildly expressionist version called *Hamletmachine* (1977); and Lee Blessing produced a fascinating version called *Fortinbras* (1991), which tells the story of the play from the point of view of the character who appears at the end of the play, when everyone but Horatio is dead.

Perception Key
EXPERIMENTAL DRAMA

Should you have the chance to experience a drama produced by any of the directors or groups mentioned above, try to distinguish its features from those of the more traditional forms of drama. What observations can you add to those made above? Consider the kinds of satisfaction you get as a participant. Is experimental drama as satisfying as traditional drama? What are the differences? To what extent are the differences to be found in the details and parts? The structure? Are experimental dramas usually episodic or organic?

SUMMARY

The subject matter of drama is the human condition as represented by action. By emphasizing plot and character as the most important elements of drama, Aristotle helps us understand the priorities of all drama. Tragedy and comedy both have archetypal patterns that help define them as genres. Some of the archetypes seem related to the natural rhythms of the seasons and focus, in the case of tragedy, on the endings of things, such as death, and, in the case of comedy, on the beginnings of things, such as marriage.

Comedy has several distinct genres. Old Comedy often abuses individual characters and revels in broad humor. New Comedy emphasizes the comedy of manners, a social commentary that often depends on type characters. Tragicomedy combines both genres to create a third genre. The ambiguity implied in tragedy joined with comedy makes this a particularly flexible genre, suited to a modern world that lives in uncertainty. The experiments in modern drama have tried to break away from traditions, the comforts of which have assured audiences of being carefully treated rather than being involved in an intense and transforming dramatic experience. The human condition may shift from period to period in the history of drama, but somehow the constancy of human concerns has helped make Shakespeare and other great dramatists our contemporaries.

CHAPTER 8 BIBLIOGRAPHY

Aristotle. *Aristotle's Theory of Poetry and Fine Art.* S. H. Butcher (trans.). New York: Dover Books, 1951.

Bentley, Eric. *The Playwright as Thinker.* New York: Harcourt Brace & World, 1967.

Bergson, Henri. *Laughter.* New York: Arden Library, 1983.

Brockett, Oscar. *History of the Theatre,* 7th ed. Boston: Allyn and Bacon, 1995.

Burkman, Katherine. *The Arrival of Godot.* Rutherford, N.J.: Fairleigh Dickinson College University Press, 1986.

Cameron, Kenneth M., and Theodore Hoffman. *A Guide to Theater Study,* 2d ed. New York: Macmillan 1974.

Dihle, Albrecht. *A History of Greek Literature.* New York: Routledge, 1994.

Esslin, Martin. *The Theatre of the Absurd,* 3rd ed. New York: Penguin, 1991.

Fergusson, Francis. *The Idea of a Theater.* Princeton: Princeton University Press, 1972.

Gassner, John. *Masters of the Drama,* 3rd ed., rev. and enl. New York: Dover Press, 1954.

———, and Ralph Allen. *Theatre and Drama in the Making.* 2 vols. Boston: Houghton Mifflin, 1964.

Gilman, Richard. *The Making of Modern Drama.* New York: Noonday, 1972.

Jacobus, Lee. *The Bedford Introduction to Drama,* 3rd ed. New York: St. Martins Press, 1997.

———. *Shakespeare and the Dialectic of Certainty.* New York: St. Martins Press, 1992.

Kernodle, George. *Invitation to the Theatre.* San Diego: Harcourt Brace Jovanovich, 1985.

Nicoll, Allardyce. *The Theory of the Drama.* New York: Crowell, 1931.

Orr, John. *Tragicomedy and Contemporary Culture: Play and Performance from Beckett to Shepard.* Ann Arbor: University of Michigan Press, 1990.

Potts, L. J. *Comedy.* London: Hutchinson, 1966.

Roose-Evans, James. *Experimental Theatre: From Stanislavsky to Today,* rev. ed. London: Studio Vista, 1973.

Steiner, George. *The Death of Tragedy.* New York: Knopf, 1961.

Wilson, Edwin. *The Theatre Experience.* New York: McGraw-Hill, 1976.

CHAPTER 8 WEBSITES

Canadian Theatre Research (mailing list)

List name: **candrama** Address: **listserv@unbvm1.csd.unb.ca**

Classical Theater (Greek and Roman theater)

World Wide Web: **http://www.warwick.ac.uk/didaskalia/Didintro.html**

Play Scripts

Gopher: Name: **Carnegie Mellon University**
Address: **English-server.hss.cmu.edu** Select: **Drama**

Stagecraft

Usenet: Newsgroup: **alt.stagecraft** or **rec.arts.theatre.stagecraft**

Theater Links (huge collection of theater links)

World Wide Web: **http://www.yahoo.com/Entertainment/Theater**

Theater, Opera, Musicals (general resources and reviews)
World Wide Web: **http://www.wiso.gwdg.de/ifbg/ent_thea.htm**

Theatre Central (links to theater groups, alternative theater, etc.)
World Wide Web: **http://www.mit.edu:8001/people/quijote/theatre-central.html**

Theatre Home Page (general information on theater)
World Wide Web: **http://www.cs.fsu.edu/projects/group4/theatre.html**

CHAPTER 9

MUSIC

Music is one of the most powerful of the arts partly because sounds—more than any other sensory stimulus—create in us involuntary reactions, pleasant or unpleasant. There is no escaping the effects of music except by turning off the source. Live concerts, whether of the Boston Symphony, or Wynton Marsalis at Lincoln Center, or Bruce Springsteen and the E Street Band on tour, usually excite delight in their audiences. Yet in all cases the audiences rarely analyze the music. It may seem difficult to connect analysis with the experience of listening to music, but everyone's listening, including the performer's, benefits from a thorough understanding of some of the basics of music.

HEARERS AND LISTENERS

Music can be experienced in two basic ways: "hearing" or "listening." Hearers do not attempt to perceive accurately either the structure or the details of the form. They hear a familiar melody such as the Beatles' "Strawberry Fields," which may trigger associations with John Lennon, early rock and roll, and perhaps even the garden in Central Park dedicated to his memory. But aside from the melody, little else—such as the details of chord progression, movement toward or away from tonic and dominant—is heard. The case is much the same with classical music. Most hearers prefer richly melodic music, such as Tchaikovsky's Fifth Symphony, whose second movement especially contains lush melodies that can trigger romantic associations. But when one asks hearers if the melody was repeated exactly or varied, or whether the melody was moved from one instrument family to another, they cannot say. They are concentrating on the associations triggered by the music rather than on the form of the music. Another kind of hearer is "suffused" or "permeated" by music, bathing in sensuous sounds, as many people will do with their earphones tuned to soft rock, new age, or easy-listening sounds. In this nonanalytic but attractive state of mind the music spreads through the body rhythmically, soothingly. It feels great, and that is enough.

The listeners, conversely, concentrate their attention upon the form, details as well as structure. They could answer the above questions about Tchaikovsky's Fifth Symphony. Listeners focus upon the form that informs, that creates content. Listeners do not just listen: they listen for something—the content.

PERCEPTION KEY
HEARING AND LISTENING

1. Play one of your favorite pieces of music. Describe its overall organization or structure. Is there a clear melody? Is there more than one melody? If so, are they similar to one another or do they contrast with each other? What elements in the piece are repeated? Is the melody repeated? Is it varied or the same? Do different instruments play it? If there are lyrics, are they repeated?
2. Describe details such as what kind of rhythm is used. Is it varied? How? Is there harmony? What kind of instruments are played? How do these details fit into the larger parts and the structure?
3. Play the first movement of Beethoven's Third Symphony (the *Eroica*). Answer the same questions for this piece as were asked in questions 1 and 2. Later, we will discuss this symphony in detail. You may wish to compare your responses now with those you have after you have studied the work.
4. Do such questions annoy you? Would you rather just experience the music as a means to daydreaming? Or as sensuously suffusing?
5. Are you basically a hearer or a listener? Are you sometimes one and then the other? Which would you rather be most of the time? And at what times? Why?

If you find that you cannot answer the first three questions or find them annoying, then indeed you are a hearer. Even the most avid listeners will be hearers under certain circumstances. No one is always "up" for concentrated attention. And although one can *hear* the Mozart in the background of a loud cocktail party, no one can *listen*. If you are usually a hearer even when the circumstances allow for listening, it is our hope that we can help you toward being a listener. And if you are a listener, we hope to make you and ourselves better ones. Music's content gives generous gifts, provided we are prepared to receive them.

THE ELEMENTS OF MUSIC

Before we go further, we will introduce some of the important terms and concepts of music essential to a clear discussion. We begin with some definitions, and then analyze the basic musical elements of rhythm, melody, counterpoint, harmony, dynamics, and contrast. A common language about music is prerequisite to any intelligible discussion.

TONE

A sound that has one definite frequency or that is dominated by one definite frequency is a tone. Most music is composed of a succession of tones. Musical patterns are heard because of our ability to hear tones and remember them as they are played in succession. Tones on a musical instrument—except for pure tones—will have subordinate, related tones, or partials, sounding simultaneously, although not as loudly as the primary tone. Our ear is used to hearing a primary tone with fainter partials; therefore, when electronic instruments produce a pure tone—that is, with no partials—it may sound very odd to us. All instruments differ in the intensity or loudness of each of the partials. Consequently, a trumpet or a piano playing C will each have its distinctive timbre, or tone color, because of the variation in intensity of the simultaneously sounding partials that accompany the primary tone.

CONSONANCE

When two or more tones are sounded simultaneously and the result is pleasing to the ear, the resultant sound is said to be consonant. The phenomenon of consonance may be qualified by several things. For example, what sounds dissonant or unpleasant often becomes more consonant after repeated hearings. Thus the sounds of the music of a different culture may seem dissonant at first but consonant after some familiarity develops. Also, there is the influence of context: a combination of notes may seem dissonant in isolation or within one set of surrounding notes and consonant within another set. In the C major scale, the strongest consonances will be the eighth (C + C′) (see Figure 9-1 for these notes) and the fifth (C + G), with the third (C + E), the fourth (C + F), and the sixth (C + A) being only slightly less consonant.

DISSONANCE

Just as some notes sounding together tend to be soothing and pleasant, other notes sounding together tend to be rough and unpleasant. This unpleasantness is a result of wave interference and a phenomenon called "beating" which accounts for the roughness we perceive in dissonance. The most powerful dissonance is achieved when notes close to one another in pitch are sounded simultaneously. The second (C + D) and the seventh (B + C) are both strongly dissonant. Dissonance is important in building musical tension, since the desire to resolve dissonance with consonance is strong in most listeners. There is a story that Mozart's wife would retaliate against

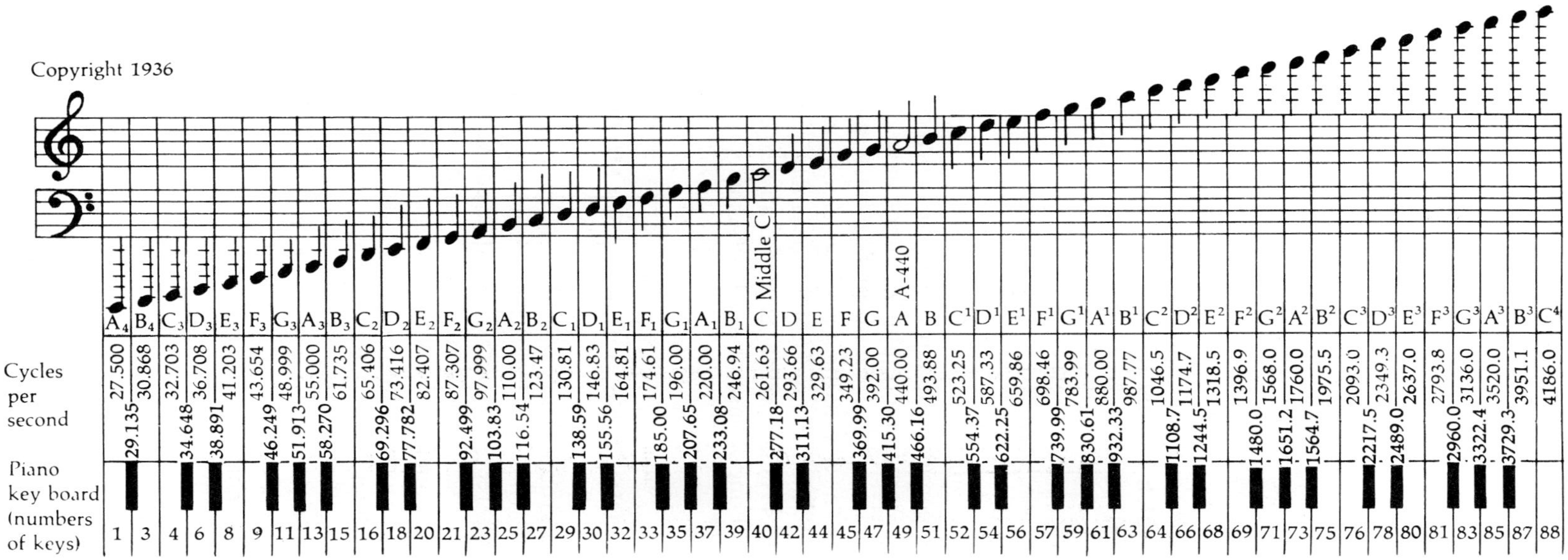

FIGURE 9-1
Pitch—the frequency of notes. Adapted from Carl Seashore, *The Psychology of Music*, 1938, McGraw-Hill, New York, p. 73.

her husband after some quarrel by striking a dissonant chord on the piano. Wolfgang would be forced to come from wherever he was to play a resounding consonant chord to relieve the unbearable tension.

RHYTHM

Rhythm is a term referring to the temporal relationships of organized sounds. Rhythm marks when a given note is to be played, and how long it is to be played (its duration). Our perception of rhythm in a composition is also affected by accent or stress on given notes. In the waltz, the accent is heavy on the first note (of three) in each musical measure. In most modern jazz, the stress falls on the second and fourth notes (of four) in each measure. Marching music, which usually has six notes in each measure, emphasizes the first and fourth note.

TEMPO

Tempo is the speed at which a composition is played. We perceive tempo in terms of beats, just as we perceive the tempo of our heartbeat as seventy-two pulses per minute, approximately. Many tempos have descriptive names indicating the general time value. *Presto* means "very fast"; *allegro* means "fast"; *andante* means "at a walking pace"; *moderato* means at a "moderate pace"; *lento* and *largo* mean "slow." Sometimes metronome markings are given in a score, but musicians rarely agree on any exact time figure. Tension, anticipation, and one's sense of musical security are strongly affected by tempo.

MELODIC MATERIAL: MELODY, LINE, THEME, AND MOTIVE

Melody is usually defined as a group of notes played one after another having a perceivable shape, or having a perceivable beginning, middle, and end. Usually a melody is easily recognizable when replayed. Vague as this definition is, we rarely find ourselves in doubt about what is or is not a melody. We not only recognize melodies easily but can say a great deal about them. Some melodies are brief, others extensive; some slow, others fast; some bouncy, others somber; some catchy, others less so, although they may bear more relistening than the catchy ones; etc. A *melodic line* is a "vague" melody, without quite as clear a beginning, middle, and end. A *theme* is a melody that undergoes significant modifications in later passages. Thus in the first movement of the *Eroica*, the melodic material is more accurately described as themes than melodies. On the other hand, the melodic material of "Swing Low, Sweet Chariot" (Figure 9-5) is clear and singable. A *motive* is the briefest intelligible and self-contained fragment or unit of a theme—for example, the famous first four notes of Beethoven's Symphony no. 5.

COUNTERPOINT

In the Middle Ages the monks composing and performing church music began to realize that powerful musical effects could be obtained by staggering the melodic lines as in folk songs such as "Row, Row, Row Your Boat." This is called *counterpoint*—a playing of one or more motives, themes, or melodies against each other. It implies an independence of simultaneous melodic lines, each of which can, at times, be most clearly audible. The opposition of melodic lines creates tension by virtue of their competition for our attention.

HARMONY

Harmony is the sounding of tones simultaneously. It is the vertical dimension, as with a chord (Figure 9-2), as opposed to the horizontal dimension, as with a melody. The harmony that most of us hear is basically chordal. A chord is a group of notes sounded together that has a specific relationship to a given key: the chord C-E-G, for example, is a major triad in the key of C major. At the end of a composition in the key of C, it will emphasize the sense of arrival—or the sense of finality—more than almost any other technique we know.

FIGURE 9-2
Harmony—the vertical element.

Chords are particularly useful for establishing cadences: progressions to resting points that release tensions. Cadences move from relatively unstable chords to stable ones. You can test this on a piano by first playing the notes C-F-A together, then playing C-E-G (consult Figure 9-1 for the position of these notes on the keyboard). The result will be obvious. The first chord establishes tension and uncertainty, making the chord unstable, while the second chord resolves the tension and uncertainty, bringing the sequence to a satisfying conclusion. You probably will recognize this progression as one you have heard in many compositions—for example, the "A-men" that closes most hymns. The progression exists in every key with the same sense of moving to stability.

In Figure 9-3 chords open the chorus of the "Battle Hymn of the Republic." Notice in the first chord the octave C interval in the bass clef and the third plus the fifth interval (E and G) in the treble clef. Clearly these are the most stable intervals in the composition, with only the third, E, being slightly less than optimum in stability. The piece thus establishes a powerful stability through its harmony at the outset. Whatever may happen in

Battle Hymn of the Republic
Attributed to William Steffe (Words by Julia Ward Howe)
CHORUS
Glo - ry, glo - ry, hal - le - lu - jah! Glo - ry, glo - ry, hal - le - lu - jah!
Glo - ry, glo - ry, hal - le - lu - jah! His truth is march - ing on.

FIGURE 9-3
"Battle Hymn of the Republic." Attributed to William Steffe (words by Julia Ward Howe).

the middle of the composition, we will expect the end to be just as stable. A glance at the last measure shows this to be the case. Whereas the opening included two Cs, an E, and a G, the final harmony dispenses with the G and substitutes another C, adding even more stability to the ending.

Harmony is based on apparently universal psychological responses. The smoothness of consonance and the roughness of dissonance seem to be just as perceptible to the non-Western as to the Western ear. The effects may be different due to cultural conditioning, but they are predictable within a limited range. One anthropologist, when told about a Samoan ritual in which he was assured he could hear original Samoan music—as it had existed from early times—hauled his tape recorder to the site of the ceremonies, waited until dawn, and when he heard the first stirrings turned on his machine and captured the entire group of Samoans singing "You are my sunshine, my only sunshine." The anthropologist was disappointed, but his experience underscores the universality of music.

DYNAMICS

One of the most easily perceived elements of music is dynamics: loudness and softness. Composers explore dynamics—as they explore keys, timbres, melodies, rhythms, and harmonics—to achieve variety, to establish a pattern against which they can play, to build tension and release it, and to provide the surprise which can delight an audience. Two terms, *piano* ("soft") and *forte* ("loud"), with variations such as *pianissimo* ("very soft") and *fortissimo* ("very loud"), are used by composers to identify the desired dynamics at a given moment in the composition. A gradual building up of loudness is called a crescendo, whereas a gradual building down is called a decrescendo. Most compositions will have some of each, as well as passages that sustain a dynamic level.

One thing that helps us value dynamics in a given composition is the composer's use of contrast. But contrast is of value in other ways. When more than one instrument is involved, the composer can contrast timbres. The brasses, for example, may be used to offer tonal contrast to a passage that may have been played by the strings. The percussion section, in turn, can contrast with both those sections, with high-pitched bells and low-pitched kettledrums covering a wide range of pitch and timbre. The woodwinds create very distinctive tone colors, and the composer writing for a large orchestra can use all of the families of instruments in ways designed to exploit the differences in the sounds of these instruments even when playing the same notes.

Composers may approach rhythm and tempo with the same attention to contrast. Most symphonies begin with a fast movement (usually labeled *allegro*) in the major key, followed by a slow movement (usually labeled *andante*) in a related or contrasting key, then a third movement with bright speed (often labeled *presto*), and a final movement that resolves to some extent all that has gone before—again at a fast tempo *(molto allegro)*, although sometimes with some contrasting sections within it. Such a symphony, examined in great detail in this chapter, is Beethoven's *Eroica*.

THE SUBJECT MATTER OF MUSIC

If music is like the other arts, it has a content that is achieved by the form's transformation of some subject matter. However, some critics have denied that music has a subject matter, while others have suggested so many different possibilities as to create utter confusion. Our theory identifies two basic kinds of subject matter: feeling (emotions, passions, and moods) and sound. The issues are extremely complex and there is little consensus, but we hope our approach at least will be suggestive.

It is difficult for music to refer to specific objects and events outside itself. Therefore it is difficult to think of music as having the same kind of subject matter as a representational painting, a figurative sculpture, or a realistic novel. Nonetheless, composers have tried to circumvent this limitation by a number of means. One is to use sounds that imitate the sounds we experience outside music: bird songs and clocks in Haydn's symphonies, a thunderstorm in Beethoven's Symphony no. 6, sirens in Charles Ives' works. Limited as such imitation may be, it represents an effort to overcome the abstract nature of music and to give it a recognizable subject matter.

Another means is a program—usually in the form of a descriptive title, a separate written description, or an accompanying narrative, as in songs or opera. *La Mer,* by Claude Debussy, has a program clearly indicated by its title, in English: *The Sea,* and its subtitles: "From Dawn to Noon at Sea," "Gambols of the Waves," and "Dialogue Between the Wind and the Sea." Debussy tried to make *La Mer* refer to specific events that happen outside music. His success depends on our knowing the program and its relationship to the music. But even if we make the connections, there is a problem involved with stating flatly that the sea is the subject matter of *La Mer*. The sea cannot be perceived in listening to *La Mer* in anything like the way it can be perceived imaginatively from a literary description or the way it can be perceived more directly in a painting. If *La Mer* were a work that used the actual sounds of the sea (as with a tape recording) or closely imitated them—the crashing of waves, the roaring of winds, and similar sounds—the problem would be simplified. But the same kind of musical sounds found in *La Mer* is also found in other compositions by Debussy that have nothing to do with the sea.

It seems, therefore, that *La Mer* is an interpretation not of the sea but, rather, of our impressions of the sea, and the fact that Debussy is often referred to as an Impressionist is supporting evidence. Thus the subject matter of *La Mer* can be said to be the feelings evoked in him by the sea. The content of the music is the interpretation of those feelings. Given close attention to the program, this suggestion seems to pose few difficulties. But much music has no program, and *La Mer* can be enjoyed by those unaware of its program. Consequently, there may be some general feelingful character to the music that can be appreciated apart from any recognition that the swelling of a theme implies the swelling of a sea wind, that the crash of the orchestra suggests the crash of a wave, or that long, quiet passages suggest the stretches of the sea. Apparently those who do not know the program may still recognize general feeling qualities in these same passages despite the fact that they do not relate these qualities to their feelings about the sea. There seems to be a general relationship, but not necessarily a strict relationship, between the structures of our feelings and the structures of music.

FEELINGS

Feelings are composed basically of sensations, emotions, passions, and moods. Any awareness of our sense organs, whether internal or external, being stimulated is a sensation. Emotions are strong sensations felt as related to a specific and apparent stimulus. Passions are emotions elevated to great intensity. Moods, on the other hand, are sensations that arise from no specific or apparent stimulus, as when one awakens with a feeling of lassitude or gloom. Generally moods, although often long-lasting, are not felt as strongly as emotions and passions. Sometimes moods are evoked by emotions and passions and mix in with them so thoroughly that we are unaware of their origin. This often seems to happen when we listen to music. For example, a number of vibrant chordal progressions may evoke joyful emotions that—taken in their entirety—evoke a mood of well-being.

Music seems to be able to interpret and thus clarify our feelings primarily because in some important ways the structures of music parallel or are congruent with the structures of feelings. A rushing, busy passage can suggest unease or nervousness so powerfully that we sense unease to be a quality of the music itself, as well as feeling unease within ourselves. A slow passage in a minor key, such as a funeral march, can suggest gloom; a sprightly passage in a major key, such as a dance, can suggest joy. These extremes, and others like them, are obvious and easy for most listeners to comprehend. But there are innumerable subtleties and variations of feelings between these extremes, none of which is as nameable or as discussable as those mentioned. How can music interpret such feelings?

First of all, the power of sound to evoke feeling has been recognized by innumerable philosophers of art. John Dewey observes:

> Sounds come from outside the body, but sound itself is near, intimate; it is an excitation of the organism; we feel the clash of vibrations throughout the whole body. . . . A foot-fall, the breaking of a twig, the rustling of underbrush may signify attack or even death from hostile animal or man. . . . Vision arouses emotion in the form of interest—curiosity solicits further examination . . . or it institutes a balance between withdrawal and forward exploring action. It is sound that makes us jump.[1]

Second, feeling is heightened when a tendency to respond is in some way arrested or inhibited. Suspense is fundamental to a feelingful response. Musical stimuli activate tendencies that are frustrated by means of deviations from the expected, and then these frustrated tendencies are usually followed by meaningful resolutions. We hear a tone or tonal pattern and find it lacking in the sense that it demands other tones, for it seems to need or anticipate following tones that will presumably resolve its "needfulness."

Third, it may be that musical structures possess, at least at times, more than just a general resemblance to the structures of feelings. Susanne Langer maintains that

> the tonal structures we call "music" bear a close logical similarity to the forms of human feelings—forms of growth and attenuation, flowing and stowing, conflict and resolution, speed, arrest, terrific excitement, calm, or subtle activation and dreamy lapses—not joy and sorrow perhaps, but the poignancy of either and both—the greatness and brevity and eternal passing of everything vitally felt. Such is the pattern, or logical form, of sentience, and the pattern of music is that same form worked out in pure, measured sound and silence. Music is a tonal analogue of emotive life.[2]

These examples of the close similarity between the structures of music and feelings are fairly convincing because they are extreme. Most listeners agree that some music has become associated with gloomy moods, while other music has become associated with exhilaration. Much of this process of association undoubtedly is the result of cultural conventions that we unconsciously accept. But presumably there is something in the music that is the basis for these associations, and Langer has made a convincing case that the basis is in the similarity of structures. It is unlikely, indeed, that a bouncy, dynamic trumpet passage would ever be associated with peaceful feelings. Such a passage is more likely to be associated with warlike alarms and uncertainties. Soft, vibrating string passages, on the other hand, are more likely to be associated with less warlike anxieties. The associations of

[1]John Dewey, *Art as Experience,* Milton Balch and Co., New York, 1934, p. 237.
[2]Susanne Langer, *Feeling and Form,* Scribner's, New York, 1953, p. 27.

feelings with music, in other words, do not seem to be entirely conventional or arbitrary. The associations are made because music sounds the way feelings feel. Music is "shaped" like the "shapes" of our feelings. Or, more precisely, the tonal structures of music and the inner or subjective structures of feelings can be significantly similar.

Music shapes in sounds characteristics of feelings separate from bodily sensation. We hear out there structures that are something like what in nonmusical experiences we feel inside. We perceive outside something of what we usually perceive inside. When we listen to the anguish of the funeral march in the second movement of Beethoven's *Eroica*, we perceive the structures of anguish but not what evoked the anguish. Beethoven interprets and, in turn, clarifies those structures, gives us insight into them. Anguish is a very unpleasant feeling, but when we listen to Beethoven's funeral march we normally feel pleasant emotions. For now we are not asked to be anguished, but to observe and interpret anguish musically. That insight dissipates—to a large extent, although probably never wholly—the pain. Understanding tragic music brings satisfaction, analogous to the satisfaction that comes from understanding tragic drama. But there is a fundamental difference: tragic drama is about what causes painful feelings; tragic music is about the structure of painful feelings. The subject matter of tragic drama is the outside world; the subject matter of tragic music is the inside world.

Music has the capacity to clarify the nuances of feeling. When we speak in terms of nuances or when we suggest that music can clarify subtle feelings, we are no longer referring to nameable feelings such as joy, sadness, uncertainty, anxiety, and security. Music is, perhaps, richest in its ability to clarify feelings for which we have no names at all. One reason we return to a favorite piece of music again and again may be that it, and it alone in many cases, can interpret for us feelings that we could not otherwise identify. One of the results of participating with such music is the revelation of the unnameable feelings that refine and enlarge our life of feeling.

Music sometimes makes us recognize feelings we do not know we had. We feel a sorrow we have no name for, but we can say that it feels like the funeral march of the *Eroica*. Or, we feel a joy we have no name for, but we can say that it feels like the exuberant last movement of Mozart's *Jupiter* symphony. And those who have participated with the *Eroica* and the *Jupiter* will understand more definitively what is meant than if we simply say: "We are sad," or "We are joyful." No art reaches into our life of feeling more deeply than music.

TWO THEORIES: FORMALISM AND EXPRESSIONISM

Music apparently not only evokes feeling in the listener but also reveals the structures of those feelings. Presumably, then, the form of *La Mer* not only evokes feelings analogous to the feelings the sea arouses in us, but the form also interprets those feelings and gives us insight into them. The Formalists of music, such as Eduard Hanslick and Edmund Gurney,[3] deny this connection of music with nonmusical situations. For them, the apprehension of the tonal structures of music is made possible by a unique musical faculty that produces a unique aesthetic effect, and they refuse to call that effect feeling since this suggests alliance with everyday feelings. They consider the grasp of the form of music so intrinsically valuable that any attempt to relate music to anything else is spurious.

As Igor Stravinsky, certainly one of the greatest composers of our century, insisted: "Music is by its very nature essentially powerless to express anything at all. . . ."[4] In other words, the Formalists deny that music has a subject matter and, in turn, this means that music has no content, that the form of music has no revelatory meaning. We think that the theory of the Formalists is plainly inadequate, but it is an important warning against thinking of music as a springboard for hearing, for nonmusical associations and sentimentalism. Moreover, much work remains—building on the work of philosophers of art such as Dewey and Langer—to make clearer the mechanism of how the form of music evokes feeling and yet at the same time interprets or gives us insight into those feelings.

Much simpler—and more generally accepted than either the Formalist theory of Hanslick and Gurney or even our own theory—is the Expressionist theory: music evokes feelings. Composers express or communicate their feelings through their music to their audience. We should experience, more or less, the same feelings as the composer. But Mozart was distraught both psychologically and physically when he composed the *Jupiter* symphony, one of his last greatest works, and melancholy was the pervading feeling of his life shortly before his untimely death. Yet where is the melancholy in that symphony? Certainly there is melancholy in his *Requiem,* also one of his last works. But do we simply undergo melancholy in listening to the *Requiem?* Is it only evoked in us and nothing more? Is there not a transformation of melancholy? Does not the structure of the music—"out there"—allow us to perceive the structure of melancholy, and thus understand it better? If so, then the undoubted fact that the *Requiem* gives extraordinary satisfaction to most listeners is given at least partial explication by our Revelational theory.

SOUND

Apart from feelings, sound, for the Formalists, might also be thought of as one of the subject matters of music, because in some music it may be that the form gives us insight into sounds. This is somewhat similar to the claim that colors may be the subject matter of some abstract painting (see pages 73–74). The tone C in a musical composition, for example, has its analogue in natural sounds, as in a bird song, somewhat the way the red in an abstract painting has its analogue in natural colors. However, the similarity

[3]Eduard Hanslick, *The Beautiful in Music,* Gustav Cohen (trans.), Novello and Co., London, 1891, and Edmund Gurney, *The Power of Sound,* Smith, Elder and Co., London, 1880.
[4]Igor Stravinsky, *An Autobiography,* Simon and Schuster, New York, 1936, p. 83.

of a tone in music to a tone in the nonmusical world is rarely perceived in music that emphasizes tonal relationships. In such music, the individual tone usually is so caught up in its relationships with other tones that any connection with sounds outside the music seems irrelevant. It would be rare, indeed, for someone to hear the tone C in a Mozart sonata and associate it with the tone C of some bird song.

Tonal relationships in most music are very different in their context from the tones of the nonmusical world. On the other hand, music that does not emphasize tonal relationships—such as many of the works of John Cage—can perhaps give us insight into sounds that are noises rather than tones. Since we are surrounded by noises of all kinds—humming machines, people talking, and banging garbage cans, to name a few—we usually "turn them off" in our conscious mind so as not to be distracted from more important matters. This is such an effective "turnoff" that we are surprised and sometimes delighted when a composer introduces such noises into a musical composition. Then, for once, we listen to rather than away from them, and then we may discover these noises to be intrinsically interesting.

Perception Key
THE SUBJECT MATTER OF MUSIC

1. Select two brief musical compositions you like and participate with them. Analyze each with the following questions in mind. Do these pieces evoke feelings? Are there passages that evoke emotions? passions? moods? Do the structures of these pieces appear similar to the structures of emotions, passions, or moods? Be as specific as possible. Do you "live through" the feelings the music evokes? In other words, are they essentially the same feelings you experience in everyday situations? Or do they differ because their structures are perceptible in the music?
2. In a small group, present a very brief piece of popular music that you think has feeling as part of its subject matter. What degree of agreement do you find concerning what that feeling is? Is there general agreement relative to whether the feeling is emotion, passion, or mood? Listen to either Tchaikovsky's *1812 Overture,* or the "Tuba Mirum" from Berlioz's *Requiem,* or Beethoven's *Grösse Fuge* (Great Fugue) Op. 133, or "Der Erlkönig" (The Erlking), a song by Franz Schubert. Ask the same questions. Are the answers more complex? If so, why? If possible, make a comparison between the piece of popular music and the suggestions mentioned above. If there any difference in the apparent complexity of feeling among the pieces?
3. Listen to a John Cage or a Spike Jones recording that uses everyday sounds, such as barking dogs or car horns. With a group, discuss the value of such music for making one more aware of the characteristics and qualities of sounds we usually take for granted.

TONAL MUSIC

Tonal music is based on scale systems that generate one tone—the tonic—around which all other tones are subordinated in varying degrees. In Western music, going back to the Greeks, various scale systems have evolved, but beginning in the early Baroque period, around 1600, through the first decades of this century, the diatonic scale system has been the fundamental organizing principle of Western music. In recent decades, however, tonality has often been supplanted by atonal and nontonal systems in which no tonic is generated. Nevertheless, tonality is still the most important force in popular music, including most blues, jazz, and rock. For purposes of simplification, we will discuss only two of the many scales available in tonal music: the C major scale, C-D-E-F-G-A-B-C, and the F major scale, F-G-A-B♭-C-D-E-F. The B is flatted (the flat sign is ♭) in the F major scale in order to lower that tone by a half step. If you refer to the piano keyboard (Figure 9-4), you will see that the distance between each adjacent key and its

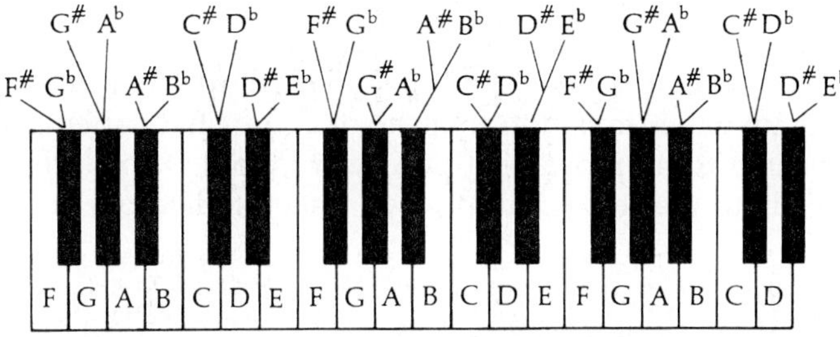

FIGURE 9-4
Notes of the piano keyboard.

touching black or white key is a half step. If there is no black key between two white keys (as in B-C), those white keys are still only a half-step apart. The major scale is built with a rigidly established order of full and half steps. The pattern is always the same, so, depending upon where you start, some notes may have to be flatted or sharped to maintain the pattern:

Step:	**Full**	**Full**	**Half**	**Full**	**Full**	**Full**	**Half**
C major	C to D	to E	to F	to G	to A	to B	to C′
F major	F to G	to A	to B♭	to C	to D	to G	to F′

By referring to a piano or Figure 9-4, you will see that if you begin with C, the piano keyboard is set up to have the right number of full and half steps to play a C major scale without resorting to any of the black keys. All other major scales, and almost all the minor scales, must use some of the black keys so as to keep the order of intervals of full and half steps.

TONAL CENTER

A composition written mainly in one scale is said to be in the key that bears the name of the tonic or tonal center of that scale. A piece in the key of F major uses the scale of F major, although in longer, more complex works, such as symphonies, the piece may use other related keys in order to achieve variety. The tonal center of a composition in the key of F major is the tone F. We can usually expect such a composition to begin on F, to end on it, and to return to it frequently to establish stability. Each return to F builds a sense of security in the listener, while each movement away usually builds a sense of insecurity or tension. The listener need not know what key the piece is in, since the tonal center is usually presented with emphasis as the piece is played. The listener perceives the tonic as the basic tone because it establishes itself as the anchor, the point of reference for all the other tones.

After beginning with A in the familiar melody of "Swing Low, Sweet Chariot" (Figure 9-5), the melody immediately moves to F as a weighty rest point. The melody rises no higher than D and falls no lower than C. (For convenience, the notes are labeled above the notation in the figure.) Most listeners will sense a feeling of completeness in this brief composition as it comes to its end. But the movement in the first four bars, from A downward to C, then upward to C, passing through the tonal center F, does not suggest such completeness; rather, it prepares us to expect something more. If you sing or whistle the tune, you will see that the long tone, C, in bar 4 sets up an anticipation that the next four bars attempt to satisfy. In bars 5 through 8 the movement downward from D to C, then upward to A, and finally to the rest point at F suggests a temporary resting point. When the

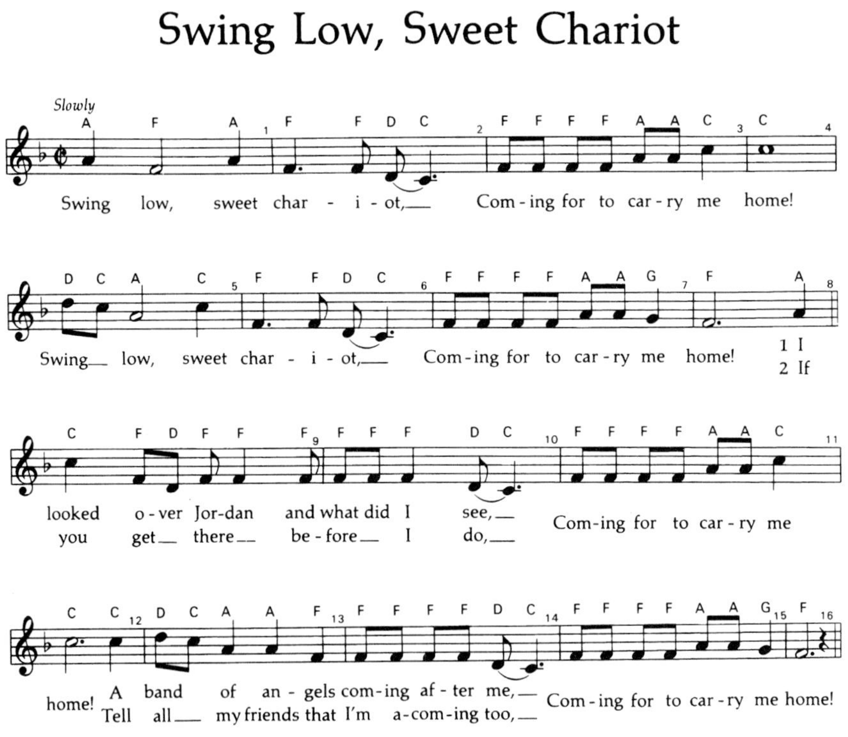

FIGURE 9-5
"Swing Low, Sweet Chariot," African-American spiritual.

A sounds in bar 8, however, we are ready to move on again with a pattern that is similar to the opening passage: a movement from A to C, and then downward through the tonal center, as in the opening four bars. Bar 13 is structurally repetitious of bar 5, moving from D downward, establishing firmly the tonal center F in the last note of bar 13 and the first four tones of bar 14. Again, the melody continues downward to C, but when it returns in measures 15 and 16 to the tonal center F, we have a sense of almost total stability. It is as if the melody has taken us on a metaphoric journey: showing us at the beginning where "home" is; the limits of our movement away from "home"; and then the pleasure and security of returning to "home."

The tonal center F is "home," and when the lyrics actually join the word "home" in bar 4 with the tone C, we are a bit unsettled. This is a moment of instability. We do not become settled until bar 8, and then again in bar 16, where the word "home" falls on the tonal center F, which we have already understood—simply by listening—as the real "home" of the composition. This composition is very simple, but also subtle, using the resources of tonality to excite our anticipations for stability and instability.

Perception Key
"SWING LOW, SWEET CHARIOT"

1. What is the proportion of tonic notes (F) to the rest of the notes in the composition? Can you make any judgments about the capacity of the piece to produce and release tension in the listener on the basis of the recurrence of F?
2. Are there any places in the composition where you expect F to be the next note but it is not? If F is always supplied when it is expected, what does that signify for the level of tension the piece creates?
3. On the one hand, the ending of this piece produces a strong degree of finality. On the other hand, in the middle section the sense of finality is much less complete. Is this difference between the middle section and the ending effective? Explain.
4. Does this music evoke feeling in you? If so, what kind of feeling? Does the music interpret this feeling, help you understand it? If so, how does the music do this?
5. Would a piece that always produces what is expected be interesting? Or would it be a musical cliché? What is a musical cliché?

ATONALITY

Atonal music abandons the tonal center. All twelve tones (including the sharps and flats—the black keys on the piano) are equal in value; thus the other name—twelve-tone music. No tone is returned to more frequently than any other, for if a system were not worked out to ensure that no tone was more frequently used than any other, the old phenomenon of the tonal center would take effect. Therefore, Arnold Schoenberg devised a tone row: a sequence of twelve tones, usually a melodic line, which constituted the basic component of the music. From the tone row all melodic and harmonic material evolved, arranged in such a way that no tone (at least ideally) was played more frequently than any other. Arnold Schoenberg's *Pierrot Lunaire* and his String Quartets nos. 1 and 3 are good examples of atonality. It is still a technique contemporary composers use, and it occasionally appears in jazz and rock.

POLYTONALITY

Polytonal music has melodies in different keys played simultaneously. The result is a curious kind of instability and, sometimes, confusion. Usually polytonal music enables us to distinguish two or more melodies being played simultaneously that probably would be undistinguished if they were all in the same key. The compression of this simultaneity can be very effective. This technique has been used by composers as different as Maurice Ravel and Charles Ives. Igor Stravinsky's *History of a Soldier* is an exceptionally interesting example of the successful use of polytonality.

NONTONAL MUSIC

Some electronic composers, such as Milton Babbitt and Karl-Heinz Stockhausen, avoid tonality most of the time. Their compositions usually depend to a large extent on other techniques for developing structure. Whereas tonal music depends on our sense of the impending tonic to help give "shape" to a musical composition, the electronic composers depend on repetition, loudness and softness, variations of speed and pitch, and sometimes silence. Often when they do produce tones—as they frequently do—the tones are pure; that is, the familiar overtones, or partials, which identify tones for most of us, are absent.

John Cage has experimented in his music with breaking panes of glass, dropping objects, dripping water, turning on and off household appliances such as the radio, and even total silence. He is committed, at times, to an exploration of noises of the everyday world. And he achieves some success by organizing them into structures that reveal the characteristics and qualities of these sounds. For instance, have you really listened to breaking glass? The fact that we are used to thinking of music only as organizations of tones may make it difficult to take Cage's work seriously. But if we think of music as organized sound rather than just as organized tones, the problem of acceptance may be eased. Since it is the opinion of many young composers that nontonal music is the music of the future, it may be useful to broaden our conceptions.

MUSICAL STRUCTURES

The most familiar musical structures are based on repetition—especially repetition of melody, harmony, rhythm, and dynamics. Even the refusal to repeat any of these may be effective mainly because repetition is usually anticipated by the listener. Repetition in music is of particular importance because of the serial nature of the medium (it is linear, with one musical moment following another). The ear cannot retain sound patterns for very long, and thus it needs repetition to help hear the musical relationships.

THEME AND VARIATIONS

A theme and variations on that theme constitute a favorite structure for composers, especially since the seventeenth century. We are usually presented with a clear statement of the theme that is to be varied. The theme is sometimes repeated so that we have a full understanding, and then modifications of the theme follow. "A" being the original theme, the structure unfolds as A^1-A^2-A^3-A^4-A^5 . . . and so on to the end of the variations. Some marvelous examples of structures built on this principle are J. S. Bach's *Art of Fugue,* Beethoven's *Diabelli Variations,* Brahm's *Variations on a Theme by Joseph Haydn,* and Edward Elgar's *Enigma Variations*.

If the theme is not carefully perceived when it is originally stated, the listener will have little chance of hearing how the variations relate to the theme. Furthermore, unless one knows the structure is theme and variations, much of the delight of the variations will be lost. Theme and variations is a structure that many arts can employ, especially the dance.

RONDO

The first section or refrain of a rondo will include a melody and perhaps a development of that melody. Then, after a contrasting section or episode with a different melody, the refrain is repeated. Occasionally, early episodes are also repeated, but usually not so often as the refrain. The structure of the rondo is sometimes in the pattern A-B-A-C-A—either B or D—and so on, ending with the refrain A. Some rondos will end on an episode instead of a refrain, although this is unusual. The rondo may be slow, as in Mozart's *Hafner Serenade,* or it may be played with blazing speed, as in Weber's *Rondo Brilliante*. The rondo may suggest a question-answer pattern, as in the children's song, "Where is Thumbkin?" Sometimes the A-B organization is reversed, so that the refrain comes second each time. The first and third movements of Vivaldi's *Seasons,* Haydn's *Gypsy Rondo,* Johann Pachelbel's *Dance Rondo,* and the second movement of Beethoven's Symphony no. 4 are all fine examples of the rondo.

FUGUE

The fugue, a specialized structure of counterpoint, was developed in the seventeenth and eighteenth centuries and is closely connected with J. S. Bach, and his *Art of Fugue*. Most fugues feature a melody—called the "statement"—which is set forth clearly at the beginning of the composition, usually with the first note the tonic of its key. Thus if the fugue is in C major, the first note of the statement is likely to be C. Then that same melody more or less—called the "answer"—appears again, usually beginning with the dominant note (the fifth note) of that same key. The melodic lines of the statements and answers rise to command our attention, and then submerge into the background as episodes of somewhat contrasting material intervene. Study the diagram in Figure 9-6 as a suggestion of how the statement, answer, and episode at the beginning of a fugue might interact. As the diagram indicates, the melodic lines often overlap, as in the popular song, "Row, Row, Row Your Boat."

The fugue, like theme and variations, is a repetitive structure, for the statements, answers, and episodes generally are similar to each other. Sometimes they share the same pattern of ascending or descending tones. Often they have similar rhythms. In some cases the answer appears like a mirror image of the statement, or sometimes the answer may be an upside-down image of the statement. Sometimes the statements and answers are jammed together, called the stretto (narrow passage), a device usually used near the conclusion of the fugue. Sometimes fugues exist not as independent compositions, but as part of a larger composition. Many symphonies, for example, have fugal passages as a means of development. Sometimes those fugal passages become the basis for independent fugues. Thus Beethoven's *Grösse Fuge* in B♭ was originally composed as a section within a string quartet.

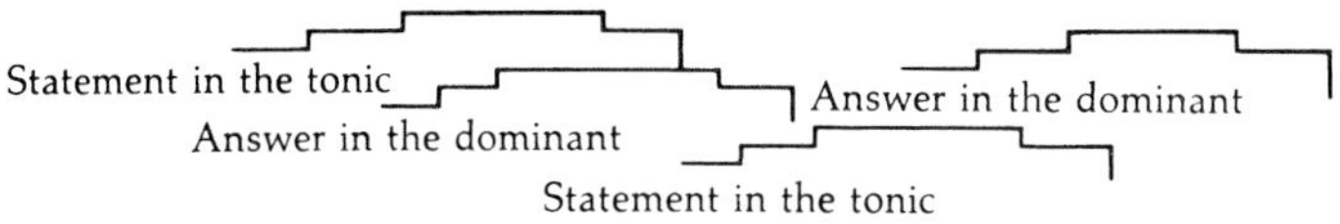

FIGURE 9-6
The fugue.

SONATA FORM

The eighteenth century brought the sonata form to full development, and many contemporary composers still find it very useful. Its overall structure basically is A-B-A, with these letters representing the main parts of the composition and not just melodies, as the letters usually represent in the rondo. The first A is the exposition, with a statement of the main theme in the tonic key of the composition and usually a secondary theme or themes in the dominant key (the key of G, for example, if the tonic key is C). A theme is a melody that is not merely repeated, as it usually is in the rondo, but is instead developed in an important way. In the A section, the themes are usually restated but not developed very far. This development of the themes occurs in the B or development section, with the themes normally played in closely related keys. The development section explores contrasting dynamics, timbres, tempos, rhythms, and harmonic possibilities inherent in the material of the exposition. In the third section or recapitulation, the basic material of the first section or exposition is more or less repeated, usually in the tonic key. After the contrasts of the development section, this repetition in the home key has the quality of return and closure.

The sonata form is ideal for revealing the resources of melodic material. For instance, the principal theme of the exposition when contrasted with a very different second theme may take on a surprisingly new quality, as in the opening movement of Beethoven's Third Symphony, the *Eroica*. We sense that we did not fully grasp the principal theme the first time. This is one of the major sources of satisfaction for the careful listener. Statement, contrasting development, and restatement is a useful pattern for revealing the resources of almost any basic musical material, especially the melodic.

The symphony is usually a four-movement structure often employing the sonata form for its opening and closing movements. The middle movement or movements normally are contrasted with the first and last movements in dynamics, tempos, timbres, harmonics, and melodies. The listener's ability to perceive how the sonata form functions within most symphonies is essential if the total structure of the symphony is to be comprehended.

PERCEPTION KEY
SONATA FORM

1. Listen to and then examine closely the first movement of a symphony by Haydn or Mozart. If a score is available it can be very helpful. Identify the exposition section—which will come first—and the beginning of the development section. Then identify the end of the development and the beginning of the recapitulation section. At these points you should perceive some change in dynamics, tempo, and movements from home key or tonic to contrasting keys and back to the tonic. You need not know the names of those keys in order to be aware of the changes. They are usually perceptible.
2. Once you have developed the capacity to identify these sections, describe the characteristics that make each of them different. Note the different characteristics of melody, harmony, timbre, dynamics, rhythm, tempo, and contrapuntal usages.
3. When you have confidence in your ability to perceive the sonata form, do some comparative studies. Take the first movement of a Haydn symphony—Symphony no. 104 in D major, the *London,* for example—and compare its first movement with any of the first movements of Brahms' four symphonies. All these movements are sonata forms, but notice how differently they are structured, and how much more difficult it is to know where you are with Brahms. The sonata form allows for great variability. For example, most of Haydn's early symphonies, up to around Symphony no. 70, are monothematic; i.e., only one theme appears in the exposition. Mozart's, Beethoven's, and Brahm's sonata forms, on the other hand, are very rarely monothematic.

FANTASIA

Romantic composers, especially in the period from 1830 to 1900, began working with much looser structures than the sonata form. We find compositions with terms such as rhapsodies, nocturnes, aubades, and fantasias. The names are impressionistic and vague, suggesting perhaps that their subject matter may be moods. The fantasia may be the most helpful of these to examine, since it is to the sonata form what free verse is to the sonnet. The word "fantasia" implies fancy or imagination, which suggests, in turn, the fanciful and the unexpected. It is not a stable structure, and its sections cannot be described in such conventional terms as A-B-A. The fantasia usually offers some stability by means of a recognizable melody of a singable quality, but then it often shifts to material that is less identifiable, tonally certain, and harmonically secure. The succession of motives (brief musical units) is presented without regard for predetermined order. However, there are controls in terms of pacing, the relationship of motives, the harmonic coloring, dynamics, and rhythms. Sometimes the fantasia will explore a wide range of feelings by contrasting fast and slow, loud and soft, rich and spare harmonies, and singable melodies with those that are less singable.

Many of Robert Schumann's best works are piano pieces he called fantasias. Mozart's Fantasia in C minor is an excellent example of the mode, but probably most of us are more familiar with Moussorgsky's fantasia: *A Night on Bald Mountain,* which was used in Walt Disney's *Fantasia,* a 1940 film.

THE SYMPHONY

The symphony marks one of the highest developments in the history of Western instrumental music. The symphony has proved to be so flexible a structure that it has flourished in every musical era since the Baroque period in the early eighteenth century, especially with the sinfonias of Handel and the symphonies of C. P. E. Bach. The word "symphony" implies a "sounding together." From its beginnings, through its full and marvelous development in the works of Haydn, Mozart, Beethoven, and Brahms, the symphony was particularly noted for its development of harmonic structures. Harmony is the sounding together of tones that have an established relationship to one another. Because of its complexity, harmony is a subject many composers must study in great depth during their apprentice years.

The symphony as it existed in the Baroque period, the Classical period of the late eighteenth and early nineteenth centuries, and the Romantic period of the nineteenth century, and as it exists in the twentieth century has undergone great changes. Many of these can be traced to developing concepts of harmony, most of which are extremely complex and not fully intelligible without considerable analysis. Triadic harmony (which means the sounding of three tones of a specific chord, such as the basic chord of the key C major, C-E-F, or the basic chord of the key F major, F-A-C) is common to most symphonies, especially before the twentieth century. Even in classical symphonies, however, such as Mozart's, the satisfaction that the listener has in triadic harmony is often withheld by the composer in order to develop musical ideas that will resolve their tensions only in a full, resounding chordal sequence of triads.

The symphony usually depends on thematic development. All the structures that we have discussed—theme and variations, rondo, fugue, and sonata form—develop melodic material, and some or all of them are often included in the symphony. Because it is a much larger structure with usually three or four movements (sections that develop thematic material), the symphony can develop melodic ideas much further. In general, as the symphony evolved into its conventional structure in the time of Haydn and Mozart, the four movements were ordered as follows: first movement, sonata form; second movement, A-B-A or rondo; third movement, minuet; fourth movement, sonata form or rondo. There were exceptions to this order even in Haydn's and Mozart's symphonies, and in the Romantic and following periods the exceptions increased as the concern for conventions decreased.

The relationships between the movements of a symphony are flexible. The same melodic or key or harmonic or rhythmic approach may not prevail in all the movements. The sequence of movements may then seem arbitrary. On the other hand, there are some symphonies that develop similar material through all movements, and then the sequence may seem less, if at all, arbitrary. This commonality of material is relatively unusual because three or four movements can rapidly exhaust all but the most sustaining and profound material. One's ear can get tired of listening to the same material for an extended time. The preferred method, until the twentieth century, was to follow the conventional patterns of tempo throughout, using appropriate melodies and harmonies in each movement, which is to say material best suited for fast or slow tempos. There is no consensus about such points, so critical discussion usually centers on the appropriateness of the material, especially the melodic, for a given movement of the symphony.

A comparison of the tempo markings of several symphonies by important composers shows several similarities: fast opening and closing movements with at least one slower middle movement. One of the most important connecting devices holding the movements of a symphony together is the convention of altering the tempo in patterns similar to those listed below. An alternation of tempo can express a profound alternation in the feeling of a movement. The predictable alternation of tempo is one of the things our ear depends upon for finding our way through the whole symphony. In such large structures, we need all the signposts we can get, since it is easy to lose one's way through a piece that may last almost an hour. The following tempo markings are translated loosely:

Haydn, Symphony in G major, no. 94, the *Surprise*
1. *Adagio, vivace* (slowly, very lively)
2. *Andante* (moderately slow)
3. *Minuet* (not fast, the dance tempo)
4. *Finale, allegro molto* (very fast)

Mozart, Symphony in C major, no. 41, the *Jupiter*
1. *Allegro vivace* (fast and lively)
2. *Andante cantabile* (slow and songlike)
3. *Minuet and trio, allegretto* (dancelike, then a little fast)
4. *Finale, allegro molto* (very fast)

Beethoven, Symphony in C minor, no. 5
1. *Allegro con brio* (fast, breezy)
2. *Andante con moto* (slowly with motion)
3. *Allegro, scherzo* (fast, with dance rhythm)
4. *Allegro, presto* (fast, very quick)

Brahms, Symphony in E minor, no. 4
1. *Allegro non assai* (fast, but not very)

2. *Andante moderato* (moderately slow)
3. *Presto giocoso* (fast and jolly)
4. *Allegro energetico e patetico* (fast, with energy and feeling)

The tempo markings in these and other symphonies, including those of modern composers, like Charles Ives and Igor Stravinsky, suggest that each movement is designed with other movements in mind. That is, each movement offers a contrast to those that come before or after it. Composers of symphonies have many means at their disposal to achieve contrast. The first, as previously discussed, is variation in tempo. This is clear in the time markings of fast and slow, but it is also present in other ways. The sonata movements are usually written in 4/4 time, which means that there are four quarter notes in each measure, with the first especially and the third usually getting accents. Minuet movements, like many other dance movements, are in 3/4 time, three quarter notes to a measure, with the first receiving the accent. March time, used in many middle movements, is usually either 6/8 time or 2/4 time. In 6/8 time there are six eighth notes to a measure, with the first and fourth receiving the accent. In 2/4 time the first of the two quarter notes receives the accent. Sometimes this produces the "oompha" sound we associate with marching bands.

Contrast is also achieved by varying the dynamics, with opposing loud and soft passages likely to be found in any movement. We might expect the middle movements, which are normally shorter than the first and last, to use less dynamic shifting. We usually expect the last movement to build to a climax that is smashing and loud. Variations in the length of movements adds to contrast. And since the symphony is usually played by a large orchestra, the composer has a variety of instrumental families to depend on for adding contrast. A theme, for instance, can be introduced by the violins, passed on to the woodwinds, then passed on to the horns, only to return to the violins. Secondary themes can be introduced by flutes or piccolos so as to contrast with the primary themes developed by other families of instruments. A secondary theme is often very different in length, pitch, and rhythmic character from a primary theme, thus achieving further contrast. Sometimes a theme or a developmental passage is played by a single instrument in a solo passage, and then with all the instruments in that family playing together. Once the theme has been introduced by a single instrument or a small group, it may be played by the entire orchestra. These contrasts should hold our attention—for otherwise we miss what is going on—helping us grasp the melodic material by showing us how it sounds in different timbres and ranges of pitch (higher in the flutes, lower in the cellos). The exceptional possibilities for achieving contrast in the symphony accounts, in part, for its sustaining success over the centuries.

We readily perceive contrasts in time signature, tempo, dynamics, and instrumentation, even if we are not trained and do not have access to the score of the composition. But there are subtler means of achieving contrast. For one thing, our discussion of tonality in music should help us appreciate the fact that, even within a specific movement, a composer will probably use a number of different keys. Usually they are closely related keys, such as C major followed by G major, or F major followed by C major. The dominant tone is the fifth tone, and one of the most convenient ways of moving from key to key is to follow the cycle of fifths, confident that each new key will clearly relate to the key that precedes it. Distant keys, A major to, say, D minor, can produce a sense of incoherence or uncertainty. Such motions between keys often are used to achieve this effect.

The average listener cannot always tell just by listening that a passage is in a new key, although practiced musicians can tell immediately. The exploration of keys and their relationship is one of the more interesting aspects of the development portions of most symphonies. The very concept of development, which means the exploration of a given material, is sometimes best realized by playing the same or similar material in different keys, finding new relationships among them. Our awareness of an especially moving passage is often due to the subtle manipulation of keys that analysis with a score might help us better understand. For the moment, however, let us concentrate on what the average listener can detect in the symphony.

Perception Key
THE SYMPHONY

Listen to a symphony by Haydn or Mozart (they established the form for us). Then analyze as you listen intermittently, jotting down notes on each movement with the following questions in mind:

1. Is the tempo fast, medium, or slow? Is it the same throughout? How much contrast is there in tempo within the movement? Between movements?
2. Can you hear differences in time signature—such as the difference between waltz time and marching time?
3. How much difference in dynamics is there in a given movement? From one movement to the next? Are some movements more uniform in loudness than others?
4. What variations do you perceive in instrumentation? If you have a difficult time distinguishing among instruments, use this guide for families of instruments, from the highest pitches to the lowest.

   Woodwinds: flutes, oboes, clarinets, bassoons
   Brass: trumpets, horns, trombones, tubas
   Strings: violins, violas, cellos, contrabasses
   Percussion: tympani, snare drum, tam-tam (melodic material is treated, if at all, by xylophone, bells, celeste, and similar instruments)

5. Is the melodic material treated by single instruments, groups of instruments, or the entire orchestra?
6. Are you aware of the melodic material establishing the tonal center, moving away from it, then returning? (This may only be answerable in the affirmative by a highly practiced listener.)
7. Are you surprised by any passage within a movement? Why?
8. As a movement is coming to an end, is your expectation of the finale carefully prepared for by the composer? Is your expectation frustrated in any fashion? Is this effective or not? Explain.
9. Can you identify or describe the subject matter of each movement? Of the whole symphony?
10. Can you describe the content of each movement? Of the whole symphony?

BEETHOVEN'S SYMPHONY IN E♭ MAJOR, NO. 3, *EROICA*

Beethoven's "heroic" symphony is universally acclaimed by musicians and critics as a symphonic masterpiece. It has some of the most daring innovations for its time, and it succeeds in powerfully unifying its movements by developing similar material throughout, especially melodic and rhythmic. The symphony was finished in 1804 and was intended to celebrate the greatness of Napoleon, whom Beethoven regarded as a champion of democracy and the common man. But when Napoleon declared himself emperor in May 1804, Beethoven, his faith in Napoleon betrayed, was close to destroying the manuscript. However, the surviving manuscript indicates that he simply tore off the dedication page and substituted the general title *Eroica*.

The four movements of the symphony follow the tempo marking we would expect of a classical symphony, but there are a number of important ways in which the *Eroica* is unique in the history of musical structures. The first movement, marked *allegro con brio* (fast, breezy) is a sonata form with the main theme of the exposition based on a triadic chord in the key of E♭ major that resoundingly opens the movement. The development section introduces a number of related keys, and the recapitulation ultimately returns to the original home key of E♭ major. There is a coda (a section added to the end of the conventional structure) so extended that it is something of a second development section as well as a conclusion. As with the development section proper, related keys come into play, but in the recapitulation the home key finally dominates. The movement is at least twice as long as the usual first movements of earlier symphonies, and no composer before had used the coda in such a developmental way. Previously the coda was quite short and repetitive. The size of the movement, along with the tight fusion of themes and their harmonic development into such a large structure, were very influential on later composers. The feelings that are evoked and revealed are profound and enigmatic.

The slow second movement is dominated by a funeral march in 2/4 time, with a very plaintive melody and a painfully slow tempo (in some performances), and an extremely tragic mood prevails. In contrast with the dramatic and vivid first movement, the second movement is sobering, diminishing the reaches of power explored in such depth in the first movement. The second movement uses a fugue in one of its later sections, even though the tempo of the passage is so slow as to seem to "stretch time." Despite its exceptional slowness, the fugue, with its competing voices and constant, roiling motion, seems appropriate for suggesting heroic, warlike feelings. The structure is a rondo: A-B-A′-C-A″-B′-D-A‴, A being the theme of the funeral march, and following A's being variations. The other material, including the fugue in C, offers some contrast, but because of its close similarity to the march theme, it offers no relief.

The relief comes in the third movement, marked *scherzo,* which is both lively (*scherzo* means a joke) and dancelike. The movement is derivative from the first movement, closely linking the two in an unprecedented way.

The time signature is the same, 3/4, and the melodic material is built on the same triadic chord as in the first movement. And there is the same rapid distribution from one group of instruments to another. However, the third movement is much briefer than the first, while only a little briefer than the last.

The finale is marked *allegro molto* (very fast). A theme and variation movement, it is a catchall. It includes two short fugues, a dance using a melody similar to the main theme of the first movement, which is not introduced until after a rather decorative opening, and a brief march. Fast and slow passages are contrasted in such a fashion as to give us a sense of a recapitulation of the entire symphony. The movement brings us "triumphantly" to a conclusion that is profoundly stable. At this point, we can most fully appreciate the powerful potentialities of the apparently simple chord-based theme of the first movement. Every tonal pattern that follows is ultimately derivative, whether by approximation or by contrast, and at the end of the symphony the last return derived from the chord-based theme is characterized by total inevitability and closure. The feelings evoked and revealed defy description, although there surely is a progression from yearning to sorrow to joy to triumph.

The following analysis will be of limited value without your listening carefully to the symphony more than once. If possible use a score, even if you have no musical training. Ear and eye can coordinate with practice.

LISTENING KEY: THE SYMPHONY

BEETHOVEN, SYMPHONY NO. 3, OPUS 55, *EROICA* 1806

Performed by George Szell and the Cleveland Orchestra. CBS Compact Disk MYK 3722. (This disk is available for use with this book.)

Consult this key while listening to the symphony. The best way to listen is with the compact disk player's timings visible.

Movement I: *Allegro Con Brio*. Fast, Breezy.

Timing: 14:46, Track 1. Theme and variations; 3/4 time, E♭ major.

FIGURE 9-7
Opening chord in E-flat major (0:01).

The first two chords are powerful, staccato, isolated, and compressed (Figure 9-7). They are one of the basic chords of the home key of E♭ major: G-E♭-B♭-G. Then at the third measure (Figure 9-8) the main theme, gener-

FIGURE 9-8
Main theme, cellos (0:04).

ated from the opening chord of the symphony, is introduced. Because it is stated in the cellos, it is low in pitch and somewhat portentous, although not threatening. Its statement is not quite complete, for it unexpectedly ends on a C♯ (♯ is the sign for sharp). The horns and clarinets take the theme at bar 15 (0:19), only to surrender it at bar 20 (0:23) to a group of ascending tones closely related to the main theme.

The second theme is in profound contrast to the first. It is a very brief and incomplete pattern (and thus could also be described as a motive) of three descending tones moved from one instrument to another in the wood-

FIGURE 9-9
Second theme, oboes at bar 45 (0:45).

winds, beginning with the oboes at bar 45 (Figure 9-9). This theme is unstable, like a gesture that needs something to complete its meaning. And the following motive of dotted eighth notes at bars 60 through 64 played by flutes and bassoons (Figure 9-10) is also unstable.

FIGURE 9-10
Flutes and bassoons at bars 60 through 64 (1:14).

This is followed by a rugged rhythmic passage, primarily audible in the violins, preparing us for a further incomplete thematic statement at bar 83, a very tentative, delicate interlude. The violin passage that preceded it (Fig-

FIGURE 9-11
Violin passage preceding bar 83 (1:19).

ure 9-11) functions here and elsewhere as a link in the movement between differing material. Getting this passage firmly in your memory will help you follow the score, for it returns dependably.

Many passages have unsettling fragments, such as the dark, brooding

FIGURE 9-12
Cello and bass motive (1:57).

quality of the cello and contrabass motive shown in Figure 9-12, which sounds as a kind of warning, as if it were preparing us for something like the funeral march of the second movement. It repeats much later in variation at bar 498, acting again as an unsettling passage. Many other passages also appear to be developing into a finished statement, only to trail off. Some commentators have described these passages as digressions, but this is misleading, because they direct us to what is coming.

The exposition starts to end at bar 148 (3:03), with a long passage in B♭, the measures from 148 to 152 hinting at the opening theme, but they actually prepare us for a dying-down action that joins with the development.

In George Szell's rendition, as in most recordings, the repeat sign at 156 is ignored. Instead, the second ending (bars 152 to 159) is played, and this passage tends to stretch and slow down, only to pick up when the second theme is played again in descending patterns from the flutes through all the woodwinds (3:16).

The development section is colossal, from bars 156 to 394, beginning at 3:18. The main theme reoccurs first at 178 (3:48) in shifting keys in the cellos, then is played again in B♭ from 186 to 194 (3:55), very slow and drawn out. Contrasting passages mix in so strongly that we must be especially alert or we will fail to hear the main theme. The momentum speeds up around bar 200 (4:16), where the main theme is again played in an extended form in the cellos and the contrabasses. The fragmented motives contribute to a sense of incompleteness, and we do not have the fullness of the main theme to hold on to. The fragmentary character of the second theme is also emphasized, especially between bars 220 and 230 (4:39). When we reach the crashing discords at bar 275 (5:44), the following quieting down is a welcome relief. The subsequent passage is very peaceful and almost without direction until we hear again the main theme in B♭ at bar 300 (6:21), then again at 312 (6:37) in the cellos and contrabasses. The music builds in loudness, quiets down, and then the main theme is stated clearly in the bassoons, preparing for an extended passage that includes the main theme in the woodwinds building to a mild climax in the strings at bar 369 (Figure 9-13).

FIGURE 9-13
Strings at bar 369 (7:53).

The remainder of this passage is marvelously mysterious, with the strings maintaining a steady tremolo and the dynamics brought down almost to a whisper. The horn enters in bar 394 (8:24), playing the main theme in virtually a solo passage. Bars 394 and 395 are two of the most significant measures of the movement because of the way in which they boldly announce the beginning of the recapitulation. The horns pick up the main theme again at bar 408 (8:32), loud and clear, and begin the restatement of the exposition section. The recapitulation begins at bar 394 (8:24) and extends to bar 575 (12:05). It includes a brief development passage, treating the main theme in several unusual ways, such as the tremolo statement in the violins at bars 559 to 565 (Figure 9-14).

FIGURE 9-14
Violins at bars 559 through 565 (11:50).

The long, slow, quiet passages after bar 575 (12:05) prepare us for the incredible rush of power that is the coda—the "tail" or final section of the movement. The triumphal quality of coda—which includes extended development, especially of the main theme—is most perceptible, perhaps, in the juxtaposition of a delightful, running violin passage from bar 631 to bar 639 (13:31), with the main theme and a minimal variation played in the horns. It is as if Beethoven is telling us that he has perceived the musical problems that existed with his material, mastered them, and now is celebrating with a bit of simple, passionate, and joyous music.

PERCEPTION KEY

MOVEMENT I

1. Describe the main theme and the second theme. What are their principal qualities of length, "tunefulness," range of pitch, rhythm, and completeness? Could either be accurately described as a melody? Which is easier to whistle or hum? Why could the second theme be plausibly described as a motive? Do the two themes contrast with each other in such a way that the musical quality of each is enhanced? If so, how?
2. What are the effects of hearing the main theme played in different keys, as in bars 3 to 7 (0:04), bars 184 to 194 (3:55), and bars 198 to 206 (4:16)? All these passages present the theme in the cellos and contrabasses. What are the effects of the appearance of the theme in other instrumental families, such as the bassoons at bar 338 (7:12) in the development section and the horns at bar 408 (8:32) in the recapitulation section? Does the second theme appear in a new family of instruments in the development section?
3. How clearly perceptible do you find the exposition, development, recapitulation, and coda sections? Can you describe, at least roughly, the feeling qualities of each of these sections?
4. The structure of the movement—exposition, development, recapitulation, and coda—presents thematic, harmonic, and rhythmic material, works with it in inventive ways, then more or less restates the original material. Does this format work in your experience in such a way that at the end of the movement you have a better understanding of the musical material than at the end of the exposition?
5. Many symphonies lack a coda. Do you think Beethoven was right in adding a coda, especially such a long and involved one? If so, what does it add?
6. If possible, record the movement on a tape recorder, but begin with the development section, then follow with the recapitulation, exposition, and coda sections. Does listening to this "reorganization" help clarify the function of each section? Does it offer a better understanding of the movement as it was originally structured? Does this "reorganization" produce significantly different feeling qualities in each section?

Movement II: *Marcia Funebra. Adagio Assai.* Funeral March, Very Slow.

Rondo, 2/4 time. Timing: 15:34; Track 2.

A funeral march in 2/4 time, the movement begins with its first theme in the opening bars shown in Figure 9-15, extremely slow, quiet, and brooding. The rhythm limps. The second theme, a plaintive descending passage in the violins beginning at bar 17 (Figure 9-16), is no less unrelieved in its sadness. Its very limited range, from B♭ to E♭, then back down to B♭, adds a closed-in quality. At bar 69 (4:19), the second, or B, section begins, ending at bar 105 (6:28). Then the funeral theme is restated very quietly in the violins. This is the A′ section of the rondo, ending at bar 113. A brief fugue appears at bar 114 (7:09), beginning the C section with material from the second theme inverted in the second violins (Figure 9-17).

FIGURE 9-15
Second movement opening bars (0:02).

FIGURE 9-16
Violins at bar 17 (1:02).

FIGURE 9-17
Beginning of a brief fugue at bar 114 (7:09).

The tempo picks up considerably at this point, with some passages echoing the full orchestral timbres of the first movement. The flutes contribute an interesting contrast in sixteenth notes in a descending pattern beginning with bar 168 (10:11), continuing through the beginning of the A″ section, which is announced by a restatement of the funeral theme at bar 172 (10:25), but this time in the bassoons, horns, cellos, and contrabasses. The second theme is restated totally in the B′ section, beginning at bar 182. The next section, D, begins at bar 211 with a surprise, a new melody in the violins (Figure 9-18).

FIGURE 9-18
New melody. Violins at bars 211 through 217 (13:37).

This melody is not developed, and thus is not a theme. The melody is relatively bright, emphasizing by contrast the plaintiveness of the themes. To emphasize this contrast, Beethoven brings back the funeral theme for the last time, A‴, at bar 238 (14:43), but in fragmented form. Now it has lost some of its power. The movement ends with no dramatic finale, but rather a simple pair of rising passages at bars 246 and 247. There remains a sense of unfulfillment. We anticipate the opening passage of the next movement.

Perception Key
MOVEMENT II

1. Are the dynamics of the second movement very different from the dynamics of the first movement? If so, in what ways?
2. The use of contrast in the second movement is much more restricted than in the first movement. What is the effect of this difference?
3. Are the sections of the rondo A-B-A′-C-A″-B′-D-A‴ as clearly defined as the exposition development, recapitulation, and coda sections of the first movement? What effect does Beethoven achieve by bringing the funeral theme back again and again? Do you begin to anticipate its return?

Movement III: *Scherzo. Allegro Vivace.* Fast and Lively.

Sonata, 3/4 time. Timing: 5:32; Track 3.

The sections of the third movement are relatively easy to hear: A-B (trio)-A′-coda. The theme of the A sections begins immediately in the first six bars with soft, rapidly paced notes, followed in bars 7 to 10 with a sharp, punctuating motive (Figure 9-19) in the oboes, succeeded by a delightful descending passage that concludes the theme in bar 14. Everything that comes after in the A section is derivative from the three parts of this theme. Notice especially the repetition of the motive in bars 85 to 88 (0:41), 265 to 268 (4:01), and 299 to 302 (4:18). The trio (named for the tradition of having three voices play in harmony) begins with its theme announced by the horns (Figure 9-20). Although the rhythmic pattern of this theme is not reminiscent of the main theme of the first movement, the notes G-C-E-G are very reminiscent. Also, the sonorities recall the first movement, especially the horns playing alone. After a contrasting woodwind interlude from bars 205 to 216 (3:03), the horns come back with a strong fanfarelike passage leading to the conclusion of the trio. The A′ section beginning in bar 255 (3:56) is essentially a repeat of the A section except that it contains more allusions to the full orchestral passages of the first movement. Because of the familiarity of this section, we feel at ease, comfortable, in recognizable territory. These allusions of A′ are more solid harmonically than in A, relying much more on the main key, E♭. The very brief finale, or coda, bars 423 to 442 (5:21), is steady in its rhythm, building to a powerful closure.

FIGURE 9-19
Beginning of third movement. Oboes at bar 7 (0:07).

FIGURE 9-20
Horn passage stating the principal theme of the trio (2:31).

PERCEPTION KEY
MOVEMENT III

1. Examine the two principal themes in this movement. Do they contrast with each other as much as the themes of the first two movements?
2. The movement is marked scherzo, a dancelike rhythm. Do you sense dancelike passages here? Does the movement suggest a dance to you?
3. What are the feelings characteristics of this movement? Compare with the first two movements.
4. How would you characterize your sense of recognition of familiar elements in this movement? How does Beethoven play with your sense of familiarity?

Movement IV: *Finale. Allegro Molto.* Very Fast.

Theme and variations, 2/4 time. Timing: 11:28; Track 4.

This theme and variation movement opens with the strings in a loud, rushing passage of eleven bars. Then the strings play a theme quite different from anything we have heard. This theme is both mysterious and suggestive of things to come, particularly as it diminishes to almost silence—followed by the plucking of single notes. The pattern of these notes (Figure 9-21) looks and sounds like a cross between the first theme of the first movement and the first theme of the third movement.

FIGURE 9-21
Fourth movement. Opening passage for violins (0:13).

This passage sounds playful, as if it were designed to represent the tread of toy soldiers. But this theme, called the bass theme, is countered by another, more important, theme, the melody theme, which begins at bar 76 (1:57), stated in the woodwinds (Figure 9-22). The violins restate this melody theme at bar 103 (2:20). We call one theme the melody theme and the other the bass theme because Beethoven used an extraordinary bit of ingenuity here. He took these themes, which were closely combined in one of his earlier contradances (Figure 9-23), varied them slightly, and separated them for use as the two distinctive themes of the movement.

FIGURE 9-22
Melody theme at bar 76 (1:57).

FIGURE 9-23
Melody and bass themes of the contradance.

Beethoven develops a fugue on the bass theme shortly thereafter, beginning at bar 117 (2:41) with the cellos (Figure 9-24), and then moving to the clarinets and bassoons. At bar 175 (3:30) the melody theme again comes into dominance. At bar 211 (3:46) the bass theme takes over in a marchlike passage, building up energy and anticipation, with rhythms that are

FIGURE 9-24
Cellos at bar 117 (2:41).

reminiscent of the ending of the first movement. The melody theme dominates again at bar 257 (4:44), in the violins and the flutes. Another fugal passage begins at bar 278 (5:09), using both themes, either entirely or in part, moving from one family of instruments to another. The effect of this passage, even though the themes are in the home key, is again to excite anticipation.

At bar 348 (6:15) an andante or slow passage begins, marked *con expressione* (with expression) meaning that the music based on the melody theme should be played lyrically, which is not quite what we might anticipate by the preceding fugue. The slow, songlike quality of this passage is something of a surprise, a distinct contrast to the marches and fugues that usually belong to a symphony celebrating the heroic. Marches, driving orchestral passages, warlike fugues, and intense rhythms seem more appropriate to a symphony inspired by Napoleon. But, quite possibly, this last songlike passage hints at a romantic quality the hero should also have. Even Napoleon had his Josephine.

But this romanticism diminishes rapidly with the descending violin passage at bar 380 (8:04). The melody theme is heard in the horns in a very stately fashion, and although the pace does not pick up quickly, the dynamics build steadily, suggesting an official ceremony. A number of brief interludes develop earlier thematic material. Despite the fragmentary quality of these interludes, the steady building of dynamic intensity and pitch by the entire orchestra suggests that we are coming to a conclusion. Yet we hardly know when to expect it. But when we hear the opening passages of the movement repeated at bar 431 (10:41), with an increase of the tempo to *presto* (extremely fast), we sense that we are coming to the end of the entire symphony. Even when the very last *presto* passages are played considerably slower than marked, the straightforwardness of the finale is inevitably complete.

PERCEPTION KEY
MOVEMENT IV

1. Many of the contrasts in this movement are achieved by using different structures—such as the fugue, march, and dance—to rework the two basic themes. Are these contrasts clearly audible to you? If not, keep listening.
2. Compare the bass and melody themes for their relative qualities of length, "tunefulness," range of pitch, rhythm, and completeness. What do you discover? If you did question 1 of the Perception Key for the first movement, you will have a basis of comparison already in your mind. What are the differences between the themes of this fourth movement and the themes of the first movement?
3. Compare your sense of closure and finality at the end of the first and fourth movements. Is there a profound difference?

Before going on to the next Perception Key, give your ear a rest for a brief time. Then, come back to the *Eroica* symphony and listen to it all the way through. In light of your analysis, sit back and enjoy it. Then consider the following issues.

Perception Key
THE *EROICA*

1. In what ways are the four movements tied together? Does a sense of relatedness develop for you?
2. Is the symphony properly named? What qualities do you perceive in it that seem "heroic"?
3. Comment on the use of dynamics throughout the whole work. Comment on variations in rhythms.
4. Is there a consistency in the thematic material used throughout the symphony? Are there any inconsistencies?
5. Do you find that fatigue affects your responses to the second movement or any other portion of the symphony? The act of creative listening can be very tiring. Could Beethoven have taken that into consideration?
6. Are you aware of a variety of feeling qualities in the music? Does there seem to be an overall "plan" to the changes in these qualities as the symphony unfolds?
7. What kind of feelings did the *Eroica* arouse in you? Did you make discoveries of your inner life of feeling because of your responses to the *Eroica*?

SUMMARY

We began this chapter by suggesting that feelings and sounds are the primary subject matters of music. This implies that the content of music is a revelation of feelings and sounds—that music gives us a more sensitive understanding of them. However, as we indicated in our opening statements, there is considerable disagreement about the subject matter of music, and, therefore, there is disagreement about the content of music. If music does reveal feelings and sounds, the way it does so is still one of the most baffling problems in the philosophy of art.

Even a brief survey of the theories about the content of music is beyond our scope here, but given the basic theory of art as revelation, as we have been presupposing in this book, a couple of examples of how that theory might be applied to music are relevant. In the first place, some music apparently clarifies sounds as noises. For example, John Cage, at times, uses devices such as a brick crashing through a glass. By putting such noises into a composition, Cage brackets out the everyday situation and helps us listen "to" rather than listen "through" such noises. In this way he clarifies those noises. His musical form organizes sounds and sometimes silences before and after the noise of the breaking glass in such a way that our perception of the noise of breaking glass is made more sensitive. Similar analyses can be made of the sounds of musical instruments and their interrelationships in the structures in which they are placed.

Second, there seems to be some evidence that music gives us insight into our feelings. It is not ridiculous to claim, for example, that one is feeling joy like that of the last movement of Mozart's *Jupiter* symphony, or sadness like the second movement—the funeral march—of Beethoven's *Eroica* symphony. In fact, joy and sadness are general terms that only very crudely describe our feelings. We experience all kinds of different joys and different sadnesses, and the names language gives to these are imprecise. Music, with its capacity to evoke feelings, and with a complexity of detail and structure that in many ways is greater than that of language, may be able to reveal or interpret feeling with much more precision than language. Perhaps the form of the last movement of the *Jupiter* symphony—with its clear-cut rising melodies, bright harmonies and timbres, brisk strings, and rapid rhythms—is somehow analogous to the form of a certain kind of joy. Perhaps the last movement of the *Eroica* is somehow analogous to a different kind of joy. And if so, then perhaps we find revealed in those musical forms clarifications or insights about joy. Such explanations are highly speculative. However, they not only are theoretically interesting but also may intensify one's interest in music. There is mystery about music, unique among the arts; that is part of its fascination.

CHAPTER 9 BIBLIOGRAPHY

Abraham, Gerald. *The Concise Oxford History of Music*. New York: Oxford University Press, 1979.

Apel, Willi. *New Harvard Dictionary of Music*. Cambridge, Mass.: Harvard University Press, 1996.

Bovers, Jane, and Judith Tick. *Women Making Music 1150–1950*. Urbana: University of Illinois Press, 1985.

Bukofzer, Manfred. *Music in the Baroque Era*. New York: Norton, 1947.

Chase, Gilbert. *America's Music*. New York: McGraw-Hill, 1955.

Copland, Aaron. *What to Listen For in Music*. New York: McGraw-Hill, 1989.

Dalhaus, Carl. *Esthetics of Music*. William Austin (trans.). Cambridge, England: Cambridge University Press, 1982.

Debussy, Claude, et al. *Three Classics in the Aesthetics of Music*. New York: Dover, 1962.

Erickson, Robert. *The Structure of Music*. New York: Farrar Straus & Giroux, 1955.

Grout, Donald. *A History of Western Music*. New York: Norton, 1988.

Haydon, Glenn. *On the Meaning of Music*. Washington, D.C.: Library of Congress, 1948.

Hindemith, Paul. *Composer's World*. Cambridge, Mass.: Harvard University Press, 1952.

Lang, Paul Henry. *Music in Western Civilization*. New York: Norton, 1941.

May, Elizabeth (ed.). *Music of Many Cultures*. Berkeley: University of California Press, 1980.

Meyer, Leonard B. *Emotion and Meaning in Music*. Chicago: University of Chicago Press, 1956.

———. *Explaining Music*. Berkeley: University of California Press, 1973.

———. *Music, the Arts, and Ideas*. Chicago: University of Chicago Press, 1994.

Nakamura, Ako. *The Interface Between Art and Music*. New Haven: Yale University Press, 1990.

Pendle, Karen. *Women and Music*. Bloomington: Indiana University Press, 1991.

Presley, Horton. *Principles of Music and Visual Arts*. Lanham, Md.: University Press of America, 1986.

Radocy, Rudolph, and J. David Boyle. *Psychological Foundations of Musical Behavior*. Springfield, Ill.: Charles C. Thomas, 1979.

Ratner, Leonard G. *Harmony: Structure and Style*. New York: McGraw-Hill, 1962.

Rosen, Charles. *The Classic Style*. New York: Viking Press, 1971.

Sachs, Curt. *The Wellsprings of Music*. New York: McGraw-Hill, 1965.

Sadie, Stanley (ed.). *The New Grove Dictionary of Music and Musicians*. London: Macmillan, 1980.

Stravinsky, Igor, and Craft, Robert. *Expositions and Developments*. Garden City, N.Y.: Doubleday, 1962.

Tovey, Donald F. *Beethoven*. New York: Oxford University Press, 1965.

———. *Essays in Musical Analysis*. New York: Oxford University Press, 1981.

Zuckerkandl, Victor. *Sound and Symbol*. Princeton, N.J.: Princeton University Press, 1956.

CHAPTER 9 WEBSITES

Classical Music (general source for classical and preclassical music)

World Wide Web: **http://www.yahoo.com/Entertainment/Music/Genres/Classical**

Ethnomusicology

Gopher: **gopher.cic.net** Select: **Electronic Serials/Alphabetic List/E/Ethnomusicology**

Indiana University Music Library

World Wide Web: **http://www.music.indiana.edu**

Library of Music Links (mailing lists and other resources on the web)

World Wide Web: **http://www-scf.usc.edu/~jrush/music/**

Music on the Web

World Wide Web: **http://www.art.net/Links/musicref.html**

Recorded Music on CDs

Usenet: Newsgroup: **rec.music.cd**

WOMAD—World of Music, Art, and Dance (schedules and assorted information)

World Wide Web: **http://www.eunet.fi/womad/**

CHAPTER 10

DANCE

Dance—with moving bodies shaping space—shares common ground with kinetic sculpture. In abstract dance the center of interest is upon visual patterns, and thus there is common ground with abstract painting. Dance, however, sometimes includes a narrative, performed on a stage with scenic effects, and thus can have common ground with drama. Dance is rhythmic, unfolding in time, and thus has common ground with music. Most dance is accompanied by music, and dance is often incorporated in opera.

SUBJECT MATTER OF DANCE

At its most basic level, the subject matter of dance is abstract motion, as in much of the work of the Pilobolus Dance Company. Pilobolus specializes in finding interrelationships of bodies in motion, often producing remarkable abstract shapes and patterns. On the other hand, the medium of the dance is the human body, whose movements on stage often produce sympathetic "movements" in the audience. Our feelings show vividly in our movements and gestures. Thus a much more pervasive subject matter of the dance is feeling. This is what, generally speaking, dance is basically about. The body exhibits feelings less abstractedly than in music, for now they are "embodied." Our instinctive ability to identify with other human bodies is so strong that the perception of feelings exhibited by the dancer often evokes something of those feelings in ourselves. The choreographer, who has created the dance, interprets those feelings. And if we participate, we understand those feelings and ourselves with greater insight. In Paul Sanasardo's *Pain,* for example, the portrayal of this feeling is so powerful that few in any audience can avoid some sense of pain. Yet the interpreta-

FIGURE 10-1
Judith Blackstone and Paul Sanasardo in *Pain*. (Paul Sanasardo Dance Company, photograph by Fred Fehl)

tion of pain by means of the dancing bodies gives us an "objective correlative," a shaping "out there" that makes it possible for us to understand something about pain rather than simply undergoing it. Figure 10-1 shows Sanasardo's depiction of pain, but only with the moving dance can its interpretation occur.

Perception Key
FEELING AND DANCE

The above claim that dance can interpret the inner life of feeling with exceptional power implies, perhaps, that no other art excels dance in this respect. Can you think of any examples—restricting your analysis to the feeling of pain—that would disprove this claim? What about feelings other than pain? Compare dance with music with reference to the power to reveal the inner life of feeling.

States of mind are a further dimension that may be the subject matter of dance. Feelings, such as pleasure and pain, are relatively transient, but states of mind involve attitudes, tendencies that engender certain feelings on the appropriate occasions. A state of mind is a disposition or habit that is not easily superseded. For example, jealousy usually involves a feeling so strong that it is best described as a passion. Yet jealousy is more than just a passion, for it is an orientation of mind that is relatively enduring. Thus José Limón's *The Moor's Pavane* explores the jealousy of Shakespeare's *Othello*. In Limón's version, Iago and Othello dance around Desdemona and seem to be directly vying for her affections. *The Moor's Pavane* represents an interpretation of the states of mind Shakespeare treated, although it can stand independently of the play and make its own contribution to our understanding of jealousy.

Since states of mind are felt as enduring, the serial structure of the dance is an appropriate vehicle for interpreting that endurance. The same can be said of music, of course, and its serial structure, along with its rhythmic nature, is the fundamental reason for the wedding of music with dance. Even silence in some dances seems to suggest music, since the dancer exhibits visual rhythm, the rising and falling of stress that we hear in music. But the showing of states of mind is achieved only partly through the elements dance shares with music. More basic is the body language of the dancing bodies. Nothing—not even spoken language—exhibits states of mind more clearly or strongly.

PERCEPTION KEY
BODY LANGUAGE AND STATES OF MIND

1. Using as little bodily motion as possible, try to represent a state of mind to a group of onlookers. Ask them to describe what you have represented. How closely does their description match your intention?
2. Represent one of the following states of mind by bodily motion: love, jealousy, self-confidence, pride. Have others do the same. Do you find such representations difficult to perceive when others do them?
3. What motions were used for the above representations? What gestures?
4. Try to move in such a way as to represent no state of mind at all. It is possible? Discuss this with your group.
5. Representing or portraying a state of mind allows one to recognize that state. Interpreting a state of mind gives one insight into that state. In any of the experiments above, did you find any examples that went beyond representation and involved revelation? If so, what made this possible? What does artistic form have to do with this?
6. Is it possible for you to recognize a state of mind such as jealousy being represented without having that state of mind being evoked in yourself? Is it possible for you not only to recognize but also to gain insight about a state of mind without that state of mind being evoked in yourself?

Narrative provides one obvious subject matter for many dances. Thus Robert Helpmann's ballet *Hamlet* uses Shakespeare's play as its subject matter. Viewers of the dance who know the play will see an interpretation of a drama, while others will see the interpretation of a tragic situation. In either case, feelings and states of mind relevant to the narrative are given vivid embodiment in the dancers' movements and gestures. Helpmann's *Hamlet* interprets the inner life of a tragic drama. Shakespeare's *Hamlet* provides the events that cause those reactions. In the dance, what is revealed is not so much why something happened, but rather the inner-life reactions to the happening.

FORM

If the subject matter of dance can be moving visual patterns, feelings, states of mind, narrative, and various combinations of these, the form of the dance—its details and parts as they function together to organize the structure—gives us insight into the subject matter. But the details, parts, and structure of the dance are not as clearly perceptible as they usually are in painting, sculpture, or architecture. The visual arts normally "sit still" long enough for us to reexamine everything. But the dance moves on relentlessly, like literature in recitation, drama, and music, preventing us from reexamining its details and parts. We can only hope to hold in memory a detail or part for comparison with a following detail or part, and those parts as they help create the structure.

Therefore, one prerequisite for a thorough enjoyment of the dance is the development of a memory for the dance movements. The dance will usually help us in this task by the use of repetitive movements and variations on them. It can do for us what we cannot do for ourselves: present once again details and parts for our renewed consideration. Often the dance builds tension by withholding movements we want to have repeated; sometimes it creates unusual tension by refusing to repeat any movement at all. Repetition or the lack of it—as in music or any serial art—becomes one of the most important structural features of the dance.

Most of the dance performed on television or produced on stage will make use of a number of basic formal qualities. Careful repetition of movements is patterned on the repetition the dancers find in the music to which they dance. The musical structure of A-B-A, in which a melody is played (A), followed by a period of development (B), finally ending with a recapitulation of the melody (A), is common to the dance. Movements performed at the beginning of a dance are often developed, enlarged, and modified in a section of the dance, only to be repeated at the end of the dance in an effort to help the viewer understand the full significance of the development.

Further, dance achieves a number of kinds of balance. In terms of the entire stage, usually a company of dancers balance themselves across the space allotted to them, moving forward, backward, left, and right as well as in a circle. Centrality of focus is important in most dances and helps us to imagine a shape for the overall dance. The most important dancers are usually at the center of the stage, holding our attention while subordinate groups of dancers balance them on the sides of the stage. Balance is also a formal consideration in both individual dancers and groups, as one can see from the balance achieved by Nureyev and Fonteyn in Figure 10-8.

The positions of the ballet dancer illustrated in Figure 10-7 also imply basic forms for the dancer, forms that can be maneuvered, interwoven, set in counterpoint, and modified as the dance progresses. Part of the experience of the dance is developing an eye for the ways in which these movements combine to create the dance. Modern dance develops a slightly different vocabulary of dance, as one can see from the illustrations in Figures 10-1, 10-10, 10-11, and 10-12. The formal elements of dance encompass the movements of the individual dancer, the dancers as they coalesce into groups, and the dance as it moves across space, horizontal, vertical, and lateral.

DANCE AND RITUAL

Since the only requirement for dance is a body in motion and since all cultures have this basic requirement, dance probably precedes all other arts. In this sense dance comes first. And when it comes first, it is usually connected to a ritual that demands careful execution of movements in precise

FIGURE 10-2
Fancy dance: powwow, Denver, Colorado. (Nicholas DeVore III/Photographers/Aspen)

ways to achieve a precise goal. The dances of most cultures were originally connected with either religious or practical acts, both often involving magic. Early dance often religiously celebrates some tribal achievement. At other times the dance is expected to have a specific practical effect. In this kind of dance—the Zuni rain dance or the ghost dance of the Sioux, for instance—the movement is ritually ordered and expected to be practically effective as long as the dance is performed properly.

Some dance has sexual origins and often is a ritual of courtship. Since this phenomenon has a correlative in nature—the courtship "dances" of birds and some other animals—many cultures occasionally imitated animal "dances." Certain movements in Mandan Indian dances, for instance, can be traced to the leaps and falls of western jays and mockingbirds who, in finding a place to rest, will stop, leap into the air while spreading their wings for balance, then fall suddenly, only to rise into the air again. Some modern dancers send their students to the zoo to observe birds, leopards, and other animals so as to represent them onstage.

Today at Native American powwows, fancy dance competitions are frequently held, giving dancers an opportunity to use complex costuming and dance steps. These dances are not ordinarily expected to produce ritual results, but they derive from such dances and echo their movements. Such dances today have important social virtues as much as they do ritual powers. (See Figure 10-2.)

Dance of all kinds draws much of its inspiration from the movements and shapes of nature: the motion of a stalk of wheat in a gentle breeze, the scurrying of a rabbit, the curling of a contented cat, the soaring of a bird, the falling of a leaf. These kinds of events have supplied dancers with ideas and examples for their own movement. A favorite shape for the dance is that of the spiral nautilus, so often seen in shells, plants, and insects:

This shape is apparent in individual movement (see Figures 10-1 and 10-7a), just as it is in the movement of groups of dancers whose floor pattern may follow the spiral pattern (see Figure 10-5). The circle is another of the most pervasive and fascinating shapes of nature. The movements of planets and stars suggest circular motion, and, more mundanely, so do the rings working out from a stone dropped in water. In a magical-religious way, circular dances have been thought to bring the dancers—and therefore humans in general—into a significant harmony with the divine forces in the universe. The planets and stars are heavenly objects in circular motion, so it was "reasonable" for early dancers to feel that they could align themselves with these divine forces by means of dance.

INDIAN DANCE

Some of the most complex and exquisite dances performed in the world today originated in India, which continues to preserve its traditional music and dance. The dancers in Figure 10-3 are performing part of a lengthy dance that retells the story of the Mahabharata, one of India's greatest epics, dealing with Lord Krishna and the primary forces of nature. The Kathakali dancers follow set movements, similar to ballet dancers, with the addition of complex finger and hand movements, all of which have individual significance. The hand gestures are called mudras. There are twenty-eight of

FIGURE 10-3
Indian Dance: A Kathakali performance from the *Mahabharata*. (© Jack Vartoogian)

them, and they can be combined to produce at least eight hundred distinctive meanings. Dancers begin working with the mudras early as children and practice endlessly in an effort to master the mudras with perfection. The control the dancers must have over their bodies to perform the complex dances matches the message of the Mahabharata: that the individual must practice self-control in order to be truly free. The dance and the drama are truly intertwined in the Kathakali renditions of epic.

THE GHOST DANCE OF THE SIOUX

The ghost dance of the Sioux (Figure 10-4) in the late nineteenth century was a circle dance performed by men and women lasting for twenty-four hours. Its purpose was to raise the spirits of dead warriors in order to reclaim the land for the native Americans who remained. In the 1880s a variety of tribes banded together in political and religious association and began the dancing. A young prophet-seer named Wovoca—or Black Elk—declared that if the dance was done properly, the dead would rise.

The dancers, about 200 at a time, formed a relatively compact circle and chanted as they danced, moving sideways to their left around a center pole. They wore bead-and-bone vests, which were called ghost shirts and thought to be impenetrable by bullets. One of the results of the dancing and chanting for hours at a time was a trancelike state resembling death. Dancers felt they were making communion with the spirit world. Unfortunately, one of the end results of the faith in the rising of the dead armies was the infamous massacre of Wounded Knee in 1890. Apparently those who died at Wounded Knee thought they were invulnerable and expected their spiritual forebears to join their struggle. The ghost dance was a visible testament of belief and an instrument of action.

FIGURE 10-4
Gilbert Gaul, *Ghost Dance* circa 1890. (The Anshutz Collection, Denver, photograph by James O. Milmoe)

FIGURE 10-5
Arapahoe and Shoshone dancers at the Windriver Reservation. (© John Running)

THE ZUNI RAIN DANCE

Tourists can see rain dances in the American Southwest even today. The floor pattern of the dance is not circular but a modified spiral, as can be seen in Figure 10-5. The dancers, properly costumed, form a line and are led by a priest, who at specific moments spreads corn meal on the ground, symbolizing his wish for the fertility of the ground. The ritual character of the dance is clearly observable in the pattern of motion, with dancers beginning by moving toward the north, then turning west, south, east, north, west, south, and ending toward the east. The gestures of the dancers, as with the gestures in most rituals, have definite meanings and functions. For example, the dancers' loud screams are designed to awaken the gods and arrest their attention, the drumbeat suggests thunder, and the dancers' rattles suggest the sound of rain.

PERCEPTION KEY
DANCE AND CONTEMPORARY RITUALS

1. Contemporary rituals such as some weddings and funerals involve motion that can be thought of as dance motion. Can you think of other contemporary rituals that involve dance motion? Do we need to know the meanings of the ritual gestures in order to appreciate the motion of the ritual?
2. How much common ground do we share with early dancers in trying to give meaning to our gestures, either in a generally accepted dance "situation" or out of it?
3. Do we have dances that can be considered as serving functions similar to those of the dances we have described? Consider, for instance, the dancing that accompanied the tearing down of the Berlin Wall, or the dancing that sometimes spontaneously breaks out at important rock concerts. Are there other instances?

FIGURE 10-6
Pieter Breughel the Elder, *The Wedding Dance*. Circa 1566. Oil on panel, 47 × 62 inches. (Photograph © 1995 The Detroit Institute of the Arts, city of Detroit purchase)

SOCIAL DANCE

Social dance is not specifically theatrical or artistic, as are ballet and modern dance. Folk and court dances are often done simply for the pleasure of the dancers. Because we are more or less familiar with square dances, round dances, waltzes, and a large variety of contemporary dances done at parties, we have some useful points of reference for the social dance in general.

COUNTRY AND FOLK DANCE

Social dance is not dominated by religious or practical purposes, although it may have secondary purposes such as meeting people or working off excess energy. More importantly, it is a form of recreation and social enjoyment. Country dance—for example, the English Playford dances—is a species of folk dance that has traces of ancient origins, because country people tended to perform dances in specific relationship to special periods in the agricultural year, such as planting and harvesting.

Folk dances are the dances of the people—whether ethnic or regional in origin—and they are often very carefully preserved, sometimes with contests designed to keep the dances alive. When they perform, the dancers often wear the peasant costumes of the region they represent. Virtually every nation has its folk dance tradition. (See Figure 10-6.)

THE COURT DANCE

The court dances of the Middle Ages and Renaissance developed into more stylized and less openly energetic modes than the folk dance, for the court dance was performed by a different sort of person and served a different purpose. Some of the favorite older dances were the volta, a favorite at Queen Elizabeth's court in the sixteenth century, with the male dancer hoisting the female dancer in the air from time to time; the pavane, a stately dance popular in the seventeenth century; the minuet, popular in the eighteenth century, performed by groups of four dancers at a time; and the eighteenth-century German allemande—a dance performed by couples who held both hands, turning about one another without letting go. These dances and many others were favorites at courts primarily because they were enjoyable—not because they performed a religious or practical function. Because the dances were also pleasurable to look at, it very quickly became a commonplace at court to have a group of onlookers as large as or larger than the group of dancers. Soon professional dancers appeared at more significant court functions, such as the Elizabethan and Jacobean masques, which were mixed-media entertainments in which the audience usually took some part—particularly in the dance sequences.

PERCEPTION KEY
SOCIAL DANCE

1. How would you evaluate rock dancing? Why does rock dancing demand loud music? Does the performing and watching of spontaneous and powerful muscular motions account for some of the popularity of rock dancing? If so, why? Why do you think the older generations generally dislike, if not hate, both rock music and rock dancing? Is rock dancing primarily a mode to be watched or danced? Or is it both? Explain what the viewer and the dancer, respectively, might derive from the experience of rock dancing.
2. Try to see an authentic folk dance. Describe the basic differences between folk dance and rock dance. Is the basic subject matter of the folk dance visual patterns, or feelings, or states of mind, or narrative? Or some combination of these? If so, what is the mix? Answer the same questions for rock dance.

BALLET

The origins of ballet usually are traced to the early seventeenth century, when dancers performed interludes between scenes of an opera. Eventually the interludes grew more important, until finally ballets were performed independently. In the eighteenth century, the *en pointe* technique was developed, with female dancers elevated on their toes to emphasize airy, floating qualities. This has remained the technique to this day and is one of the important distinctions between ballet and modern dance, which avoids *en pointe* almost entirely.

Today there is a vocabulary of movements that all ballet dancers must

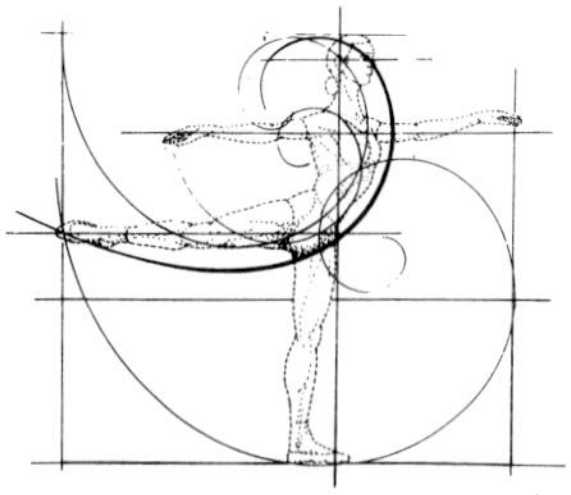

(a)

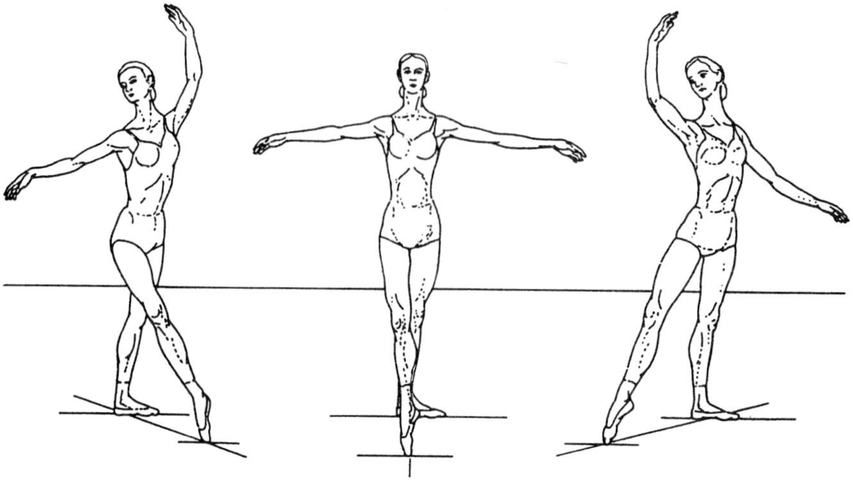

(b)

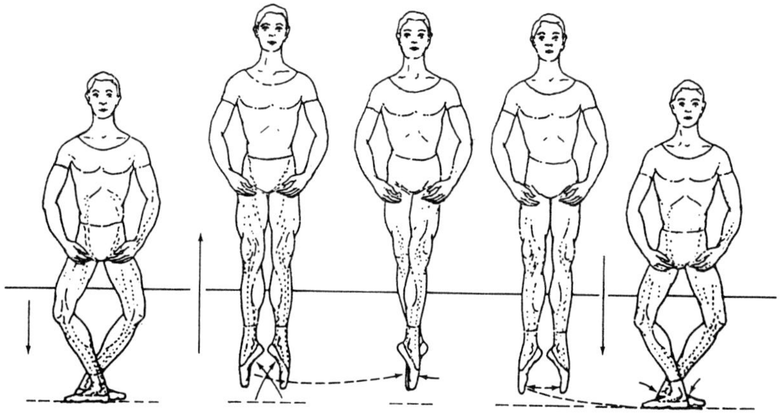

(c)

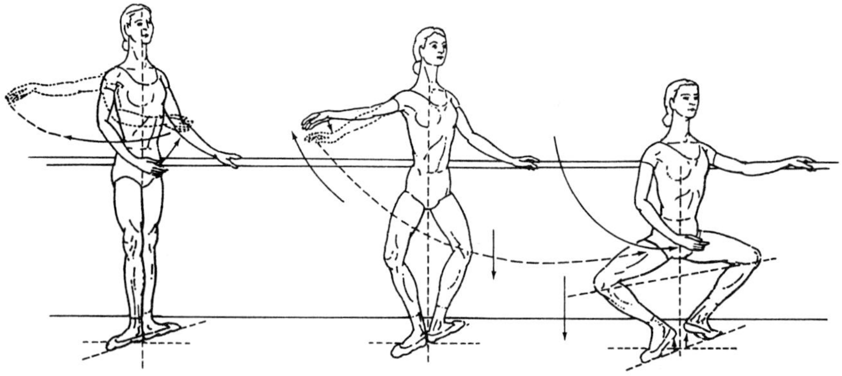

(d)

FIGURE 10-7
Derived from drawings by Carlus Dyer of some important positions. (a) The arabesque spiral; (b) basic positions of the body; (c) entrechat quatre; (d) grande plié.

learn, since these movements constitute the fundamental details of every ballet. In this sense they are as important as the keys and scales in music, the vocabulary of tones constantly employed in most musical composition. Figure 10-7 shows a number of the more important ballet positions. There are, of course, many more.

A considerable repertory of ballets has been built up in the last 290 years, but many ballets have been lost to us through the lack of a system of notation with which to record them. The same was true of music until a system of notation was adopted. Today most dance is recorded on videotape and film, although there is a system—Labanotation—that can be used effectively by experts for recording a dance. Some of the ballets many of us are likely to see are Lully's *Giselle; Les Sylphides,* with music by Chopin; Tchaikovsky's *Nutcracker, Swan Lake,* and *Sleeping Beauty; Coppelia,* with music by Delibes; and *The Rite of Spring,* with music by Stravinsky. All these ballets—like most ballets—have a pretext, a narrative line or story around which the ballet is built. In this sense, the ballet has as its subject matter a story that is interpreted by means of stylized movements such as the arabesque, the bourrée, and the relévé to name a few. Our understanding of the story is basically conditioned by our perception of the movements that present the story to us. It is astounding how, without having to be obvious and without having to resort very often to everyday gestures, ballet dancers can present a story to us in an intelligible fashion. Yet it is not the story or the performance of specific movements that constitutes the ballet: it is the meld of narrative and movement.

Perception Key

NARRATIVE AND BODILY MOVEMENT

1. Without training we cannot perform ballet movements, but all of us can perform some dance movements. By way of experiment and simply to increase understanding of the meld of narrative and bodily movement, try representing a narrative by bodily motion to a group of onlookers. Choose a narrative poem from our chapter on literature, or choose a scene from a play that may be familiar to you and your audience. Let your audience know the pretext you are using, since this is the normal method of most ballets. Avoid movements that rely exclusively on facial expressions or simple mime to communicate story elements. After your presentation, discuss with your audience their views about your success or failure in presenting the narrative. Discuss, too, your problems as a dancer and what you felt you wanted your movement to reveal about the narrative. Have others perform the experiment, and discuss the same points.
2. Even the most rudimentary movement attempting to reveal a narrative will bring in interpretations that go beyond the narrative alone. As a viewer, discuss what you believe the other dancers added to the narrative.

SWAN LAKE

One of the most popular ballets of all time is Tchaikovsky's *Swan Lake* (*Le Lac des Cygnes*), composed from 1871 to 1877 and first performed in 1894

FIGURE 10-8
Margot Fonteyn and Rudolf Nureyev in *Swan Lake*. (Dance Collection, The New York Public Library for the Performing Arts, Lincoln Center)

(Act II) and 1895 (complete). The choreographers were Leon Ivanov and Marius Petipa. Tchaikovsky originally composed the music for a ballet to be performed for children, but its fascination has not been restricted to young audiences. With Margot Fonteyn and Rudolf Nureyev, the reigning dancers in this ballet in modern times, *Swan Lake* has been a resounding favorite on television and film, not to mention repeated sellout performances in dance theaters the world over (Figure 10-8).

Act 1 opens with the principal male dancer, the young Prince Siegfried, attending a village celebration. His mother, the Queen, finding Siegfried sporting with the peasants, decides that it is time for him to marry someone of his own station and settle into the nobility. After she leaves, a *pas de trois*—a dance with three dancers, in this instance Siegfried and two maids—is interrupted by the Prince's slightly drunk tutor, who tries to take part in some of the dancing but is not quite able. When a flight of swans is seen overhead, the prince resolves to go hunting.

The opening scene of Act 2 is on a moonlit lake, with the arch magician, Rothbart, tending his swans. The swans, led by Odette, are maidens he has enchanted. They can return to human form only at night. Odette's movements are imitated by the entire group of swans, movements that are clearly influenced by the motions of the swan's long neck and by the movements we associate with birds—for example, an undulating motion executed by the dancers' arms and a fluttering executed by the legs. Siegfried comes upon the swans and restrains his hunters from shooting at them. He falls in love with Odette, all of whose motions are characterized by the softness and grace of the swan. Siegfried learns that Odette is enchanted and that she cannot come to the ball at which the Queen has planned to arrange his marriage. Siegfried also learns that if he vows his love to her and keeps his vow, he can free her from the enchantment. She warns him that Rothbart will do everything to trick him into breaking the vow, but Siegfried is determined to be steadfast. As dawn arrives, the lovers part and Rothbart retrieves his swans.

Act 3 commences with the ball the Queen has arranged for presenting to Siegfried a group of princesses from whom he may choose. Each princess, introduced in lavish native costume with a retinue of dancers and retainers, dances the folk dance of her country, such as the allemande, the czardas, the tarantella. But suddenly Rothbart enters in disguise with his own daughter, Odile, who looks exactly like Odette. Today most performances require that Odette and Odile be the same dancer, although the parts were originally written for two dancers. Siegfried and Odile dance the famous Black Swan *pas de deux,* a dance notable for its virtuosity. It features almost superhuman leaps on the part of Siegfried, and it also involves thirty-two rapidly executed whipping turns (fouettés) on the part of Odile. Her movement is considerably different in character from that of Odette. Odile is more angular, less delicate, and in her black costume seems much less the picture of innocence Odette had seemed in her soft white costume. Siegfried's movements suggest great joy at having Odette, for he does not realize that this is really Odile, the magician's daughter.

When the time comes for Siegfried to choose among the princesses for his wife, he rejects them all and presents Odile to the Queen as his choice. Once Siegfried has committed himself to her, Rothbart exults and takes Odile from him and makes her vanish. Siegfried, who has broken his vow to Odette, realizes he has been duped and ends the act by rushing out to find the real Odette.

Like a number of other sections of the ballet, Act 4 has a variety of versions that interpret what is essentially similar action. Siegfried, in finding Odette by the lake at night, sacrifices himself for her and breaks the spell. They are joined in death and are beyond the power of the magician. Some versions of the ballet aim for a happy ending and suggest that though Siegfried sacrifices himself for Odette, he does not die. In this happy-ending version, Odette, upon realizing that Siegfried had been tricked, forgives him. Rothbart raises a terrible storm in order to drown all the swans, but Siegfried carries Odette to a hilltop, where he is willing to die with her if necessary. This act of love and sacrifice breaks the spell and the two of them are together as dawn breaks.

Another version concentrates on spiritual victory and reward after death in a better life than that which was left behind. Odette and the swans dance slowly and sorrowfully together, with Odette rising in a stately fashion in their midst. When Siegfried comes, he begs her to forgive him, but nothing can break the magician's spell. Odette and he dance, they embrace, she bids him farewell and casts herself mournfully into the lake, where she perishes. Siegfried, unable to live without her, follows her into the lake. Then, once the lake vanishes, Odette and Siegfried are revealed in the distance, moving away together as evidence that the spell was broken in death.

The late John Cranko produced a more tragic version with the Stuttgart Ballet in the 1970s. Siegfried is drowned in the rising of the lake—presented most dramatically with long bolts of fabric undulating across the stage. Odette is whisked away by Rothbart and condemned to keep waiting for the hero who can be faithful to his vow. This version is particularly gloomy, since it reduces the heroic stature of Siegfried and renders his sacrifice useless. The hero who can rescue Odette must be virtually superhuman.

The story of *Swan Lake* has archetypal overtones much in keeping with the Romantic age in which it was conceived. John Keats, who wrote fifty years before this ballet was created, was fascinated by the ancient stories of men who fell in love with supernatural spirits, which is what the swan-Odette is, once she has been transformed by magic. Likewise, the later Romantics were fascinated by the possibilities of magic and its implications for dealing with the forces of good and evil. In his *Blithedale Romance,* Nathaniel Hawthorne wrote about a hypnotist who wove a weird spell over a woman. The story of Svengali and his ward Trilby was popular everywhere, seemingly attesting to the fact that strange spells could be maintained over innocent people. This interest in magic and the supernatural is coupled with the Wagnerian interest in heroism and the implications of the sacrifice of the hero for the thing he loves. Much of the power of the idea of sacrifice derives from the sacrifice of Christ on the cross. But Tchaikovsky—like Wagner, whose hero in the *Ring of the Niebelungs* is also a Siegfried, whose end with Brunnhilde is similar to the ending in *Swan Lake*—concentrates on the human valor of the prince and its implication for transforming evil into good.

PERCEPTION KEY

SWAN LAKE

1. If you can see a production of *Swan Lake,* focus on a specific act and comment in a discussion with others on the suitability of the bodily movements for the narrative subject matter of the act. Are feelings or states of mind interpreted as well as the narrative? If so, when and how?
2. If you cannot see the ballet, recordings are easily available; and you should be able to comment on the possibilities for movements that would be effective for specific portions of the dance. For instance, how should Odette and the swans move at the opening of Act 4? How should Siegfried move in his last *pas de deux* in the same act?
3. Whether or not you have a chance to see the ballet, try to move in such a way as to present your interpretation of a specific moment in the ballet. You might try something as simple as Odette fluttering with the swans in Act 2 or as complicated as Siegfried or Odette casting himself or herself into the lake in Act 4.
4. If someone who has had training in ballet is available, you might try to get him or her to present a small portion of the ballet for your observation and discussion. What would be the most important kinds of questions to ask such a person?

FIGURE 10-9
George Balanchine's *Apollo*, with Peter Martins and, from the left, Suzanne Farrell, Kyra Nichols, and Karin von Arnoldingen. (Martha Swope © Time, Inc.)

GEORGE BALANCHINE

Born in pre-revolution Russia as Georgi Balanchivadze, Balanchine was the son of an important composer. He studied ballet but was also a very competent pianist, so his understanding of music was unusual. When he left Russia in 1923, he became part of Serge Diaghilev's Ballets Russes and began to choreograph for Diaghilev. He worked with Igor Stravinsky and Serge Prokofiev, two of the most important modern composers. Two of his earliest dances, still performed regularly today by the New York City Ballet, are *Apollo* (Figure 10-9) and *The Prodigal Son*. Balanchine choreographed for the Ballets Russes until Diaghilev died, then came to New York to found a school and a company in 1934. He also created important dances for films and shows on Broadway, such as "Slaughter on Tenth Avenue" for the show *On Your Toes*. That dance is still performed by the New York City Ballet. Since his death, Balanchine has been especially visible on television because his dances are clear, are formally strong, and demand exceptional technique from the dancers. These qualities come across on television, and since Peter Martins has continued the legacy of Balanchine at the New York City Ballet, Balanchine's work has become more and more available to audiences.

MODERN DANCE

The origins of modern dance are usually traced to the American dancers Isadora Duncan and Ruth St. Denis. They rebeled against the stylization of

FIGURE 10-10
Isadora Duncan in *La Marseillaise*. (Dance Collection, The New York Public Library for the Performing Arts, Lincoln Center)

ballet, with ballerinas dancing on their toes and executing the same basic movements in every performance. Duncan insisted on natural movement, often dancing in bare feet with gossamer drapery that showed her body and legs in motion (see Figure 10-10). She felt that the emphasis ballet places on the movement of the arms and legs was wrong. Her insistence on placing the center of motion just below the breastbone was based on her feeling that the torso had been neglected in the development of ballet. She felt, too, that the early Greek dancers, whom she wished to emulate, had placed their center of energy at the solar plexus. Her intention was to return to natural movement in dance, and this was one effective method of doing so.

The developers of modern dance who followed Duncan (she died in 1927) built on her legacy. In her insistence on freedom with respect to clothes and conventions, she infused energy into the dance that no one had ever seen before. Although she was a native Californian, her successes and triumphs were primarily in foreign lands, particularly in France and Russia. Her performances differed greatly from the ballet. Instead of developing a dance built on a pretext of the sort that underlies *Swan Lake,* Duncan took more abstract subject matters—especially states of mind and moods—and expressed her understanding of them in dance.

Duncan's dances were lyrical, personal, and occasionally extemporaneous. Since she insisted that there were no angular shapes in nature, she would permit herself to use none. Her movements tended to be ongoing and rarely came to a complete rest. An interesting example of her dance, one in which she does come to a full rest, is recounted by a friend. It was performed in a salon for close friends, and its subject matter seems to be human emergence on the planet:

> Isadora was completely covered by a long loose robe with high draped neck and long loose sleeves in a deep muted red. She crouched on the floor with her face resting on the carpet. In slow motion with ineffable effort she managed to get up on her knees. Gradually with titanic struggles she rose to her feet. She raised her arms toward heaven in a gesture of praise and exultation. The mortal had emerged from primeval ooze to achieve Man, upright, liberated, and triumphant.[1]

Martha Graham, Erick Hawkins, José Limón, Doris Humphrey, and other innovators who followed Isadora developed modern dance in a variety of directions. Graham, who was also interested in Greek origins, created some dances on themes of Greek tragedies, such as her *Medea.* In addition to his *Moor's Pavane,* Limón is well known for his interpretation of Eugene O'Neill's play *The Emperor Jones,* in which a black slave escapes to an island only to become a despised and hunted tyrant. These approaches are somewhat of a departure from Duncan, as they tend to introduce the balletic pretext into modern dance. Humphrey, who was a little older than Graham and Limón, was closer to the original Duncan tradition in such dances as *Water Study, Life of the Bee,* and *New Dance,* a 1930s piece that was successfully revived in 1972.

Perception Key
PRETEXT AND MOVEMENT

1. Devise a series of movements that will take about thirty seconds to complete and that you are fairly sure do not tell a story. Then "perform" these movements for a group and question them on the apparent pretext of your movement. Do not tell them in advance that your dance has no story. As a result of this experiment, ask yourself and the group whether it is possible to create a sequence of movements that will not suggest a story line to some viewers. What would this mean for dances that try to avoid pretexts? Can there really be abstract dance?
2. Without explaining that you are not dancing, represent a familiar human situation to a group by using movements that you believe are not dance movements. Is the group able to understand what you represented? Do they think you were using dance movements? Do you believe it possible to have movements that cannot be included in a dance? Are there, in other words, nondance movements?

[1]From Kathleen Cannell, "Isadorable Duncan," *Christian Science Monitor,* December 4, 1970.

FIGURE 10-11
The Alvin Ailey City Center Dance Theater, New York. *Revelations,* "Wading in the Water." Photo: Jack Vartoogian. From Jonas, *Dancing*, p. 229 bottom.

ALVIN AILEY'S *REVELATIONS*

One of the classics of modern dance is Alvin Ailey's *Revelations* (Figure 10-11), based largely on African-American spirituals and experience. It was first performed in January 1960, and hardly a year has gone by since without its having been performed to highly enthusiastic crowds. Ailey refined *Revelations* somewhat over the years, but its impact has brought audiences to their feet for standing ovations at almost every performance. Since Ailey's early death, the company has been directed by Judith Jamison, one of the great dancers in Ailey's company.

Some of the success of *Revelations* stems from Ailey's choice of the deeply felt music of the spirituals to which the dancers' movements are closely attuned. But, then, this is also one of the most noted qualities of a ballet like *Swan Lake,* which has one of the richest orchestral scores of any ballet. Music, unless it is program music, is not, strictly speaking, a pretext for a dance, but there is a perceptible connection between, say, the rhythmic characteristics of a given music and a dance composed in such a way as to take advantage of those characteristics. Thus in *Revelations* the energetic movements of the dancers often appear as visual, bodily transformations of the rhythmically charged music.

Although it is not useful to describe the entire dance, we will try to point out certain general qualities of which an awareness may prove helpful for refining your experience not only of this dance but of modern dance in general. Beyond the general pretext of *Revelations*—that of African-American experience as related by the spirituals—each of its separate sections has its own pretext. But none of them is as tightly or specifically narrative as is usually the case in ballet. In *Revelations* only generalized situations act as pretexts.

The first section of the dance is called "Pilgrim of Sorrow," with three parts: "I Been Buked," danced by the entire company (about twenty dancers, male and female); "Didn't My Lord Deliver Daniel," danced by only a few dancers; and "Fix Me Jesus," danced by one couple. The general pretext is the suffering of African-Americans at the hands of their tormentors, like the Israelites of the Old Testament, but taking refuge in their faith in the Lord. The most dramatic moments in this section are in "Didn't My Lord Deliver Daniel," a statement of overwhelming faith characterized by close ensemble work. The in-line dancers parallel the rhythms of the last word of the hymn: "Dan´-i-el´," accenting the first and last syllables with powerful rhythmic movements.

The second section, titled "Take Me to the Water," is divided into "Processional," danced by eight dancers, "Wading in the Water," danced by six dancers, and "I Want to Be Ready," danced by a single male dancer. The whole idea of "Take Me to the Water" suggests baptism, a ritual that affirms faith in God—the source of energy of the spirituals. "Wading in the Water" is particularly exciting, with dancers holding a stage-long bolt of light-colored fabric to represent the water. The dancers shimmer the fabric to the rhythm of the music and one dancer after another crosses over the fabric, which symbolizes at least two things: the waters of baptism and the Mosaic waters of freedom. It is this episode that originally featured the charismatic Judith Jamison in a long white gown holding a huge parasol as she danced (Figure 10–11). Donna Wood performs the role in the illustration.

The third section is called "Move, Members, Move," with the subsections titled "Sinner Man," "The Day Is Past and Gone," "You May Run Home," and the finale, "Rocka My Soul in the Bosom of Abraham." In this last episode a sense of triumph over suffering is projected, suggesting the redemption of a people by using the same kind of Old Testament imagery and musical material that opened the dance. The entire section takes as its theme the life of people after they have been received into the faith, with the possibilities of straying into sin. It ends with a powerful rocking spiritual that emphasizes forgiveness and the reception of the people (the "members") into the bosom of Abraham, according to the prediction of the Bible. This ending features a large amount of ensemble work and is danced by the entire company, with rows of male dancers sliding forward on their outspread knees and then rising all in one sliding gesture, raising their hands high. "Rocka My Soul in the Bosom of Abraham" is powerfully sung again and again until the effect is almost hypnotic.

The subject matter of *Revelations* is in part that of feelings and states of mind. But it is also more obviously that of the struggle of a people as told—on one level—by their music. The dance has the advantage of a powerfully engaging subject matter even before we witness the transmutation of that subject matter. And the way in which the movements of the dance are closely attuned to the rhythm of the music tends to give most viewers a very intense participation, since the visual qualities of the dance are so powerfully reinforced by the aural qualities of the music. Not all modern dance is characterized by this reinforcement, but most show dance and most dance in filmed musicals encourage a similar closeness of movement and music.

Perception Key
AILEY'S *REVELATIONS*

1. A profitable way of understanding the resources of *Revelations* is to take a well-known African-American spiritual such as "Swing Low, Sweet Chariot," part of which appears on page 274, and supply the movements that it suggests to you. Once you have done so, ask yourself how difficult it was. Is it natural to move to such music?
2. Instead of spirituals, try the same experiment with popular music such as rock. What characteristics does such music have that stimulate motion?

MARTHA GRAHAM

Quite different from the Ailey approach is the "Graham technique," taught in Graham's own school in New York as well as in colleges and universities across the country. Like Ailey, Graham was a virtuoso dancer and organized her own company. After Isadora Duncan, no one has been more influential in modern dance. Graham's technique is reminiscent of ballet in its rigor and discipline. Dancers learn specific kinds of movements and exercises designed to be used both as preparation for and part of the dance. Graham's contraction, for example, is one of the commonest movements one is likely to see. It is the sudden contraction of the diaphragm with the resultant relaxation of the rest of the body. This builds on Duncan's em-

FIGURE 10-12
Martha Graham in *Phaedra*. (Martha Swope © Time, Inc.)

phasis on the solar plexus, but adds to that emphasis the systolic and diastolic rhythms of heartbeat and pulse. The movement is very effective visually as well as being particularly flexible in depicting feelings and states of mind. It is a movement unknown in ballet, from which Graham always wished to remain distinct.

At times Graham's dances have been very literal, with narrative pretexts quite similar to those found in ballet. *Night Journey,* for instance, is an interpretation of *Oedipus Rex* by Sophocles. The lines of emotional force linking Jocasta and her son-husband Oedipus are strongly accentuated by the movements of the dance as well as by certain props on stage, such as ribbons that link the two together at times. In Graham's interpretation, Jocasta becomes much more important than she is in the original drama. This is partly because Graham saw the female figures in Greek drama—such as *Phaedra* (Figure 10-12)—as much more fully dimensional than we have normally understood them. By means of dancing their roles, she was able to develop the complexities of their character. In dances such as her *El Penitente,* Graham experimented with states of mind as the subject matter. Thus the featured male dancer in loose white trousers and tunic, moving in slow circles about the stage with a large wooden cross, is a powerful interpretation of penitence.

PILOBOLUS DANCE COMPANY

The more innovative dance companies, such as Pilobolus and the Mark Morris Company, often surprise audiences with abstract dances and moving bodies creating visual patterns as the primary subject matter. The dances of these companies usually have no pretexts—or at least none that could be interpreted in the narrative fashion of *Swan Lake.* The Pilobolus Company began in 1970 at Dartmouth, with four gymnastic male dancers. The choreographer Alison Chase directed the company in a series of dances that depended on the balance and leverage principles of gymnastics, producing shapes and movement that startled the dance world. The principle of balance and leverage is illustrated in Figure 10-13, a moment from *Monkshood's Farewell* (1974), one of their first efforts at producing a dance that had an extended development suggesting a narrative.

In later experiments implied narratives are taken further. But the distinctive visual vocabulary of interlocking bodies continues. Something of this can be seen in the series of photographs joined together in a continuum representing part of the dance *Ciona* (Figure 10-14).

If you let your eyes scan the "frames" rapidly from left to right as if they were lines of print, you may see the way in which the forms shift and grow. The dances of Pilobolus are infectious. After concerts at colleges, one sometimes may see students balancing each other on their knees or backs, attempting to imitate the movements they have seen.

MARK MORRIS DANCE GROUP

The Mark Morris Dance Group was created—"reluctantly," he has said—in 1980 because he found he could not do the dances he wanted with other

FIGURE 10-13
Monkshood's Farewell.
Pilobolus Dance Company.
(Tim Matson)

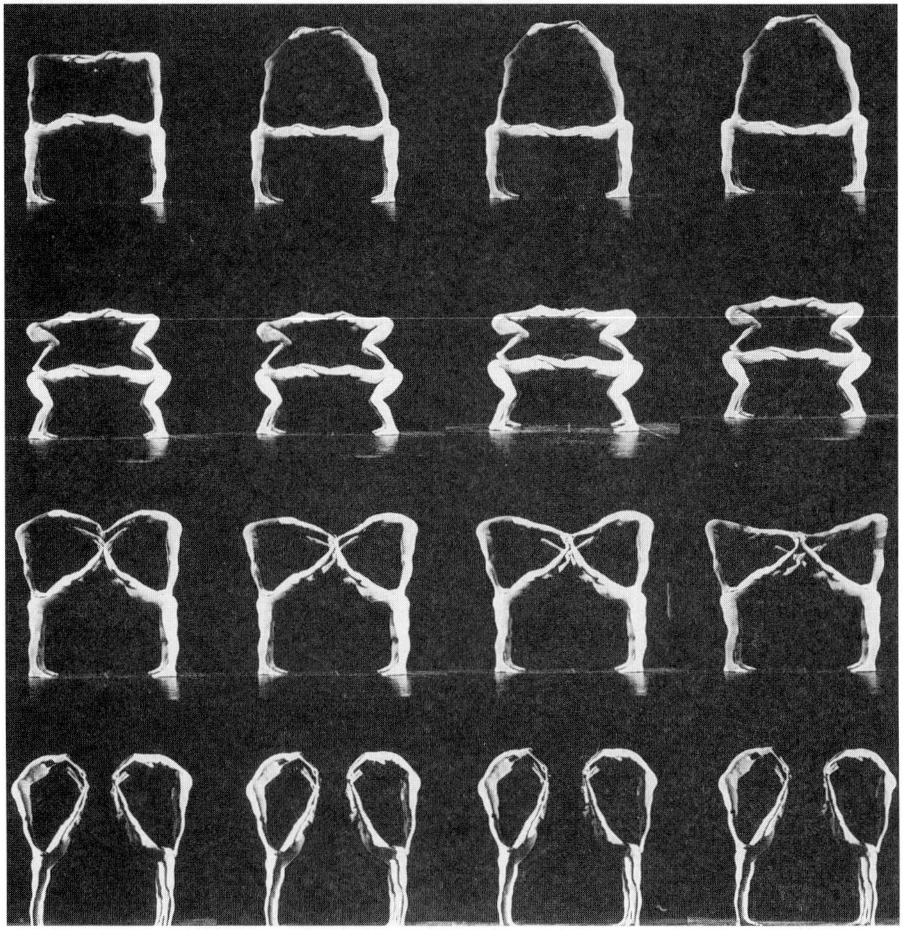

FIGURE 10-14
Ciona. Pilobolus Dance
Company. (Tim Matson)

existing companies. Morris was a sensation from the first. His company performed in New York from 1981 to 1983, then at the Brooklyn Academy of Music in their "Next Wave" series, beginning in 1984. Since then he has been considered the most promising American dancer of his generation. His company was based at the University of Washington in Seattle, performing regularly to extraordinary reviews in New York City. In 1988 the company shocked the dance world by accepting an invitation from Brussels to take up residence at Théâtre Royal de la Monnaie, where the famed and well-loved ballet company of Maurice Béjart had thrilled a very demanding audience.

Morris' first dance in Brussels was a theatrical piece with an intricate interpretation of Handel's music to John Milton's lyric poems: *L'Allegro, il Penseroso ed il Moderato.* The title refers to three moods: happiness, melancholy, and restfulness. The interpretation of the state of mind associated with happiness is clearly evident in the movement patterns in Figure 10-15. The dance was produced again in Edinburgh in 1994 and Lincoln Center in 1995. David Dougill commented especially on the "absolute rightness to moods and themes" the dance was in correlating with Milton's poems and Handel's music. Morris left Brussels in 1991 and now centers his work in New York.

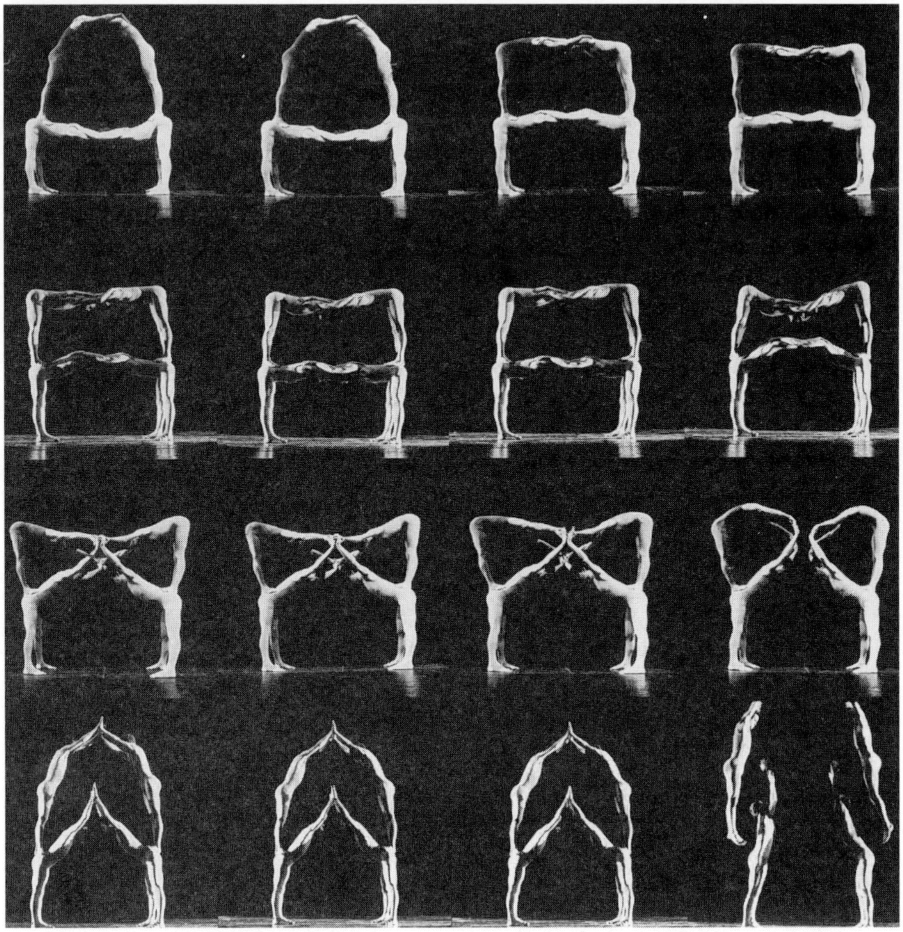

FIGURE 10-15
L'Allegro, il Penseroso ed il Moderato. Mark Morris Dance Group. (Klaus Lefebvre)

FIGURE 10-16
Sue's Leg. Choreography, Twyla Tharp; costumes Santo Loquasto; lighting, Jennifer Tipton; dancers (l. to r.) Kenneth Rinker, Rose Marie Wright, Twyla Tharp, Tom Rawe. (Courtesy Twyla Tharp Dance Foundation, photograph by Tom Berthiaume)

TWYLA THARP

Tharp has developed a style pleasing to both serious critics and dance amateurs. A thoughtful student of the philosophy of dance, she includes a playfulness that seems appropriately modern. She also has taken advantage of the new opportunities for dance on television, particularly the Public Broadcasting Corporation's *Dance in America* series, which has been very popular and critically successful. For television productions, she often uses cuts from newsreel films along with her dancers' interpretations of 1930s dances. She has been particularly successful in adapting jazz of the 1920s and 1930s to dance; for example, *Sue's Leg* features the music of "Fats" Waller (Figure 10-16). *Bix Pieces* was inspired by the cornetist, Bix Beiderbecke, the first romantic, self-destructive young man with a horn. *Eight Jelly Rolls,* premiered in 1971, and also televised, is a brilliant series of interpretations of eight songs written by the legendary Jelly Roll Morton, who claimed to have invented jazz. Tharp's interest in sequential dances—*Ocean's Motion,* a suite of dances to the music of Chuck Berry; *Raggedy Dances,* to ragtime tunes; and *Assorted Quarters,* to classical music—shows a virtuoso ability to explore feelings and states of mind as related to music.

Television has had a significant impact on dance performances since the early 1970s. Tharp has been foremost among those experimenting with that medium, choreographing famous dancers, such as Rudolf Nureyev, the former star of the Russian Kirov ballet. Nureyev was interested in working with her partly because she had learned how to interpret the relatively restricted spaces available to the television camera, and partly because her vocabulary of movements is very different from that of classical ballet. He welcomed a new dance challenge. Tharp choreographed *The Sinatra Suite,* a duet with Nureyev and Elaine Kudo, set to a group of songs sung by Frank Sinatra. The sultry style that Nureyev brought to this American music and choreography was striking. Nureyev again showed his versatility by dancing in Tharp's *Push Comes to Shove,* set to ragtime music interwoven with selections from Haydn symphonies. These dances have no explicit pretext.

PERCEPTION KEY
DANCE AND TELEVISION

The dance is becoming more available through television. Take advantage of these performances and keep asking yourself—after participation—three basic questions:

1. What was the subject matter?
2. Did the form give you insight into the subject matter?
3. If so, in what ways? Discuss what you think was revealed.
4. Consider, in addition to these three questions, issues concerning form in the dance: how congruent is the form with the music that accompanies the dance? Examine the dance and the music for patterns of repetition and development: in what ways do these patterns produce a sense of completeness and satisfaction in the dance?

Having a mental set of such questions should help focus your attention for the next performance and lead to more intense participations.

SUMMARY

Through the medium of the moving human body, the form of dance can reveal visual patterns or feelings or states of mind or narrative or, more probably, some combination. The first step in learning to participate with dance is to learn the nature of its movements. The second is to be aware of its different kinds of subject matter. The content of dance gives us insights about our inner life, especially states of mind, that supplement the insights of music. Dance has the capacity to transform a pretext, the narrative which it enacts, whether the pretext is a story or a state of mind or a feeling. Our attention should be drawn into participation with this transformation. The insight we get from the dance experience is dependent on our awareness of this transformation.

CHAPTER 10 BIBLIOGRAPHY

Amberg, George. *Ballet.* New York: Mentor Books, New American Library, 1949.

Cohen, Selma Jean. *Dance as a Theatre Art.* New York: Dodd Mead, 1974.

———. *Doris Humphrey: An Artist First.* Middletown, Conn.: Wesleyan University Press, 1972.

——— (ed.). *The International Encyclopedia of Dance.* Berkeley: University of California Press. Forthcoming.

——— (ed.). *The Modern Dance.* Middletown, Conn.: Wesleyan University Press, 1965.

Copeland, Roger, and Marshall Cohen (eds.). *What Is Dance?* New York: Oxford University Press, 1983.

DeMille, Agnes. *Dance to the Piper.* Boston: Houghton Mifflin, 1952.

Duncan, Isadora. *Art of the Dance,* 2d ed. New York: Theatre Arts, 1977.

———. *My Life.* New York: Liveright, 1972.

Emery, Lynne Fauley. *Black Dance in the U.S. from 1619 to Today.* 2d ed. Salem, New Hampshire: Ayer Co., 1988.

Fergusson, Erna. *Dancing Gods: Indian Ceremonials of New Mexico and Arizona.* Albuquerque: University of New Mexico Press, 1966.

Friedman, James Michael. *Dancer and Spectator: An Aesthetic Distance.* San Francisco: Balletmonographs, 1976.

Horst, Louis. *Modern Dance Forms in Relation to the Other Modern Arts.* New York: Dance Horizons, 1961.

Humphrey, Doris. *The Art of Making Dances.* Barbara Pollack (ed.). New York: Grove Press, 1959.

Jonas, Gerald. *Dancing: The Pleasure, Power, and Art of Movement.* New York: Harry N. Abrams, 1992.

Jowitt, Deborah. *Time and the Dancing Image.* New York: William Morrow, 1988.

Kirstein, Lincoln, et al. *Ballet: Bias & Belief.* New York: Dance Horizons, 1983.

———. *The Classic Ballet.* New York: Knopf, 1969.

Magriel, Paul (ed.). *Nijinsky, Pavlova, Duncan.* New York: Da Capo, 1977.

McDonagh, Don. *The Rise and Fall and Rise of Modern Dance.* New York: New American Library, 1970. Reprinted Chicago Review Press, 1990.

Migel, Parmenia. *The Ballerinas.* New York: Macmillan, 1972.

Miller, David Humphreys. *Ghost Dance.* Lincoln: University of Nebraska Press, 1959.

Nadel, Myron, and Constance Miller (eds.). *The Dance Experience.* New York: Universe Books, 1978.

Percival, John. *Modern Ballet.* New York: Dutton, 1970.

Prabhavananda, Swami. *The Spiritual Heritage of India.* Garden City, N.Y.: Doubleday, 1963.

Reynolds, Nancy. *In Performance: A Companion to the Classics of the Dance.* New York: Harmony Books, 1980.

Sachs, Curt. *World History of the Dance.* New York: Norton, 1965.

Sorell, Walter. *The Dance Through the Ages.* New York: Grosset & Dunlap, 1967.

Sparshott, Francis. *Off the Ground: First Steps to a Philosophical Consideration of the Dance.* Princeton: Princeton University Press, 1988.

Stearns, Marshall. *Jazz Dance: The Story of American Vernacular Dance.* New York: Macmillan, 1968.

Note: Dance Films Catalogue (Sara Menke, 5746 Gabbert Road, Moorpark, CA 93021) and Index to 16mm Educational Films (New York: McGraw-Hill, 1967) list dance films and sources. For *Dance in America* and other series, contact the local PBS TV Station or PBS in Washington, D.C. Also, distributors of dance films include Harris Communications, 45 East 66th Street, New York, NY 10021; Encyclopedia Britannica Films, 1150 Wilmette Avenue, Wilmette, IL 60091; Audio Films, 406 Clement Street, San Francisco, CA 94118; and Museum of Modern Art, Dept. of Film, 11 West 53rd Street, New York, NY 10019. Some of the dances mentioned in this chapter are available on videotape from KULTUR, 121 Highway 36, West Long Branch, NJ 07764. Among them are *Swan Lake* (No. 1162); Alvin Ailey's *Revelations* (No. 1152); Twyla Tharp's *Sinatra Suite* and *Push Comes to Shove,* with Rudolf Nureyev and Elaine Kudo (No. 1167); *Martha Graham: An American Original in Performance* (No. 1177).

CHAPTER 10 WEBSITES

Ballet
Usenet: Newgroup: **alt.arts.ballet**

Ballet Terms
World Wide Web: **http://sleepless.acm.uiuc.edu/signet/JHSI/dance.html**

Ballroom Dancing (competitive ballroom dancing)
World Wide Web: **http://w.chat.on.ca/dance/pages/dscape1.htm**

Break Dancing (history and images of the '80s dance craze)
World Wide Web: **http://rowlf.cc.wwu.edu:8080/~n9344199/bd/bd.html**

Dance Information
Anonymous FTP: Address: **ftp.std.com** Path: **/pub/dance/***

Dance Links (links to various dance forms)
World Wide Web: **http://www.cyberspace.com/vandehey/dance.html**

Dance Links (nightclubs, studios)
World Wide Web: **http://zeus.ncsa.uiuc.edu:8080/~hneeman/dance_hotlist.html**

Dance Mailing List
Name: **Ballroom** Address: **ballroom-request@mitvma.mit.edu**

Dance on the Internet (miscellaneous information on the Internet)
World Wide Web: **http://www.cs.fsu.edu/projects/group4/dance.html**

Events (schedule of international events)
World Wide Web: **http://www.weblink.com/nyibc/Events/events.html**

World Dance
Anonymous FTP: Address: **ftp.std.com** Path: **/customers2/nonprofits/dance/***

CHAPTER 11

FILM

Most of the discussion that follows can be considered descriptive criticism, although in the area of film, what most of us practice most of the time is evaluative criticism. Most of us decide a film is good or bad, satisfying or unsatisfying, and we do so in a public way, sharing our evaluation readily with our friends. The basis on which we make evaluative judgments of films is, to a large extent, also the subject of this chapter. Our concerns are to point to cinematic excellence in several areas: cinematography, the care with which a film is photographed; structure, the completeness and excellence of the script or story line; acting and character development; editing, the care with which separate "shots" (see below) are joined together to achieve a satisfying form for the film; music, the way in which sound evokes emotion or establishes mood.

When we evaluate a film, all of these elements come into play. It is also true that the qualities discussed in Chapter 8 on drama apply to most films, since most feature films are forms of dramatic literature. This chapter examines each of these elements in enough depth to make us aware of their demands, their resources, and their obligations in a film. The majority of films made will handle all these elements in a serviceable fashion—only a few will handle any of them badly enough for us to notice. However, it is also true that only a few will handle them well enough for us to think of them as great classics, such as *Casablanca, Jules and Jim, Citizen Kane, A Wonderful Life,* or *The Searchers*. The films we discuss below are all in this category of achievement.

THE SUBJECT MATTER OF FILM

In a scant century, the film has become the most popular art form around the world. From the beginning, it borrowed principles of visual organization from painting. Even today, as films are planned a "storyboard" is created with drawings of scenes that are realized on film often just as they were designed. But unlike the image of the painting, the images of the film "move," because they are projected on a screen at twenty-four frames per second and the eye merges them as if they were continuous action. The indebtedness of the film to drama and literature is also great, since virtually all films have narrative structure for the characters to follow. When films were young and silent, a pianist, organist, or sometimes an entire symphony orchestra provided "mood" music to intensify visual scenes. After 1926, many films incorporated a soundtrack not only with the dialogue, but with background music that has now become virtually indispensable. Because the film is relatively inexpensive to see, it reaches millions and millions of people and provides them with what may be their primary experience in art, and, by extension, their primary experience in the arts on which it depends.

Except in its most reductionist form, the subject matter of most great films is very difficult to isolate and restate in words. You could say that death is the subject matter of Bergman's *The Seventh Seal* (1957), but you would also need to observe that the knight's sacrifice to save the lives of others—which he accomplishes by playing chess with Death—is also part of the film's subject matter. You might say that crime is the subject matter of *The Godfather* (1972), or perhaps power, or perhaps even loyalty and honor. All these are part of the subject matter of the film, and we can see that the complexity of subject matter in film rivals that of any art except literature.

It may be that the very popularity of film and the ease with which we can access it has led to ignoring the form that may be creating insights about the subject matter. For example, is it really possible to catch the subtleties of form of a great film in one viewing? Yet how many of us see a great film more than once? Audiences generally enjoy, but rarely analyze, films. Some of the observations that follow may help you both to enjoy and to analyze the best films you see.

Except perhaps for opera, the film more than any of the other arts involves collaborative effort. Most films are written by a scriptwriter, then planned by a director who may make many changes. However, even if the director is also the scriptwriter, the film needs a producer, camera operators, an editor, designers, researchers, costumers, actors, and actresses. Auteur criticism regards the director as equivalent to the auteur, or author, of the film. For most moviegoers, the most important persons involved with the film will almost surely be not the director, but the stars who appear in the film. Meryl Streep, Uma Thurman, Robert Redford, John Travolta, or Morgan Freeman will be far more famous than such directors of stature as Ingmar Bergman, Federico Fellini, Lina Wertmuller, Akira Kurosawa, Jane Campion, or Krzyzstof Kieslowski.

DIRECTING AND EDITING

The two dominant figures in early films were directors who did their own editing: D. W. Griffith and Sergei Eisenstein, unquestionably the great early geniuses of filmmaking. They managed to gain enough control over the production of their works so that they could craft their films into a distinctive rather than a subservient medium. Some of their films are still considered among the finest ever made. *Birth of a Nation* (1916) and *Intolerance* (1918) by Griffith, and *Potemkin* (1925) and *Ivan the Terrible* (1941–1946) by Eisenstein are still being shown and are still influencing contemporary filmmakers. These men were more than just directors. With many of their films they were responsible for almost everything: writing, casting, choosing locations, handling the camera, directing, editing, and financing.

Directing and editing are probably the most crucial phases of filmmaking. Today most directors control the acting and supervise the photography, carried out by skilled technicians who work with such problems as lighting, camera angles, and focusing, as well as the motion of the camera itself (some sequences use a highly mobile camera, while others use a fixed camera). Some of the resources of the director when making choices about the use of the camera involve the kinds of shots that may eventually be edited together. A shot is a continuous length of film exposed sequentially in the camera without a break. Some of the most important kinds of shots are:

Establishing shot: usually a distant shot establishes important locations or figures in the action.

The close-up: the face of a character or an important object fills the screen.

The long shot: the camera is very far distant from the most important character or object in the shot.

Medium shot: neither up close nor far distant shot. There can be medium close-ups and medium long shots too.

Following shot: camera keeps a moving figure in the frame, usually keeping pace with the figure.

Point-of-view shot: the camera records what the character must be seeing; when the camera moves, it implies the character's gaze moves.

Tracking shot: a shot in which the camera moves forward, backward, or sidewise.

Crane shot: the camera is on a crane or movable platform and moves upward or downward through the shot.

Hand-held shot: the camera is carried, sometimes on a special harness, by the camera operator.

If you have been watching television or seeing films, you have seen all these shots hundreds of times. Add to these specific kinds of shots the variables of camera angles, types of camera lenses, variations in lighting, variations in approach to sound, and you can see that the technical resources of the director are enormous. The addition of script and actors enriches the director's range of choices so that they become almost dizzying.

The editor, usually assisted by the director, puts the shots in order after the filming is finished. The editor trims the shots to an appropriate length, then joins them with other shots to create the final, edited film. Edited sequences sometimes shot far apart in time and place are organized into a unity. Films are rarely shot sequentially, and only a part of the total footage is ever shown in a film. The old saying of the bit-part actor—"I was lost on the cutting-room floor"—attests to the fact that much interesting footage is omitted. Often some of the most bitter arguments in filmmaking are between the director and the editor, who can frequently disagree on how to edit a film. Sometimes, especially in video stores, you will see the term "Director's Cut" on a film, meaning that the director edited or reedited the film to please his or her original vision—usually adding sequences omitted to conform to the perceived needs of the exhibiting theaters.

It helps to know the resources of the editor, who "cuts" the film to create certain relationships between takes. These relationships, or cuts, are often at the core of the director's distinctive style. Some of the most familiar of the editor's choices are:

Continuity cut: editing so as to produce a sense of narrative continuity, following the action stage by stage with different shots. The editor can also use a discontinuity cut to break up the narrative continuity for effect.

Cheat cut: using the technique of the continuity cut, but showing the characters or physical properties in different relationships to one another.

Jump cut: sometimes just called a cut, the jump cut moves abruptly from one shot to the next, with no preparation, and often with a shock.

Cut-in: an immediate move from a wide shot to a very close shot of the same scene; the editor may cut-out, as well.

Cross-cutting: alternating shots of two or more distinct actions occurring in different places (but often at the same dramatic time).

Dissolve: one scene disappears slowly while the next scene appears as if beneath it.

Fade: fade-in shows a dark screen growing brighter to reveal the shot; fade-out darkens the screen, effectively ending the shot.

Wipe: transition between shots, with a line moving across or through the screen separating one shot from the next.

Graphic match: joining two shots that have similar composition, color, or scene.

Montage sequence: a sequence of rapidly edited images designed to build tension and reveal a passage of time.

Shot, reverse shot: first shot shows a character looking at something; reverse shot shows what the character sees.

Our responses to film depend largely on the choices that directors and editors make regarding shots and editing almost as much as they do on the nature of the narrative and the appeal of the actors. In a relatively short time film editing has become almost a form of language of imagery that has close to universal significance.

When editing is handled well, it can be profoundly effective, because it is impossible in real-life experience to achieve what the editor achieves. By eliminating the irrelevant, good editing accents the relevant. We cannot go instantly from an airport, where we are watching a hired assassin from Chicago landing at Los Angeles, to the office of the political candidate he has come to kill. Film can do this with ease. The montage—dramatically connected but physically disconnected images—can be made without a word of dialogue. You can undoubtedly recall innumerable instances of this kind of editing. When done well, this tying together of images that could not possibly be together in real-life experience enhances the meaning of the images we see.

PERCEPTION KEY
TECHNIQUES OF DIRECTING AND EDITING

1. Study the next film you see and record the kinds of shots and cuts you see. How many of the ones listed above are used?
2. Keep track of the length of time spent in any given shot in minutes and seconds. Is there a major difference between the length of shots in older films and in newer films? In action films and romantic films? In dramatic films and comedies? In horror films and cartoon films? Which kinds of cuts seem preferred in each kind of film?
3. What is the emotional effect of the various cuts available to editors? Does one kind of cut affect your central nervous system more than another?
4. Do certain choices in shots or cuts produce predictable emotional reactions?

THE PARTICIPATIVE EXPERIENCE AND FILM

Our participation with the film is often virtually involuntary. For one thing, most of us know exactly what it means to lose our sense of place and time in a movie. This loss seems to be achieved rapidly in all but the most awkwardly conceived films. In a film like *Black Orpheus* (1958), shot in Rio, the intensity of tropical colors, Latin American music, and the dynamics of the carnival produce an imaginary reality so intense and vital that actual reality seems dull by comparison. But then there are other films that create the illusion of life itself. Aristotle analyzed the ways in which drama imitates life and the ways in which an audience identifies with some of the actors on the stage. Yet the film seems to have these powers to an even greater degree than the stage. (See discussion of Aristotle's mimesis in Chapter 8.)

Cinematic realism makes it easy for us to identify with actors who represent our values (a kind of participation). For instance, in *Forrest Gump* (1994), Tom Hanks plays what seems to be, on the surface, a mentally defective person. But Gump is not just dumb—he is good at heart and positive in his thinking. He is a character in whom the cunning—not just the intelligence—has been removed, and in him the audience sees their lost innocence. It would be very doubtful that anyone in the audience consciously identified with Gump, but it was clear from the film's reception that it found something in him that touched a nerve and that was, in the final analysis, both appealing and cheering. Gump is an unlikely hero primarily because he is trusting, innocent, and good-hearted. When the audience participates with that film, it is in part because the audience sees in Gump what it would like to see in itself.

PERCEPTION KEY
FILM, DRAMA, TELEVISION, AND PARTICIPATION

1. Observe people coming out of a movie theater. Can you usually tell by their behavior whether the film was a western, comedy, tragedy, melodrama, etc.?
2. Does it make a significant difference whether you experience a film in an empty or a packed theater? Is laughter somehow enhanced in a crowd? Yet is the humor of a comic film significantly depressed if you see it alone?
3. Compare your experiences of the same film in the theater and on television. Which presentation engages your participation more intensely? Is the difference in the sizes of the screens mainly responsible for any difference in the intensity of participation? Or is it, perhaps, the stronger darkness that usually surrounds you in the theater? What other factors might be involved?
4. Do you think it would be easier to make a television film or a theater film? What would the basic differences be?

Other forms of identification happen in films all the time. In the *Rambo* films of the 1970s and 1980s America seemed to identify with Sylvester Stallone, who did single-handedly what the nation could not: win the Vietnam war. It may be that we naturally identify with heroes in films, as we do in books. The characters played by extremely charismatic actors like Paul Newman, Tom Cruise, Clint Eastwood, Robert Redford, John Travolta, Brad Pitt, Whoopie Goldberg, Denzel Washington, Eddie Murphy, Rosanna Arquette, Jack Nicholson, Emma Thompson, Anthony Hopkins, to name only a few—and primarily those known to an American audience—almost always appeal to some aspect of our personality, even if sometimes that aspect is frightening. Such may be the source, for instance, of the appeal of Hannibal Lector in *The Silence of the Lambs* (1992), in which Anthony Hopkins not only appears as a cannibal, but actually gets away with it, identifying his former doctor as his next victim, whose liver he plans to eat with some "fava beans and a nice Chianti."

There are problems with this kind of loss of self, which is often a veiled appeal to the worship of self. Film can inform us about ourselves, or it can cause a short circuit of self-awareness: we simply indulge in hero worship with ourselves as the hero. The other arts may also cause this short circuit, of course, but the temptation seems most likely with film.

There are two kinds of participative experiences with film. One is not principally filmic in nature and is represented by a kind of self-indulgence that depends upon self-justifying fantasies. We imagine ourselves as James Bond, for example, and ignore the interrelationship of the major elements of the film. The other kind of participation evolves from an awareness of all the parts and their interrelationships. This second kind of participative experience means much more to us ultimately because it is significantly informative: we "get" the content by means of the form.

Just a word more about the first kind of participation. It is usually referred to as "escapism." Escape films give us the chance to see ourselves complimented in a movie, thus satisfying our desire for self-importance. Unhappily, escape films often help us avoid doing anything about achieving something that would really make us more important to ourselves. In some ways these films help rob people of the chance to be something in their own right. Most television depends on this effect for its success. Perhaps it is true that large masses of people need this kind of entertainment in order to avoid the despair that would set in if they had to face up to the reality of their lives. It may be cynical to think so, yet it is highly possible that many people who make motion pictures believe this to be a justification for what they are doing.

The fact that film may cause such an intense sense of participation of the wrong kind prevents our perception of the content of the film. We can see a film and know nothing about the finer points of its form and meaning—the nuances that make a film worth experiencing and then pondering over because of its impact on us. Most films, unfortunately, are hardly worth seeing more than once (or even once), while there are a few that are rightly called classics because of their humanizing achievement through formal excellence. We want to get a sense of how to appreciate a film that is a classic. Questions of criticism, as we hope we established in Chapter 3, are always implicitly operative when we view a film or any work of art.

THE FILM IMAGE

The starting point of film is the image. Just as still photographs and paintings can move us profoundly by their organization of visual experience, so can such images when they are set to motion. Indeed, many experts insist that no artistic medium ever created has the power to move us as deeply as the medium of moving images. They base their claim not just on the mass audiences who have been profoundly stirred but also on the fact that the moving images of the film are similar to the moving images we perceive in life. We rarely perceive static images except when viewing such things as paintings or photographs. Watching a film closely can help us perceive much more intensely the visual worth of many of the images we experience outside film.

Many early filmmakers composed their films by adding single photographs to each other, frame by frame. Movement in motion pictures is caused by the physiological limitations of the eye. It cannot perceive the black line between frames when the film strip is moved rapidly. All it sees is the succession of frames minus the lines that divide them, for the eye cannot perceive separate images or frames that move faster than one-thirtieth of a second. This is to use the "language" of the camera, which can take a picture in much less time than that. Motion picture film is usu-

FIGURE 11-1
From Jean Renoir's *The Grand Illusion* with Erich von Stroheim, Jean Gabin, and Marcel Dalio. (A Continental Distributing, Inc., release, National Film Archive)

ally projected at a speed of twenty-four frames per second, and the persistence of vision merges the images.

Because of this, many filmmakers, both early and contemporary, attempt to "design" each individual frame as carefully as they might a photograph. (See "Photography and Painting: The Pictorialists" in Chapter 12, pp. 362–365.) Jean Renoir, the famous French filmmaker and son of painter Pierre-August, sometimes composed frames like a tightly unified painting, as in the *Grand Illusion* (1936, Figure 11-1) and *The Rules of the Game* (1939). Serge Eisenstein also framed many of his images carefully, notably in *Potemkin.* David Lean, who directed *Brief Encounter* (1945), *Bridge Over the River Kwai* (1957), *Lawrence of Arabia* (1962, re-released 1988), *Dr. Zhivago* (1965), and *Ryan's Daughter* (1970), also paid very close attention to the composition of individual frames.

PERCEPTION KEY
STILL FRAMES AND PHOTOGRAPHY

Study Figures 11-1,11-2, and 11-3.

1. How would you evaluate these stills with reference to tightness of composition? For example, do the details and parts interrelate so that any change would disrupt the unity of the totality? Compare with Figure 2-2 and discuss.
2. Compare the stills with Figures 12-17, 12-18, and 12-19. Are the stills as tightly organized as the photographs? Discuss.

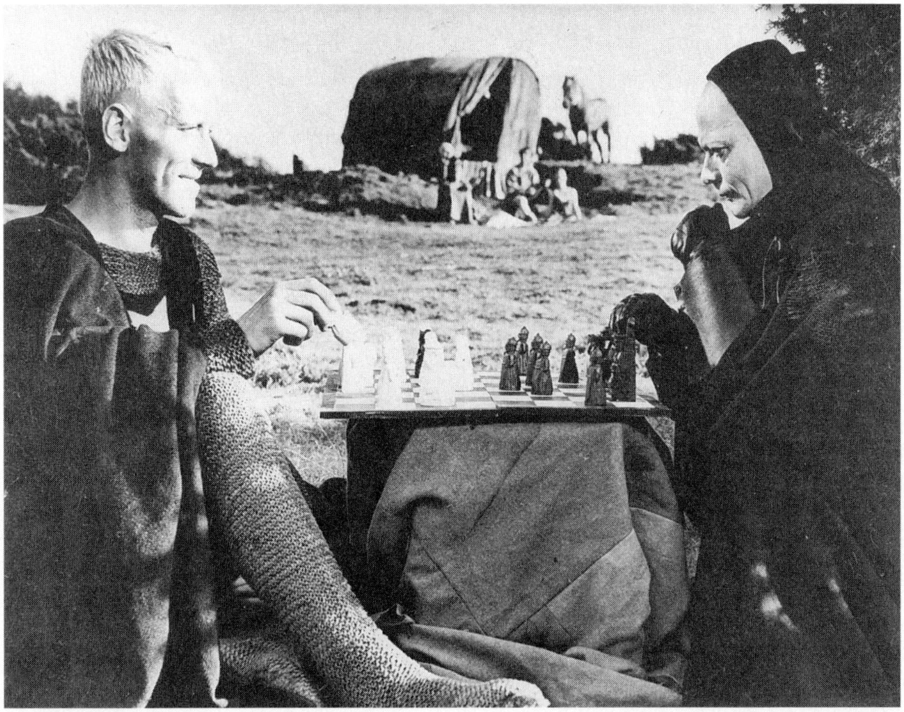

FIGURE 11-2
From Ingmar Bergman's *Seventh Seal*. (© Svensk Film Industry, Stockholm; National Film Archive)

FIGURE 11-3
Gianni de Venanzo's powerful recessional shot for *8½*. Guido (Marcello Mastroianni) greets his mistress Carla (Sandra Milo) at the spa train station. Federico Fellini, *8½*. (© 1963, Embassy Pictures Corp. Museum of Modern Art Film Stills Archive)

FIGURE 11-4
From *Citizen Kane* (1941) with Orson Welles and Dorothy Comingore, directed by Orson Welles. (Museum of Modern Art Film Stills Archive)

For some directors, the still moments of the film must be as exactly composed as a painting. The theory is that if the individual moments of the film are each as perfect as can be, the total film will be a cumulative perfection. This seems to be the case only for some films. In films that have long meditative sequences, such as Orson Welles' *Citizen Kane* (1941) (Figure 11-4) or Bergman's *Cries and Whispers* (1972), or sequences in which characters or images are relatively unmoving for significant periods of time, such as Robert Redford's *The River Runs Through It* (1994), the carefully composed still image may be of real significance. However powerful, most stills from fine films will reveal very little of the power of the entire film all by themselves: it is their sequential movement that brings out their effectiveness.

The still frame and the individual shot are the building blocks of film. Controlling the techniques that produce and interrelate these blocks is the first job of the film artist. We can see from the storyboard sketches by Steve Burg and Leonard Morganti from Kevin Costner's *Dances with Wolves* (1990) (Figure 11-5) that planning individual images even before shooting begins is an important part of making a film.

CAMERA POINT OF VIEW

Obviously the motion in the motion picture can come from numerous sources. The actors can move toward, away from, or across the field of camera vision. When something moves toward the camera it moves with astonishing speed, as we all know from watching the images of a moving

FIGURE 11-5
Storyboard images from Kevin Costner's *Dances with Wolves* (1990), by Steve Burg and Leonard Morganti. (From *Dances with Wolves: The Illustrated Story of the Epic Film*, Kevin Costner, Michael Blake, and Jim Wilson. Compilation and design © 1990 by Newmarket Press. Reprinted by permission of Newmarket Press, New York)

locomotive (the favorite vehicle for this technique so far) rush at us and then "catapult over our heads." The effect of the catapult is noteworthy because it is characteristic of the film medium.

People move before us the way they move before the camera, but the camera (or cameras) can achieve visual things that our unaided eye cannot: showing the same moving action from a number of points of view simultaneously, for instance, or showing it from a camera angle the eye cannot achieve. The realistic qualities of a film can be threatened, however, by being too sensational, with a profusion of shots that would be impossible in a real-life situation. Although such virtuoso effects can dazzle us at first, the feeling of being dazzled can degenerate into being dazed.

Another way the film portrays motion is by the movement or tracking of the camera. In a sequence in John Huston's *The Misfits* (1961), cowboys are rounding up wild mustang horses to sell for dog food, and some amazing scenes were filmed with the camera mounted on a pickup truck chasing fast-running horses. The motion in these scenes is overwhelming because Huston combines two kinds of rapid motion—of trucks and horses. Moreover, the motion is further increased because of the narrow focus of the camera and the limited boundary of the screen. The recorded action excludes vision that might tend to distract or dilute the motion we are permitted to see. Much the same effect was achieved in the buffalo run in *Dances with Wolves* thirty years later. The screen in motion pictures always constrains our vision, even when we imagine the space beyond the screen that we do not see, as when a character moves off the filmed space. Eliminating the space beyond the images recorded by the camera circumscribes and fixes our attention. And such attention is bound to enhance the rapidity and intensity of the moving images.

A final basic way film can achieve motion is by means of the camera lens. Even when the camera is fixed in place, a lens that affords a much wider, narrower, larger, or smaller field of vision than the eye normally supplies will give the illusion of motion, since we instinctively feel the urge to be in the physical position that would supply that field of vision. Zoom lenses which change their focal length along a smooth range—thus bringing images gradually closer or farther away—are even more effective for suggesting motion, especially for small-screen viewing of movies on television. One of the favorite shots on television is that of a figure walking or moving in some fashion, which looks, at first, as if it were a medium shot but which is actually revealed as a long shot when the zoom is reversed. Since our own eye cannot imitate the action of the zoom lens, the effect the lens has can be quite dramatic when used creatively. It is something like the effect that slow motion or stop motion has on us. It interrupts our perceptions of something—something that had seemed perfectly natural—in a way that makes us aware of the film medium itself. On the other hand, with many people experimenting with 8X zooms on video cameras, it is clear that zoom shots are quick to become very tedious.

Sometimes technique can "take over" a film by becoming the most interesting aspect of the cinematic experience. The Academy Award winner, *2001: A Space Odyssey* (1968, Figure 11-6), *Star Wars* (1977), *Close Encounters of the Third Kind* (1977), and the seven Star Trek films of the 1970s

Perception Key
CAMERA VISION

Make a mask with two small cutout rectangles, approximately ⅜ inch long × ½ inch wide, as shown:

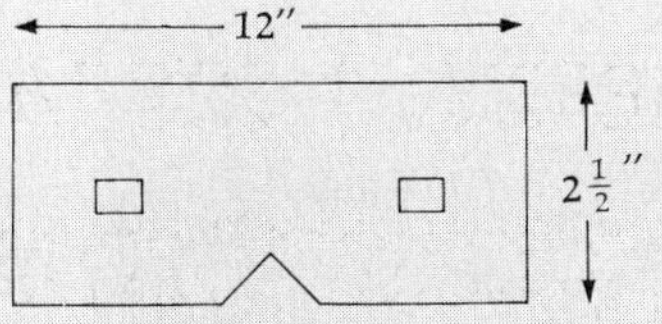

Place the mask so that you can see only out of the slits. This experiment can be conducted almost as effectively by using simple pinholes in place of cutout rectangles. In fact, for those who wear glasses it may be more effective, because the pinholes are actually "lenses" and may permit some people with defective vision to see fairly clearly without their glasses.

1. Does the "framing" of the cutouts make you unusually sensitive to the way things look?
2. What effect does moving your head have on the composition of the things you see?
3. What are some of the differences between using one eye, then both eyes? Which is more the way the camera sees? What do you learn from viewing a scene first with one eye, then the other?
4. An important feature of this experiment is the analogy with the motion of the camera. Be sure you get a sense of what happens to your visual field when you move your head in the fashion a camera would move. Are you capable of any motion that is impossible for the camera?
5. If the camera is the principal tool of filmmaking, do directors give up artistic control when they have photographers operate the machines? Does your experimenting in the questions above suggest there may be a camera "language" that directors should be controlling themselves? Given your experience with film and cameras, how might camera "language" be defined?

FIGURE 11-6
From Stanley Kubrik's MGM release *2001: A Space Odyssey*. Dr. Floyd (William Sylvester), one of the scientists from the Clavius moon base, descends the ramp into the TMAi excavation and, for the first time, the visiting scientist from earth has a close look at the strange object, which has been hidden beneath the lunar surface for millions of years. (© 1968 Turner Entertainment Company. All rights reserved)

FIGURE 11-7
Star Wars. (Lucasfilm/20th Century Fox/The Kobol Collection)

and 1980s have similar themes, concentrating on space, the future, and fantastic situations. All include shots of marvelous technical achievements, such as the images of the computer-guided cameras that follow the space vehicles of Luke Skywalker and Hans Solo in the dramatic conclusion of *Star Wars* (Figure 11-7). But some critics have argued that these technical achievements were ends rather than means to artistic revelation.

PERCEPTION KEY
TECHNIQUE AND FILM

1. Are the technical triumphs of films such as *Star Wars* used as means or ends? If they are the ends, then are they the subject matter? What kind of problem does such a possibility raise for our appreciation of the film?
2. In *Tom Jones* (1963) a technique called the "double take" was introduced. After searching for his wallet everywhere, Tom turns and looks at the audience and asks whether we have seen his wallet. Is this technique a gimmick, or artistically justifiable? Why could you make a defensible judgment about this without seeing the film?
3. Recently old black-and-white films have been "colorized," a technique espoused by Ted Turner. In the case of *It's a Wonderful Life,* James Stewart protested vigorously before a congressional committee, and Frank Capra, the director, issued a passionate sickbed plea. Do you agree with Turner or Stewart and Capra? Why? Try to see a colorized version of *Casablanca* and compare it with the original. Which do you prefer? Why?

AUDIENCE RESPONSE IN FILM

Because it is so easy to shoot a scene in various ways, a good director is constantly choosing the shot that he or she hopes has the most meaning within the total structure. When Luis Buñuel briefly shows us the razoring of a woman's open eyeball in *Un Chien Andalou* (1928) (it is really a slaughtered cow's eyeball), he is counting on our personal horror at actually seeing such an act, but the scene is artistically justifiable because Buñuel carefully integrated the scene into the total structure of the film. Unfortunately, many films show sheer violence without any attempt to inform—for example, *Halloween* (1979); *Friday the 13th* (1979) and its many sequels; and *Nightmare on Elm Street* (1985) and its many sequels. The violence is used strictly for shock value, but it is so overdone that the audience is rarely moved by it. A curious phenomenon about experiencing film as well as drama is that the imagination of the audience is often a much more reliable instrument for the interpretation of horror than the fully realized visual scene.

Clever directors can easily shock responses from their audiences. But the more complex responses, some of which are as difficult to control as they are to attain, are the aim of the enduring filmmakers. When Ingmar Bergman shows us the rape scene in *The Virgin Spring* (1959), he does not saturate us with horror. And the murder of the rapists by the girl's father is preceded by an elaborate purification ritual that relates the violence and horror to profound meaning. In any art, control of audience response is vital. We can become emotionally saturated just as easily as we can become bored. The result is indifference.

SOUND

Al Jolson's *Jazz Singer* (1927) introduced sound, although it was not welcomed by everyone. Sergei Eisenstein feared, as did many others, that sound might kill the artistic integrity of film. He was afraid that with sound no one would work with the images that create a film language, and that film would once again become subservient to drama. Eisenstein knew that images in motion could sustain the kind of dramatic tension that was once thought limited to the dramatic stage. This is a point of consummate importance. First of all, a film is images in motion. Great filmmakers may exploit sound and other elements, but they will never make them the basic ingredients of the film. On the other hand, some filmmakers will rely on the dialogue of the film almost exclusively, using the camera to do little more than visually record people talking to one another.

Sound in film may involve much more than the addition of dialogue to the visual track. Music had long been a supplement of the silent films, and special portfolios of piano and organ music were available to the accompanist who played in the local theater while coordinating the music with

FIGURE 11-8
Religious services held in the field while a tank flamethrower destroys crops in the background in *Apocalypse Now*. (© 1979 United Artists Corp. Museum of Modern Art Film Stills Archive)

the film. They indicated the kind of feelings that could be produced by merging special music with chase, love, or suspense scenes. D. W. Griffith's *Birth of a Nation* (1916) features a "rescue" charge by the Ku Klux Klan, which was cut to the dynamics of Richard Wagner's *Die Walküre*. Francis Ford Coppola may have had that in mind when he made the incredible helicopter battle scene in *Apocalypse Now* (1979, Figure 11-8) to Wagner's "Ride of the Valkyries." *Apocalypse Now,* a film about the Vietnam war, used sound in exceptionally effective ways, especially in scenes such as the skyrocket fireworks battle deep in the jungle.

Sound may intensify our experience of film. Not only do we expect to hear dialogue, but we also expect to hear the sounds we associate with the action on screen, whether it is the quiet chirping of crickets in a country scene in *Sounder* (1972) or the dropping of bombs from a low-flying Japanese Zero in *Empire of the Sun* (1987). Subtle uses of sound sometimes prepare us for action that is yet to come, such as when in *Rain Man* (1989) we see Dustin Hoffman and Tom Cruise walking toward a convertible, but we hear the dialogue and road sounds from the next shot, when they are driving down the highway. That editing technique might have been very unsettling in the 1930s, but filmmakers have had sixty years to get our sensibilities accustomed to such disjunctions.

A very famous disjunction occurs in the beginning of *2001: A Space Odyssey* when, watching images of one tribe of apes warring with another tribe of apes in prehistoric times, we hear the rich modern harmonies of Richard Strauss's dramatic tone poem *Also Sprach Zarathustra*. The music suggests one very sophisticated mode of development inherent in the future of these primates—whom we see in the first phases of discovering how to use tools. They already show potential for creating high art. Eventually the sound and imagery coincide when the scene changes to 2001, with scientists on the moon discovering a monolithic structure identical to one the apes had found on earth.

PERCEPTION KEY
SIGHT AND SOUND

1. Analyze carefully the next film you see on television. Examine the frames for their power as individual compositions, recalling some of the points made in the chapters on painting and sculpture. How strong is the film in this respect?
2. Do the size and shape of the television screen inhibit intense visual experience? Is your participation with film stronger with television or in the theater? Why?
3. Turn off the sound entirely. Can you follow clearly what is going on? Is much of importance lost?
4. Block out the video portion of the program and listen to the sound only. Can you follow clearly what is going on? Is much of importance lost? When you come right down to it, you may find that in all but the more impressive films not terribly much is lost when the images are eliminated.

IMAGE AND ACTION

These experiments probably indicate that most contemporary film is a marriage of sight and sound. Yet we must not forget that film is a medium in which the moving image—the action—is preeminent, such as in Federico Fellini's *8½* (1963). The title refers to Fellini's own career, ostensibly about himself and his making a new film after seven and a half previous films. *8½* is about the artistic process. Guido, played by Marcello Mastroianni (Figure 11-3), brings a group of people to a location to make a film. But from the first shot of his having a nervous breakdown in a car in heavy Rome traffic, crosscut with the helicoptered statue of Christ, the action points inward, to Guido's mind. His worldlessness combined with the claustrophobia produced by the intense sound reveals something of his inner state.

What follows centers on Guido's loss of creative direction, his psychological problems related to religion, sex, and his need to dominate women. As he convalesces from his breakdown, he brings people together to make a film, but he has no clear sense of what he wants to do, no coherent story to tell. *8½* seems to mimic Fellini's situation so carefully that it is difficult to know whether Fellini planned out the film or not. He has said "I appeared to have it all worked out in my head, but it was not like that. For three months I continued working on the basis of a complete production, in the hope that meanwhile my ideas would sort themselves out. Fifty times I nearly gave up."[1] And yet, most of the film is described in a single letter

[1]John Kobal, *The Top 100 Movies,* New American Library, New York, 1988.

to Brunello Rondi (a writer of the screenplay), written long before the start of production.

The film is episodic, with memorable dream and nightmare sequences, some of which are almost hallucinatory. Such scenes focus on the inward quest of the film: Guido's search for the source of his creative block so that he can resolve it. By putting himself in the center of an artistic tempest, he mirrors his own psychological confusion in order to bring it under control. Indeed, he seems intent on creating artistic tension by bringing both his wife and mistress to the film's location.

The film abandons continuous narrative structure in favor of episodic streams of consciousness in the sequences that reveal the inner workings of Guido's mind. In a way they may also reveal the inner workings of the creative mind if we assume that Fellini projected his own anxieties into the film. *8½* seems revelatory of the psychic turmoil of creativity.

FILM STRUCTURE

Michael Cimino's portrayal of three hometown men who fight together in Vietnam, *The Deer Hunter* (1979, Figure 11-9), has serious structural problems because the film takes place in three radically different environments, and it is not always clear how they are related. Yet it won several Academy Awards and has been proclaimed one of the great antiwar films. Cimino took great risks by dividing the film into three large sections: sequences of life in Clairton, Pennsylvania, with a Russian Orthodox wedding and a last hunting expedition for deer; sequences of war prisoners and fighting in Vietnam; sequences afterward in Clairton, where only one of the three men,

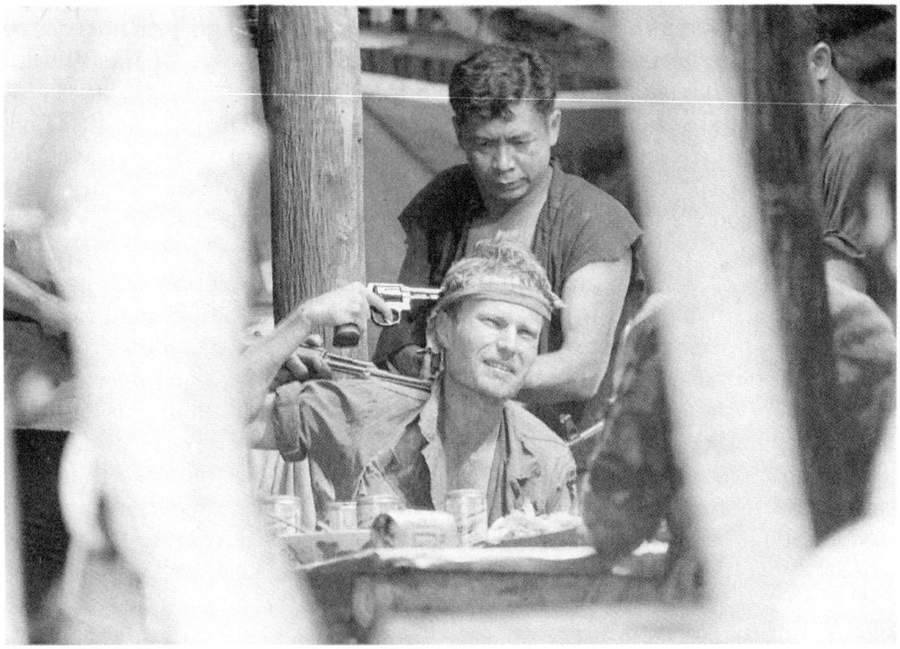

FIGURE 11-9
John Savage in a scene from *The Deer Hunter*. (EMI/Columbia/Warners/ The Kobol Collection)

FIGURE 11-10
Susan Sarandon and Geena Davis in *Thelma & Louise*. (MGM/Pathe/The Kobol Collection)

Mike, played by Robert DeNiro, is able to live effectively. Mike finally sets out to get Steven to return from the wheelchair ward of the VA hospital to his wife. Then he sets out to find his best friend, Nick, a heroin addict still in Saigon, playing Russian roulette for hardened Vietnamese gamblers. Russian roulette was not an actual part of the Vietnam experience, but Cimino made it a metaphor for the senselessness of war.

Cimino relied in part on the model of Dante's *Divine Comedy,* also divided into three sections—Hell, Purgatory, and Paradise. In *The Deer Hunter* the rivers of molten metal in the steel mills and, more obviously, the war scenes suggest the ghastliness of Hell. The extensive and ecstatic scenes in the Russian Orthodox church suggest Paradise, while life in Clairton represents an in-between, a kind of Purgatory. In one of the most stirring episodes, when he is back in Saigon during the American evacuation looking for Nick, Mike is shown standing up in a small boat negotiating his way through the canals. The scene is a visual echo of Eugene Delacroix's *Dante and Virgil in Hell,* a nineteenth-century painting. For anyone who recognizes the allusion to Dante, Cimino's structural techniques become clearer, as do his views of war in general and of the Vietnam war in particular.

The function of photography in films such as *8½* and *The Deer Hunter* is sometimes difficult to assess. If we agree that the power of the moving image is central to the ultimate meaning of the motion picture, we can see that the most important structural qualities of any good film develop from the choices made in the editing stage. Sometimes different versions of a single action will be filmed, the editor and the director deciding which will be in the final mix after testing each version in relation to the overall structure.

The episodic structure of Ridley Scott's *Thelma and Louise* (1991, Figure 11-10) lends itself to contrasting the interiors of a seamy Arkansas nightclub and a cheap motel with the magnificent open road and dramatic landscape of the Southwest. Louise, played by Susan Sarandon, and Thelma, played by Geena Davis, are on the run in Louise's 1956 Thunderbird convertible after Louise shoots and kills Harlan, who has attempted to rape Thelma. Knowing their story will not be believed, they head for Mexico and freedom, but never get there. Callie Khouri wrote the script for this feminist film, casting women as deeply sympathetic outcasts and desperadoes—roles traditionally reserved for men. In one memorable scene, a truck driver hauling a gasoline rig makes lecherous faces at the women and generally harasses them. The cross-cutting builds considerable tension which is relieved, at first, when the women pull over as if they were interested in him. As the driver leaves his truck to walk toward them, they shoot his rig and it explodes like an inferno. The editing in this film is quite conventional, but everyone who has seen it remembers this scene, whose power depends on the use of montage.

The editor's work gives meaning to the film just as surely as the scriptwriter's and the photographer's. Observe, for instance, the final scenes in Eisenstein's *Potemkin* (1925). The battleship *Potemkin* is steaming to a confrontation with the fleet. Eisenstein rapidly cuts from inside the ship to outside: showing a view of powerfully moving engine pistons, then the ship cutting deeply into the water, then rapidly back and forth, showing occasional anxiety-ridden faces, all designed to raise the emotional pitch of anyone watching the movie. This kind of cutting or montage was used by Alfred Hitchcock in the shower murder scene of the 1960 horror thriller *Psycho*. He demonstrated that the technique could be used to increase tension and terror, even though no explicit murderous actions were shown on screen. Ironically, the scene was so powerful that its star, Janet Leigh, avoids showers as much as possible, always preferring the bath.

CONTENT

We cannot completely translate filmic meaning into language, any more than we can completely translate any artistic meaning into language. We can only approximate a "translation" by describing the connections—emotional, narrative, or whatever—implied by the sequence of images. When we watch the overturning coffin in Bergman's *Wild Strawberries* (1957), for example, we are surprised to find that the figure in the coffin has the same face as Professor Borg, the protagonist, who is himself a witness to what we see. Borg is face to face with his own death. That this scene has a meaningful content is clear, yet we cannot completely articulate this scene into language. The meaning is embodied in the moving images. Moreover, this scene and others like it achieve full meaning only in relation to other dramatic moments in the film. The scene has a strong tension and impact, and yet it is apparent that the full meaning depends on the context of the whole film in which it appears. The relation of part to structure exists in every art, of course, but that relation in its nuances often may more easily be missed in our experiences of the film. For one thing, we are not accustomed to permitting images to build their own meanings apart from the meanings we already associate with them. Second, we do not always observe the way one movement or gesture will mean one thing in one context and an entirely different thing in another context. Third, moving images generally are more difficult to remember than still images, as in painting, and thus it is more difficult to become aware of their connections.

The filmmaker is the master controller of contexts, just as the dramatist is. In Eric Rohmer's film *Claire's Knee* (1970), a totally absurd gesture, the caressing of an indifferent and relatively insensitive young woman's knee, becomes the fundamental focus of the film. This gesture is loaded with meaning throughout the entire film, but loaded only for the main masculine character and us. The young woman is unaware that her knee holds such power over the man. Although the gesture is absurd, in a way it is plausible, for such fixations can occur to anyone. But this film is not concerned solely with plausibility; it is mainly concerned with the gesture in a context that reveals what is unclear in real-life experience—the complexities of some kinds of obsessions. And this is done primarily through skillful photography and editing rather than through a spoken narrative.

PERCEPTION KEY
CONTEXTS

1. Examine the next film you watch for its power to give meaning to gesture through the contexts which are established for it. If certain gestures are repeated, do they accumulate greater meaning? Do they achieve different meaning?
2. To what extent do the gestures in this film tie the images together, making them coherent?
3. Compare the gestures in film with the gestures of sculpture. How do they differ? Do you see film sometimes "borrowing" familiar gestures, such as the posture of Michelangelo's *David?*
4. To what extent is the film you have watched meaningful because of its relationship to the world we inhabit?

THE CONTEXT OF FILM HISTORY

All meanings, linguistic or nonlinguistic, are within some kind of context. Most first-rate films exist in many contexts simultaneously, and it is our job as sensitive viewers to be able to decide which are the most important. Film, like every art, has a history, and this history is one of the more significant contexts in which every film takes place. In order to make that historical context fruitful in our filmic experiences, we must do more than just read about that history. We must accumulate a historical sense of film by seeing films that have been important in the development of the medium. Most of us have a very rich personal backlog in film; we have seen a great many films, some of which are memorable and many of which have been influenced by landmark films.

Furthermore, film exists in a context that is meaningful for the life work of a director and, in turn, for us. When we talk about the films of Orson Welles, Ingmar Bergman, or Federico Fellini, we are talking about the achievements of artists just as much as when we talk about the paintings of Rembrandt or Van Gogh. Today we watch carefully for films by Francis Ford Coppola, Michelangelo Antonioni, Michael Cimino, Woody Allen, Robert Altman, Martin Scorsese, Spike Lee, Jane Campion, Quentin Tarantino, and Lina Wertmuller—to name only a few of the most active current directors—because their work has shown a steady development and because they, in relation to the history of the film, have shown themselves in possession of a vision that is transforming the medium. In other words, they are altering the history of film in significant ways. In turn, we should be interested in knowing what they are doing because they are providing new contexts for increasing our understanding of film.

But these are only a few contexts in which films exist. Every film exists in a social context, in relation to the social system it springs from and portrays or idealizes or criticizes. We do not usually judge films specifically on the basis of their ability to make social comment, but if we lived in China we would probably judge a film on the basis of its ability to make a positive contribution to the building of a new society. Obviously, the context of the society would then outweigh the context of internal parts: the relation of detail to part to structure.

Our concerns in this book have not been exclusively with one or another kind of context, although we have assumed that the internal context of a work of art is necessarily of first importance to begin with. But no work can be properly understood without resorting to some external contextual examination. A visual image, a contemporary gesture, even a colloquial expression will sometimes show up in a film and need explication in order to be fully understood. Just as we sometimes have to look up a word in a dictionary—which exists outside a poem, for instance—we sometimes have to look outside a film for explanations. Even Terence Young's James Bond thriller movies need such explication, although we rarely think about that. If we failed to understand the political assumptions underlying such films, we would not fully understand what was going on.

FRANCIS FORD COPPOLA'S *THE GODFATHER*

Coppola's *The Godfather* (Figures 11-11 to 11-14), produced in 1971, was based on Mario Puzo's novel about an Italian immigrant fleeing from Sicilian Mafia violence who eventually grew to be a Don of a huge crime family in New York City. The film details the gradual involvement of Michael Corleone, played by Al Pacino, in his father's criminal activities during the years from 1945 to 1959. His father Vito, played by Marlon Brando, suffers the loss of Sonny, an older son, and barely survives an assassination attempt. As Michael becomes more and more a central figure in his family's "business," he grows more frightening and more alienated from those around him until, as Godfather, he becomes, it seems, totally evil.

Although some critics complained that the film glorified the Mafia, almost all have praised its technical mastery. A sequel, *Godfather II,* was produced in 1974, and while not as tightly constructed as the first film, it

FIGURE 11-11
Johnny sings to the bride in the wedding sequence in *The Godfather*. (© 1972 Paramount Pictures Corporation. Museum of Modern Art Film Stills Archive)

FIGURE 11-12
Sonny (James Caan) is riddled with bullets at the toll booth in *The Godfather*. (© 1972 Paramount Pictures Corporation/ Photofest)

FIGURE 11-13
Don Vito Corleone, the Godfather (Marlon Brando), confers with a wedding guest who requests an important favor in *The Godfather*. (© 1972 Paramount Pictures Corporation/Photofest)

fleshes out the experience of Vito as he slowly developed into a criminal. Both films center on the ambiguities involved in the conversion of the poverty-ridden Vito into a wealthy and successful gangster.

The Godfather both engages our sympathy with Michael and yet increasingly horrifies us with many of his actions. We admire Michael's personal valor, and his respect for father, family, and friends. But we also see the corruption and violence that are the bases of his power. Inevitably, we have to work out for ourselves the ambiguities that Coppola sets out.

THE NARRATIVE STRUCTURE OF *THE GODFATHER*

The narrative structure of most films supplies the framework on which the filmmaker builds the artistry of the imagery, shots, sound, and editing. An overemphasis on the artistry, however, can distract a viewer from the narrative, whereas a great film avoids allowing technique to dominate a story. Such is the case with *The Godfather,* we believe, because the artistry produces a cinematic lushness that helps tell the story.

The film begins with Michael Corleone, as a returning war hero in 1945, refusing to be part of his father's criminal empire. The immediate family enjoys the spoils of criminal life—big cars, a large house in a guarded compound, family celebrations, and lavish weddings. Although Michael's brothers are active members of the crime family, they respect his wishes to remain apart.

In a dispute over whether to add drug-running to the "business" of gambling, prostitution, extortion, and labor racketeering, Vito is gunned down, but not killed. Michael comes to the aid of his father and so begins his career in the Mafia. It takes him only a short time to rise to the position of Godfather when Vito is too infirm to continue. When he marries Kay, played by Diane Keaton, Michael explains that the family will be totally legitimate in five years. She believes him, but the audience already knows better. It is no surprise that seven years later, the family is more powerful and ruthless than ever.

In a disturbing and deeply ironic sequence, Michael acts as godfather in the church baptism of his nephew, while at the same time his lieutenants are murdering the heads of the five rival crime families. Coppola jump cuts back and forth from shots of Michael in the church promising to renounce the work of the devil to shots of his men turning the streets of New York into a bloodbath. This perversion of the sacrament of baptism illustrates the depths to which Michael has sunk.

As the family grows in power, Michael moves to Tahoe, gaining control of casino gambling in Nevada. He corrupts the governor, who even while demanding kickbacks expresses contempt for Italians. However, when the governor is compromised by killing a prostitute, he cooperates fully with the Corleones. The point is made again and again that without such corrupt officials, the Mafia would be significantly less powerful.

As the film draws to a close, Michael survives an assassination attempt made possible by his brother Fredo's ignorant collusion with another gangster who is Michael's nemesis. At first he does nothing but refuse to talk to Fredo, but when their mother dies, Michael has Fredo murdered. Meanwhile, Kay has left him, and those who were close to him, except his step-

FIGURE 11-14
Michael Corleone, with his father dead, is now the Godfather, reflecting on the world he has created for himself. (© 1972 Paramount Pictures Corporation/The Kobol Collection)

brother Tom Hagen (Robert Duvall), have been driven away or murdered. The last images we have of Michael show him alone in his compound staring into a darkened room. We see how far he has fallen since his early idealism.

COPPOLA'S IMAGES

Coppola chooses his frames with great care, and many would make an interesting still photograph. He balances his figures carefully, especially in the quieter scenes, subtly using asymmetry to accent movement, and sometimes using harsh lighting that radiates from the center of the shot, focusing attention and creating tension. He rarely cuts rapidly from one shot to another but depends on conventional establishing shots—such as showing a car arriving at a church, a hospital, a home—before showing us shots of their interiors. This conventionality intensifies our sense of the period of the 1940s and 1950s, since most films of that period relied on just such techniques.

Darkness dominates, and interiors often have a tunnellike quality, suggesting passages to the underworld. Rooms in which Michael and others conduct their business usually have only one source of light, and the resulting high contrast is disorienting. Bright outdoor scenes are often marked by barren snow, or winds driving fallen leaves. The seasons of fall and winter predominate, suggesting loneliness and death.

COPPOLA'S USE OF SOUND

The music in *The Godfather* helps Coppola evoke the mood of the time the film covers. Coppola used his own father, Carmine Coppola, as a composer of some of the music. There are some snatches of Italian hill music from small villages near Amalfi, but sentimental dance music from the "big band" period of the 1940s and 1950s predominates.

An ingenious and effective use of sound occurs in the baptism/murder scene discussed earlier. Coppola keeps the sounds of the church scene—the priest reciting the Latin liturgy, the organ music, the baby crying—on the soundtrack even when he cuts to the murders being carried out. This accomplishes two important functions—it reinforces the idea that these two scenes are actually occurring simultaneously, and it underscores the hypocrisy of Michael's pious behavior in church. Because such techniques are used sparingly, this instance works with great power.

THE POWER OF *THE GODFATHER*

Those critics who felt the film glorified the Mafia seem not to have taken into account the fated quality of Michael. He begins like Oedipus: running away from his fate. He does not want to join the Mafia, but when his father is almost killed, his instincts push him toward assuming the role of Godfather. The process of self-destruction consumes him as if it were completely out of his control. Moreover, despite their power and wealth, Michael and the Corleones seem to have a good time only at weddings, and even then the Godfather is doing business in the back room. Everyone in the family suffers. No one can come and go in freedom—everyone lives in an armed camp. All the elements of the film reinforce that view. The houses are opulent, but vulnerable to machine guns. The cars are expensive, but they blow up. Surely such a life is not a glory.

In shaping the film in a way that helps us see Mafia life as neither glamorous nor desirable, Coppola forces us to examine our popular culture—one that seems often to venerate criminals like Bonnie and Clyde, Jesse James, Billy the Kid, and John Dillinger. At the same time Coppola's refusal to treat his characters as simply loathsome, his acknowledgment that they are in some sense victims as well as victimizers, creates an ambiguity that makes his film an impressive achievement.

EXPERIMENTATION

Because of the complex technical problems involved in filmmaking, much experimentation has occurred. Many of the early filmmakers, such as D. W. Griffith, had technical training and interests, helping to account for this experimentation. Today the experimental work is less technical, perhaps, and more a trying out of the technical advances. For example, Andy Warhol, originally a painter and sculptor, did some interesting work in raising questions about film, especially about the limits of realism. Realism is often praised in films. But when Andy Warhol puts a figure in front of a camera to sleep for a full eight hours, we get the message: we want a transformation of reality that gives us insight into reality, not reality itself. The difference is important because it is the difference between reality and art. We all have reality in front of us most of the time. We have art much less frequently. Realistic art is a selection of elements that convey the illusion of reality. When we see Warhol's almost direct transcription of reality on film, we understand that selecting—through directing and editing—is crucial to film art. The power of most striking films is often their ability to condense experience, to take a year, for example, and portray its most intense ninety minutes. This condensation is what Marcel Proust, one of the greatest of novelists, expected from the novel:

> Every emotion is multiplied ten-fold, into which this book comes to disturb us as might a dream, but a dream more lucid, and of a more lasting impression, than those which come to us in sleep; why, then, for a space of an hour he sets free within us all the joys and sorrows in the world, a few of which, only, we should have to spend years of our actual life in getting to know, and the keenest, the most intense of which would never have been revealed to us because the slow course of their development stops our perception of them. It is the same in life; the heart changes . . . but we learn of it only from reading or by imagination; for

in reality its alteration . . . is so gradual that . . . we are still spared the actual sensation of change.[2]

Some interesting modern films address the question of the creation of reality. Antonioni's *Blow Up* (1966), for example, had the thread of a narrative holding it together: a possible murder and the efforts of a magazine photographer, through the medium of his own enlargements, to confirm the reality of that murder. But anyone who saw the film would know that the continuity of the narrative was not the most important part of the film. The basic content came out of what were essentially disconnected "moments": a party, some antiquing while driving around London in a convertible Rolls-Royce, and some unusual tennis played without a ball. What seemed most important was the role of the film itself in creating certain "realities." In a sense the murder was a reality only after the film uncovered it. Is it possible that Antonioni is saying something similar about the reality that surrounds the very film he is creating? There is a reality, but where? Is *Blow Up* more concerned with the film images as reality than it is with reality outside the film? If you have a chance to see this film, be sure you ask that puzzling question.

Some more extreme experimenters remove the narrative entirely and simply present successions of images, almost in the manner of a nightmare or a drug experience. Sometimes the images are abstract, nothing more than visual patterns, as with abstract painting. Some use familiar images, but modify them with unexpected time-lapse photography and distortions of color and sound. Among the more successful films of this kind are *Koyaanisqatsi* (1983) and *Brooklyn Bridge* (1994). The fact that we have very little abstract film may have several explanations. Part of the power of abstract painting seems to depend on its "all-at-onceness" (see Chapter 4), precisely what is missing from film. Another reason may be tied in, again, with the popular nature of the medium: masses of people do not prefer abstraction.

The public generally is convinced that film, like drama and literature, must have characters, themes, and narrative lines. Thus even filmic cartoons are rarely abstract, although they are not photographs but drawings. Such animated films as *Pinnochio* (1940), *Dumbo* (1941), and *Fantasia* (1940) have yielded to enormously successful contemporary films such as *The Yellow Submarine* (1968), *Beauty and the Beast* (1993), *The Lion King* (1994), *Toy Story* (1995), and *Pocahontas* (1995). It may be unreasonable to consider animated films as experimental, and it is certainly unreasonable to think of them as children's films, since adult audiences have made them successful. What they seem to offer an audience is a realistic approach to fantasy that has all the elements of the traditional narrative film. This may also be true of animated films using clay figures and puppets for actors. These have had a narrower audience than cartoon and computer animations and have been restricted to film festivals, which is where most experimental films have been seen.

[2]Marcel Proust, *Swann's Way,* C. K. Scott Moncrieff (trans.), The Modern Library, Random House, New York, 1928, p. 119.

Perception Key
MAKE A FILM

The easy availability of video recorders makes it possible to suggest that you make a film (actually a video). On the other hand, you may also have access to an 8mm film camera and projector. In either case, be sure to create your shots after you have made a storyboard. Then, when you review your shots, try experiments with editing. For a video camera this may involve rerecording on a VCR and reorganizing your visual material to take advantage of various shot techniques and various editing techniques.

1. Take the opportunity of making a film seriously. Emulate the role of the director, and experiment with your role as editor. Try to invent ways to give a meaningful unity to the succession of images you photograph. You may even wish to substitute another organizing principle for the usual one of narrative. For example, take a musical composition that is especially interesting to you, and then fuse moving images with the music.
2. Assuming you do not want to abandon narrative as an organizing principle, try to use narrative "lines" that you do not usually find in films. We all know the formulas for a western, for instance. Can you free yourself from such formulas and invent a different kind of narrative?
3. Short of making a film, try some editing by finding and clipping from twenty to thirty "stills" from magazines, brochures, newspapers, or other sources. Choose stills or frames you believe may have some coherence, and then arrange them in such a way as to make a meaningful sequence. How is your sequence affected by rearrangement? This project will be much more interesting if you use or make slides for viewing. Then add a "soundtrack" to heighten interest and to clarify the meaning of the sequence. While projecting the slides you might videotape them, then add the sound in order to produce a more convincing sequence.

SUMMARY

The making of film is exceptionally complex because of the necessary and often difficult collaboration required among many people, especially the director, scriptwriter, actors, photographer, and editor. The range of possible subject matters is exceptionally extensive for film. The resources of the director in choosing shots and the imagination of the editor in joining shots and images provide the primary artistic control over the material. Such choices translate into evoking emotional responses from the audience. The point of view that can be achieved with the camera is similar to that of the unaided human eye, but because of technical refinements, such as the wide-angle and zoom lens and moving and multiple cameras, the dramatic effect of vision can be intensified. Because it is usually easy to block out everything irrelevant to the film in a dark theater, our participative experiences with film tend to be especially intense. The temptation to identify with a given actor or situation in a film may distort the participative experience by blocking our perception of the form of the film, and thus missing the content. The combination of sound, both dialogue and music (or sound effects), with the moving image helps engage our participation. The film is the most modern and popular of our arts.

CHAPTER 11 BIBLIOGRAPHY

Allen, Robert C. *Film History: Theory and Practice.* New York: Random House, 1985.

Andrew, Dudley. *Concepts of Film Theory.* New York: Oxford University Press, 1984.

Arnheim, Rudolf. *Film as Art.* London: Faber and Faber, 1983.

Barthes, Roland. *The Semiotic Challenge.* New York: Hill and Wang, 1988.

Bazin, André. *What Is Cinema?* Berkeley: University of California Press, 1974.

Bobker, Lee R. *Elements of Film,* 3d ed. New York: Harcourt Brace Jovanovich, 1981.

Bordwell, David. *Narration in the Fiction Film.* Madison: University of Wisconsin Press, 1985.

———, and Kristin Thompson. *Film Art: An Introduction,* 4th ed. New York: Knopf, 1993.

Branigan, Edward. *Point of View in the Cinema.* Berlin: Mouton, 1984.

Braudy, Leo. *The World in a Frame.* Garden City, N.Y.: Doubleday, 1976.

Cavell, Stanley. *World Viewed.* Cambridge, Mass.: Harvard University Press, 1979.

Dick, Bernard. *Anatomy of Film.* New York: St. Martin's Press, 1978.

Eisenstein, Sergei. *Film Form and Film Sense.* Jay Leyda (trans.). New York: Harcourt Brace Jovanovich, n.d.

Giannetti, Louis. *Understanding Movies,* 7th ed. Upper Saddle River, N.J.: Prentice Hall, 1996.

Huss, Roy, and Norman Silverstein. *The Film Experience.* New York: Dell, 1969.

Jacobs, Diane. *Hollywood Renaissance: The New Generation of Filmmakers and Their Works.* New York: Dell, 1980.

Jacobs, Lewis. *The Emergence of Film Art,* 2d ed. New York: W. W. Norton, 1979.

Jameson, Fredric. *Signatures of the Visible.* New York: Routledge, 1992.

Kracauer, Siegfried. *Theory of Film.* New York: Oxford University Press, 1960.

Lehman, Peter (ed.). *Close Viewings: An Anthology of New Film Criticism.* Tallahassee: Florida State University Press, 1990.

Lindgren, Ernest. *The Art of the Film.* London: Allen & Unwin, 1963.

Mast, Gerald. *Film/Cinema/Movie: A Theory of Experience.* New York: Harper & Row, 1977.

———, and Marshall Cohen (eds.). *Film Theory and Criticism,* 4th ed. New York: Oxford University Press, 1992.

Monaco, James. *How to Read a Film.* New York: Oxford University Press, 1981.

Nichols, Bill (ed.). *Movies and Methods.* 2 vols. Berkeley: University of California Press, 1976 and 1985.

Pudovkin, V. I. *Film Technique and Film Acting,* I. Montagu (ed. and trans.). New York: Grove Press, 1960.

Rothman, William. *The "I" of the Camera: Essays in Film Criticism, History, and Aesthetics.* New York: Cambridge University Press, 1989.

Stephenson, Ralph, and J. R. Debrix. *The Cinema as Art,* rev. ed. London: Penguin Books, 1989.

Weis, Elizabeth, and John Belton (eds.). *Film Sound: Theory and Practice.* New York: Columbia University Press, 1985.

Weiss, Paul. *Cinematics.* Carbondale: Southern Illinois University Press, 1975.

Note: Some distributors of films for classroom use are Audio-Brandon, 34 MacQuesten Parkway South, Mount Vernon, NY 10550; Contemporary/McGraw-Hill, Princeton Road, Hightstown, NJ 08520; Janus Films, 745 Fifth Avenue, New York, NY 10022; United Artists 16, 729 Seventh Avenue, New York, NY 10019; Universal 16, 445 Park Avenue, New York, NY 10003; and Warner Brothers, Inc., Non-Theatrical Division, 4000 Warner Boulevard, Burbank, CA 91522.

CHAPTER 11 WEBSITES

Film Database (large database filled with information about film)

World Wide Web: **http://www.cm.cf.ac.uk/Movies/moviequery.html**

General Information about Film (film and video reviews and information)

World Wide Web: **http://www.ivg.com/~marb**

MPEG Films (huge collection of short movie excerpts)

World Wide Web: **http://www.c.ucl.ac.uk/movies/**

The National Museum of Photography, Film & Television (material from England)

World Wide Web: **http://www.nmsi.ac.uk/nmpft/**

Previews (movie previews, posters, and information)

World Wide Web: **http://movieweb.com/movie/**

CHAPTER 12

PHOTOGRAPHY

THE CAMERA BEFORE PHOTOGRAPHY

Before the invention of film and light-sensitive paper, Renaissance painters sometimes used a camera obscura (see Figure 12-1) to help achieve realistic representations of space and depth. The camera obscura was a large box with a lens to control light, and a ground glass at the back on which the image could be traced. Louis J. M. Daguerre (1789–1851) invented the first practical system for producing permanent photographic prints in 1839. Daguerre had originally used a camera obscura to help him paint gigantic backdrops for opera, which in turn led him to experiment with photography.

In addition to its capacity to produce accurate perspective and great detail, the camera lens "crops" (or restricts) the visual field before it, especially with portraits. When the photograph became widely available in the 1840s and 1850s the images printed on paper were in black-and-white or sepia (brown-and-white). Daguerreotype images were direct silver positives on metal, which when looked at from one direction revealed a negative image. Monochrome images transform their subject in complex ways, but modern color prints produce such faithful renditions of the scene that it is difficult for some viewers to perceive the image as something other than what it represents. For that reason contemporary photographers constantly search for new means of transformation in order to expand the resources of photography as art.

FIGURE 12-1
A camera obscura: The image formed by the lens is reflected by the mirror on the ground glass and then traced. (Culver Pictures)

THE POWER OF REPRESENTATION

The success of photography in reproducing realistic scenes and people had an instant impact on painting. Paul Delaroche, a French academic painter (1795–1856), was widely admired for his realistic technique, as in his *Execution of Lady Jane Grey* (1834, Figure 12-2), a massive painting (97 × 117 inches). When he saw the daguerreotype process first demonstrated in 1839, he declared: "From today painting is dead." He was quite wrong, but he was responding to the realistic detail Daguerre's almost instant process (like the modern Polaroid) could extract from the world. Even today realism remains among the most important resources of the photographic medium.

PERCEPTION KEY
EXECUTION OF LADY JANE GREY

1. What qualities of Delaroche's style of painting would have made him think of photography as a threat? In what ways is this painting similar to a photograph?
2. Is it surprising to learn that this painting was exhibited five years before Delaroche saw a photograph—actually before the invention of photography?
3. Like some painters before him, Delaroche may have used the camera obscura to compose his figures and render them exactly as they appeared. Does this painting become less a work of art if in fact Delaroche used such an instrument to assist him?

The capacity of the camera to capture and control details is exhibited in many early photographs. Robert Howlett's portrait of Isambard Kingdom Brunel (1857), a builder of steamships (Figure 12-3), uses the power of the lens to isolate Brunel from his surroundings. He set his lens so that only Brunel's body is in focus. The depth of field (range of sharpness of focus)

FIGURE 12-2
Paul Delaroche, *Execution of Lady Jane Grey*. Reproduced by courtesy of the trustees, National Gallery, London.

of the lens was, therefore, only about twenty inches or less. The wood pilings in the lower right are in soft focus because they are just out of that depth of field. The pile of anchor chains, which serves as background, is even farther out of focus, thus softening their massive, fascinating pattern. By being out of focus, the chains are rendered subservient to Brunel and help establish his mastery as a famous designer of great steamships. The huge chains make this image haunting, whereas rendering them sharply (which Howlett could easily have done) would have weakened the effect. In *Execution of Lady Jane Grey* everything is in sharp focus, which may simply mean that Howlett's style of selective focus was not part of Delaroche's repertoire. It would be difficult to imagine Howlett's photograph in color, although if Delaroche had painted it, the gold watch chain and fob would have been a prominent distraction.

Brunel's posture is typical of photographs of the period. We have many examples of men lounging with hands in pockets and cigar in mouth, but few paintings portray men this way. Few photographs of any age show us a face quite like Brunel's. It is relaxed, as much as Brunel could relax, but it is also impatient, "bearing with" the photographer. And the eyes are sharp, businessman's eyes. The details of the rumpled clothing and jewelry do not compete with the sharply rendered face and the expression of control and power. Howlett has done, by simple devices such as varying the focus, what many portrait painters do by much more complex means: reveal the essence of the model.

Julia Margaret Cameron's portrait of Sir John Herschel (1867, Figure 12-4), and Étienne Carjat's portrait of the French poet Charles Baudelaire (1870, Figure 12-5), unlike Howlett's portrait, ignore the background entirely. But their approaches are also different from each other. Cameron, who reports being interested in the way her lens could soften detail, isolates Herschel's face and hair. She drapes his shoulders with a black velvet shawl so that his clothing will not tell us anything about him or distract us from his face. Cameron catches the stubble on his chin and permits his hair to "burn out," so we perceive it as a luminous halo. The huge eyes, soft and bulbous with their deep curves of surrounding flesh, and the downward curve of the mouth are depicted fully in the harsh lighting. While we do not know what he was thinking, the form of this photograph reveals him as a thinker of deep ruminations. He was the chemist who first learned how to permanently fix a photograph.

The portrait of Baudelaire, on the other hand, includes simple, severe clothing, except for the poet's foulard, tied in a dashing bow. The studio

FIGURE 12-3
Robert Howlett, *Isambard Kingdom Brunel*. (International Museum of Photography at George Eastman House, Rochester)

FIGURE 12-4
Julia Margaret Cameron, *Sir John Herschel*. (International Museum of Photography at George Eastman House, Rochester)

FIGURE 12-5
Étienne Carjat, *Charles Baudelaire*. (International Museum of Photography at George Eastman House, Rochester)

backdrop is set far out of focus so it cannot compete with the face for our attention. Baudelaire's intensity creates the illusion that he sees us. Carjat's lens was set for a depth of field of only a few inches. Therefore Carjat chose to have the eyes in focus, but not the shoulders. What he could not control, except by waiting for the right moment to uncover the lens (at this time there was no shutter because there was no "fast" film), is the exact expression he would catch.

One irony of the Carjat portrait is that Baudelaire, in 1859, had condemned the influence of photography on art, declaring it "art's most mortal enemy." He thought that photography was adequate for preserving visual records of perishing things, but that it could not reach into "anything whose value depends solely upon the addition of something of a man's soul." Baudelaire was a champion of imagination and an opponent of realistic art: "Each day art further diminishes its self-respect by bowing down before external reality; each day the painter becomes more and more given to painting not what he dreams but what he sees."[1]

Some philosophers of art and critics argued that photography is not an art—or at least not a major art—on different grounds than Baudelaire's. The images could be selected and controlled, of course, but after their "taking" what could be done with them was restricted. Therefore the photographer's ability to transform subject matter was also restricted. Painters, on the other hand, created their images and in doing so had much greater flexibility in organizing their media—color, light, line, and texture. Today this argument falters because of the computer's capacity to alter, distort, and totally transform the image of the camera. But even without the computer's magical capacities, the photograph is rich with artistic possibilities. It is not restricted only to recording slices of life.

[1]*The Mirror of Art,* Phaidon, London, 1955, p. 230.

Perception Key
PHOTOGRAPHY AND ART

1. Do you agree with Baudelaire that photography is "art's most mortal enemy"? What reasons might lead Baudelaire to express such a view?
2. Baudelaire felt that art depended on imagination and that realistic art was the opponent of imagination. Why would he hold such an opinion? Is it one that you hold yourself?
3. Read a poem from Baudelaire's most celebrated volume—*The Flowers of Evil.* You might choose "Twilight: Evening" from the group he called "Parisian Scenes." In what ways is his poem unlike a photograph (consider the questions of representation of visual imagery and allusion to visual structures). Is it possible that Baudelaire's artistic temperament set him in opposition to photography?
4. Considering his attitude toward photography, why would he have sat for a portrait such as Carjat's? Do you regard his portrait as a work of art?

Compare Carjat's and Cameron's portraits with Rembrandt's *Self Portait* (Figure 4-11). Both photographers were familiar with Rembrandt's stylistic choices about lighting and background. Neither photograph has imitated Rembrandt's pose, but the use of a rich dark background in Cameron's photograph, and the direct, frank stare of Carjat's subject demonstrate an awareness of style and a carefulness of expression that parallel Rembrandt's. Indeed, the photographs and the painting seem to have a similar purpose: to reveal the personality of the subject. They all share a sense of dramatic purpose, as if each subject were caught in an instant of time at a moment of meditation. The use of lighting is similar and Rembrandt's use of color is earthy and in some ways almost monochromatic: the canvas seems to have been painted in one basic color: a reddish brown.

An impressive example of the capacity of the photographic representation is Timothy O'Sullivan's masterpiece, *Canyon de Chelley, Arizona,* made in 1873 (Figure 12-6). Many photographers go back to this scene, but none have treated it quite the way O'Sullivan did, although most, like Ansel Adams (see Figure 12-14), pay homage to O'Sullivan. O'Sullivan chose a moment of intense sidelighting, which falls on the rock wall but not on the nearest group of buildings. He waited for that moment when the great rock striations and planes would be most powerfully etched by the sun. The closer group of buildings is marked by strong shadow. Comparing it to the more distant group shows a remarkable negative-positive relationship. The groups of buildings are purposely contrasted in this special photographic way. One question you might ask of this photograph is whether it reveals the "stoniness" of this rock wall in a manner similar to the way Cézanne's painting *Mont Sainte Victoire* (Figure 2-5) reveals the "mountainness" of the mountain.

The most detailed portions of the photograph are the striations of the rock face, whose tactile qualities are emphasized by the strong sidelighting. The stone buildings in the distance have smoother textures, particularly as they show up against the blackness of the cave. The men standing in the ruins show us that the buildings are only twelve to fifteen feet high.

FIGURE 12-6
Timothy O'Sullivan, *Canyon de Chelley, Arizona*. (International Museum of Photography at George Eastman House, Rochester)

Nature dwarfs the work of humans. By framing the canyon wall, and by waiting for the right light, O'Sullivan has done more than create an ordinary "record" photograph. He has concentrated on the subject matter of the puniness and softness of humans, in contrast with the grandness and stoniness of the canyon. The content centers on the extraordinary sense of stoniness—symbolic of permanence—as opposed to the transience of humanity, revealed by the capacity of the camera to render realistic detail.

PHOTOGRAPHY AND PAINTING: THE PICTORIALISTS

Pictorialists are photographers who use the achievements of painting, particularly realistic painting, in their effort to realize the potential of photography as art. The early pictorialists tried to avoid the "head-on" directness of Howlett and Carjat, just as they tried to avoid the amateur's "mistakes" in composition, such as including distracting and asymmetrical elements. The pictorialists controlled details by subordinating them to structure, thus producing compositions that usually relied on the same underlying structures found in most late nineteenth-century paintings. Normally the most important part of the subject matter was centered in the frame. Pictorial lighting, also borrowed from painting, was often Rembrandt-like, with dramatic effects of the sort we sometimes associate with the stage.

Generally, the pictorialist photograph was soft in focus, centrally weighted with its subject, and carefully balanced symmetrically across the frame. By relying on the formalist qualities of some nineteenth-century paintings, pictorialist photographers were able to evoke emotions that centered on sentimentalism. Indeed, one of the complaints modern commentators have about the development of pictorialism is that it was too sentimental, too predictable in its emotional range.

Although rarely criticized for sentimentalism, Alfred Stieglitz was, in his early work, a master of the pictorial style. His *Paula* (Figure 12-7), done in 1889, places his subject at the center in the act of writing. The top and bottom of the scene are printed in deep black. The light falls and centers on Paula, while also creating an interesting pattern on the venetian blind. Paula's profile is strong against the dark background partly because Stieglitz has removed in the act of printing one of the strips which would have fallen on her lower face. The candle, ordinarily useless in daylight, is a beacon of light because of its position. The strong vertical lines of the window frames reinforce the verticality of the candle and echo the back of the chair.

A specifically photographic touch is present in the illustrations on the wall: photographs arranged symmetrically in a triangle. Two prints of the same lake-skyscape are on each side of a woman in a white dress and hat. The same photograph of this women is on the writing table in an oval frame.

FIGURE 12-7
Alfred Stieglitz, *Paula*.
(International Museum of Photography at George Eastman House, Rochester)

FIGURE 12-8
Sally Mann, *The Last Time Emmett Modeled Nude.* 1987. (© Sally Mann, courtesy Houk Friedman, New York)

Is it Paula? The light in the room echoes the light in the oval portrait. The three hearts in the arrangement of photographs are balanced; one heart touches the portrait of a young man. We wonder if Paula is writing to him. The cage on the wall has dominant vertical lines, crossing the lines cast by the venetian blind. Stieglitz may be suggesting that Paula, despite the open window, may be in a cage of her own. Stieglitz has kept most of the photograph in sharp focus because most of the details have something to tell us. If this were a painting of the early nineteenth century, for example one by Delaroche, we would expect much the same style. By implication, we see Paula in a dramatic moment, with dramatic light, and with an implied narrative suggested by the artifacts surrounding her. It is, however, up to the viewer to decide what, if anything, the drama implies.

Pictorialism is still an ideal of many good photographers, although we associate it mainly with those working at the beginning of the twentieth century. One of the most controversial of contemporary photographers, Sally Mann, has produced an interesting body of work using her children as her models. Not all of her work would fit the pictorialist ideal, but *The Last Time Emmett Modeled Nude* (Figure 12-8) provides us with a visual drama: what is this nude child doing? and why is his countenance so disturbed? The darkness of the water and shoreline, with the lyrical nimbus of light to the left of the child, suggests a foreboding, perhaps threatening moment. But however one interprets the light and the composition, Sally Mann has implied a dramatic moment. Something is about to happen. Her isolation of the figure and the drama of the setting produce a psychological moment, with the image itself suggesting the mystery of a dream. Some who have commented on her work question her use of her children as models as if implying that she is abusing them.

Perception Key
PICTORIALISM AND SENTIMENTALITY

1. Pictorialists are often condemned for their sentimentality. Write down your definition of sentimentality. Compare it with a dictionary definition.
2. Are *Paula* and *The Last Time Emmett Modeled Nude* sentimental? Is their subject matter sentimental, or does their formal treatment make a neutral subject matter sentimental?
3. Is Delaroche's *Execution of Lady Jane Grey* sentimental? Does its sharpness of detail contribute to its sentimentality? Would softening the lines and textures make the painting more or less sentimental? Why?
4. Is sentimentality desirable in paintings, photographs, or any art form?

Both paintings and photographs can be sentimental in subject matter. The severest critics of such works complain that sentimentality falsifies feelings by demanding emotional responses that are cheap or easy to come by. Sentimentality is usually an oversimplification of complex emotional issues. It also tends to be mawkish and self-indulgent. The case of photography is special because we are accustomed to the harshness of the camera. Thus when the pictorialist finds tenderness, romance, and beauty in everyday occurrences, we become suspicious. We may be more tolerant of painting doing those things, but in fact we should be wary of any such emotional "coloration" in any medium if it is not restricted to the subject matter.

The pictorialist approach, when not guilty of sentimentalism, has great strengths. The use of lighting that selectively emphasizes the most important features of the subject matter often helps in creating meaning. Borrowing from the formal structures of painting also may help clarify subject matter. Structural harmony (or disharmony) of the kind we look for in representational painting is possible in photography. Although it is by no means limited to the pictorialist approach, it is clearly fundamental to that approach.

THE EMOTIONAL POWER OF PHOTOGRAPHY

Photography has the power to evoke horror as well as pleasant sentiments. Joel-Peter Witkin has built a reputation for images that explore the grotesque in ways in which some painting and sculpture have done, although it may be difficult to see the connection between his work and those arts. In Figure 12-9, *La Bête,* Witkin has presented an image of a tormented looking animal—or animal-like figure—with grotesque encrustation, standing on a display table or structure as if part of a freak exhibit. The curtains to each side, along with the drawstring at the top of the frame, imply ex-

FIGURE 12-9
Joel-Peter Witkin, *La Bête* (The Beast), *New Mexico*. 1989. Gelatin silver print (© Joel-Peter Witkin, courtesy PaceWildensteinMacGill, New York)

hibition. The scratches on the negative suggest the same kind of finish one might find on an old daguerreotype. Freak shows in the nineteenth century often created impossible animals by means of makeup and manipulation, and in this photograph Witkin presents a figure without comment. The emotions demanded by the photograph may be those associated with disgust, fright, or concern for the animal's rights. Witkin leaves it to us to deal with the emotional content of the photograph.

By contrast, Lewis Carroll's *Alice Liddell as "The Beggar Maid"* (circa 1859, Figure 12-10) produces an entirely different emotional response. To some extent, a viewer's response will be shaped by the knowledge that Lewis Carroll (his real name was Rev. Charles Lutwidge Dodgson) wrote *Alice in Wonderland* specifically for Alice Liddell, the girl in this photograph. Carroll was a highly sophisticated photographer, especially of young girls. The practice of having photographic subjects dress up in costume as if they were in a play was common in the mid-1800s. But here we have a barefoot child looking at the camera in a manner that we may interpret in any number of ways: impatiently or perhaps even alluringly. Her right hand was in motion, and therefore is slightly blurred. But her visage is clear and sharp because she held her gaze as steadily on the camera as it was held on her. Much of the right side of the photograph is soft in focus, while the sharpness of detail on the left side—which is closer to the camera—emphasizes the stone wall and the ground cover plants. Alice Liddell's face is thoroughly expressive, but who can say of what? Other photographs of ordinary people in this period usually show blank stares. But the emotional core of this photograph centers on the question: What is Alice Liddell thinking?

Kevin Carter's short life was spent in photojournalism, much of it in Africa. See his photograph of a vulture and child (Figure 2-6). The horror

FIGURE 12-10
Lewis Carroll (Charles Lutwidge Dodgson), *Alice Liddell as "The Beggar Maid."* Circa 1859. Albumen silver print from glass negative, 6⅜ × 4¼ inches. (Gilman Paper Company Collection)

of *Untitled* (Figure 12-11) resides in the fact that the viewer knows the man crouched by his automobile will be killed almost instantly—indeed, he was killed, and Carter photographed him dead as well. But this moment, what the great French photographer Robert Cartier-Bresson would call "the decisive moment," balances the death of comrades with the impending death of a man who looks resigned to his fate. The details to this story are important to the politics of South Africa, but unimportant in face of the image of impending death. Carter revealed that the men in the car were part of a group of extreme right-wingers who had threatened journalists only hours before. They were cut off from their comrades, wounded, then executed by members of the Bophuthatswana army. Carter's life was in jeopardy every moment of this "shoot."

The natural question to be asked is whether a journalistic photograph of this kind can be considered from the point of view of art. Does Goya's painting of an execution serve a journalistic purpose? Were you to examine Carter's photograph from the point of view of its organization of individual details, you would see that the intersection of lines flowing from body to body, including the body of the Bophuthatswana soldier, link each figure conclusively and emotionally, while the open doors divide the photograph into powerful visual units. The lighting is harsh, the colors earthy and bleached, intensifying the mercilessness of the scene.

FIGURE 12-11
Kevin Carter, *Untitled*. March 12, 1994. (Kevin Carter/Sygma)

PERCEPTION KEY
WITKIN, *LA BÊTE*; CARROLL, *ALICE LIDDELL AS "THE BEGGAR MAID"*; AND CARTER, *UNTITLED*

1. Which of these photographs most emulates the pictorialist ideals? Which emulates them least?
2. Can any of these photographs be said to be sentimental? Which and why?
3. Compare these photographs for their reliance on principles of centrality of organization; use of symmetry and balance of composition; reliance on asymmetry or apparent disorder.
4. Does the use of color intensify or reduce the emotional impact of Kevin Carter's photograph?
5. In which of these photographs does "the decisive moment" seem best illustrated? In which is it least illustrated? What is the difference in the power of these photographs when examined from the point of view of "the decisive moment"?

STRAIGHT PHOTOGRAPHY: AN END TO SENTIMENTALISM

As one can see from the work of Witkin and Carter, the reactions of straight photography to the pictorialist approach have helped reshape modern photography. Alfred Stieglitz, in his later work, pioneered the movement of straight photography beginning in 1905. The F/64 Group, working in the 1930s, and the second school, the ongoing and current documentarist tradition (of which Carter is a part) continue the tradition. Straight photography respected photographic techniques and happily separated itself from the ideals of painting. It de-emphasized pictorialism, taking the position that, as Aaron Siskind said later, "Pictorialism is a kind of dead end making everything look beautiful." The straight photographer wanted things to look as they do, even if they are ugly.

Straight photography aimed toward excellence in photographic techniques, independent of painting. Susan Sontag summarizes: "For a brief time—say, from Stieglitz through the reign of Weston—it appeared that a solid point of view had been erected with which to evaluate photographs: impeccable lighting, skill of composition, clarity of subject, precision of focus, perfection of print quality."[2] Some of these qualities are shared by pictorialists, but new principles of composition—not derived from painting—and new attitudes toward subject matter helped straight photography reveal the world straight, as it really is.

ALFRED STIEGLITZ: PIONEER OF STRAIGHT PHOTOGRAPHY

One of the most famous straight photographs leading to the F/64 Group was Stieglitz's *The Steerage* (1907, Figure 12-12). It was taken under conditions that demanded quick action.

[2]*On Photography,* Farrar, Straus & Giroux, New York, 1977, p. 136.

FIGURE 12-12
Alfred Stieglitz, *The Steerage*. 1907. Photogravure (artist's proof) from *Camera Work* No. 36, 1911, 7¾ × 6½ inches. The Museum of Modern Art, New York. Gift of Alfred Stieglitz. (Copy print © 1997 The Museum of Modern Art, New York)

Perception Key
The Steerage

1. How many of the qualities Susan Sontag lists above can be found in this photograph?
2. What compositional qualities make this photograph different from the pictorialist examples we have discussed? How does the structural organization control the details of the photograph?
3. What is the subject matter of the photograph? Is the subject matter made to seem beautiful? Should it be?
4. Does the framing cut off important figural elements of the photograph? If so, is this effective?
5. Does the photograph have content? If so, how does the form achieve it? And what is the content?

The Steerage portrays poor travelers huddled in the "budget" quarters of the *Kaiser Wilhelm II,* which is taking this group of disappointed immigrants who, because of economic hardship, sailed back to their native lands. Ironically, the New York Public Library uses his photograph to celebrate the arrival of immigrants to America. Stieglitz wrote that while strolling on deck he was struck by a

> round straw hat, the funnel leaning left, the stairway leaning right, the white drawbridge with its railing made of circular chains, white suspenders crossing on the back of a man in the steerage below, round shapes of iron machinery, a mast cutting into the sky, making a triangular shape. . . . I saw a picture of shapes and underlying that the feeling I had about life.[3]

The Steerage shares much with the pictorialist approach: dramatic lighting and soft focus. But there is much that the pictorialist would probably avoid. For one thing, the framing omits important parts of the funnel, the drawbridge, and the nearest people in the lower-right quadrant. Moreover, the very clutter of people—part of the subject matter of the photograph—would be difficult for the pictorialist to tolerate. And the pictorialist certainly would be unhappy with the failure to use the center of the photograph as the primary region of interest. Certain focal points have been used by Stieglitz to stabilize the composition: the straw hat attracts our eye, but so too does the white shawl of the woman below. The bold slicing of the composition by the drawbridge sharpens the idea of the separation between the well-to-do and the poor. On the other hand, the leaning funnel, the angled drawbridge and chains, the angled ladder on the right, and the horizontal boom at the top of the photograph are rhythmically interrelated. This rhythm is peculiarly mechanical and modern. The stark metal structures are in opposition to the softer, more random assortment of the people. Photographs like this one can help teach us how to see and appreciate formal organizations.

[3]Quoted in Beaumont Newhall, *The History of Photography,* Museum of Modern Art, New York, 1964, p. 111.

FIGURE 12-13
Edward Weston, *Nude*. 1936. (© 1981 Center for Creative Photography, Arizona Board of Regents, Used by permission.)

THE F/64 GROUP

The name of the group derives from the small aperture, F/64, which ensures that the foreground, middle ground, and background will all be in sharp focus. The group declared its principles through manifestos and shows by Edward Weston, Ansel Adams, Imogen Cunningham, and others. It continued the reaction against pictorialism, adding the kind of nonsentimental subject matter that interested the later Stieglitz. Edward Weston, whose early work was in the soft focus school, developed a special interest in formal organizations. He is famous for his nudes and his portraits of vegetables, such as artichokes, eggplants, and green peppers. His nudes rarely show the face, not because of modesty, but because the question of the identity of the model can distract us from contemplating the formal relationships.

Weston's *Nude* (Figure 12-13) shows many of the characteristics of the F/64 Group. The figure is isolated and presented for its own sake, the sand being equivalent to a photographer's backdrop. The figure is presented not as a portrait of a given woman, but rather as a formal study. Weston wanted us to see the relationship between legs and torso, to respond to the rhythms of line in the extended body, and to appreciate the counterpoint of the round, dark head against the long, light linearity of the body. Weston enjoys some notoriety for his studies of peppers, because his approach to vegetables was similar to his approach to nudes. We are to appreciate the sen-

FIGURE 12-14
Ansel Adams, *Antelope House Ruin*. Canyon de Chelley National Monument, Arizona. 1942. (Photograph by Ansel Adams. © 1995 by the Trustees of the Ansel Adams Publishing Rights Trust. All Rights Reserved.)

sual curve, the counterpoints of line, the reflectivity of skin, the harmonious proportions of parts.

Weston demanded objectivity in his photographs. As he said, "I do not wish to impose my personality upon nature (any of life's manifestations), but without prejudice or falsification to become identified with nature, to know things in their very essence, so that what I record is not an interpretation—my ideas of what nature should be—but a revelation."[4] One of Weston's ideals was to capitalize on the capacity of the camera to be objective and impersonal, an ideal that the pictorialists usually rejected.

The work of Ansel Adams establishes another ideal of the F/64 Group: the fine print. Even some of the best early photographers were relatively casual in the act of printing their negatives. Adams spent a great deal of energy and skill in producing the finest print the negative would permit, sometimes spending days to print one photograph. He developed a special system (the Zone System) to measure tonalities in specific regions of the negative so as to control the final print, keeping careful records so that he could duplicate the print at a later time. In even the best of reproductions it is very difficult to point to the qualities of tonal gradation that constitute the fine print. Only the original can yield the beauties that gradations of silver or platinum can produce. In his *Antelope House Ruin* (Figure 12-14), Adams aimed for a print of textural subtleties. Unlike O'Sullivan, Adams

[4]*The Daybooks of Edward Weston,* Nancy Newhall (ed.), 2 vols., Aperture, New York, 1966, vol. 2, p. 241.

did not stress the contrast between the rock and the houses. He chose a canyon face and a lighting that emphasized the textural gradations that would yield a print of tonal brilliance. In Weston's terms, he renders the essence of the rock and ruin. But the important thing to Adams is that the print be all it can be; in essence, the print takes precedence over the scene it represents.

PERCEPTION KEY
O'SULLIVAN AND ADAMS

1. Compare O'Sullivan's photograph of the Canyon de Chelley (Figure 12-6) with Adams' version (Figure 12-14). Is the subject matter the same in both photographs? Explain.
2. How do the formal organizations of the photographs differ? What does their organization emphasize in each case?
3. To what extent is the content of both photographs similar? To what extent is it different?

BEYOND STRAIGHT PHOTOGRAPHY: THE SYMBOL

Aaron Siskind and Harry Callahan were never members of the F/64 Group, but their techniques are close in spirit, for they emphasize objectivity and mastery of the fine print. However, unlike the F/64 Group, their images sometimes take on symbolic significance—by means of isolation or juxtaposition—which was not apparent in the objects before they were photographed. Such images are visual symbols (compare with literary symbols, pp. 216–219) that go beyond the essence of things, as in Weston's work.

Siskind's image *Gloucester, Massachusetts* (Figure 12-15) is evidence that the camera can invest even very ordinary objects with symbolic power. He tells us that in Gloucester he deliberately sought out everyday objects (like Kurt Schwitters, see Figure 5-26) rather than obviously important subject matter. But the fascinating thing is that the glove—although it had apparently been cast aside or lost—seems to have a living spirit of its own. It takes on the vitality of the hand that, only a while before, animated it. Isolated on the board, the glove becomes a pulsing symbol of absent life that can be felt but not accurately described. The isolation of the glove from its normal environment helps create a significance it would not otherwise have.

FIGURE 12-15
Aaron Siskind, *Gloucester, Massachusetts*. 1944. (© Aaron Siskind Foundation, Courtesy Robert Mann Gallery)

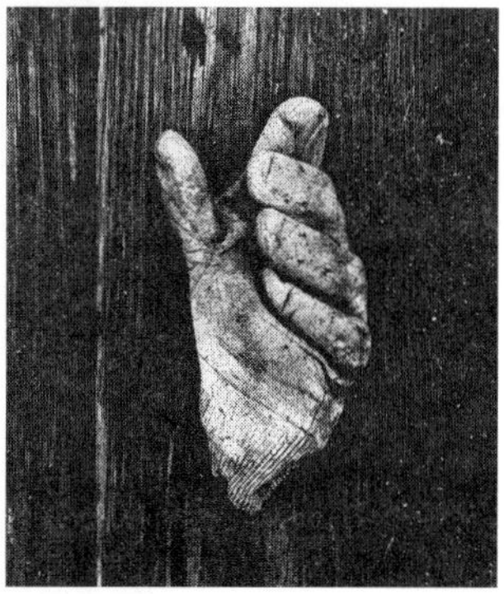

The symbolic power of Callahan's *Chicago* (Figure 12-16) depends on the juxtaposition of images as well as the low camera angle connecting the nearest woman (and the people behind her) with some of the architectural forces of the city. Behind her is a black building. It is just past noon and the light is intense. Near the woman is a sprouting metal lamppost—suggesting a sorry substitute for a tree. The woman reveals strength and determination, adding to the uprightness and stability of her environment. In turn, something of the power of Chicago seems to radiate through her. Yet it would be difficult to limit that significance to a single meaning. We see a mixture of forces: human, mechanical, temporal, architectural, metropolitan. Their interaction is complex and exciting.

FIGURE 12-16
Harry Callahan, *Chicago*. 1961. (© Harry Callahan, courtesy PaceWildensteinMacGill, New York)

PERCEPTION KEY
SISKIND AND CALLAHAN

1. Can either photograph by Siskind or Callahan be clearly related to the pictorialist tradition?
2. Which photograph emphasizes detail more than the other?
3. What is the subject matter of these photographs? What is their content, if any? If there is content, how do the visual symbols function in the content?
4. Symbolic meanings are not limited to photographs, of course. Examine paintings in the first four chapters for their symbolic significance. How are they like or unlike the photographs of Siskind and Callahan? Are there visual symbols in Eddie Adams' *Execution in Saigon* (Figure 2-2)?

THE DOCUMENTARISTS

Time is critical to the documentarist, who portrays a world that is disappearing so slowly (or quickly) we cannot see it go. Cartier-Bresson's "decisive moment" defines that crucial interaction of shapes formed by people and objects that tells him when to snap his shutter. Not all his photographs are "decisive"; they do not all catch the action at its most intense point. But the best documentarists develop an instinct—nurtured by years of visual education—for the powerful formal statement even in the midst of disaster, as one can see in Kevin Carter's *Untitled.*

Eugène Atget spent much of his time photographing in Paris in the early morning (when no one would bother him). The balcony and storefront in Figure 12-17 are shot from an acute angle, to avoid reflecting himself in the glass. Everything is in sharp focus. The importance of this photograph is not in the way the shapes are organized (Stieglitz), nor its objectivity (Weston), nor its symbolism (Siskind), but because, as Beaumont Newhall has said, "this work has no reference to any graphic medium other than photography."[5] The innocence of this photograph links Atget with the contemporary photographer Gary Winogrand, who said, "I photograph to see what something will look like photographed." Atget's work did not refer to painting: it created its own photographic reference. We see a photograph, not just a thing photographed.

Tina Modotti was known in several circles as a political activist—specifically a Communist in the 1930s—and as a companion of the photographer Edward Weston. She modeled for him as well as sometimes managed his studio in Mexico in the 1920s. When she left Weston, she displayed considerable talent as a photographer and has been published and shown frequently in recent years. The power of her work is increased by her attention to formal organization of visual details, as in *Woman of Tehuantepec* (circa 1929, Figure 12-18), which emphasizes the circular form on the woman's head with the prominent centralized earring and the circular pen-

[5]Newhall, *History of Photography,* p. 137.

FIGURE 12-17
Eugène Atget, *Balcon. 17 rue du Petit-Pont*. 1913. Albumen-silver print, $9\frac{3}{8} \times 7$ inches. The Museum of Modern Art, New York. Abbott-Levy Collection. Partial gift of Shirley C. Burden. (Copy print © 1997 The Museum of Modern Art, New York)

FIGURE 12-18
Tina Modotti, *Woman of Tehuantepec*. Circa 1929. Gelatin silver print. Philadelphia Museum of Art. Gift of Mr. and Mrs. Carl Zigrosser.

dant hanging from her neck. Modotti may have had a political message for the photograph, but it is secondary to our sense that she has aimed at a painterly perfection without involving sentimentalism or extraneous emotional issues.

Much the same may be said of Laura Gilpin's portrait of a Pueblo Indian woman in *Old Woman of Acoma* (1939, Figure 12-19). Both these photographs were taken with large cameras (not the conventional 35 mm of today), so some time had to be taken in composition and thought before tripping the shutter. Both photographers were concerned with the expression of the subject; both were interested in the costume and jewelry. In the *Old Woman of Acoma,* Gilpin uses a classic composition for the figure: a straight-on look, the hands balanced in front of the woman's waist, the necklaces falling naturally, and the light harsh and revealing. Gilpin spent many years with the Pueblo, and her thousands of negatives attest an understanding and a response to Native American life that has been shared by many photographers. She documented a passing way of life in a tender and responsive manner.

FIGURE 12-19
Laura Gilpin, *Old Woman of Acoma*. 1939. Amon Carter Museum, Fort Worth, Texas. Pueblo Indians: 2969.1 © 1981 Laura Gilpin Collection.

James Van Der Zee worked in a somewhat different tradition from Atget, Modotti, and Gilpin. His studio in Harlem was so prominent that many important black citizens felt it essential that he take their portrait. Like Atget, he was fascinated with his community, photographing public events and activities from the turn of the century into the 1930s. *Couple in Raccoon Coats* (Figure 12-20) is reminiscent of Howlett as well as of Atget. Like Howlett, there is the contrast of soft focus for the background and sharp

FIGURE 12-20
James Van Der Zee, *Couple in Raccoon Coats*, 1932. © 1997 All rights reserved by Donna Van Der Zee.

FIGURE 12-21
Henri Cartier-Bresson, *Lisbon*. 1955. (Henri Cartier-Bresson/Magnum Photos)

focus for the foreground. Thus the couple and their new car stand out brilliantly. On the other hand, the interaction of formal elements is so complex that it reminds us of Atget: there has been no reduction of shapes to a simpler geometry. We must take these shapes as they are. The car has been selectively framed front and rear, reminding us that this is, first, a portrait of a couple. Their style and elegance are what Van Der Zee was anxious to capture. Our familiarity with the chief elements in the photograph—brownstones, car, and fur-coated people—helps make it possible for him to be direct, avoiding the soothing formal order the pictorialist might have used. If anything, Van Der Zee is moving toward the snapshot aesthetic that was another generation in the making. His directness of approach puts him in the documentary tradition.

Unlike Atget and Van Der Zee, who used large cameras, Cartier-Bresson used the 35-mm Leica and specialized in people. He preset his camera in order to work fast and instinctively. His *Lisbon* (Figure 12-21) shows his instinct for tight formal organization, with the sharp diagonal of the cannon merging with the diagonal formed by the three aligned men. The umbrella and the left arm of the man holding it are poised at the right place to cap this arrangement. The angle of the wall echoes this triangulation, establishing a clear relationship among the basic elements of the composition. The men have been caught in a moment of reflection, as if they, like the defunct cannon, are parts of the ancient history of Lisbon. The formal relationship of elements in a photograph can produce various kinds of significance or apparent lack of significance. The best documentarists search for the strongest coherency of elements while also searching for the decisive moment. That moment is the split-second peak of emotional intensity (as Newhall puts it), and it is defined especially with reference to light, action, and expression.

Perception Key
THE DOCUMENTARY PHOTOGRAPHERS

1. Which of these documentary photographs most completely rejects the pictorialist approach to formal organization? Is any of these photographs sentimental?
2. Some critics assert that these photographers have made interesting social documents, but not works of art. What arguments might support their views? What arguments might contest their views?
3. Contemporary photographers and critics often value the work of Atget highly because it is "liberated" from the influence of painting. What does it mean to say that his work is more purely photographic than it is painterly?
4. What is the subject matter of each photograph? What is the content of each photograph?

Walker Evans and Dorothea Lange took part in a federal program to give work to photographers during the Depression of the 1930s. Both photographers use framing, although it is much more evident in the Lange photograph. And both created careful formal organizations. Lange (Figure 12-22) stresses centrality and balance by placing the children's heads next to the mother's face, which is all the more compelling because the children's faces do not compete for our attention. The mother's arm leads us upward to her face, emphasizing the other triangularities of the photograph. Within ten minutes, Lange took four other photographs of this woman and her children, but none could achieve the power of this photograph. Lange caught the exact moment when the children's faces turned and the mother's anxiety comes forth with utter clarity, although the lens mercifully softens its focus on her face, while leaving her shabby clothes in sharp focus. This softness helps humanize our relationship with the woman. Lange gives us an unforgettable image that brutally and yet sympathetically gives us a deeper understanding of what the Depression was for many.

Evans' photograph (Figure 12-23) shows us a view of Bethlehem, Pennsylvania, and the off-center white cross reminds us of what has become of the message of Christ. The vertical lines are accentuated in the cemetery stones, repeated in the telephone lines, porch posts, and finally in the steel-mill smokestacks. The aspirations of the dominating verticals, however, are dampened by the strong horizontals, which, through the low angle of the lens, tend to merge from the cross to the roofs. Evans equalizes focus, which helps compress the space so that we see the cemetery on top of the living space, which is immediately adjacent to the steel mills where some of the people who live in the tenements work and where some of those now in the cemetery died. This compression of space suggests the closeness of life, work, and death. We see a special kind of sadness in this steel town that we may never have seen before. Evans caught the right moment for the light, which intensifies the white cross, and he aligned the verticals and horizontals for their best effect.

FIGURE 12-22
Dorothea Lange, *Migrant Mother*. 1936. (© Dorothea Lange Collection, The Oakland Museum of California, The City of Oakland. Gift of Paul Taylor)

THE MODERN EYE

The art of photography is young, and the mood is often rebellious. The successes of the pictorialist and straight photographic movements have led to reactions. Some rebellion has produced unusual subject matter, as in the work of Diane Arbus, who specialized in photographing dwarfs, aberrants, and freaks for their surprise, shock, and compassion value. Some rebellion has produced novel approaches to the composition of shapes, such as the

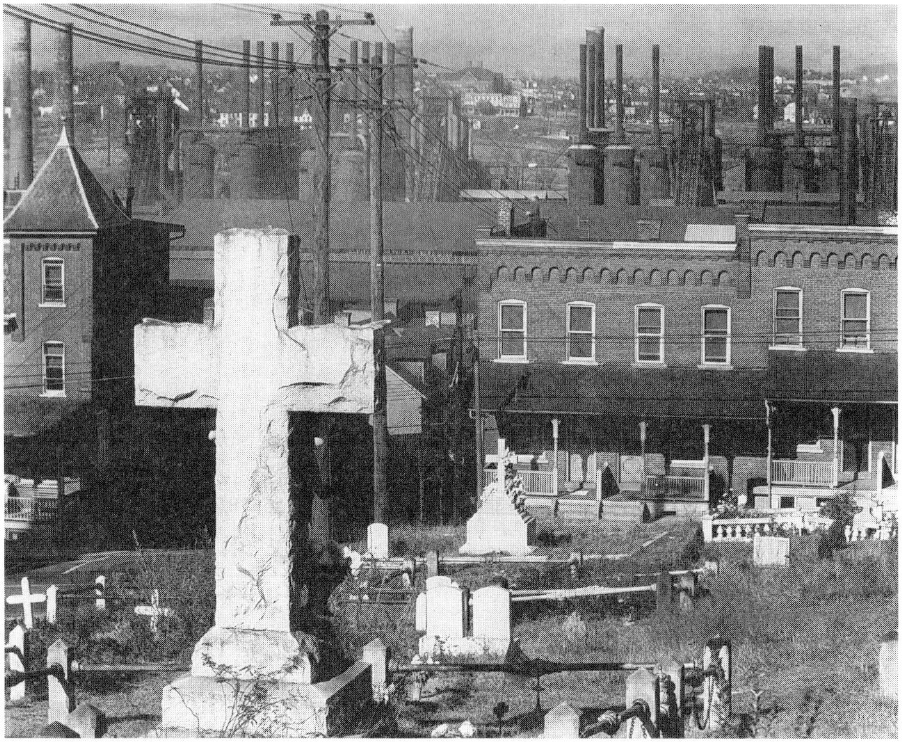

FIGURE 12-23
Walker Evans, *A Graveyard and Steel Mill in Bethlehem, Pennsylvania*. 1935. Silver print, 7⅞ × 9⅝ inches. The Museum of Modern Art, New York. Gift of the Farm Security Administration. (Copy print © 1997 The Museum of Modern Art, New York)

work of Robert Frank, a Swiss documentarist famous for his study of America in 1958. And some rebellion has produced serial photography. Thus Duane Michals' sequences of prints form a narrative that sometimes contrasts the subconscious with the conscious.

Diane Arbus was drawn to people who were outcasts, and her personality permitted her to establish a liaison that produced frank and remarkable images. Her photograph of the Jewish giant with his parents (Figure 12-24) is striking primarily because of the strangeness of the subject matter. Arbus has organized the details carefully. The giant is standing, bent over against the ceiling. His parents stand beside him looking up in wonderment. The simplicity and ordinariness of this room are significant when we think of how unordinary this scene is. In one way, Arbus is feeding our curiosity for looking at freaks, but in another way she is showing us that freaks are like us. We know this, of course, but Arbus' images make us feel its truth. Arbus brought exceptional sensitivity to her work and great sympathy for her subjects.

Although it is not quite accurate to associate Robert Frank with the snapshot, his work fits in well with that practice. Janet Malcolm claims: "Photography went modernist not, as has been supposed, when it began to imitate modern abstract art but when it began to study snapshots."[6] John Szarkowski of the Museum of Modern Art has praised the snapshot as one of the great resources of the medium. Its low technical demands, its

[6]*Diana and Nikon: Essays on the Aesthetics of Photography,* David Godine, Boston, 1980, p. 113.

FIGURE 12-24
Diane Arbus, *A Jewish Giant at Home with His Parents in the Bronx, N.Y.* (© 1971 by the estate of Diane Arbus. Photograph courtesy Robert Miller Gallery, New York.)

unself-consciousness, its potential for cluttered composition, and its refusal to attend to the standards of pictorialism all offered a way to rebel against the photographic establishment. No school of photography established a snapshot canon. It seems to be the product of amateurs, while the studied photograph is the product of professionals. In that sense the snapshot is more primitive, spontaneous, and accidental, and occasionally more exciting.

Frank's *Gallup, New Mexico* (Figure 12-25) gives the impression of being unplanned, with little attention to the Weston dogma concerning the fine print (the book it appeared in was wretchedly printed). However, despite its unconventional composition, it may achieve content. Judge for yourself. The light is brutal, befitting a tough, male-dominated environment. The sharp angle of presentation is unsettling and contributes to our lack of ease. The main figure, posed with his hands in his pockets, seems at home in this environment, while the menacing black forms of the men in the foreground shadow us from the scene. We cannot tell what is going on, but we are given a "feel" of the place. One of Weston's concerns—rendering the essence of the scene—perhaps is satisfied. However, Weston's

FIGURE 12-25
Robert Frank, *Gallup, New Mexico*. 1955–1956. (© Robert Frank, courtesy PaceWildensteinMacGill, New York)

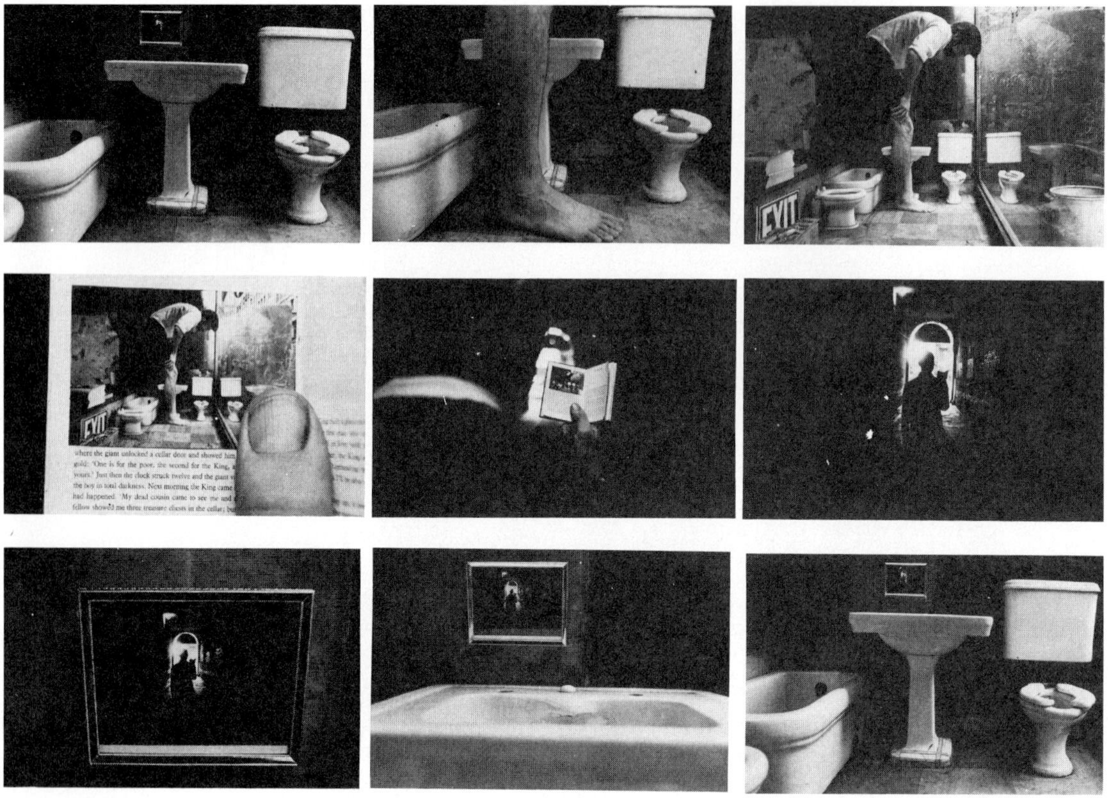

FIGURE 12-26
Duane Michals, *Things Are Queer*. (Courtesy Duane Michals)

concern for objectivity, the impersonal rendering of the subject matter, is partially ignored. We are presented with a scene with violence lurking just beneath the surface, and this seems an objective representation, but we also sense Frank's personal statement in the exceptionally low camera angle and the unusual framing.

Duane Michals has experimented with surrealist techniques, using a frame-by-frame sequential approach to a kind of storytelling that is almost cinematic. Yet it is not translatable into a literary explanation, nor does it imply cinematic development. Michals' *Things Are Queer* (Figure 12-26), from his book *Real Dreams,* has a dreamlike quality. When we follow the images from left to right, beginning at the top, we are constantly surprised. The images become images within images, like Chinese boxes, until we return to the first image, realizing that we are in a sealed continuum of visual experience. Michals' images are both playful and serious—playful because they are amusing and confounding, serious because they imply something of the "closed system" that is everyone's psychic experience. Michals' work is witty but informative. His use of photographic images would seem to answer some of the "charges" of Baudelaire and others who would relegate photography to recording "facts."

When he died of AIDS in 1989 at age 42, Robert Mapplethorpe was arguably the best-known young photographer in America. Six months after his death he became even better known to the public because of an exhibit of his work, supported by a grant from the National Endowment for the Arts, caused Senator Jesse Helms (R-NC) to add an amendment to an important appropriations bill that would make it almost impossible for the NEA to fund exhibitions of the work of artists like Mapplethorpe. The amendment reads:

> None of the funds authorized to be appropriated pursuant to the Act may be used to promote, disseminate, or produce—(1) obscene or indecent materials, including but not limited to depictions of sadomasochism, homo-eroticism, the exploitation of children, or individuals engaged in sex acts; or (2) material which denigrates the objects or beliefs of the adherents of a particular religion or nonreligion; or (3) material which denigrates, debases, or reviles a person, group, or class of citizens on the basis of race, creed, sex, handicap, age, or national origin.

The provisions of this bill—which was defeated—would essentially apply to every federal granting or exhibition agency, including the National Gallery of Art. The exhibit that triggered this response included Mapplethorpe's photographs of the homosexual community of New York to which he belonged. Some of his work portrays bondage, sadomasochistic accoutrements, and nudity. At this same exhibit, Andres Serrano provided a photograph of a crucifix in a beaker of what he said was his own urine. Such works so angered Senator Helms (apparently) that his proposed law would make it difficult, if not impossible, for photographers such as Mapplethorpe to get the kind of government support that artists of all kinds have been given since World War II. The decision to withhold support would not be made by experts in the arts, but by government functionaries.

Despite the defeat of the bill, federal support to public radio, public television, public institutions such as the most prominent museums in the United States, and all the public programs designed to support the arts has been curtailed so profoundly as to jeopardize the careers of dancers, composers, symphony orchestras, and virtually all arts organizations that are not part of pop culture. Interestingly, similar pressure was put on the arts in the governments of Francisco Franco, Josef Stalin, Adolf Hitler, and Chairman Mao. The outcome of the United States' political reactions to arts is still in doubt.

Mapplethorpe's double portrait (Figure 12-27) might well be considered controversial in the light of Helm's amendment. Who is to say that this is not a homosexual portrait? Are there racial implications to this photograph? These are questions that may impinge on the photographic values of the portrait. Mapplethorpe has interpreted these heads almost as if they were sculptured busts. There is no hair. The surfaces are cool, almost stonelike. The tonal range of darks and lights is a marvel, and one of the most important challenges of this photograph was in making the print manifest the range of the paper from the brightest white to the darkest black. Unlike Howlett, Carjat, and Emerson, Mapplethorpe portrayed the coolness and detachment of his subjects. Instead of revealing their personality, Mapplethorpe seems to aim at revealing their physical qualities by inviting us to compare them not only with each other, but with the images we have in our minds of conventional portrait busts.

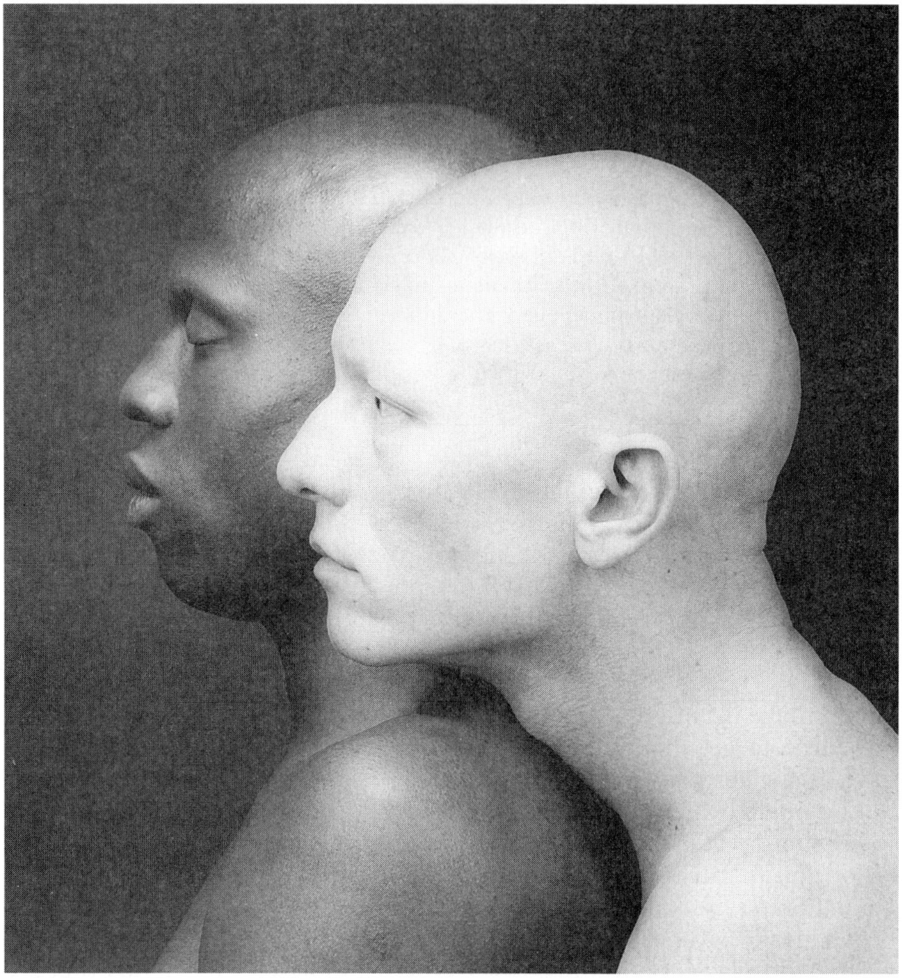

FIGURE 12-27 Robert Mapplethorpe, *Ken Moody and Robert Sherman, 1984*. (© 1984 The Estate of Robert Mapplethorpe)

PERCEPTION KEY
ART AND CENSORSHIP

1. Should governments support the arts as a means of improving the life of the public? Government supports education; is art a form of education?
2. Would you vote for the Helms amendment? Are there works in this book that you believe would fall under one of the three categories that it restricts from support? Is it right for the government of the United States to restrict support of art, however presumably obscene, sacrilegious, or immoral? If a work of art enlightens, then is not obscenity, the sacrilegious, and the immoral transformed? If so, then would you agree that these undesirables may be the subject matter of a work of art but never the content?
3. Why would artists feel it appropriate to shock the public rather than to pander to its tastes? Is it possible that artists who pander to public taste ought to be censored on the basis that they are unoriginal, greedy, and socially destructive?
4. If the U.S. government has the right to reject art that offends, should it not also imprison the offending artist (as was done in the Soviet Union and China)?
5. What are the alternatives to censorship of the arts?

COLOR PHOTOGRAPHY

Color photography has special problems because color tends to limit the photographer's ability to transform the subject matter. Therefore serious photographers often choose apparently inconsequential subject matter in order to release the viewer from the tyranny of the scene, thereby permitting the viewer to concentrate on structure and nuances of lighting and texture. These are expressly photographic values. In a sense such photographers follow Atget's lead.

An example of the opposite approach is the pictorialism of the typical journalistic photograph of the kind seen in *National Geographic,* a publication whose photographs are celebrated, but almost always because they are excellent examples of a picturesque subject. In the color photographs of Thomas Höpker, Joel Myerowitz, and Cindy Sherman, we are in worlds far removed from journalism.

Thomas Höpker's image from *Sculpture Safaris* (Figure 12-28) is mysteriously tantalizing. The contrast between the man-made object and the naturally sculptured sand dunes of the Sahara is matched by the contrast in light patterns, both on the mirrored cube and in the dunes themselves. The softness of lighting and color—and especially its limited range of tonalities—make this a complex image whose allusion to sculpture is part of its subtle subject matter.

Joel Myerowitz's solution to the problem of color is to make the scene

FIGURE 12-28
Thomas Höpker, *Sculpture Safaris*. 1978. (Thomas Höpker/Magnum Photos.)

FIGURE 12-29
Joel Meyerowitz, *Red Interior, Provincetown*. 1977. (Courtesy Joel Meyerowitz)

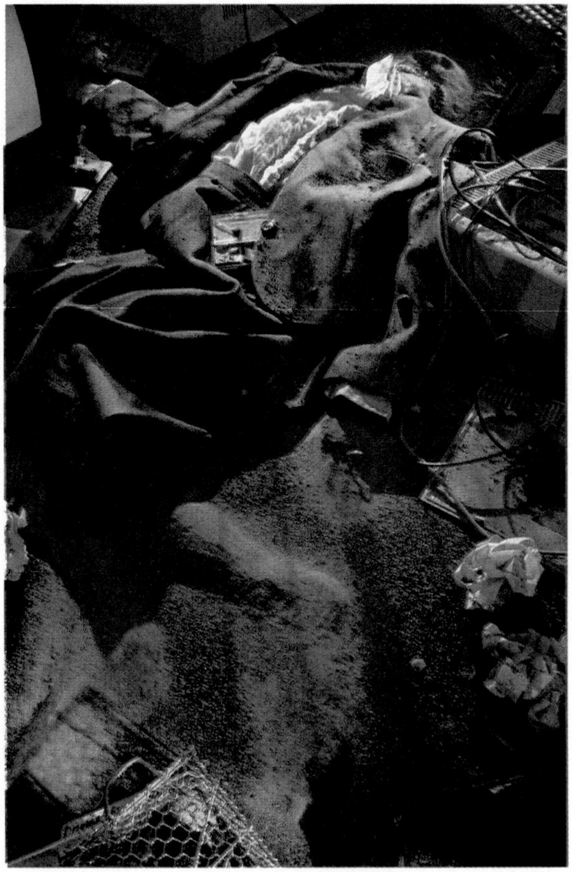

FIGURE 12-30
Cindy Sherman, *Untitled*. 1987. Color photograph, 86⅛ × 61⅛ inches. (Courtesy Metro Pictures)

secondary to the color, so that the subject matter of *Red Interior, Provincetown* (1977, Figure 12-29) is more the play of the red and white and blues than of the moon, cars, and cottages. Yet the cars and the cottages are there, and the complex interrelationship between them and Myerowitz's hymn to color and light makes this photograph a fascinating study in lyric sensuality.

Cindy Sherman is one of the few American photographers to have had a one-woman show at the prestigious Whitney Museum in New York City (1987). Her work has annoyed, confounded, and alarmed many people both ignorant and well informed about photography as an art. For many years she photographed herself in various costumes, with various makeup and guises that showed her almost limitless capacity to interpret her personality. Those color photographs often had a snapshot quality, and they were most interesting when seen as a group rather than individually.

Some of Sherman's work is often condemned because it seems designed to "gross out" the audience with images of garbage, offal, vomit, and body parts. The crumpled suit and assorted garbage in *Untitled* (Figure 12-30) seems to be the residue of a life. In the middle of the carpet is a small pile of ashes that may suggest the mortal remains of a cremated person (Cindy Sherman?). This photograph should not be read only in terms of its objects. Color is also part of the subject matter, as it is in *Red Interior, Provincetown,* and can be appreciated somewhat the way one appreciates the color of a Cézanne or a Renoir. The objects she photographed have been purposely simplified and limited. This is not the kind of photograph of which anyone would ask: "Where was this taken?"

Perception Key
THE MODERN EYE

1. Which of the black-and-white images (Figures 12-24 to 12-27) is least like a snapshot?
2. Compare the photographic values of Robert Mapplethorpe's *Ken Moody and Robert Sherman* with those of Duane Michals' *Things Are Queer.* In which are the gradations of tone from light to dark more carefully modulated? In which is the selectivity of the framing more consciously and apparently artistic? In which is the subject matter more obviously transformed by the photographic image?
3. Which of the color photographs best combines the colors with the objects they help interpret? What do the colors suggest about those objects?
4. Xerox one of the color photographs to produce a black-and-white image. What has been lost? Is the color essential to the success of the photograph?

SUMMARY

Photography's capacity to record reality faithfully is both a virtue and a fault. It makes many viewers of photographs concerned only with what is presented (the subject matter) and leaves them unaware of the way it has been represented (the form). Because of its fidelity of presentation, photography seems to some to have no transformation of subject matter (the content). This did not bother early photographers, who were delighted at the ease with which they could present their subject matter. The pictorialists, on the other hand, relied on nineteenth-century representational painting to guide them in their approach to form. Their soft focus, sometimes sentimental subject matter, and carefully composed images are still valued by many photographers. But the reaction of the straight photographers, who wished to shake off any dependence on painting and disdained sentimental subject matter, began a revolution that emphasized the special qualities of the medium: especially the tonal range of the silver or platinum print (and now color print), the impersonality of the sharply defined object (and consequent lack of sentimentality), spatial compression, and selective framing. The revolution has not stopped there, but has pushed on into unexpected areas, such as the exploration of the random snapshot and the rejection of the technical standards of the straight photographers. Many contemporary photographers are searching for new ways of photographic seeing based on the capacity of the computer to transform and manipulate images.

CHAPTER 12 BIBLIOGRAPHY

Barthes, Roland. *Camera Lucida.* New York: Hill and Wang, 1981.

Bayer, Jonathan. *Reading Photographs: Understanding the Aesthetics of Photography.* New York: Pantheon Books, 1977.

Berger, John, and Jean Mohr. *Another Way of Telling.* New York: Pantheon, 1982.

Doty, Robert. *Photo-Secession.* New York: Dover, 1978.

Galassi, Peter. *Before Photography.* New York: Museum of Modern Art, 1981.

Gernsheim, Helmut. *Creative Photography.* London: Faber and Faber, 1962.

Hambourg, Maria Morris, et al. (eds.). *The Waking Dream: Photography's First Century.* New York: Metropolitan Museum of Art, 1993.

Jeffrey, Ian. *Photography.* London: Thames & Hudson, 1985; 1991.

Lyons, Nathan. *Photographers on Photography.* Englewood Cliffs, N.J.: Prentice Hall, 1966.

Malcolm, Janet. *Diana and Nikon: Essays on the Aesthetics of Photography.* Boston: David Godine, 1980.

Newhall, Beaumont. *The History of Photography,* 5th ed., rev. and enl. New York: Museum of Modern Art, 1994.

——— (ed.). *Photography: Essays and Images.* New York: Museum of Modern Art, 1980.

Petruck, Peninah R. (ed.). *The Camera Viewed.* 2 vols. New York: E. P. Dutton, 1979.

Rosenberg, Harold. *The Tradition of the New.* New York: McGraw-Hill, 1965.

Sandler, Martin W. *The Story of American Photography.* Boston: Little, Brown, 1979.

Scharf, Aaron. *Art and Photography.* New York: Penguin, 1974.

Sontag, Susan. *On Photography.* New York: Farrar, Straus & Giroux, 1977.

Time-Life Books. *Life Library of Photography.* New York: Time-Life, 1970–1972; rev., 1980.

CHAPTER 12 WEBSITES

Ansel Adams (exhibits and essays)

World Wide Web: **http://bookweb.cwis.uci.edu:8042/AdamsHome.html**

California Museum of Photography (University of California at Riverside collections)

World Wide Web: **http://www.cmp.ucr.edu/**

Canadian Journal of Photojournalism and Documentary Photography (exhibitions of Canadian photography)

World Wide Web: **http://cadvision.com/Home_Pages/accounts/galbrair/deadline.html/**

The Civil War Collection (Brady, Gardner, and other masters of Civil War photography)

World Wide Web: **http://rs6.loc.gov/cwarquery.html**

Digital Photography (view annual contest winners; contest information)

World Wide Web: **http://www.bradley.edu/exhibit95/**

George Eastman House (classic photos, exhibitions)

World Wide Web: **http://www.it.rit.edu:80/~gehouse/**

The National Museum of Photography, Film & Television (exhibits from England)

World Wide Web: **http://www.nmsi.ac.uk/nmpft/**

Photo Perspectives Museum (special exhibits)

World Wide Web: **http://www.i3tele.com/photoperspectives**

Planet Earth Art and Photography (links to various sites and images)

World Wide Web: **http://www.nosc.mil/planet_earth/art.html**

Smithsonian Image Archive

Anonymous FTP: Address: **photo1.si.edu** Path: **/images/gif89a** or **/images/jpeg**

Stereograms and 3D Images (links to great images and archives)

World Wide Web: **http://www.yahoo.com/Art/Computer_Generated/Stereograms**

Time Life Photo Sight (great archives, historical photos)

World Wide Web: **http://pathfinder.com/photo/sighthome/html/** or **http://pathfinder.com/Life/lifehome.html**

The Zone 1 Gallery (African-American photography)

World Wide Web: **http://www.gate.net/~eak3/**

C H A P T E R 13

THE INTERRELATIONSHIPS OF THE ARTS

THE LANGUAGES OF THE ARTS

The arts express themselves through various media: paint, stone, sounds, words, film, and much more. Certain media have been refined over thousands of years so that they become appropriate in the hands of the artist for exploring issues and impressions of great complexity. To some extent it may be reasonable to think of the resources of the sculptor, for example, as constituting a type of language expressing itself in terms of three-dimensional space, volume, and color. The painter, with the resources of two-dimensional space, light, color, and line, works within another artistic language. The writer creates imaginary space, sound, action, and landscape using the resources of words. The various languages of art ordinarily circumscribe themselves with reference to the senses. Therefore, one may say the primary sense relating to music is sound; the primary sense relating to painting is sight; the primary senses relating to sculpture are sight and touch, as we have suggested in our discussions of these arts.

Different arts sometimes share the same senses, as, for example, architecture and sculpture depend upon sight, touch, and the perception of space as real volume. Yet they do so in quite different ways: architectural volume will be perceived differently from sculptural volume. Our sense of touch will attract us virtually to caress a given sculpture, while certain architecture will excite our tactile imagination with its remote surface coarseness or exceptional smoothness. Occasionally, the distinctions between the two art forms will become shadowy, as when, for example, one can walk inside a colossal sculpture such as Alexander Calder's *Gates of Spoleto* (Figure 5-16), or when, as in the case of the great pyramid (Figure 5-10), one cannot gain access to the inside of what appears to be a colossal architectural statement. However, those are exceptions. Usually, we feel that arts differ in terms of their appeal to various senses in their various specialized fashions.

However different the languages of specific arts may be, they communicate with each other. Indeed, a great deal of important art speaks to or about arts in different media. A great many poems have been written on works of art—or have been inspired by them. In a sense, we see poets taking the subject matter of painters and using the formal means of poetry to discover a new content. The same is true of painting inspired by music, for example, Mondrian's *Broadway Boogie Woogie* (Figure 5-5). Unfortunately, much illustration fails to achieve artistic form because it restates—rather than interprets—its source. Our concern here will be with works that have an independent vitality as art while maintaining art as their referent.

PAINTING AND PHOTOGRAPHY: VISUAL EXPRESSION

Two-dimensional arts such as painting and photography depend on the visual for their effect. It is possible to have paintings whose canvases are stretched in such a way as to bulge in the middle or stick out sharply. It is also possible to have photographs on irregular surfaces. But we also know when we see these works that their primary appeal is to the visual. External noises would not ruin our experience of viewing such works, but turning out the lights would definitely damage our experience.

SCULPTURE: TACTILE AND VISUAL EXPRESSION

Sculpture depends on visual expression—we see sculpture. Sometimes we can walk around it to find a privileged position from which to view it. Our sense of sight is intensely involved with sculpture, just as it is with painting. But there are times when the roughness of its metal surface or the smoothness of its wood or marble surfaces invites us to touch it and sense it in a more visceral way. Some sculptures invite us to think of how much they weigh, while at the same time they impress us with a sense of the space or volume they displace in air. When walking around Alexander Liberman's *Iliad* (Figure 5-35) one participates with the sculpture in a special way. Its size is gigantic, its color is bold and fresh in a setting that is green and lush in summer, bright and cold in winter. The appeals to the visual sense are intense. But one is also aware of the size and sheer volume of the tanks he has used to construct his work. A synaesthesia—an appeal to several senses simultaneously—is at work in such sculpture.

ARCHITECTURE: SPATIAL AND VISUAL EXPRESSION

Antonio Gaudí's *Sagrada Familia* (Figures 6-22 to 6-24) is a cross between sculpture and architecture. One walks before the church and sees the huge, towering spires looming suddenly in a crowded cityscape. They are unlike any nearby physical structure. At first they appear to be modern sculpture thrusting, like Liberman's, dramatically upward. Then one realizes they are continued by walls and portals. But when one is inside the church, again there is a confusion, since with no roof to cover the interior, and with circular steps leading upward in the spires, one's sense that this is a piece of architecture is confounded. Of course, other buildings, such as the Pantheon in Paris, present us with a more conventional interior space marked with arcs, curves, and soaring columns leading our eyes upward to heaven. We are aware, as at St. Peter's in Rome (Figure 6-1) and St. Paul's in London (Figure 3-7), of a huge volume of space available for our contemplation. In these buildings it is an articulated space that seems calculated for precise effects on the viewer. But the viewer perceives the building with more than the eyes. One sees the walls, the physical fabric of the building, but one "feels" the space that the fabric not only contains, but controls.

MUSIC: AURAL EXPRESSION

Music is as much aural in its appeal as painting is visual. The basic "material" of music is sound. Yet, as John Cage demonstrated in a brief composition during which a performer sits motionlessly at a piano for a little more than a minute, silence is also an element of sound. Just as the absence of color is useful in painting, the absence of sound can be important in music. Still, our primary responses are given to tones articulated in specific ways to achieve specific results. Some of our satisfaction in music comes from our awareness of the perfection achieved by the composer in terms of having found the logical relations among tones. In other words, some music satisfies by its sheer formal perfection. But most music satisfies by exploring and clarifying feelings recognized by the listener. Sounds evoke those feelings and the form of the musical organization controls them.

LITERATURE: REPLICATING THE SENSES

Literature uses the language we speak, but it evokes images derived from all the senses. The poet can evoke aromas, as when one speaks of "lilies redolent of perfume." Literature can cause us to "see" characters as if they were present, as in this description:

> He was a manic little fellow, with a twitchy face and febrile arms that gestured meaninglessly in several directions at once as he attempted to articulate a thought whose stopping and starting reflected his own unstable postures.

The writer can describe things in such a way as to help us imagine them.

In the same sense, literature can appropriate other arts by describing them in a way that helps us see the originals more clearly. When the poet describes a painting, in the sense that Anne Sexton describes Vincent van Gogh's *The Starry Night* (see p. 404), part of her purpose is to help us see the painting differently, in the terms in which she establishes her own perception.

DRAMA AND FILM: VISUAL, AURAL, SPATIAL EXPRESSION

The drama and film are very different, to be sure. Film replicates the spatial dimension as literature replicates the five senses. We know the screen is flat, but the experience of the film makes us feel that we observe interiors with spatial dimensions similar to architecture. We know the characters in action are also projected on a flat screen, but we are encouraged to imagine a genuine action involving real people moving before us. The film experience is not limited by a single setting, as in drama, and therefore its expansiveness seems more lifelike even though, paradoxically, it is actually more of an illusion of reality. By contrast, drama generally gives us the real thing: real people moving in real space in front of an audience. Yet the use of the visual, aural, and spatial serves to perpetuate the illusion that the action unfolding onstage is real rather than contrived by a playwright and actors. The two media are similar in that most plays and most films encourage us to observe the lives of people who undergo important changes.

DANCE: KINETIC AND VISUAL EXPRESSION

Dance, whether modern, ballet, jazz, tap, or folk, depends on visual expression, but unlike painting, stable sculpture, or architecture, it adds movement. The usual form of ballet involves an interaction with music, with the dancer moving in such a manner as to interpret the kinetic potential of the music. Much the same is true of modern dance. Alvin Ailey's *Revelations* (Figure 10-11) openly interprets gospel music, especially the great African-American spirituals that dominate each segment of the dance. One of Ailey's lasting achievements is implied in the fact that it is difficult to listen to one of those spirituals without remembering (perhaps even re-imagining) his dance. One can say the same about *Swan Lake* and the ever-popular *Nutcracker.* After seeing the ballet, when we later hear the music, we almost inevitably re-imagine dance movements to accompany it.

WHEN THE LANGUAGES OF THE ARTS INTERPRET EACH OTHER

Each of the arts exists in an environment of awareness of the other arts. Sculptors read literature; painters see sculpture; filmmakers enjoy architecture; all of them contemplate the others and most of them sooner or later interact with art that is different from their specific chosen medium. Some, such as dramatists, dancers, opera composers, and other performing artists, will draw upon the arts liberally to incorporate them into a production. Scenic stage designers use the methods of architects; lighting designers borrow from painting and photography; stage sets are sometimes painted to resemble landscapes. Such interaction is worth examining. The arts articulate their own artistic form, and when they borrow from other arts they alter that artistic form in ways that are sometimes surprising.

FILM INTERPRETS LITERATURE: *HOWARDS END*

E. M. Forster's novel, *Howards End* (1910), was made into a remarkable film in 1992 by producer Ismail Merchant and director James Ivory. Ruth Prawer Jhabvala wrote the screenplay. The film starred Anthony Hopkins and Emma Thompson, who along with Jhabvala won an Academy Award. The film itself was nominated as best picture, and its third Academy Award went to the art direction of Luciana Arrighi and Ian Whittaker. (See Figures 13-1 to 13-3.)

The team of Merchant–Ivory, producer–director, has become distinguished for period films set in the late nineteenth century and the time of the First World War. Part of the reputation won by Merchant–Ivory films is due to the detailed artistic direction. Thus, in any Merchant–Ivory film one expects to see Edwardian costumes meticulously reproduced, Edwardian interiors with period prints and paintings on the walls, authentic architecture, both interior and exterior, and authentic period details sumptuously photographed so that the colors are rich and saturated and the

FIGURE 13-1
James Wilby, Jemma Redgrave, Vanessa Redgrave, and Joseph Bennett in *Howards End*. (© 1992 Merchant Ivory Productions)

FIGURE 13-2
Anthony Hopkins and Emma Thompson in *Howards End*. (© 1992 Merchant Ivory Productions)

atmosphere appropriately that of another era from ours. (See Figures 13-1 to 13-3.)

All of that is true of the production of *Howards End*. But the subtlety of the interplay of the arts in the film is intensified because of the subtlety of the interplay of the arts in the original novel. E. M. Forster wrote his novel in such a way as to emulate in part contemporary drama. His scenes are dramatically conceived, with characters acting in carefully described settings, speaking lines of dialogue to one another, and forwarding the action by their responses to people and circumstances. Moreover, Forster's special interest in music and the role culture in general plays in the lives of his characters makes the book especially interesting to interpret in a film.

The novel examines the English middle-class as it represents itself in two families, that of Margaret Schlegel, who is sensitive and responsive to others—especially those in need—and Henry Wilcox, whose family is concerned with money, position, and securing itself in the world. The Wilcoxes are insensitive and careless of others—except for Henry's first wife Ruth, who, when she is ill, comes to know Margaret. Ruth dies and leaves a handwritten note giving her own home, Howards End, to Margaret. But the Wilcoxes decide to suppress the bequest, not because they like the house, but because they do not want to give Margaret something they think she does not deserve. Ironically, and much later, Margaret and Henry marry, only to find that their sensibilities and values are so diametrically opposed that they cannot continue, and the novel ends with their separation.

The film is quite faithful to the novel in that it preserves the plot, represents the characters carefully, and presents a similar impression of the families and the problems that are uncovered in the original. What it adds to

FIGURE 13-3 Emma Thompson and Helena Bonham Carter in *Howards End.* (© 1992 Merchant Ivory Productions)

the novel is on the one hand quite welcome: music, for the scene early in the novel when the Schlegels meet Leonard Bast, a penniless young man married to a woman who was once Henry Wilcox's mistress. They have all been at a concert listening to Beethoven's Fifth Symphony. The film supplies the Beethoven as well as the atmosphere of Queens Hall, helping to bring the scene to life.

E. M. Forster describes the experience of listening to the music—which the film does not do, and probably could only do by quoting this passage in a "voice-over":

> It will be generally admitted that Beethoven's Fifth Symphony is the most sublime noise that has ever penetrated into the ear of man. All sorts and conditions are satisfied by it. Whether you are like Mrs. Munt, and tap surreptitiously when the tunes come—of course, not so as to disturb the others; or like Helen, who can see heroes and shipwrecks in the music's flood; or like Margaret, who can only see the music; or like Tibby, who is profoundly versed in counterpoint, and holds the full score open on his knee; or like their cousin, Fräulein Mosebach, who remembers all the time that Beethoven is "echt Deutsch" [pure German]; or like Fräulein Mosebach's young man, who can remember nothing but Fräulein Mosebach: in any case, the passion of your life becomes more vivid, and you are bound to admit that such a noise is cheap at two shillings.

Forster reminds us that Beethoven's Fifth Symphony not only appeals to many different kinds of listeners, but that their act of listening will be very different from one another. Some people like Margaret hear the music and respond to it; others, like her younger sister Helen, imagine a dramatic pretext of heroes and shipwrecks and respond thus to their imagination. The film cannot provide such analysis despite its efforts because such analysis can only be suggested by the visual language of film, but not articulated in Forster's fashion in anything but words. Fortunately, James Ivory does not worry us over such an issue. Instead, he focuses on the contrast of Margaret and Leonard Bast, whose umbrella she takes by error from the concert hall, only to meet him later at her home, where she returns it. Bast is living in squalor, working at a low-level office job, hardly able to get by. But he craves access to the cultured life that the Schlegels take virtually for granted, and that the Wilcoxes tolerate only so long as it does not prevent them from making money.

The film of *Howards End* achieves something in 1992 that the novel could not have achieved in its own time, and probably not even in our time. It creates a sense of nostalgia for an elegant way of life in a time long past and totally unrecoverable. The very beauty of the art direction undoubtedly glamorizes the era and makes it look more glowing, more beautiful, more desirable than it really was. The novel, since it cannot represent the scenes before our eyes, could not achieve that goal unless it were to use very different means. Simply setting the characters in their carefully described houses and rooms and describing their environment does not produce in the reader a sense of longing for a time past. The novel forces us to focus much more intensely on the values of the characters and the implications of those values for the development of social responsibility. The motto of the novel, on the front cover, is "Only connect," which is used later in the novel as a reprimand against the Wilcoxes, who cannot "connect" themselves with those in a lesser position in life. They cannot sympathize with others because they have isolated themselves from anyone except themselves and others like them.

Perception Key

FORSTER'S AND MERCHANT–IVORY'S *HOWARDS END*

1. View the film's scenes set in Queens Hall listening to Beethoven's Fifth Symphony. Compare them with Chapter V of the novel. In which is the music more significant to the action? In which is the music more valued?
2. After reading some or all of the novel, compare your expectations of how the characters would look and behave with the film's presentation of Margaret Schlegel and Henry Wilcox. In what ways does the film disappoint you? In what ways does it surprise and delight you?
3. In which work, the film or the novel, are the social issues of greater importance? Which seems to stress more the class distinctions between the Basts and both the Schlegels and the Wilcoxes? Which seems to have a clearer social "message"?
4. How does the film, by supplying the materials your imagination supplies in reading the novel, affect your understanding of the lives of the Schlegels, Wilcoxes, and Basts? Can you return to the novel after seeing the film and read the novel the same way?

FIGURE 13-4
Dawn Upshaw as Susanna and Ferruccio Furlanetto as Figaro in the 1992 Metropolitan Opera production of *The Marriage of Figaro* (Winnie Klotz, Metropolitan Opera Association)

MUSIC INTERPRETS DRAMA: *THE MARRIAGE OF FIGARO*

Perhaps in the age of Wolfgang Amadeus Mozart (1756–1791) the opera performed a function for literature somewhat equivalent to what the film does today. Opera, in combining orchestral music, singing, speech, beautiful sets, and dramatic plots, was held in highest esteem in Europe in the eighteenth century. And despite the competition from ambitious theater and eventually film and musical comedy, opera is still performed to large audiences in theaters and larger audiences on television. Among the world's greatest operas, few are more popular than Mozart's *The Marriage of Figaro* (1786) written when Mozart was only thirty. (See Figure 13-4.)

Mozart's opera interprets a French play by Pierre Augustin de Beaumarchais, *The Marriage of Figaro* (1784). Beaumarchais was then a highly successful playwright, who was known to Mme. Pompadour, mistress of Louis XVI, during the period of the American revolution. Beaumarchais began as an ordinary citizen, bought his way into the aristocracy, survived the French revolution, went into exile, and later died in France. His plays were the product of, yet comically critical of, the aristocracy. *The Marriage of Figaro,* written in 1780, was held back by censors as an attack on the government. Eventually produced to great acclaim, it was seditious

FIGURE 13-5
Helen Donat as the Countess and Dwayne Croft as the Count in the 1994 Metropolitan Opera production of *The Marriage of Figaro* (Winnie Klotz, Metropolitan Opera Association)

enough for later commentators to claim that it was an essential ingredient in fomenting the French revolution of 1789.

Mozart, with Lorenzo da Ponte, who wrote the book (the libretto, or text, of the opera), remained generally faithful to the play, changing some names and changing the occupations of some characters. They reduced the opera to four acts from Beaumarchais' five, although the entire opera is three hours long. (See Figure 13-5.)

In brief, it is the story of Figaro, servant to Count Almaviva, and his intention of marrying the countess's maid Susanna. The count has given up feudal tradition, which would have permitted him to sleep with Susanna first, before her husband. However, he regrets his decision because he has fallen in love with Susanna and now tries to seduce her. When his wife, the countess, young and still in love with him, discovers his plans, she throws in with Figaro and Susanna to thwart him. Cherubino, a very young man—sung by a female soprano—feels the first stirrings of love and desires both the countess and Susanna in turn. He is a page in the count's employ and when his intentions are discovered, he is sent into the army. One of the greatest arias in the opera is "Non più andrai," "From now on," which Figaro sings to Cherubino, telling him that his amorous escapades are now over.

Mozart's nine-page aria is derived from part of a single speech of Beaumarchais' Figaro:

> No more hanging around all day with the girls, no more cream buns and custard tarts, no more charades and blind-man's-bluff; just good soldiers, by God: weatherbeaten and ragged-assed, weighed down with their muskets, right face, left face, forward march.[1]

Mozart's treatment of the speech demonstrates one of the resources of opera as opposed to straight drama. In the drama, it would be very difficult to expand Figaro's speech to intensify its emotional content, but in the opera the speech or parts of it can be repeated frequently and with pleasure, since the music that underpins the words is delightful to hear and rehear. Mozart's opera changes the emotional content of the play because it invokes feelings and associates them with key moments in the action.

The aria contains a very simple musical figure that has nonetheless a great power in the listening. Just as Mozart is able to repeat parts of dialogue, he is able to repeat notes, passages, and patterns. The pattern repeated most conspicuously is that of the arpeggio (a chord whose notes are played separately): C-E-G; E-G-C; G-C-E, then returning to C: three forms of the most basic chord in the key of C (Figure 13-6). Mozart's genius was marked by a way of finding the simplest, yet most unexpected, solutions to musical problems. The arpeggio is practiced by every student of a musical instrument, so it is familiar to all, yet it is thought of as something appropriate to practice rather than performance, and thus comes as a surprise.

FIGURE 13-6
Arpeggio from "Non più andrai," *The Marriage of Figaro.*

The very essence of the arpeggio is constant repetition, and in using the pattern of the arpeggio Mozart finds yet another way to repeat elements to intensify the emotional circumstance of the music. The listener hears the passage, is impressed by the emotional effect, yet hardly knows in any conscious way why it is as impressive and as memorable as it is. There are ways of doing similar things in drama—repeating image patterns, for example—but there are very few ways of repeating elements in such close proximity without risking boredom.

The plot of the opera, like that of the play, is based on thwarting the plans of the count with the use of disguise and mixups. Characters are hidden in bedrooms, thus overhearing important conversations they ought not hear. They leap from bedroom windows, hide in closets, and generally add to a comic confusion. The much older Marcelina and her lawyer Bartholo introduce the complication of a breach of promise suit between her and

[1]Beaumarchais, *The Marriage of Figaro,* tr. Bernard Sahlins. Copyright 1994. Chicago: Ivan R. Dee 1332 North Halsted Street, Chicago 60622, p. 29.

Figaro just as Figaro is about to marry. The count uses it to his advantage while he can, but the difficulty is resolved in a marvelously comic way: Marcelina sees a birthmark on Figaro and realizes he is her son and the son of Bartholo, with whom she had an affair. That finally clears the way for Figaro and Susanna, who, once they have shamed the count into attending to the countess, can marry.

Mozart's musical resources include techniques that cannot easily be duplicated in straight drama. For example, his extended use of duets, quartets, and sextets, in which characters interact and sing together, would be impossible in the original drama. Mozart's libretto gave him a chance to have one character sing a passage while another filled in with an aside. Thus, there are moments when one character sings what he expects others want him to say, while another character sings his or her inner thoughts, specifically designed for the audience to hear. Mozart reveals the duplicity of characters by having them sing one passage "publicly" while revealing their secret motives "privately."

The force of the quartets and the sextets in *The Marriage of Figaro* is enormous, adding wonderfully to the comic effect that this opera always achieves. Their musical force, in terms of sheer beauty and subtle complexity, is one of the hallmarks of the opera. In the original drama by Beaumarchais it would be impossible to have six characters speaking simultaneously, but with the characters singing, such a situation is quite possible. Yet it is also enormously difficult for the composer to work out the harmonies and melodies in a way that sustains the clarity of the thoughts and emotions of the characters.

The resources that Mozart had in orchestration helped him achieve effects that the stage could not produce. The horns, for example, are sometimes used for the purposes of poking fun at the pretentious count, who is a hunter. The discords found in some of the early arias resolve themselves in later arias as the countess smooths them out, as in the opening aria in Act II: *Porgi Amor* (Pour forth, O Love). The capacity of the music to emulate the emotional condition of the characters is a further resource that permits Mozart to emphasize tension, as when, for example, strong chords seem to jab or stab in the air to reflect the anxiety of the count. Further, the capacity to bring the music quite low (pianissimo) and then contrast it with brilliant loud passages (fortissimo) adds a dimension that the stage can barely even suggest.

Mozart's *The Marriage of Figaro* has been successful not only because of its political message, which is essentially democratic in nature. The opera presents us with a delightful character, Figaro, a barber become a servant, who is level-headed, somewhat innocent of the evil ways of the world, and a smart man when he needs to be. He loves Susanna, who is much more worldly wise than he, but who is also a thoughtful, intelligent young woman. They contrast as a couple with the count, an unsympathetic man who resents the fact that his servant Figaro can have what he wants but cannot possess. The count is outwitted by his servant and his wife at almost every turn. The countess is a sympathetic character. She loves her husband, knows he wants to be unfaithful, but plays along with Susanna and Figaro in a scheme involving assignations and disguises in order to shame him into doing the right thing. The audiences of the age loved the play because they reveled in the amusing way that Figaro manipulates his aristocratic master. Beaumarchais' play was as clear about this as the opera. However, the opera continues to be produced because the music adds a dimension of humor and pathos that the play could not produce as efficiently.

PERCEPTION KEY

BEAUMARCHAIS' AND MOZART'S *THE MARRIAGE OF FIGARO*

1. Compare Act I of Beaumarchais' play with Act I of Mozart's opera. In the original production of the opera the aria "Non più andrai," at the end of Act I, was a huge sensation even to those who knew the play in its original form. Compare the effects achieved by play and opera. Unfortunately, there is no video available of the Beaumarchais play, but there are several videos of the opera. The Deutsche Grammophone version, with Dietrich Fisher-Dieskau as the count, Herman Prey as Figaro, Mirella Freni as Susanna, and Kiri Te Kanawa as the countess, is excellent and has English subtitles. Listening to the opera while following the libretto is also of great value. Listen for the use of individual instruments, such as the clarinets on the off-beat, the power of horns and drums, and the repetition of phrases. The simplicity of the final aria nonetheless builds tension and provides the listener with great amusement. Are such emotions developed in the play?
2. Compare the clarity of the development of character in both play and opera. What differences in feeling do the respective works produce? Is character or plot foremost in Beaumarchais' work? Which is foremost in Mozart's?

POETRY INTERPRETS PAINTING: *THE STARRY NIGHT*

Poetry often interprets famous paintings, since paintings are wordless and in a sense invite a commentary. Vincent van Gogh was a tormented man whose slide into madness has been chronicled in letters, biographies, romantic novels, and films. His painting *The Starry Night* (Figure 13-7) is an eloquent, tortured image filled with dynamic swirls and rich colors, portraying a night that is not peaceful and calm, but one that is intense, active, and perhaps even threatening.

The first poem, by Robert Fagles (b. 1933), speaks from the point of view of van Gogh, imagining a psychic pain that has somehow been relieved by the act of painting:

THE STARRY NIGHT

Long as I paint
I feel myself
less mad
the brush in my hand
a lightning rod to madness

FIGURE 13-7
Vincent van Gogh, *The Starry Night.* 1889. Oil on canvas, 29 × 36¼ inches. The Museum of Modern Art, New York. Acquired through the Lillie P. Bliss Bequest. (Photograph © 1997 The Museum of Modern Art, New York)

But never ground that madness
execute it ride the lightning up
from these benighted streets and steeple up
with the cypress look its black is burning green

I am that I am it cries
it lifts me up the nightfall up
the cloudrack coiling like a dragon's flanks
a third of the stars of heaven wheeling in its wake
wheels in wheels around the moon that cradles round the sun

and if I can only trail these whirling eternal stars
with one sweep of the brush like Michael's sword if I can
cut the life out of the beast—safeguard the mother and the son
all heaven will hymn in conflagration blazing down
    the night the mountain ranges down
    the claustrophobic valleys of the mad

            Madness
    is what I have instead of heaven
    God deliver me—help me now deliver
    all this frenzy back into your hands
    our brushstrokes burning clearer into dawn

Anne Sexton (1928–1975) was one of America's most powerful poets, but her brief life was cut short by insanity and then suicide. She may have seen the painting as an emblem of madness from a perspective that most sane people cannot. In light of her personal journey, it is especially painful to see how she interprets the painting:

THE STARRY NIGHT

That does not keep me from having a terrible need of—shall I say the word—religion. Then I go out at night to paint the stars.

Vincent van Gogh in a letter to his brother

The town does not exist
except where one black-haired tree slips
up like a drowned woman into the hot sky.
The town is silent. The night boils with eleven stars
Oh starry starry night! This is how
I want to die.

It moves. They are all alive.
Even the moon bulges in its orange irons
to push children, like a god, from its eye.
The old unseen serpent swallows up the stars.
Oh starry starry night! This is how
I want to die:

into that rushing beast of the night,
sucked up by that great dragon, to split
from my life with no flag,
no belly,
no cry.

Both poets offer only the briefest description of the painting. If one had not seen it, no reader could know quite what the painting looks like. Yet both poets move directly to the emotional core of the painting, its connection with madness and psychic pain. For Fagles, the effort was intensely imaginative. For Sexton, perhaps, less so. Shortly before she wrote her poem her father had died and she had an illegal abortion because she feared the baby she was about to have was not fathered by her husband. Her personal life was tormented for several months before she wrote the poem, but she continued to write all the time, producing her most widely read volume: *All My Pretty Ones,* which, for a book of modern poetry, had extraordinary sales and a great popularity. Interestingly, both poets see in the painting the form of a dragon, the biblical beast that hounded humanity to make a hell of life.

PERCEPTION KEY

FAGLES' AND SEXTON'S *THE STARRY NIGHT*

1. Does either poem reflect the forms found in the painting? Is the shape of Fagles' poem similar to the cypress tree?

2. How relevant is the imagery of the beast in the poems to an understanding of the forms in the painting?
3. Do the poems help you interpret the imagery of the painting in ways that are richer than before you read the poems? Or do the poems distract you from the painting?
4. How effective would the poems be if there were no painting for them to refer to? Could they stand on their own or must they always be referenced to the painting?
5. Does the painting profit from having had these poems written about it?
6. If you feel it does profit from these poems, write your own poem about this painting. Or, if you like, choose another painting in this book and write a poem that you feel has an independent integrity, but is inspired by the painting.

PAINTING INTERPRETS ARCHITECTURAL SPACE: *DIDO BUILDING CARTHAGE, SEAPORT: THE EMBARKATION OF THE QUEEN OF SHEBA,* AND *SCHOOL OF ATHENS*

Painters have represented buildings of all kinds in their work over the entire history of painting. During the romantic period, the late eighteenth and early nineteenth centuries, painters were attracted to ruined castles, ruined abbeys, and ruins in general. The neoclassical period (the early 1700s), which held classical Greek and Roman values in high esteem, produced paintings with columns, pediments (the triangular, decorated space above the columns over the entrance), and other signs of the great Greek period of architecture. But since most modern examples were in a state of ruin, these paintings often picture buildings that are incomplete and partially worn by time. Yet, artists beginning with the Renaissance realized that classical civilizations had built magnificently and that to a large extent the values that dominated their culture were most powerfully expressed in their great temples and public buildings.

Claude Lorrain (1600–1682), one of the most venerated of the old masters, pictured paintings in a classical mode (Figure 13-8), celebrating classical subjects and settings. J. M. W. Turner (1775–1851) was a romantic and his *Dido Building Carthage* (Figure 13-9) was painted in deliberate competition with Claude's neoclassical painting, using a similar point of view, similar lighting, and a similar veneration for architecture. Turner's purpose was to demonstrate that he was superior to one of the most acknowledged "old masters." He gave his painting to the National Gallery on condition that it be hung beside *Seaport: The Embarkation of the Queen of Sheba* so that posterity would see how right he was.

The paintings have some interesting differences. Claude's includes completed architecture featuring the great achievement of the Roman arch as well as the details of tower, rising pediments, and sculptural ornament. All is proportioned according to classical models, receding grandly into the distance. The contemporary sailing ship to the right implies that the imaginary landscape is still in existence, refined and complete. Turner's approach is ingenious in that by imagining Carthage in the process of being built, he can make his buildings resemble the ruins that travelers in his time saw—

FIGURE 13-8
Claude Lorrain. *Seaport: The Embarkation of the Queen of Sheba.* 1648. Oil on canvas, 58½ × 76¼ inches. National Gallery, London. (Bridgeman/Art Resource, New York)

FIGURE 13-9
J. M. W. Turner, *Dido Building Carthage.* 1815. Oil on canvas, 61¼ × 91¼ inches. National Gallery, London. (Bridgeman/Art Resource, New York)

they are incomplete. He, too, represents columns and the Roman arch, two unmistakable achievements of the classical architecture that people would have seen. Like Claude, he celebrates the harmonic relationship of parts, the perfect proportions that marked classical architecture.

PERCEPTION KEY
TURNER AND CLAUDE

1. Compare the role of architecture in the Turner and the Claude. In which painting does architecture play a greater role? In which does it seem more commanding, more suggestive of cultural greatness?
2. In which painting do human beings seem less significant in relation to the architecture: the Turner or the Claude? What do the people seem to be doing in each of their paintings? In which is human achievement more celebrated?
3. Compare the left and right portions of the Turner and the Claude. Do they complement each other or do they sharply contrast with each other?

The Renaissance painter Raphael Sanzio (1483–1520) produced quite a different hymn to architecture in his *School of Athens* (Figure 13-10). One might say that this is a testament to "pure" classical architecture, or perhaps the "idea" of classical architecture. It would have been difficult to imagine any Greek building looking like the building Raphael painted. Historians have long wondered what kind of building Raphael had in mind. It may be intended as a temple, although it seems to be a gigantic public

FIGURE 13-10
Raphael, *School of Athens.* Stanza della Segnatura, Vatican. 1509–1511. Fresco, 25 feet 3 inches long. (Erich Lessing/Art Resource, New York)

building celebrating the Roman arch, with its arches receding into the distance and its coffered ceilings punctuating space around which must have been a dome of the kind Renaissance architects created. The illusion of recessional space and accurate perspective are central to the achievement of the painting.

Standing before this massive work you have the feeling that you are looking into a true receding architectural space. Part of the illusion is supported by the fact that the primary arch is like a proscenium for a great stage. Within we see figures posed in the foreground in two groups, one on the left and one on the right. The major group of figures is posed above them on an elevation, all spread across the top step.

Raphael represents the School of Athens in terms of the Greek philosophers Plato and Aristotle, both of whom came back into prominence in the fifteenth century and both of whose works became the core of training in Renaissance schools. The figure standing on the main step just to the left of center, robed in red, is Plato, said to be modeled on the aging Renaissance artist Leonardo da Vinci. Plato's right hand points upward toward the heavens. His best known book, *Timaeus,* is in his other hand.

The symbolism is clear: Plato is best known for his concepts of the ideal, the perfection of heaven. His studies were aimed at the cosmos, and those figures who stand with him on the left of the fresco are his disciples. On the right, as we face the painting, is Aristotle, garbed in blue. His hand points down, earthward. In his hand is his *Nichomachaean Ethics*. The symbolism is again clear: Aristotle was more confident in the value of the human senses for gaining a true knowledge of experience. Consequently, those figures to the right of the center of the fresco are involved in the sciences of engineering and architecture. On the left are those involved in mathematics and music, which is why in the niche above the figures on the left stands a giant statue of Apollo with his lute, an instrument that Plato admitted into his perfect Republic. On the right is a large statue of Athena, goddess of wisdom or reason. Raphael included a portrait of himself—the figure in profile at the edge of the lower right foreground group.

The two groups of figures are united under one arch and in one architectural space in part because the pure mathematics of Plato's world is made "visible" in the physical expression of the proportions of classical architecture. The arches express relationships and repetitions much as musical phrases or geometrical figures do. The illusion of recessional space is profound in this painting, which interprets architecture in a symbolic manner as well as in a realistic manner. Architecture is symbolic order. As von Schilling said, "architecture is frozen music," and this painting seems to demonstrate his claim. We are impressed with the rhythms of the repeated and balanced "physical phrases," not just of groups of figures, but of the architectural columns, ornaments, and primary structures. As one stands before it, the painting makes the ideal relationships of architectural space seem real—and yet they are all the more ideal for the very fact that they are not at all "real." The painterly space is, in fact, ideal, yet its "realization" depends on the virtues which we accord our physical senses, particularly the sense of sight, and the combination of sight and touch that permits us to imagine physical space where there is none.

PERCEPTION KEY
RAPHAEL

1. What does Raphael seem to be saying about the architectural space in which he has placed his figures? Is he praising the artistic achievement of the architecture? The technical achievement?
2. Compare the human figures in the architectural space of Raphael's painting. How do they compare in importance with the architecture? Do they hold your attention or does the illusion of interior space hold your attention? How does Raphael use color to achieve a balance in the painting?
3. Examine the focal point of the painting. What is the effect of having such a strong single point of centrality dominate the painting? How does the architecture help produce that point of centrality?

SCULPTURE AND THE INTERPRETATION OF POETRY: *APOLLO AND DAPHNE*

The Roman poet Ovid (43 B.C.–17 A.D.) inspired writers and artists throughout the Renaissance and into modern times. His masterpiece, *The Metamorphoses,* collected a large number of myths that were of interest to his own time, and that have inspired readers of all ages. The title implies changes, virtually all kinds of changes imaginable in the natural and divine world. The sense that the world of Roman deities intersected with humankind had its Greek counterpart in Homer, whose heroes often had to deal with the interference of the gods in their lives. Ovid inspired Shakespeare in literature, Botticelli in painting, and, perhaps most impressively, the renowned sculptor Gian Lorenzo Bernini (1598–1680).

Bernini's technique as a sculptor was without peer in his age. His purposes were quite different from those of modern sculptors in that he was not interested in "truth to materials." If anything, he was interested in showing how he could defy his materials and make marble appear to be flesh, make stone pillows seem to be soft and inviting, and make figures frozen in stone appear to be in motion. His carvings of human figures defy the marble, although they profit from its ability to reproduce the smoothness of human flesh.

Apollo and Daphne (1622–1625) represents a section of *The Metamorphoses* in which the god Apollo falls in love with the nymph Daphne (Figure 13-11). Cupid had previously hit his heart with an arrow to inflame him, while he hit Daphne with an arrow designed to make her reject love entirely. Cupid did this in revenge for Apollo's having killed the python with a bow and arrow. Apollo woos Daphne fruitlessly, she resists, and he attempts to rape her. As she flees from him she pleads with her father, the river god Peneus, to rescue her, and she turns into a laurel tree as Apollo reaches her. Here is the moment in Ovid:

The god by grace of hope, the girl, despair,
Still kept their increasing pace until his lips
Breathed at her shoulder; and almost spent,

FIGURE 13-11
Gian Lorenzo Bernini, *Apollo and Daphne.* 1622–1625. Marble, 8 feet high. Galleria Borghese, Rome. (Scala/Art Resource, New York)

The girl saw waves of a familiar river,
Her father's home, and in a trembling voice
Called, "Father, if your waters still hold charms
To save your daughter, cover with green earth
This body I wear too well," and as she spoke
A soaring drowsiness possessed her; growing
In earth she stood, white thighs embraced by climbing
Bark, her white arms branches, her fair head swaying
In a cloud of leaves; all that was Daphne bowed
In the stirring of the wind, the glittering green
Leaf twined within her hair and she was laurel.

Ovid portrays the moment of metamorphosis as a moment of drowsiness as Daphne becomes rooted and sprouts leaves. It is this instant that Bernini has chosen, an instant during which we can see the human forms of the gods, with Daphne's thighs enclosed in bark, her hair and hands growing leaves as Apollo reaches her. The detail of his sculpture, whose figures are life-size, is extraordinary. In the Borghese Gallery one can walk around the sculpture and examine it up close. The moment of change is so astonishingly wrought that one virtually forgets that it is a sculpture. In some ways, Bernini has converted the poem into a moment of drama through the medium of sculpture.

Certainly Bernini's sculpture is an "illustration" of a specific moment in *The Metamorphoses,* but it goes beyond illustration. Bernini has brought the moment into a three-dimensional space, with the illusion of the wind blowing Apollo's garments and with the pattern of formal, swooping lines producing a sense of motion. From almost any angle, this is an arresting work even for those who do not know the Ovidian reference.

PERCEPTION KEY
OVID'S *THE METAMORPHOSES* AND BERNINI'S *APOLLO AND DAPHNE*

1. Read Book I of *The Metamorphoses* of Ovid. Its theme is creation, and, to an extent, Ovid has told a fanciful tale about the creation of the laurel. Many cultures have similar stories explaining the creation of animals, plants, and trees. Which is more important in Ovid, the laurel itself or the person of Daphne? What is most important about the story?
2. Bernini's sculpture was famous in its time (as was he) for its virtuoso performance. Compare your reaction to the sculpture before you knew the story of Apollo and Daphne and after. What do you notice about the sculpture after reading the story that you did not notice before?
3. Bernini assumed that his audience would realize he was interpreting Ovid's story. Did Bernini choose the right moment for conveying the full power of Ovid's passage on Apollo and Daphne? Is there any other moment that might be of equal power?
4. If you did not know Ovid's *Metamorphoses,* what would your interpretation of the sculpture be? What would you find in it to interpret? What could it mean to you? What would you make of its formal qualities and its use of materials? How would you evaluate it? Is it possible to conclude that it is a less interesting work if you do not know Ovid?
5. Assuming that one knows Bernini is interpreting Ovid, would you conclude that Ovid takes precedence in your response to the sculpture? Does Bernini make the experience of reading Ovid more intense for you? Why? What does Bernini add to the experience of reading Ovid?

PAINTING INTERPRETS DANCE AND MUSIC: *THE DANCE* AND *MUSIC*

Henri Matisse (1869–1954) was commissioned to paint *The Dance* and *Music* (both 1910) by Sergey Shchukin, a Russian businessman in Moscow who had been a constant patron. The works were murals for a staircase and have, since the Russian revolution of 1917, been moved to the Hermitage in Leningrad. In Matisse's time Shchukin entertained lavishly and his guests were sophisticated, well-traveled, beautifully clothed patrons of the arts who went regularly to the ballet, opera, and lavish orchestral concerts. Matisse made his work stand in stark contrast to the world of experience of his potential viewers.

According to Matisse, *The Dance* (Figure 13-12) derived originally from observation of local men and women dancing on the beach in a fishing village in France in which Matisse lived for a short time. Their *sardana* was

FIGURE 13-12
Matisse, *The Dance.* 1910. Decorative panel, oil on canvas, 102¼ × 125½ inches. The Hermitage, St. Petersburg. (Photograph Scala/Art Resource, New York; art © 1997 Succession H. Matisse/Artists Rights Society [ARS], New York)

a formal traditional circle dance, but the energy and essential joy of that dance is transformed in Matisse's image. It is possible to say that *The Dance* interprets the idea of dance rather than any particular dance. Moreover, it is clear that Matisse reaches into the earliest history of dance, portraying naked women and men on a green mound dancing almost ritualistically against a dark blue sky. Their sense of movement is implied in the gesture of each leg, the posture of each figure, the instability of pose, and the sense that the action is ongoing. The figures have been described as "primitive," but the simplicity of their form and hairdos suggests more that they are contemporary dancers merely returning to nature and dancing in accord with a natural sense of motion.

Another version of *The Dance* done in 1909 hangs in the Museum of Modern Art in New York, and while it is very similar in most respects to the version in the Hermitage, it differs in some important ways. First, all of the dancers are clearly women, whereas in the 1910 version the dancer to the far left is not clearly female. Second, in the 1909 version the figures are painted in a much "whiter" flesh tone, and, finally, the dancers all have stark black hair. In the 1910 version, the reddish flesh tones merge with the reddish-brown hair, creating a tonal unity missing in the 1909 version. The impression of movement is much more evident in the 1910 painting, in part because of subtle differences in the postures of the dancers, and in part because of subtle lines demarcating body shape.

Music is similarly primitive, with a fiddler and pipes player (who look as if they were "borrowed" from a Picasso painting) and three singers sitting on a mound of earth against a dark blue sky (Figure 13-13). They are painted in the same flat reddish tones as the dancers, and it seems as if they are playing and singing the music that the dancers are themselves hearing. Again, the approach to the art of music is as basic as the approach to the

FIGURE 13-13
Matisse, *Music.* 1910. Decorative panel, oil on canvas, 102¼ × 153 inches. The Hermitage, St. Petersburg. (Photograph Scala/Art Resource, New York; art © 1997 Succession H. Matisse/Artists Rights Society, New York)

art of dance: there is very little added to the equipment that people in a state of nature would find. The violin represents the strings and the pipes the woodwinds of the modern orchestra, whereas the majority of the musicians use the most basic of instruments, the human voice. The figures are placed linearly as if they were notes on a staff: a chord with three rising tones and one falling tone.

The two panels, *The Dance* and *Music,* seem designed to work together to imply an ideal for each art. Instead of interpreting a specific artistic moment, Matisse appears to be striving to interpret the essence of both arts.

PERCEPTION KEY

PAINTING AND THE INTERPRETATION OF DANCE AND MUSIC

1. Must these paintings be hung near each other for both to achieve their complete effect? If they are hung next to one another would they need to have their titles evident for the viewer to respond fully to them?
2. What qualities of *The Dance* make you feel that kinetic motion is somehow "present" in the painting? What is dance-like here?
3. What does Matisse do to make *Music* somehow congruent with our ideas of music? Is the painting musical? Which forms within the painting most suggest music?
4. Suppose the figures were totally realistic and the setting were painted realistically. How would that stylistic change affect our perception of the essential nature of dance and music?
5. How does seeing these paintings and reflecting on their achievement help you respond better to dance and music?

THE ARTS AND THE INTERPRETATION OF EXPERIENCE

One function of art is the interpretation of experience, whether the experience is perceiving something, being somewhere, or doing something. In that sense, the arts are always transforming experience into something new. A landscape is transformed into a painting, which in turn helps organize the ways in which we later perceive landscapes. The vistas of Claude and Turner, for example, organize visual spaces in particular ways, and the next time we see a genuine view of a riverhead and architecture, we may well respond more strongly for the fact that it resembles the organization chosen by those painters. The same is true for photography, especially the modern photography of documentarists such as Walker Evans, who in finding formal beauty in otherwise ugly small-town scenes has given us a new way to look at our own experience. Some of us see "Walker Evanses" in our everyday drives and walks through town.

Much the same may be said of literature, which gives us ways of interpreting experience by means of example. Susan Glaspell's *Trifles* reminds us that women and men see different things by virtue of their specific life experiences. The women in the play unravel the mystery of why John Wright was killed by examining the quilt that Mrs. Wright had been working on. They understood the frustration of being dominated by a man and living in rural solitude without so much as a birdsong to lighten the day. The men empowered to do the investigation see only what their acculturation will permit them to see, and they remain baffled. *Trifles* helps us see our own experience in a different way. The arts interpret experience on many levels.

Since art is a large part of our experience, it is natural that the arts should be influenced by one another and that they should interpret each other. Obviously, paintings represent dance in a way that is much different from what dance itself will do and be. The same is true for the subject matter of dance. For example, a reading of the story line, the pretext, of *Swan Lake* can hardly represent anything but an aspect of the ballet. Likewise, a painting or still photograph of a moment in *Swan Lake* will resemble the ballet, but not be it. Instead, it re-presents a crucial moment in the ballet that can contribute to our fuller understanding of the dance. Paintings or photographs may even reveal something of the spirit of the ballet that will surprise and inspire us. They may also, in their own right, be very powerful works of art. Art has long been entranced by other art, and seeing how the arts interrelate helps us understand why this is so.

SUMMARY

Each of the arts interprets experience in languages related to the senses that are dominant in that art. Painting and photography are mainly visual; sculpture is visual and tactile; architecture is visual, tactile, and spatial; music is aural; literature invokes the imagination to replicate all the senses. Specific arts are capable of interpreting other works of art by responding directly to them, as in the case of Robert Fagles and Anne Sexton in responding to *Starry Night*. Or they can interpret the same subject matter, as in the case of Mozart's *The Marriage of Figaro* and Beaumarchais' original play of the same name. Both versions have almost the same plot, most of the same characters, and the same setting. Mozart, however, adds music and song to the original. All the arts have the capacity to interpret another work of art, or even, as in the case of Matisse, to interpret the essence of other arts.

CHAPTER 13 BIBLIOGRAPHY

Beaumarchais, Pierre Augustin de. *The Marriage of Figaro*. Bernard Sahlins (trans.). Chicago: Ivan Dee, 1994.

Biancolli, Louis. *The Mozart Handbook*. New York: Grosset & Dunlap, 1954.

Braunbehrens, Volkmar. *Mozart in Vienna: 1781–1791*. New York: Grove Weidenfeld, 1986.

Butler, Christopher. *Early Modernism*. Oxford: Clarendon Press, 1994.

Fleming, William. *Concerts of the Arts: Their Interplay and Modes of Relationship*. Pensacola: University of West Florida Press, 1990.

Hunt, John Dixon. *Poetry, Painting, and Gardening During the Eighteenth Century*. Baltimore: The Johns Hopkins University Press, 1976.

Lange, Art, and Nathaniel Mackey (eds.). *Moment's Notice: Jazz in Poetry and Prose*. Minneapolis: Coffee House Press, 1993.

Liebner, János. *Mozart on Stage*. London: Calder and Boyars, 1972.

Mozart, Leopold Wolfgang. *The Marriage of Figaro*. London: John Calder, 1983.

North, Michael. *The Final Sculpture: Public Monuments and Modern Poets*. Ithaca, N.Y.: Cornell University Press, 1985.

Pearce, Lynne. *Woman/Image/Text*. Toronto: University of Toronto Press, 1991.

Sachs, Curt. *The Commonwealth of Art*. New York: Norton, 1946.

Sungolowsky, Joseph. *Beaumarchais*. New York: Twayne, 1974.

CHAPTER 13 WEBSITES

Art Network for Integrated Media Applications (digital art, online arts, discussion groups)

World Wide Web: **http://www.anima.wis.net/**

ArtResources (galleries, art publications, museums)

World Wide Web: **http://www.ftgi.com/**

Brian Eno (multi-subject discussion forum)

World Wide Web: **http://140.148.1.16/nerve_net.shtml**

Mythology in Western Art (pictures, general resource)

World Wide Web: **http://www-lib.haifa.ac.il/www/art/mythology_westart.html**

Opera (schedules, links, opera synopses)

World Wide Web: **http://web.metronet.com/~elektra/operal.html** or **http://www.physics.su.oz.au/~neilb/operah.html**

CHAPTER 14

THE INTERRELATIONSHIPS OF THE HUMANITIES

THE HUMANITIES AND THE SCIENCES

In the beginning pages of Chapter 1, we referred to the humanities as the broad range of creative activities and studies that are usually contrasted with mathematics and the "hard" sciences, mainly because in the humanities strictly objective or scientific standards do not usually dominate.

Most college and university catalogs contain a grouping of courses called the humanities. First, studies such as literature, the visual arts, music, history, philosophy, and theology are almost invariably included. Second, studies such as psychology, anthropology, sociology, political science, economics, business administration, and education may or may not be included. Third, studies such as physics, chemistry, biology, mathematics, and engineering are never included. The reason the last group is excluded is obvious—strict scientific or objective standards are clearly applicable. With the second group, these "hard" standards are not always so clearly applicable. There is an uncertainty about whether they belong with the sciences or the humanities. For example, most psychologists who experiment with animals apply the scientific method as rigorously as any biologist. But there are also psychologists—C. G. Jung, for instance—who speculate about such phenomena as the "collective unconscious" and the role of myth. To judge their work strictly by scientific methods is to miss their contributions. Where then should psychology and the subjects in this group be placed? In the case of the first group, finally, the arts are invariably listed under the humanities. But then so are history, philosophy, and theology. Thus, as the title of this book implies, the humanities include subjects other than the arts. Then how are the arts distinguished from the other humanities? And what is the relationship between the arts and these other humanities?

These are broad and complex questions. Concerning the placement of the studies in group two, it is usually best to take each department case by case. If, for example, a department of psychology is dominated by experimentalists, as is most likely in the United States, it would seem most useful to place that department with the sciences. And the same approach can be made to all the studies in group two. In most cases, probably, you will discover that clear-cut placements into the humanities or the sciences are impossible. Furthermore, even the subjects that are almost always grouped within either the humanities or the sciences cannot always be neatly cataloged. Rigorous objective standards may be applied in any of the humanities. Thus, painting can be approached as a science—the historian of medieval painting, for example, who measures, as precisely as any engineer, the evolving sizes of haloes. On the other hand, the beauty of mathematics—its economy and elegance of proof—can excite the lover of mathematics as much as, if not more than, painting. Edna St. Vincent Millay noted that "Euclid alone has looked on beauty bare." And so the separation of the humanities and the sciences should not be observed rigidly. The separation is useful mainly because it indicates the dominance or the subordinance of the strict scientific method in the various disciplines.

THE ARTS AND THE OTHER HUMANITIES

Artists differ from the other humanists primarily because they create works that reveal values. Artists are sensitive to the important concerns or values of their society. That is their subject matter in the broadest sense. They create artistic forms that clarify these values. That is their content. The other humanists—such as historians, philosophers, and theologians—reflect upon, rather than reveal, values. They study values as given, as they find them. They try to describe and explain values—their causes and consequences. Furthermore, they may judge these values as good or bad. Thus like artists they, too, try to clarify values; but they do this by means of discussion, criticism, and analysis (see Chapter 2).

CONCEPTION KEY
ARTISTS AND OTHER HUMANISTS

1. Explain how the work of an artist might be of significance to the historian, philosopher, and theologian.
2. Select works of art that we have discussed in this book that you think might be of greatest significance respectively to historians, philosophers, and theologians. Ask others to do the same. Then compare and discuss your selections.
3. Can you find any works of art we have discussed that you think would have no significance whatsoever to any of the other humanists? If so, explain.

The other humanists in their studies do not transform values as in artistic revelation. If they take advantage of the revealing role of the arts, their studies often will be enhanced because, other things being equal, they will have a more penetrating understanding of the values they are studying. This is basically the help that the artists can give to some of the other humanists. Suppose, for example, a historian is trying to understand the bombing of Guernica by the Fascists in the Spanish Civil War. Suppose he or she has explored all factual resources. Even then something very important may be left out: a vivid awareness of the suffering of the noncombatants. To gain insight into that pain, Picasso's *Guernica* (Figure 1-4) may be a great aid.

Conception Key
OTHER HUMANISTS AND ARTISTS

1. Is there anything that Picasso may have learned from historians that he used in painting *Guernica*?
2. Explain how the work of the other humanists might be of significance to the artist. Be specific.

Other humanists, such as critics, historians, and sociologists, may aid artists by their study of values. For example, in this book we have concerned ourselves in some detail with criticism—the description, interpretation, and evaluation of works of art. Criticism is a humanistic discipline because it studies values—those revealed in works of art—without strictly applying scientific or objective standards. Good critics aid our understanding of works of art. We become more sensitively aware of the revealed values. This deeper understanding brings us into closer rapport with artists, and such rapport helps sustain their confidence in their work.

The arts reveal values; the other humanistic disciplines study values. That does not mean that artists may not study values, but rather that such study, if any, is subordinated to revealing values in an artistic form that attracts our participation.

PERCEIVING AND THINKING

Another basic difference between the arts and the other humanities is the way perceiving dominates in the arts whereas thinking dominates in the other humanities. Of course, perceiving and thinking almost always go together. When we are aware of red striking our eyes, we are perceiving, but normally our brain is also conceiving, more or less explicitly, the idea "red." On the other hand, when we conceive the idea "red" with our eyes closed, we almost invariably remember some specific or generalized image of some perceptible red. Probably the infant only perceives, and as we are sinking into unconsciousness from illness or a blow on the head it may be that all ideas or concepts are wiped out. It may be, conversely, that conceiving sometimes occurs without any element of perceiving. Descartes, the great seventeenth-century philosopher, thought so. Most philosophers and psychologists believe, however, that even the most abstract thinking of mathematicians, since it still must be done with perceptible signs such as numbers, necessarily includes residues of perception. In any case, the question of the relationships and interdependence of perception and thought, which has been puzzling thinkers from the beginnings of civilization, still remains open.

Conception Key

PERCEPTION AND CONCEPTION

1. Think of examples in your experience in which percepts dominate concepts, and vice versa. Which kind of experience do you enjoy the most? Does your answer tell you anything about yourself?
2. Is it easily possible for you to shift gears from conceptually dominated thinking to perceptually dominated thinking? For example, if you are studying intensely some theoretical or practical problem—"thinking at"—do you find it difficult to begin to "think from" some work of art? Or, conversely, if you have been participating with a work of art, do you find it difficult to begin to "think at" some theoretical or practical problem? Do your answers tell you anything about yourself?
3. Select from the chapter on literature (Chapter 7) the poem that seems to demand the most from your perceptual faculties and the least from your conceptual faculties. Then select the poem that seems to demand the most from your conceptual faculties and the least from your perceptual faculties. Which poem do you like better? Does your answer tell you anything about yourself?
4. Which of the arts that we have studied seems to demand the most from your perceptual faculties? Your conceptual faculties? Why? Which art do you like better? Does your answer tell you anything about yourself?

It seems evident that perceiving without some thinking is little more than a blooming, buzzing confusion. Thus, all our talk about art in the previous chapters has been a conceptualizing that we hope has clarified and intensified your perception of specific works of art. But that is not to suggest that conception ought to dominate perception in your participation with a work of art. In fact, if conception dominates, participation will be weakened or prevented—we will be thinking *at* rather than thinking *from*. If, as we listen to the sonata form, we only emphasize conception, or thought, by identifying the exposition, development, and recapitulation sections, we could lower the sensitivity of our listening. Yet, if you were to ask trained music lovers *after* their listening, they probably could easily name the sections and tell you where such sections occurred. In other words, to experience the arts most intensely and satisfactorily, conception is indispensable, but perception must remain in the foreground. When we come to the other humanities, conception usually comes to the foreground. The other humanities basically reflect about values rather than reveal values, as in the case of the arts. With the other humanities, therefore, concepts or ideas become more central than percepts.

VALUES

A value is something we care about, something that matters. A value is an object of an interest. The term "object," however, should be understood as including events or states of affairs. A pie is obviously an object and it may be a value, and the course of action involved in obtaining the pie may also be a value. If we are not interested in something, it is neutral in value or valueless to us. Positive values are those objects of interest that satisfy us or give us pleasure, such as good health. Negative values are those objects of interest that dissatisfy us or give us pain, such as bad health.

When the term "value" is used alone, it usually refers to positive values only, but it may also include negative values. In our value decisions, we generally seek to obtain positive values and avoid negative values. But except for the very young child, these decisions usually involve highly complex activities. To have a tooth pulled is painful, a negative value, but doing so leads to the possibility of better health, a positive value. *Intrinsic values* involve the feelings, such as pleasure and pain, we have of some value activity, such as enjoying good food or experiencing nausea from overeating. *Extrinsic values* are the means to intrinsic values, such as making the money that pays for the food. *Intrinsic–extrinsic values* not only evoke immediate feelings but also are means to further values, such as the enjoyable food that leads to future good health. For most people, intrinsic–extrinsic values of the positive kind are the basis of the good life. Certain drugs may have great positive intrinsic value, but then extrinsically they may have powerful negative value, leading to great suffering.

CONCEPTION KEY
PARTICIPATION WITH ART AND VALUES

1. Do you think that the value of a participative experience with a work of art is basically intrinsic, extrinsic, or intrinsic–extrinsic? Explain.
2. Dr. Victor Frankl, a medical doctor and psychiatrist, writes in *The Doctor and the Soul,*

   > The higher meaning of a given moment in human existence can be fulfilled by the mere intensity with which it is experienced, and independent of any action. If anyone doubts this, let him consider the following situation. Imagine a music lover sitting in the concert hall while the most noble measures of his favorite symphony resound in his ears. He feels that shiver of emotion which we experience in presence of the purest beauty. Suppose now that at such a moment we should ask this person whether his life has meaning. He would have to reply that it had been worthwhile living if only to experience this ecstatic moment.[1]

   Do you agree with Frankl, or do you consider this an overstatement? Why?
3. It has been variously reported that some of the most sadistic guards and high-ranking officers in the Nazi concentration camps played the music of Bach and Beethoven during or after torturings. Goering was a great lover of excellent paintings. Hitler loved architecture and the music of Wagner. What do you make of this?

[1]Victor E. Frankl, *The Doctor and the Soul,* Richard and Clara Winston (trans.), Alfred A. Knopf, New York, 1955, p. 49.

Participation with a work of art not only is immediately satisfying but also is usually extrinsically valuable because it leads to deeper satisfactions in the future. To participate with one poem is likely to increase our sensitivity to the next poem. Moreover, by enhancing our sensory receptivity, participation with art can sometimes help in our practical activities, as in the case of the unsure surgeon. But most important of all, the understanding of values we achieve through participating with works of art may be extrinsically very valuable because such understanding helps us face our moral dilemmas with sounder orientation and deeper sympathy for others. And yet again, as implied by the last question of the last Conception Key, it is also clear that some people can compartmentalize their lives and emotions through an act of will, thereby ignoring the insights that arts can provide. Our hope is to avoid such compartmentalization.

CONCEPTION KEY
THE ORIGIN OF VALUE

1. Select the work of art discussed in this book that is the most valuable to you. Why is it so valuable?
2. Do you believe that value is projected into things by us, or that we discover values in things, or that in some way value originates in the relationship between us and things? Explain.

Values, we propose, involve a valuer and something that excites an interest in the valuer. Subjectivist theories of value claim, however, that it is the interest that projects the value on something. The painting, for example, is positively valuable only because it satisfies the interest of someone. Value is in the valuer. If no one is around to project interest, then there are no valuable objects. Value is entirely relative to the valuer. Beauty is in the eye of the beholder. Objectivist theories of value claim, conversely, that it is the object that excites the interest. Moreover, the painting is positively valuable even if no one has any interest in it. Value is in the object independently of any subject. Jane is beautiful even if no one is aware of her beauty.

The relational theory of value—which is the one we have been presupposing throughout this book—claims that value emerges from the relation between an interest and an object. A good painting that is satisfying no one's interest at the moment possesses only potential value. A good painting possesses properties that under proper conditions are likely to stimulate the interests of a valuer. The subjectivist would say that this painting has no value whatsoever until someone projects value on it. The objectivist would say that this painting has actualized value inherent in it whether anyone enjoys it or not. The relationalist would say that this painting has potential value; that when it is experienced under proper conditions, a sensitive, informed participant will actualize the potential value. To describe a painting as "good" is the same as saying that the painting has positive potential value. Furthermore, for the relationalist, value is realized only when objects with potential value connect with the interests of someone.

Values are usually studied with reference to the interaction of various kinds of potential value with human interests. For example, criticism tends to focus on the intrinsic values of works of art; economics focuses on commodities as basically extrinsic values; and ethics focuses on intrinsic–extrinsic values as they are or ought to be chosen by moral agents.

Values that are described scientifically as they are found we shall call "value facts." Values that are set forth as norms or ideals or what ought to be we shall call "normative values." The smoking of marijuana, for instance, is a positive value for some. Much research is being undertaken to provide descriptions of the consequences of the use of marijuana, and rigorous scientific standards are applicable. We would place such research with the sciences. And we would call the values that are described in such research value facts. A scientific report may describe the relevant value facts connected with the use of marijuana, showing, for instance, that people who smoke marijuana generally have such-and-such pleasurable experiences but at the same time incur such-and-such risks. Such a report is describing what is the case, not what ought to be the case (that is, normative values). When someone argues that marijuana should be prohibited or someone else argues that marijuana should be legalized, we are in a realm beyond the strict application of scientific standards. Appeal is being made not to what "is" or to factual value—this the sciences can handle—but to the "ought" or normative value.

CONCEPTION KEY
FACTUAL VALUE AND NORMATIVE VALUE

1. Do you see any possible connection between factual and normative value? For example, will the scientific studies now being made on the use of marijuana have any relevance to your judgment as to whether you should or should not smoke marijuana?
2. Do you think that the artist can reveal anything relevant to your judgment about using marijuana?
3. Do you think humanists other than artists might produce anything relevant to your judgment about the use of marijuana?

There is a very close relationship between factual and normative value. If scientists were to assert that anyone who uses marijuana regularly cannot possibly live longer than ten more years, this obviously would influence the arguments about its legalization. Yet the basis for a well-grounded decision about such a complex issue—for it is hardly likely that such a clear-cut fact as death within ten years from using marijuana regularly will be discovered—surely involves more than scientific information. Novels such as Aldous Huxley's *Brave New World* reveal aspects and consequences of drug experiences that escape the nets of scientific investigation. They clarify features of value phenomena which supplement the factual values as discovered by science. After exposure to such literature, we may be in a better position to make well-grounded decisions about such problems as the legalization of marijuana.

The arts and the other humanities often have normative relevance. They may clarify the possibilities for value decisions, thus clarifying what ought to be and what we ought to do. And this is an invaluable function, for we are creatures who must constantly choose among various value possibilities. Paradoxically, even not choosing is often a choice. The humanities can help enlighten our choices. Artists help by revealing aspects and consequences of value phenomena that escape scientists. The other humanists help by clarifying aspects and consequences of value phenomena that escape both artists and scientists. For example, the historian might trace the consequences of drug use in past societies. Moreover, the other humanists—especially philosophers—can take account of the whole value field, including the relationships between factual and normative values. This is something we are trying to do, however briefly and oversimply, right here.

Conception Key
VALUE DECISIONS

1. You probably have made a judgment about whether or not to use marijuana. Was there any kind of evidence—other than the scientific—that was relevant to your decision? Explain.
2. Reflect about the works of art that we have discussed in this book. Have any of them clarified value possibilities for you in a way that might helpfully influence your value decisions? How? Be as specific as possible. Do some arts seem more relevant than others in this respect? If so, why? Discuss with others. Do you find that people differ a great deal with respect to the arts that are most relevant to their value decisions? If so, how is this to be explained?
3. Do you think that in choosing its political leaders a society is likely to be helped if the arts are flourishing? As you think about this, consider the state of the arts in societies that have chosen wise leaders, as well as the state of the arts in societies that have chosen unwise leaders.
4. Do you think that political leaders are more likely to make wise decisions if they are sensitive to the arts? Back up your answer with reference to specific leaders.
5. Do you think there is any correlation between a flourishing state of the arts and a democracy? A tyranny? Back up your answers with reference to specific governments.

Factual values are verified experimentally, put through the tests of the scientific method. Normative values are verified experientially, put through the tests of living. Satisfaction, for ourselves and the others involved, is an experiential test that the normative values we chose in a given instance were probably right. Suffering, for ourselves and the others involved, is an experiential test that the normative values we chose were probably wrong. Experiential testing of normative values involves not only the immediacy of experience but the consequences that follow. If you choose to try heroin, you cannot escape the consequences. And, fortunately, certain novels—Nelson Algren's *Man with the Golden Arm,* for instance—can make you vividly aware of those consequences before you have to suffer them. Science can also point out these consequences, of course, but science cannot make them so forcefully clear and present, and thus so thoroughly understandable.

The arts are closely related to the other humanities, especially history, philosophy, and theology. In conclusion, we shall give only a brief sketch of these relationships, for they are enormously complex and require extensive analyses that we can only suggest.

THE ARTS AND HISTORY

Historians try to discover the *what* and the *why* of the past. Of course, they need as many relevant facts as possible in order to describe and explain the events that happened. Often they may be able to use the scientific method in their gathering and verification of facts. But in attempting to give as full an explanation as possible as to why some of the events they are tracing happened, they function as humanists, for here they need understanding of the normative values or ideals of the society they are studying. Among their main resources are works of art. Often such works will reveal the norms of a people—their views of birth and death, blessing and disaster, victory and disgrace, endurance and decline, themselves and God, fate and what ought to be. Only with the understanding of such values can history become something more than a catalog of events.

CONCEPTION KEY
THE ARTS AND HISTORY

1. Can works of art be of great significance to the work of a historian? Explain.
2. Suppose an ancient town were being excavated but, aside from architecture, no works of art had been unearthed. And then some paintings, sculpture, a few musical scores, and some poems come to light—all from the local culture. Is it likely that the paintings would give the historian information different from that provided by the architecture or the sculpture? Or what might the music reveal that the other arts do not? The poems? As you reflect on these questions, reflect also on the following description by Heidegger of a painting by Van Gogh of a pair of peasant shoes:

> From the dark opening of the worn insides of the shoes the toilsome tread of the worker stares forth. In the stiffly rugged heaviness of the shoes there is the accumulated tenacity of her slow trudge through the far-spreading and ever-uniform furrows of the field swept by a raw wind. On the leather lie the dampness and richness of the soil. Under the soles slides the loneliness of the field-patch as evening falls. In the shoes vibrates the silent call of the earth, its quiet gift of the ripening grain and its unexplained self-refusal in the fallow desolation of the wintry field. This equipment is pervaded by uncomplaining anxiety as to the certainty of bread, the wordless joy of having once more withstood want, the trembling before the impending childbed and shivering at the surrounding menace of death. This equipment belongs to the earth, and it is protected in the world of the peasant woman.[2]

[2]Martin Heidegger, "The Origin of the Work of Art," in Albert Hofstadter (trans.), *Poetry, Language, Thought,* Harper & Row, New York, 1971, pp. 33ff.

THE ARTS AND PHILOSOPHY

Philosophy is, among other things, an attempt to give reasoned answers to fundamental questions that, because of their generality, are not treated by any of the more specialized disciplines. Ethics, aesthetics, and metaphysics or speculative philosophy, three of the main divisions of philosophy, are very closely related to the arts. Ethics in part is often the inquiry into the presuppositions or principles operative in our moral judgments, and the study of norms or standards for value decisions. If we are correct, an ethic dealing with norms that fails to take advantage of the insights of the arts is inadequate. John Dewey even argued

> that art is more moral than moralities. For the latter either are, or tend to become, consecrations of the status quo, reflections of custom, reenforcements of the established order. The moral prophets of humanity have always been poets even though they spoke in free verse or by parable.[3]

CONCEPTION KEY
ETHICS AND THE ARTS

1. In the quote above, Dewey might seem to be thinking primarily of poets when he speaks of the contribution of artists to the ethicist. Or do you think he is using the term "poets" to include all artists? In any case, do you think that literature has more to contribute to the ethicist than the other arts? If so, why?
2. Reflect on the works of art which we have discussed in this book. Which ones do you think might have the most relevance to an ethicist? Why?

Throughout this book we have been elaborating an aesthetics or philosophy of art. We have been attempting to account to some extent for the whole range of the phenomena of art—the creative process of the artist, the work of art, the experience of the work of art, criticism, and the role of art in society—from a philosophic standpoint. On occasion we have avoided restricting our analysis to any single area within that group, considering the interrelationships of these areas. And on other occasions we have tried to make explicit the basic assumptions of some of the restricted studies. These are typical functions of the aesthetician or philosopher of art. For example, much of our time has been spent doing criticism, analyzing and appraising particular works of art. But at other times, as in Chapter 3, we tried to make explicit the presuppositions or principles of criticism. Critics, of course, may do this themselves, but then they are functioning more as aestheticians than as critics. Furthermore, we have also reflected on how criticism influences artists, the participants, and society. This, too, is a function of the aesthetician.

Finally, the aim of the metaphysicians or speculative philosophers, roughly speaking, is to understand reality as a totality. Therefore they must take into account the artifacts of the artists as well as the conclusions and

[3]John Dewey, *Art as Experience,* Minton, Balch and Co., New York, 1934, p. 348.

reflections of the other humanists and the scientists. Metaphysicians attempt to reflect on the whole in order to achieve some valid general conclusions concerning the nature of reality and our position and prospects in it. A metaphysician who ignores the arts will have left out some of the most useful insights about value phenomena, which are very much a fundamental part of our reality.

THE ARTS AND THEOLOGY

The practice of religion, strictly speaking, is not a humanistic activity or study, for basically it neither creates values in the way of the arts nor studies values in the way of the other humanities. A religion is an institution that brings people together for the purpose of worship. These people share certain religious experiences and beliefs about those experiences. Since the beliefs of various people differ, it is more accurate to refer to religions than to religion. Nevertheless, there is a commonsense basis, reflected in our ordinary language, for the term "religion." Despite the differences about their beliefs, religious people generally agree that their religious values—for example, achieving, in some sense, communion with God—are ultimate—that is, more important than any other values. They have ultimate concern for these values. Moreover, a common nucleus of experience seems to be shared by all religious people: (1) uneasy awareness of the limitations of human moral and theoretical powers; (2) awe-full awareness of a further reality—beyond or behind or within the world of our sense experience; (3) conviction that communion with this further reality is of supreme importance.

Theology involves the study of religions. As indicated in Chapter 1, the humanities in the medieval period were studies about humans, whereas theology and related studies were studies about God. But in present times theology, usually broadly conceived, is placed with the humanities. Moreover, for many religious people today, ultimate values or the values of the sacred are not necessarily ensconced in another world "up there." In any case, some works of art reveal ultimate values in ways that are relevant to the contemporary situation. Theologians who ignore these revelations cannot do justice to their study of religions.

Conception Key
RELIGIOUS VALUES AND THE ARTS

Reflect about the works of art you know best. Have any of them revealed ultimate values to you in a way that is relevant to your situation? How? Are they necessarily contemporary works?

Dietrich Bonhoeffer, in one of his last letters from the Nazi prison of Tegel, noted that "now that it has become of age, the world is more Godless, and perhaps it is for that very reason nearer to God than ever before." Our artists, secular as well as religious, not only reveal our despair but also, in the depths of that darkness, open paths back to the sacred.

At the end of the last century, Matthew Arnold intimated that the aesthetic or participative experience, especially of the arts, would become the religious experience. We do not think this transformation will happen because the participative experience lacks the outward expressions, such as worship, that fulfill and in turn distinguish the religious experience. But Arnold was prophetic, we believe, in sensing that increasingly the arts would provide the most direct access to the sacred. Iris Murdoch, the contemporary Irish novelist, describes such an experience:

> Dora had been in the National Gallery a thousand times and the pictures were almost as familiar to her as her own face. Passing between them now, as through a well-loved grove, she felt a calm descending on her. She wandered a little, watching with compassion the poor visitors armed with guidebooks who were peering anxiously at the masterpieces. Dora did not need to peer. She could look, as one can at last when one knows a great thing very well, confronting it with a dignity which it has itself conferred. She felt that the pictures belonged to her. . . . Vaguely, consoled by the presence of something welcoming and responding in the place, her footsteps took her to various shrines at which she had worshipped so often before.[4]

Such experiences are rare. Most of us still require the guidebooks. But one hopes the time will come when we no longer just peer but participate. And when that time comes, a guidebook like this one may have its justification.

SUMMARY

The various arts, despite their autonomy, often interrelate in mixed media for two basic reasons. In the first place, the media of the arts are each subject to systematic ordering, thus lending themselves to mixing. Second, the arts are a commonwealth because they serve the same purpose: to reveal something significant in their form-content that has never been made explicit before. This common purpose, moreover, often allows the arts to be performed and exhibited in close juxtaposition.

The arts and the other humanities are distinguished from the sciences because in the former, generally, strictly objective or scientific standards are irrelevant. In turn, the arts are distinguished from the other humanities because in the arts values are revealed, whereas in the other humanities values are studied. Furthermore, in the arts perception dominates, whereas in the other humanities conception dominates.

In our discussion about values, we distinguish between (1) intrinsic values—activities involving immediacy of feeling, positive or negative, (2) extrinsic values—activities that are means to intrinsic values, and (3) intrinsic–extrinsic values—activities that not only are means to intrinsic values but also involve significant immediacy of feeling. The theory of value presupposed in this book has been relational: that is, value emerges from the

[4] *The Bell,* by Iris Murdoch, copyright © 1958 by Iris Murdoch. Reprinted by permission of The Viking Press, Inc., New York, and Chatto and Windus Ltd., London, p. 182.

relation between a human interest and an object or event. Value is not merely subjective—projected by human interest on some object or event—nor is value merely objective—valuable independently of any subject. Values that are described scientifically we call "value facts." Values set forth as norms or ideals or what ought to be we call "normative values." The arts and the other humanities often have normative relevance: by clarifying what ought to be and thus what we ought to do.

Finally, the arts are closely related to the other humanities, especially history, philosophy, and theology. The arts help reveal the normative values of past cultures to the historian. Philosophers attempt to answer questions about values, especially in the fields of ethics, aesthetics, and metaphysics. Some of the most useful insights about value phenomena for the philosopher come from artists. Theology involves the study of religions, and religions are grounded in ultimate concern for values. No human artifacts reveal ultimate values more powerfully to the theologian than works of art.

CHAPTER 14 BIBLIOGRAPHY

Andrews, Michael S. *Creativity and Psychological Health*. Syracuse, N.Y.: Syracuse University Press, 1961.

Fleming, William. *Arts and Ideas*, 9th ed. Fort Worth: Harcourt Brace College Publishers, 1995.

Gotshalk, D. W. *Art and the Social Order*. New York: Dover, 1962.

Greenberg, Clement. *Art and Culture*. Boston: Beacon, 1989.

Hall, James B., and Barry Ulanov. *Modern Culture and the Arts,* 2d ed. New York: McGraw-Hill, 1972.

Hauser, Arnold. *The Philosophy of Art History*. Evanston, Ill.: Northwestern University Press, 1985.

Heidegger, Martin. *Poetry, Language, Thought*. Albert Hofstadter (trans.). New York: Perennial Library, Harper Colophon, 1975.

Kepes, György (ed.). *Education of Vision*. New York: Braziller, 1965.

Koestler, Arthur. *The Act of Creation*. New York: Macmillan, 1964.

Kroeber, A. L. *Style and Civilization*. Berkeley: University of California Press, 1963.

Martin, F. David. *Art and the Religious Experience*. Cranbury, N.J.: Associated University Press, 1972.

Maslow, Abraham. *New Knowledge in Human Values*. Chicago: Henry Regnery, Gateway, 1970.

Murdoch, Iris. *The Fire and the Sun: Why Plato Banished the Artists*. New York: Oxford, 1977.

Panofsky, Erwin. *Idea: A Concept in Art*. New York: Harper and Row, 1975.

Porter, Burton F. *Philosophy: A Literary and Conceptual Approach,* 2d ed. New York: Harcourt, Brace, Jovanovich, 1980.

Rader, Melvin, and Bertram Jessup. *Art and Human Values*. Englewood Cliffs, N.J.: Prentice-Hall, 1976.

Read, Herbert. *Education Through Art,* 3d ed. London: Faber and Faber, 1958.

———. *Icon and Idea*. Cambridge, Mass.: Harvard University Press, 1955.

Sachs, Curt. *The Commonwealth of Art*. Washington, D.C.: U.S. Government Printing Office, 1960.

Tillich, Paul. *The Courage to Be*. New Haven: Yale University Press, 1952.

Wilson, Robert N. *The Arts in Society*. Englewood Cliffs, N.J.: Prentice-Hall, 1964.

Wolterstorff, Nicholas. *Art in Action*. Grand Rapids, Mich.: William B. Eerdmans, 1980.

CHAPTER 14 WEBSITES

Humanities Hub (gender studies, philosophy, languages)

World Wide Web: **http://www.gu.edu.au/qwis/hub/hub.home.html**

Humanities Resources (great collection of general resources)

World Wide Web: **http://www.hum.gu.se/w3vl/w3vl.html**

Resource Guides to the Humanities

Gopher: Name: **University of Michigan** Address: **una.hh.lib.umich.edu**
Choose: **inetdirs** Choose: **Guides on the Humanities**

GLOSSARY

Abstract painting Painting that has sensa or the sensuous as its primary subject matter. *See* Representational painting.

Aesthetics The philosophy of art: the examination of the creative process, the work of art, the aesthetic experience, principles of criticism, and the role of art in society.

Ambiguity Uncertain meaning, a situation in which several meanings are implied. Ambiguity sometimes implies contradictory meanings.

Archetype An idea or behavioral pattern, usually formed in prehistoric times, that becomes a part of the unconscious psyche of a people. The archetype is embedded in the "collective unconscious." The term comes from Jungian psychology, and has been associated by Jung with myth. In the arts, the archetype is usually expressed as a narrative pattern, such as the quest for personal identity. *See* Myth.

Aristotle's elements of drama Plot, character, thought, diction, spectacle, and music. *See* entries under individual elements.

Artistic form The organization of a medium whereby values are separated from irrelevancies and clarified. *See* Decorative form; Work of art.

Artistic medium The elements or material out of which works of art are made. These elements either have an inherent order, such as colors, or permit an imposed order, such as words; and these orders, in turn, are organizable by artistic form.

Assemblage The technique of sculpture, such as welding, whereby preformed pieces are attached. *See* Modeling.

Auteur In film, the idea that a director (usually) is the author or primary maker of the total film.

Avant-garde Those who break sharply with traditional conventions and styles.

Axis mundi A vertically placed pole used by some primitive people to center their world.

Centered space A site—natural or manmade—that organizes other places around it.

Character In drama, that which reveals the moral purpose of the agents (according to Aristotle).

Comedy A form of drama that is usually light in subject matter and ends happily. Comedy that is art is not void of seriousness.

Conception Thinking that focuses on concepts or ideas.

Configurational center A place of special value, a place to dwell.

Connotation Use of language to suggest ideas and/or emotional colorations in addition to the explicit or denoted meaning. "Brothers and sisters" denotes relatives, but the words may also connote people united in a common effort or struggle, as in the expressions "Brotherhood of Teamsters" or "Sisterhood Is Powerful." *See* Denotation.

Content Subject matter detached by means of an artistic form from its accidental or insignificant aspects, and thus clarified and made more meaningful.

Decorative form The organization of a medium that pleases or distracts or entertains but does not inform about values. *See* Artistic form.

Denotation The direct, explicit meaning or reference of a word or words.

Detail Elements of structure.

Diction In literature, drama, and film the choice of words with special care for their expressiveness.

Earth-resting architecture Buildings that accent neither the earth nor the sky, using the earth as a platform with the sky as a background.

Earth-rooted architecture Buildings that bring out with special force the earth and its symbolisms. *See* Sky-oriented architecture.

Earth sculpture Sculpture that makes the earth the medium, site, and subject matter.

Editing In film, the process by which the footage is cut, the best version of each scene chosen, and these versions joined together for optimum effect. *See* Montage.

Embodiment The meshing of medium and ideas in a work of art.

Emotion Strong sensations felt as related to a specific and apparent stimulus. *See* Passion; Mood.

Epic A lengthy narrative poem, usually episodic, with heroic action and great cultural, political scope.

Episodic narrative A story composed of separate incidents (or episodes) tied loosely together. *See* Organic narrative.

Flaws in character In drama, the prominent weakness of character that leads to the protagonist's tragic end.

Form-content The fusion of the meaning of a work of art with the form.

Framing The photographic technique whereby important parts of figures or objects in a scene are cut off by the edges of the photograph.

Frieze Figurative, low-relief sculpture on a wall or walls of a building, usually in a horizontal band.

Genre Kind.

High relief Sculpture with a background plane from which the projections are relatively large.

Humanities Broad areas of human creativity and study essentially involved with values and generally not using strictly objective or scientific standards.

Imagery Use of language to represent objects and events with strong appeal to the senses.

Intentional fallacy In criticism, the assumption that what the artists say they intended to do outweighs what they in fact did.

Irony Saying the opposite of what one means. Dramatic irony plays on the audience's capacity to perceive the difference between what the characters expect and what they will get.

Low relief Sculpture with a background plane from which the projections are relatively small.

Lyric A poem, usually brief and personal, with an emphasis on feeling as part of the subject matter.

Machine sculpture Sculpture that reveals the machine and/or its powers.

Meta-art Art that challenges traditional presuppositions about art, especially embodiment. *See* Embodiment.

Metaphor An implied comparison between different things. *See* Simile.

Mixed media The merger of two or more artistic media.

Modeling The technique of building up a sculpture piece by piece with some plastic or malleable material. *See* Assemblage.

Montage The joining of physically different but usually psychologically related scenes. *See* Editing.

Mood Feelings that arise from no specific or apparent stimulus.

Motive In music, a brief but intelligible and self-contained fragment of a melody or theme.

Myth Ancient stories rooted in primitive experience. *See* Archetype.

Narrative The story line of a work of art.

Narrator The teller of a story.

New Comedy Subject matter centered on the foibles of social manners and mores. Usually quite polished in style, with bright and incisive humor.

Normative values Norms or ideals about values; what "ought to be."

Old Comedy Subject matter centered on ridiculous and/or highly exaggerated situations. Usually raucous, earthy, and satirical.

Organic narrative A story composed of separable incidents that relate to one another in tightly coherent ways, usually causally and chronologically. *See* Episodic narrative.

Paradox An apparent contradiction that, upon reflection, may seem reasonable.

Participative experience "Thinking from" something, letting that thing initiate and control everything that comes into awareness.

Passion Emotions elevated to great intensity.

Pediment The triangular space formed by roof jointure in a Greek temple or Roman building on the Greek model.

Perception The awareness of something stimulating our sense organs.

Plot The sequence of actions or events.

Pop art Art that incorporates mass-produced articles.

Presentational immediacy The awareness of something that is presented in its entirety with an "all-at-onceness."

Pretext Usually the underlying narrative as the basis for a dance, but occasionally feelings or states of mind.

Protagonist The chief character in drama and literature.

Representational painting Painting that has specific objects or events as its primary subject matter. *See* Abstract painting.

Satire Literature that ridicules people or institutions.

Sciences Disciplines that for the most part use strictly objective standards.

Sculpture in the round Sculpture freed from any background plane.

Sensa The qualities of objects or events that stimulate our sense organs.

Setting In literature, drama, dance, and film, the time and place in which the work of art occurs. The setting is established mainly by means of description in literature, and spectacle in drama, dance, and film.

Simile An explicit comparison between different things, using comparative words such as "like," and "as." *See* Metaphor.

Sky-oriented architecture Buildings that bring out with special force the sky and its symbolisms. *See* Earth-resting architecture; Earth-rooted architecture.

Space The power of the positioned interrelationships of things.

Space sculpture Sculpture that emphasizes spatial relationships and thus tends to de-emphasize the density of its materials.

Spectacle The visual ingredients of a work of art.

Stereotype A completely predictable character. *See* Type character.

Structure Overall organization of a work of art.

Style Characteristics of form which are peculiar to a certain work or a group of works.

Subject matter What the work of art "is about"; some value *before* artistic interpretation. *See* Content.

Sunken relief Sculpture made by carving grooves of various depths into the surface plane of the sculptural material, the surface plane remaining perceptually distinct.

Surface relief Sculpture with a flat surface plane as the basic organizing plane of the composition, but no clear perceptual distinction is perceivable between the depths behind the surface plane and the projections in front.

Symbol Something perceptible that means something more abstract.

Tactility Touch sensations, both inward and outward.

Technologies Disciplines that apply for practical purposes the theoretical knowledge produced by the sciences.

Texture The "feel" of a material, such as "smooth" bronze or "rough" concrete.

Theme In music, a melodic line or motive of considerable importance because of later repetition or development. In the other arts, a theme is a main idea or general topic.

Thought The ideas expressed in works of art.

Tragedy Drama that treats a serious subject matter and ends unhappily.

Tragic flaw *See* Flaws in character.

Tragicomedy Drama that includes characteristics of both tragedy and comedy.

Tympanum The space above an entranceway to a building, usually containing a painting or frieze.

Type character A predictable character. *See* Stereotype.

Value facts Values described scientifically. *See* Normative values.

Values Objects and events important to human beings.

Work of art An artifact that informs about values by means of an artistic form. *See* Artistic form.

PERMISSIONS ACKNOWLEDGMENTS

Giovanni Boccaccio: "The Pot of Basil" from *The Decameron* translated by G. H. McWilliam (Penguin Books Ltd.) copyright © G. H. McWilliam, 1972.

E. E. Cummings: "l(a", copyright © 1958, 1986, 1991 by the Trustees for the E. E. Cummings Trust, from *Complete Poems: 1904–1962* by E. E. Cummings, Edited by George J. Firmage. Reprinted by permission of Liveright Publishing Corporation.

Emily Dickinson: "After Great Pain, a Formal Feeling Comes." From *The Complete Poems of Emily Dickinson* edited by Thomas H. Johnson. Copyright 1929, 1935 by Martha Dickinson Bianchi; Copyright © renewed 1957, 1963 by Mary L. Hampson. By permission of Little, Brown and Company.

Fyodor Dostoevsky: excerpt from *Crime and Punishment* by Fyodor Dostoevsky, trans. Jessie L. Coulson. Oxford: Oxford University Press, 1953. By permission of Oxford University Press.

Clayton Eshleman: "Tehuana Frida by Victorian Horrah." Copyright © 1994 by Clayton Eshleman. Reprinted from *Under World Arrest* with the permission of Black Sparrow Press.

Robert Fagles: "The Starry Night" from *I, Vincent: Poems from the Pictures of Van Gogh* by Robert Fagles. Copyright 1978 by Princeton University Press. Reprinted with permission of Robert Fagles.

Martin Heidegger: excerpt from *Poetry, Language, Thought* by Martin Heidegger and translated by Albert Hofstadter. Copyright © 1971 by Martin Heidegger. Reprinted by permission of HarperCollins Publishers, Inc.

Donald Justice: "A Map of Love" from *New and Selected Poems* by Donald Justice. Copyright © 1995 by Donald Justice. Reprinted by permission of Alfred A. Knopf, Inc.

D. H. Lawrence: "Piano" from *The Complete Poems of D. H. Lawrence* by D. H. Lawrence, edited by V. de Sola Pinto & F. W. Roberts. Copyright © 1964, 1971 by Angelo Ravagli and C. M. Weekley, Executors of the Estate of Frieda Lawrence Ravagli. Used by permission of Viking Penguin, a division of Penguin Books USA Inc.

Li Ho: "The Grave of Little Su" from *Poems of the Late T'ang* translated by A. C. Graham (Penguin Classics, 1965) copyright © A. C. Graham, 1965.

Audre Lorde: "Coal," copyright © 1973, 1970, 1968 by Audre Lorde, from *Undersong: Chosen Poems Old and New* by Audre Lorde. Reprinted by permission of W. W. Norton & Company, Inc.

Wolfgang Amadeus Mozart: excerpt from "Non più andrai" from *Le Nozze di Figaro (The Marriage of Figaro)*, English translation and vocal score by Thomas and Ruth Martin. Copyright © 1947, 1948, 1951, 1959 (Renewed) by G. Schirmer, Inc. (ASCAP). International Copyright Secured. All Rights Reserved. Reprinted by Permission.

Gabriel Okara: "Piano and Drums" from *The African Assertion,* ed. Austin J. Shelton. New York: Odyssey, 1968. Originally in *Black Orpheus* #6, 1959. Reprinted by permission of Gabriel Okara.

Ovid: from *The Metamorphoses* by Publius Ovidius Naso, translated by Horace Gregory, Translation copyright © 1958 by The Viking Press, Inc., renewed 1986 by Patrick Bolton Gregory. Used by permission of Viking Penguin, a division of Penguin Books USA Inc.

Sylvia Plath: "Paralytic" from *The Collected Poems of Sylvia Plath* by Sylvia Plath. Copyright © 1963 by Ted Hughes. Copyright renewed. Reprinted by permission of HarperCollins Publishers, Inc., and Faber and Faber Ltd.

Ezra Pound: "In a Station of the Metro" from *Personae* by Ezra Pound. Copyright © 1926 by Ezra Pound. Reprinted by permission of New Directions Publishing Corp.

Anne Sexton: "The Starry Night" from *All My Pretty Ones* by Anne Sexton. Copyright © 1962 by Anne Sexton, renewed 1990 by Linda G. Sexton. Reprinted by permission of Houghton Mifflin Company. All rights reserved.

Tu Mu: "The Retired Official Yüan's High Pavilion" from *Poems of the Late T'ang* translated by A. C. Graham (Penguin Classics, 1965) copyright © A. C. Graham, 1965.

Virginia Woolf: excerpt from "Kew Gardens" in *A Haunted House and Other Short Stories* by Virginia Woolf, copyright 1944 and renewed 1972 by Harcourt Brace & Company, reprinted by permission of the publisher.

INDEX